PREVENTING WORLD WAR III

BOOKS BY DAVID M. ABSHIRE

Preventing World War III: *A Realistic Grand Strategy*

Foreign Policy Makers: *President vs. Congress*

International Broadcasting: *A New Dimension of Western Diplomacy*

The South Rejects a Prophet

National Security (ed.)

The Growing Power of Congress (ed.)

Portuguese Africa (ed.)

PREVENTING
WORLD WAR III

A REALISTIC GRAND STRATEGY

DAVID M. ABSHIRE

A Cornelia & Michael Bessie Book

HARPER & ROW, PUBLISHERS, New York
Cambridge, Philadelphia, San Francisco, London
Mexico City, São Paulo, Singapore, Sydney

FIRST EDITION

Designed by Sidney Feinberg

Library of Congress Cataloging-in-Publication Data

Abshire, David M.
  Preventing World War III.

  "A Cornelia & Michael Bessie book."
  Includes index.
  1. United States—National security. 2. North Atlantic Treaty Organization. 3. Europe—Defenses. 4. World War III. I. Title.
UA23.A4297 1988   355'.033073   88-45171
ISBN 0-06-015986-3

---

88 89 90 91 92 AC/HC 10 9 8 7 6 5 4 3 2 1

To my wonderful wife, Carolyn, and our children
Lupton, Anna, Mary Lee, Phyllis, and Caroline

Contents

Acknowledgments

Many friends have contributed neverending time and talent to this endeavor, and this book would not have been possible without their support. From my earliest drafts, Michael Moodie contributed excellent editorial and substantive suggestions, especially in those areas of the book concerning NATO. John Reichart, Andrew Gilmour, Ian Lesser, and John Vondracek supplied a broad base of substantive input and editorial comment. My executive assistant, Jay Collins, worked closely with me throughout the book, especially on economic and Asia-related issues. Robert Neumann, Edward Luttwak, Tom Callaghan, Steve Ledogar, and Brock Brower gave frank critiques at various stages of the manuscript.

I appreciate the critiques and keen commentary given me on individual chapters: Walter Laqueur and Bob Frowick on early versions of several chapters; Dennis Kloske on "Resources Strategy" and "Technology Strategy"; Stan Burnett and Walter Roberts on "Political Strategy" and "Public Strategy"; Stephen Sestanovich, Gregory Guroff, and John Evans on "Gorbachev's Superpower"; David Bradford and Georges Fauriol on "Global Perspectives"; Penelope Hartland-Thunberg, Nat Samuels, John Yochelson, and Cynthia Wallace on economic aspects; Martin Weinstein, Susan Pharr, and Eugene Lawson on "The Power Balancers"; Jim Woolsey on naval aspects and "Global Perspectives"; Wayne Berman for helpful comments on a broad range of issues.

Bill Stokes worked diligently and untiringly on the details of every chapter and coordinated the critiques and footnotes. Elise Callaghan, my long-time assistant both in and out of government, was as usual helpful in many ways. Donna Chamberlain, Dexter Congbalay, and Brent Fischmann assisted in pulling together data and proofing later versions of several chapters. Connie O'Reilly and John Novick gave skilled typing support. Much appreciation goes to the many interns who gave me essential support.

My Harper & Row editors have been of immeasurable help: it has been my extraordinary good fortune to have Michael Bessie for overall guidance; Brooke Drysdale Samuels was masterful in tightening the book, dramatically reducing unnecessary history and background; Gina Heiserman ably coordinated with my staff to meet deadlines.

Finally, I cannot adequately stress that the views herein are my own and by no means necessarily those of the persons mentioned above. Indeed, we have had lively debates amongst ourselves as to whether Lee or Grant was a greater general and on judgments related to nuclear strategy. It would have been more diplomatic of me not to have attacked so many sacred cows, but I was convinced that only by frank talk—with constructive recommendations—could I help move forward the agenda of the United States and our allies. If I disturbed any of my friends overseas, I can only say that I would not have met the requirements of friendship had I not been frank in my views.

Prologue:
How War Comes

As a schoolchild I learned John McCrae's poem "In Flanders Fields," written in homage to those who lost their lives in World War I:

> If ye break faith with us who die,
> We shall not sleep, though poppies grow
> In Flanders fields.

It was a sunny Memorial Day, 1986. As U.S. ambassador to NATO, I stood next to the Belgian prime minister at a World War I American cemetery in Flanders, where white tombstones stood row upon row. Wreaths were laid, shots were fired, "Taps" played. Why did these men fight and die? Supposedly it was to make the world safe for democracy and to keep the peace. It was called the Great War, the War to End All Wars.

Weeks later I stood at the vastly larger, much more sweeping cemetery in Normandy. More tombstones stood, row upon row, overlooking the steep chalk banks over which Americans had to climb, through withering fire, to regain a foothold on the continent. Why did our soldiers fight and die in another war that the Great War was to have eliminated? To liberate Europe, destroy Hitler, to make the world safe . . . no more wars. Yet, I ask myself, would my children or grandchildren ever so stand, mourning our dead of World War III?

Contemporary people now face not only the fear of death of the individual but of humankind itself—so wrote the Jesuit scientist Teilhard de Chardin. Yet after forty years of peace in Europe, there are influential Americans—some neoconservatives on the right, some revisionist historians on the left, some in a quandary over the need for deep cuts in the budget, some who say Europe is getting a free ride—who want to set off a process that would take us out of the Europe for whose freedom those soldiers fought and died.

"It is time to pull back and let Europe build its own defense," one increasingly hears. Other critics argue that the cost of America's defense effort overseas, for Europe and Japan together, totals about $150 billion; that is just about the size of the deficit; cut off NATO and Japan and balance the budget.

Our new isolationists say a world war will never happen again. Some revisionist historians say there is no threat anyway, that we caused the Cold War in the first place. Some neoconservatives say that the Soviets stalk us elsewhere around the world and that there is no danger in Europe. They recommend we reduce the commitment to Europe and to the collective defense stipulated in the North Atlantic Treaty. They believe the Pacific Basin is what counts, but add that after we reduce our commitments to Europe we must do the same elsewhere.

Today there is a dramatic new ingredient overarching all these arguments: Gorbachev's *perestroika* fills the air, and *glasnost* is seen as the wave of the future. Many Westerners see a Soviet Union absorbed in reform, and they proclaim that the East–West confrontation is a thing of the past. People write of both superpowers declining from imperial overstretch and internal ills. Such observers argue that alliances are also in decline, both the Warsaw Pact and NATO, and that perhaps democracies should not have such commitments anyway. There is a new era of summitry and disarmament, and there is talk of the emergence of a bright multipolar world and new stability for the millennium.

Sarajevo, 1914. Gavrilo Princip's gunshot on June 28 triggered a series of events that culminated in two world wars, the devastating loss of 58 million lives,[1] the invention of the atomic and hydrogen bombs, and the destruction of international order. The real catalyst, however, was not Princip's bullet but uncertainty: unclear alliances, secret agreements, differing perceptions. No one national leader ever thought a worldwide catastrophe would result from his decisions in the summer of 1914. World War I was a world war by miscalculation— not an accident, but a serious error in human judgment.

There had been previous Balkan crises in 1908 and 1912, which were resolved without major power conflicts. Most rulers of Europe were related. Many commentators even said that important European trading relationships made war impossible. The deterrence system of the Concert of Europe, instituted after Napoleon's defeat, had prevented general war for nearly one hundred years. Just believe in that deterrent, it was felt, and everything would be all right.

All of these assumptions proved tragically wrong. British sentiment to stay out of a continental conflict was reversed with the German invasion of Belgium. The Kaiser believed that King Albert would permit him a peaceful passageway to France and that Britain would not respond to the violation of Belgian neutrality. He was wrong on both counts. When Albert fought, Britain entered the war in an emotional reaction to stories of Belgian heroism and German atrocities.[2]

The perception in Europe that the United States would not fight was another miscalculation. In 1916, Woodrow Wilson was campaigning on a platform to stay out of the war. By 1917, the United States was committed to the fight in Europe. The world suffered its first global war—the result of a series of misperceptions.[3] The aftermath was devastating. The upheavals and depressions provoked by World War I ultimately were responsible for the rise of a Communist Soviet Union and a Nazi Germany. The first steps on the road to World War II had been taken.

Historians and statesmen tend to argue that World War II was different. That, they say, was a consequence of Hitler's calculation. I don't believe this. Hitler wanted conquest without war if he could get it and was not preparing to fight a major world war. The Allies had backed down over the 1936 remilitarization of the Rhineland and the violation of the treaty provisions limiting the German army and navy. They had backed down over the *Anschluss* in 1938 and the incorporation of Czech Sudentenland. After "peace with honor" at Munich, Hitler took the rest of Czechoslovakia and was met only by harsh British and French words.

Why should Hitler have expected a different response to the division of Poland in concert with Russia in September 1939? If Britain did fight, it could only be briefly, for Poland was indefensible. Besides, Hitler knew his military capabilities would not reach their peak until 1942. It was certainly not his intention to set off a general war when he was not fully prepared.

He miscalculated, not only about Britain but also about the avow-
edly neutralist United States, which had sent very mixed signals about
its willingness to fight for Europe. The unwitting contributors to
Hitler's aggression subsequently became defenders who too late made
clear their will to resist.[4]

What are the lessons of these dreadful miscalculations? What can
we learn about preventing World War III and achieving world peace?
Shall we repeat history, complacent in a mistaken belief that people,
after forty years of nuclear peace, have achieved a new rationality? Is
that rationality more valid than that of 1914, which was fostered by
interdependent trade or a century of peace? Can summit meetings of
the two superpowers now make unnecessary our alliance systems?
Will *perestroika* guarantee the peace?

The image of international politics as a rational chessboard with
cool logic behind every move does not hold in our age. One of the
themes of this book is that it is possible to repeat history, despite the
summits, *perestroika* and *glasnost*, and nuclear deterrence. The lessons of history, written in the blood of nearly 60 million lives, are
already being forgotten or benignly reinterpreted. Such complacency
could be fatal once again but on a scale far worse than the past two
world wars.

The North Atlantic Treaty alliance was born out of these tragic
wars. It was precisely owing to these two global conflicts, the product
of unclear national commitments, that Article V became the centerpiece of the North Atlantic Treaty. It boldly stated that an attack
against one ally would be considered an attack against all. For the
United States, the commitment to the alliance was clear. It broke from
the warning of George Washington against "entangling alliances" and
a century of isolationism. We were now committed in advance to
defending Western Europe.

At a key 1952 meeting in Lisbon, NATO governments decided
collectively to provide fifty divisions, four thousand aircraft, and strong
naval forces for Europe's defense. But the money was not forthcoming
to support such goals, and they were abandoned in 1954 with the
adoption of the strategy of massive nuclear retaliation. This pleased
the Europeans. Because nuclear weapons were far cheaper than conventional forces, they received "more bang for the buck." And since
the nuclear forces were American, this had the additional advantage
for the Europeans of being supported by the U.S. dollar. As for

conventional forces, they would not be strong enough to hold back or defeat the enemy, but would serve only as a "trip wire," setting off a massive nuclear response.

This massive retaliation strategy, easy and cheap as it was for the Europeans, regrettably transformed NATO from a mutual security alliance to an alliance of guarantee. With its nuclear weapons, the United States guaranteed the security of Europe. Over time, in place of Europe's initial appreciation of U.S. involvement, resentment and other negative attitudes toward the American protector were to rise out of this dependency.

Very soon after the strategy's introduction, the credibility of massive retaliation began to wear thin. Was it rational to meet a quick Soviet land-grab in Europe with a nuclear war? This kind of nagging question became a burning issue by 1957, when the launch of Sputnik made it clear that the Soviets would be able to respond with nuclear strikes of their own. After retiring as army chief of staff, General Maxwell Taylor wrote an incisive book, *The Uncertain Trumpet*, about the illogic of an inflexible nuclear strategy. He proposed a flexible, rather than a massive, nuclear response, with that flexibility based on strong conventional forces. Taylor very much impresssed young Senator John F. Kennedy, who was looking for new ideas for his presidential campaign. During the campaign, Kennedy began to claim that since Sputnik, the Soviets had made so much progress producing missiles that there was a "missile gap" between the Soviets and the Americans—a contention later proved wrong. But Kennedy also argued that there needed to be a conventional weapons buildup and a more flexible strategy.

Kennedy's secretary of defense, Robert McNamara, began to press NATO for just such a flexible-response strategy—the opposite of a "trip wire." The Europeans did not like McNamara's idea because a flexible strategy would force them to spend money on conventional forces. Nevertheless, after five years of wrangling, the strategy of a flexible response was accepted by NATO in 1967, after France (which had bitterly opposed it) withdrew from NATO's Military Command. Thus a massive credibility gap was closed—for the time being.

Flexible response was designed to deter aggression by providing not just one alliance response to such aggression (the strategic nuclear one) but a range of possible responses proportional to the challenge. The possible responses included: (1) direct initial defense by conventional forces; (2) if that failed, deliberate escalation using a range of nuclear weapons stationed on European soil; and (3) only finally, a general strategic nuclear option. NATO's three-legged deterrent depended on conventional forces, theater nuclear forces, and strategic nuclear forces. This made sense at the time, given America's nuclear superiority.

If one thing is certain about "the art of war," it is that things never stay the same. Technologies evolve and opponents seek ways to gain a new advantage. It is not surprising, then, that over time and in the face of continued Soviet buildup of conventional, theater nuclear, and strategic nuclear forces in the 1970s, each component of the NATO deterrent developed vulnerabilities. By the 1970s, the Soviet nuclear force equaled and in some cases threatened ours.

In the early to mid-1980s the United States began to take several important steps designed to restore equilibrium on the strategic level, including introduction of the Trident submarine, the B-1 bomber, and the MX missile and the pursuit of meaningful arms negotiations to cut back Soviet first-strike heavy missiles.

It was in the midst of the second round of U.S.–Soviet strategic arms negotiations in 1977 that West German Chancellor Helmut Schmidt sounded the alarm regarding theater nuclear forces: Soviet deployment of a very advanced, three-warhead solid-fuel missile, the SS-20, threatened to decouple Europe from the United States. This weapon was thought to have a unique potential for political blackmail, since NATO had no counterpart. The ominous SS-20s were not being included in the SALT II negotiations. Europeans like Schmidt feared that their defense interests were being relegated to second place as the superpowers negotiated over their heads.

This concern was addressed by NATO in 1979, in the "two track" decision of the NATO Foreign and Defense Ministers' Meeting in Brussels. According to this now-famous decision, the preferred solution, the so-called first track, was one of negotiated reductions of these weapons. If that could not be achieved, NATO would move to the second track: It would deploy its own theater nuclear forces, the Pershing II and ground-launched cruise missiles. When NATO began to deploy, the Kremlin walked out of the negotiations.

Then came the stunning Soviet turnabout. In 1987, the Soviets under Gorbachev agreed to eliminate all intermediate-range weapons. This led to a sudden new focus on superior Soviet conventional forces.

I had always said in my speeches across Europe that the deterrent was like a three-legged stool, with the conventional leg much shorter than the others so that the stool was badly out of balance. In light of the Intermediate-Range Nuclear Forces (INF) Treaty, the conventional leg of the deterrent stool, now more than ever, must be made longer and sturdier.

The conventional imbalance is the heart of the problem. NATO has never properly strengthened the third, conventional leg of the deterrent. In certain parts of the NATO defense, there have not been, for example, adequate ammunition stocks and manpower reserves to sustain combat for more than a few days on certain parts of the front. Nor has there been sufficient commonality among allies of ammunition, weapons, and communications. Forces are not stationed where they are supposed to fight. The problem is not that the NATO front is universally weak; rather, it is uneven and contains vulnerabilities that could invite Soviet miscalculation in the 1990s. Many people at NATO really don't want to look at these weaknesses. They would rather believe that nuclear weapons automatically deter war, regardless of the condition of conventional forces. Some Europeans thought I was much too worried about all these unpleasant things as NATO ambassador. I secretly felt that they were like Europeans who wanted blindly to believe that royal family relationships, trade relations, and the one hundred years of peace since the Congress of Vienna would prevent any world war.

If the lessons of two world wars tell us anything, it is that conflicts start at low, not high, levels and are often caused by little moves, not big ones. A nuclear Pearl Harbor is not our greatest danger. And yet military and diplomatic planners and politicians simply do not understand this. They look at the situation at the top strategic level, counting nuclear numbers, playing with the tantalizing nuclear "endgame." They do not look at the lowest level, conventional forces, where deterrence is put on the line first. It is mind-boggling that a fascination with counting nuclear weapons as a part of the negotiations game has so distracted us from what is by far the most fundamental issue: where and how war might begin. Indeed, it is the need to compensate for the basic imbalance in conventional forces that has driven much of the nuclear arms race.

In the event the Soviets ever move toward war, their doctrine and military behavior seem to envision a kind of short, quick attack reminiscent of General Guderian's blitzkrieg in World War II. Part of the German miscalculation in both world wars was that the Germans had believed in rapid victory. It is a dangerous trend that Soviet military doctrine and their military formations increasingly contemplate rapid victory. Recently there have been Soviet pronouncements about changing that doctrine, but this has yet to show up in the configuration of their forces.

Plainly, if present trends continue, Soviet blitzkrieg forces in the 1990s will have a new potential to intimidate Western Europe. They can retain this capability despite their overall need to economize. Gorbachev recognizes that the role of nuclear weapons is declining and thus has given up the SS-20s, which the Kremlin had said it would never do. However, lightninglike forward deployed conventional forces could offer a new form of political suasion.

The very presence of a Soviet northern fleet, capable of operating in the Norwegian Sea and standing between NATO reinforcement of Norway and Denmark, would give the Soviets the capability to exercise power and influence without firing a shot. In the worst case, this influence could be exercised at the same time that it became known that Soviet armed forces had the power to overwhelm NATO's Northern Army Group within days. Such a capability in Europe could even be used to limit our freedom of action during a Third World crisis, for example, in the Middle East or even the Caribbean.

The biggest danger, however, comes not from bad intentions but from instabilities on both sides: on the NATO side if maldeployments remain, if the United States withdraws some troops or if the alliance becomes looser; and on the other side, if the Soviet Union and Eastern Europe are in turmoil. There can be consequences that neither side has planned. During a crisis, a precautionary move by one side could be taken as provocative by the other. More specifically, the beginning of mobilization in Europe and massive reinforcement by America could be used by Soviet marshals to argue for a flash preemptive move on the ground, confident that their nuclear deterrence of our nuclear weapons would work. Such crisis instability could take us back to the summer of 1914. It would be the fault of both superpowers and to the ultimate advantage of neither.

The experts say that the leaders of the Soviet Union do not want world war. I believe that. But no one in the summer of 1914 wanted war. In the 1930s, few realized how the deterioration of economic relations would contribute to the coming of war. Yet in the 1990s, forces of profound change will be at play, with the power to unravel both the East and the West. Ironically, a shifting multipolar world of the late 1990s would add to the lack of predictability. We must ensure that war comes neither by calculation nor by mistake, and that blackmail short of war cannot be successful. Then the Soviets will have no recourse but to change their failing system and its authoritarian form of government. Never before has there been such extraordinary promise in what is happening in the Soviet Union, but there is a new kind of potential peril.

This book offers a grand strategy to develop the promise and avoid the peril, to ensure that war does not occur and that peace, prosperity, and freedom are achieved. The strategy is global rather than regional and encompasses economics, technology, arms control, and leadership as well as the need for military stability. It also offers a grand strategy that seeks to place our policies on a higher moral ground and inspire confidence both at home and abroad.

PART I
THE WORLD THEATER

1   In Search of
    a Grand Strategy

I GREW up on a tall hill overlooking the winding Tennessee River and Missionary Ridge in the Chattanooga Valley. On a clear November day in 1863, my great grandfather, a Union officer, was among the thousands of blue-coated soldiers who charged that ridge to dislodge surprised Confederate forces. My other ancestors fought with Robert E. Lee's army in northern Virginia. The nation was, as Lincoln said, a house divided. General Grant commanded at Chattanooga, and by his victory, he won such acclaim that Lincoln soon made him commander of all Union forces.

Grant always had more resources and he used them well. It was Lee, though, with inferior forces who displayed a genius for classical strategy perhaps unmatched in all American history, a gift of knowing how to do more with less. Had Lee been given the overall Confederate command at the beginning of the war (as Lincoln had offered command of the North in 1861), the country might permanently have become a house divided. Instead, it became a house united—and the hope of the world.[1]

Or did it? In many ways, the United States is still a house divided, even subdivided—incapable of devising an integrated grand strategy or achieving a unity of vision and purpose. In 1987, there were two dramatic examples. The Speaker of the House of Representatives conducted diplomacy with Nicaragua independent of the White House; the secretary of state complained to a Senate committee that life in Washington is a battle royal, a kind of guerrilla warfare with

3

increasing conflict over policy. The usually stoic George Shultz lamented that, "Nothing ever gets settled in this town."[2] Overextended and often wasteful in its expenditures, misunderstood, at times discredited abroad, often stalemated and divided between the Congress and the executive, our now-debtor nation must impose the organization and exercise the leadership of a house reunited. This may well be necessary to prevent a global financial crisis and even the possibility of World War III.

The balkanization of Washington did not begin during the Reagan or Carter administrations. It was much longer in the making. To fully understand its meaning, one must go back to what now seems like a golden age. Having left the regular army in 1955, I arrived in the capitol city to pursue graduate studies in history at Georgetown University. The leader of our great crusade to victory in Europe—the enormously popular General Dwight Eisenhower—was in the White House. He was courtly and deferential to Congress in his style. At the same time, he really did not have to deal with "the Congress" but rather with equally courteous, powerful committee chairmen, most of whom were Southern. Ike shrewdly obtained a resolution of support before undertaking any foreign initiative.

While completing my doctorate I went to work on Capitol Hill for the last two years of that Eisenhower administration, to experience history in the making. As a member of the Republican staff, I often ran missions to the White House, the State or Defense departments, or the CIA. Once I went to see Allen Dulles, the debonair head of the Central Intelligence Agency—an agency much praised at the time and filled with the "best and brightest" from Ivy League schools. On his desk was an array of different colored telephones. In awe, I drank up his explanation of how he was capable of operating in a crisis. No one on Capitol Hill, or even in the White House, questioned his budget, his authority, or his judgment. Unlike today, Washington's governmental institutions were admired, not debunked, and the governance process was trusted.

Although there were tensions and divisions in Washington, it was a completely different ball game from today. Not only were the institutions and processes of American government in good shape but there was a "grand strategy" in place that commanded a bipartisan consensus including the support of the powerful Eastern Establishment. People perceived the threat of communism and the fallacy of appeasement; they recognized the importance of global leadership, and the naïveté of isolationism; the Truman Doctrine, the Marshall Plan, our global alliance structure—it all worked, including the U.N. action responding to North Korea's aggression.

In fact, as an infantry company commander on a Korean hillside in the spring of 1953, I could carry out my assigned mission of troop education by simply explaining why we were there: the line of freedom versus communism—the 38th parallel—had to be defended. The arguments of some conservatives about "rolling back" or "winning" the Cold War were highly controversial, but no one argued against containment as a minimum requirement. The troops all understood the simple concept presented by their company commander. The concept of containment started in Europe but came to be applied globally. After Eisenhower, containment was carried further and interpreted more vigorously. By 1961, the young, idealistic president, John F. Kennedy, said that Western freedom must be defended anywhere, everywhere.

This stirring philosophy was to be swept away with hurricane force. The painful experience of the televised Vietnam War, and the breakdown of consensus it fostered, contributed to the Balkanization not only of the executive branch and the Congress but of the nation at large. The "best and brightest" of the Eastern Establishment who led us into the Vietnam commitment not only abandoned it but largely turned vehemently against it. In the same period, the rise of special interests and single-issue politics, of mass mail and television, produced a revolution in politics. Structures and consensus were broken. New forms of direct political action developed, first in civil rights issues, then against the war in Vietnam and the military-industrial complex in general. CIA recruiters and ROTC were run off college campuses. In Congress, committee chairmen were overthrown by freshman congressmen while fights within the executive branch increased.

My early career education took place in the middle of this brewing maelstrom, in both the world of Washington think tanks, one of which I helped establish in 1962, and the world of executive-legislative relations as I became assistant secretary of state for congressional relations ten years later. That Congress was very different from the one on whose staff I had served in 1959–60. If nothing else, the "new" Congress was more assertive about foreign policy. In the golden years of the 1950s, two of the Senate's strongest proponents of presidential powers—individuals who indeed showed deference to the presidency—were former Rhodes scholar William Fulbright and former secretary of the Air Force Stuart Symington.

Senator Fulbright helped sponsor the Gulf of Tonkin Resolution in 1964 which gave President Johnson the power to react to a reported attack on two U.S. vessels. But Johnson took the resolution to give him vast authority to enlarge the war effort. Later, Fulbright felt deceived over the circumstances and the resolution's follow-up. He and Symington turned on their commander-in-chief's war effort. The senators launched hearings on U.S. commitments abroad and attempted to cut off support for many of them.

When I became assistant secretary of state in the spring of 1970, I was thrown into the management of these hearings for the executive branch. Other senators introduced amendments to end the war in Southeast Asia, stop funding certain covert efforts, or withdraw troops from NATO. Whenever Congress was out of session I went to trouble spots to see them for myself. I recall a dinner conversation with the prime minister of Laos. He asked again and again for my estimate of the chances of Congress passing an amendment cutting off the financing of the war there. That showed me how far the power of Congress had stretched! In 1975, over a White House toast, the prime minister of Singapore asked for a "restoration of confidence in the capacity of the United States [the president and the Congress] to act in unison in a crisis."[3] His toast was in vain.

That same year, out of government again, I served on a commission to study the organization of the government for the effective conduct of foreign policy. The legislation for this commission actually had been initiated by the Senate Foreign Relations Committee to see if there was a better way for the government in Washington to conduct its business. In these latter years of the Vietnam War, relations between the executive and legislative branches were often inflamed and the commission approach seemed a very constructive one.

Appointments were made by the Congress and the president, and the commission was chaired by famed diplomat Robert Murphy. In the commission's early days there was considerable harmony, as we met in the gilded office of the taciturn but highly hospitable Senate Majority Leader Mike Mansfield. Then a few differences among the group began to emerge. Congressmen tilted more toward a stronger presidency than did the senators. The White House was concerned that the commission would not be critical enough of such things as the War Powers Resolution. Later, President Ford appointed his own vice president, Nelson Rockefeller, to a commission vacancy to try to tilt the commission more toward the presidency. Rockefeller hired a crack staff, including General Andrew Goodpaster and naval Captain Jonathan Howe, destined to be an admiral. I recall how the commanding vice president swept into the room at his first meeting, shaking hands with everyone in sight, and settled into his chair ready for combat over any and every word in the draft. Perhaps no American in history chaired or served on so many commissions, bringing his brand of Eastern Establishment internationalism.

Neither Rockefeller's style nor his message impressed Senator Mansfield, who ceased coming to meetings and sent a representative. Divisions became deep and biting between the Montana-based Democrat and the Eastern Establishment Republican. They had little in common in their views of the world and the U.S. role in it, and this only exacerbated their biases toward the institutions they represented. The commission's recommendations, some of which will be discussed later in this book, had little impact, in part because of the Mansfield-Rockefeller disputes.

The Watergate scandal and the aborted Nixon presidency brought public disillusionment and distrust of Washington to a new high. Gerald Ford, a wise caretaker president and a healer of wounds, was later to be defeated by a previously little known presidential nominee who successfully ran against Washington. Jimmy Carter's single foreign policy experience had been serving on David Rockefeller's Trilateral Commission. Despite bright beginnings, however, the problem of consensus and governance worsened under the Carter administration. As Anatoly Dobrynin wrote, President Carter was "fundamentally unpredictable."[4] After the failed efforts of the administration's official representatives, the Panama Canal Treaty was ratified only because of the coordinated efforts of Republican Senate Leader Howard Baker and Washington Democratic lawyer William Rogers, operating out of channels. The SALT II agreement never made it through the Senate, and the hostage crisis in Teheran paralyzed the Carter administration. The exception was the conclusion of the Tokyo trade round, which was a tribute to the extraordinarily skilled Texan Robert Strauss. He knew how to negotiate both internationally and domestically in a balkanized environment. However, this achievement was unusual.

In the spring of 1978, the dean of Washington columnists, Scottie Reston, wrote a piece titled "Is Anybody in Charge?"[5] The general frustration was so great that Carter's White House counsel, veteran Washington lawyer Lloyd Cutler, wrote an article calling for a constitutional amendment to reestablish presidential leadership.[6] Allies also had cause to wonder about the leader of the alliance.

Then came the tall, square-shouldered, former governor from California. With not a hair out of place, Ronald Reagan strode jauntily into the future. It was this man from the West who restored for Americans much of their idealism. He inspired the kind of admiration that, in my youth, I felt for movie heroes like John Wayne. He was a straight-shooter, riding tall in the saddle, quite sure of his mission against the bad men. With a magnetic ability to communicate to the American public, a sense of optimism and personal decency, of simplicity so different from a Johnson or Nixon, Reagan won over the public. Above all, he inspired personal trust.

Perhaps because the new crowd came from the West, they initially brought a sense of can-do unilateralism, a willingness to act alone and the courage to call the "evil empire" just that. There was certainly none of the post-Vietnam defeatism or European equivocation that had characterized foreign policy during the previous decade. But there was one problem. Although the U.S. actions against Grenada and Libya had immense appeal to Americans, this was hardly the case in Europe. Nevertheless, for all the objections and snide criticisms about the former actor, everyone knew that after a series of plagued presidencies Ronald Reagan had restored the strength of the American presidency.

Ronald Reagan's personal attributes, however, by no means substituted for a grand strategy, a grand consensus, or grand governance. Underneath the optimism, trust, and admiration the problems of governance remained. This fundamental fact was driven home to me in 1986, when as NATO ambassador I made four hundred phone calls to Congress and spent cumulatively thirty days walking the marble halls on the Hill to buttonhole Members or to give strategy briefings on what we at NATO were doing, and the need for members of Congress to support our needs with their votes. After the defense buildup peaked, the struggle over the defense budget intensified.

There was no consensus on strategy, too few funds after the Reagan military buildup turned downward, and the NATO programs often took a back seat among our military services.

The problem of dealing with the executive branch, however, was even more difficult. Serious battles within and between the State and Defense departments and the National Security Council staff were profuse—Shultz vs. Weinberger, Vance vs. Brzezinski, Kissinger vs. Schlesinger—and these became reflected through the already fractionalized bureaus. Debate is good, for the president must have options; but permanent divisions and civil wars are not. When I came to NATO in 1983, there were two groups of governmental experts from NATO capitals chaired by two brilliant, but highly competitive young Americans: the Special Consultative Group on Intermediate Nuclear Forces Negotiations was chaired by the State Department's Richard Burt, and the High Level Task Force was chaired by the Defense Department's Richard Perle. It was State against Defense. A tight-lipped NATO ambassador broke his diplomatic rule over his evening Scotch to say, "Don't you think it extraordinary that Burt and Perle use these two groups to play out their differences all over Europe?"

The problem is deeper than any one administration. Washington government is compartmentalized rather than integrated, reactive rather than anticipatory. As a result, it lacks a common, long-range strategy. We must put together the house divided if we are to realize our "last best hope" and peace in the world of the 1990s and beyond. Indeed, the first requirement of a grand strategy relates to the institution of the presidency itself. How can the executive branch be moved from division to unity, and how can the president and Congress reunite their divided house?

I pondered such questions during the bleak winter days of 1987. I had been called back from my NATO ambassadorial post to be the president's Special Counselor on the Iran-Contra inquiry. If the Iran-Contra controversy had been the result of a flawed process, it was essential to the survival of the Reagan presidency that the investigators and the White House follow due process in the aftermath. It was as if a recurring Greek tragedy had descended over the last quarter-century of the presidency to sap its strength: Kennedy's assassination, Johnson's Vietnam, Nixon's Watergate, Carter's Tehran, and now

Reagan's Iran-Contra. Two Select Committees of Congress were investigating, in addition to Judge Lawrence Walsh, the Independent Counsel, and the president's own panel chaired by former Senator John Tower. Much of the world held its breath and wondered once again what was happening to Washington.

I outlined to President Reagan a plan to enhance the presidency. I explained why it was necessary to go beyond the forthcoming Tower Board report on the Iran-Contra affair to bold new measures of leadership, organization, and strategy.

As a follow-up for the White House staff, I put some of my thoughts in an action memorandum: "The President must go beyond the Tower Board reforms, and must be seen to do so by taking strong, decisive actions with his direct personal involvement. Nothing less will be adequate, especially in view of the fact that his party does not control the Congress, and in the foreign policy area, Gorbachev has shown a capacity quite unparalleled in Soviet leadership." The memorandum argued that "the Presidency will face its most severe challenge following the release of the Tower Board Report. We have a window of opportunity of about thirty days—opportunity to escape the danger of a more permanent image of a weakened Presidency. This cannot be done incrementally, or by tidying-up things a bit." The president and his administration, I said, "must act immediately, boldly, and dramatically; the action must be real, not just show."[7]

What I was also saying was that the national security process should be reorganized, that it had to have a team that worked together. I believed we had to take this catastrophe and turn it to advantage. A broader sense of comprehensive strategy should be developed, and the chronic divisions on almost all national security questions between the State and Defense departments had to end. Needless to say, the director of the Central Intelligence Agency should never conduct his own secret foreign policy. Gorbachev's comprehensive strategy could not be met by a piecemeal, divided administration, or by a Congress divided from an administration.

Because there were those in the White House who said I would raise false expectations or, worse yet, false obstacles, I wrote, "We must risk that danger of raising expectations, for if we do not do so and seek to justify them, the first two-term Presidency since Eisenhower—one that has reinforced the strength of the Presidency after a series of

Presidential failures—would itself be put at risk." Time was of the essence. On top of the Iran-Contra disillusionment, we had divided government. Furthermore, the president's party had lost control of the Senate. This made a bipartisan approach more important than ever. My extensive consultations on Capitol Hill convinced me it was possible to reinforce strength if the president took broad initiatives before we entered the partisanship of the forthcoming election.

I made a number of suggestions. I argued that the vice president should be put in charge of a new process with Congress. His office next to the Senate chamber should become the symbol of that new partnership, to overcome congressional distrust resulting from the withholding of information on Iran-Contra activities. The vice president should be responsible for restoration and renewal. Second, the entire national security process should be examined, going far beyond Iran-Contra issues. The president should reassert his role as commander in chief, taking the secretary of defense with him on a visit to the State Department, and taking the secretary of state to the Defense Department. The president personally should bring the leaders of the Intelligence Committee to the CIA to visit with its new head. We should require teamwork throughout, at a time when America's international leadership ability was under question.

Some of the minor parts of the plan were adopted, but not the major and fundamental ones. President Reagan supported it, but before long there was overconfidence that a few excellent changes in personnel would remedy the process. Frank Carlucci, who was highly effective with bureaucracies, had taken over the National Security Council. Then, the arrival of Howard Baker as chief of staff was taken throughout the White House as the requisite reorganization—indeed, as the "second coming," following the problems and controversy over his predecessor Donald Regan. After all, Baker was the former Majority Leader of the Senate. One might conclude that all problems were soon to be solved, but despite an initial and glorious honeymoon, they were not. In retrospect, the talented Howard Baker would be the first to say so and point out the limitations of the chief of staff position.

For the long term, only consensus on a realistic grand strategy can overcome the deleterious effects of Balkanization in the executive branch, distrust, and governance by amendment on the Hill. It is clear that a coordinated, comprehensive approach is badly needed. Only with such an approach can a consensus between the executive and legislative branches reemerge. We also need a grand strategy to rally people around and to guide our resource priorities at a time of budget cuts and debtor-nation status.

What is at issue is the strategy making itself. It is easy to talk about and hard to do and perhaps this is why the task is easy for academics having no accountability in the real world of governance. The problem with governmental practitioners, however, is that few of them understand what strategy really is. Originally it was a military subject concerned with using the instruments of war to achieve victory. Today, however, the dimensions of strategy have expanded, and it must be a peacetime pursuit. Board-room discussions shape "corporate strategies," economists argue about "development strategies," and sports fans debate the merits of "game strategy." Many people think a strategy is simply a plan. I disagree vehemently. The term was derived from the Greek *strategos*, meaning the "art" of the general, not the "plan" of the general. Art is an arrangement of elements in a manner that creates a whole that is far greater than the sum of its elements. This is just as true of peacetime strategies as of wartime ones. A plan, if it is fixed and stereotyped, is in fact the opposite of a truly good strategy. Strategy involves having a concept, priorities, and a direction—ones that are flexible and adaptable to changing situations—for the rational and disciplined allocation of resources to achieve specific objectives.

There is no set formula to strategy, although strategists have offered certain general principles. At the turn of the century much was written about "classical" strategy in a way that emphasized it as an art rather than an exact science. Of course in the military realm, where there is an opponent, one is always dealing with the maximization of resources that can be brought to bear on an opponent's vulnerabilities. In war, the good strategist attempts to break his opponent's equilibrium and will to fight. In peace, the successful strategy prevents war from ever breaking out and keeps an opponent from taking adverse action. The ultimate aim of strategy is to influence the will of opponents, the will and commitment of allies, and the allocations and harmonization of economic measures to accomplish objectives. The classical art of strategy—in peace or war—is often to rearrange and redirect what is already available to produce a favorable outcome.

The problem is that today's modern military is characterized by huge structures that tend to produce managers, not strategists. This is not to say that good management is unessential in military structures, but rather that it must not be pursued to the exclusion of good strategy. Managers tend toward a wartime strategy of attrition—winning by superior resources directly applied, as Americans tried in Vietnam, as the Allied generals did for much of World Wars I and II, or as Grant did in the Civil War. They tend to forget the lessons of history about the art of using inferior resources more skillfully. In their frontal approach, they frequently do not allow for changing conditions, either technological or psychological, nor for the role of perceptions. The good strategist is not reactive and compartmentalized but integrative and anticipatory, seeking ways to multiply his strength. The good strategist must be a psychologist and never forget the human factor in war, as we did in Vietnam.[8]

What of grand strategy? Today more than ever, security is both military and economic, and the two must be interrelated in a grand strategy. Western grand strategy, however, must do even more. It must embrace political and diplomatic, technological, and even cultural and moral factors. It must be a comprehensive way to deal with all the elements of national power, matching ends and means, relating them to commitments and diplomacy, and ensuring that they work in harmony. For example, a protectionist trade strategy against our security allies would undercut the military strategy of our alliance. It is for this very reason that Edward Luttwak, that profound writer on this subject, so emphasizes the element of consistency: "It is the peculiar reward of grand strategy that a mere untalented adequacy in each of its dimensions could result in large success if there is consistency across the board."[9]

Just this consistency has been the hallmark of Soviet strategy, a strategy that otherwise can appear quite drab. In fact, Marxists have been better attuned for grand-strategy formulation than have capitalists. Together, Karl Marx's pamphlet of 1848, the *Communist Manifesto*, and Lenin's extensive writings represent a basic strategic concept the Kremlin has consistently pursued. If today the true believers in communism may be fewer, the Soviet method of organizing power, internally and externally, remains despite the "time of troubles" facing the world's last empire. The Soviets hold to the requirement for the long view of grand strategy, like the Romans and their empire. Unlike undisciplined "decadent" democracies, they maintain the conviction that ends justify means, whether in Eastern Europe or elsewhere. Unlike Hitler, the Soviets know the difference between power and force: maximize power and it will not be necessary to use force so long as it hovers in the background. This was a strategy carried out effectively in the attempted suppression of Solidarity in Poland.

Communists speak of the "correlation of forces," and the very idea conveys a grand strategy. Their long-term view that history works in their favor gives them patience, especially since they must feel the West is incapable of a long-term, integrated grand strategy. They know, and we know, that the Western democracies live from election to election. What kind of alliance is it anyway, they must speculate, when the ambassador of the weakest NATO nation can prevent consensus, as compared to the Warsaw Pact, where only one nation decides?

In Moscow in 1983, I visited the Institute for the Study of the United States and Canada, headed by Georgi Arbatov. In the conference room, I sat at a table with a range of Soviet experts on America. What struck me most was that our discussion focused almost entirely on the conflicting forces and crosscurrents in the United States and Europe. To them it seemed impossible that out of such "democratization run wild" there could ever be a long-range, integrated strategy in the West.

Strategy Making

Are the naysayers and skeptics correct? Can there be a grand strategy? This is the central question of this book.

The Soviets certainly know the West had a strategy after World War II. Ironically, they helped trigger it. Containment, the Truman Doctrine, the Marshall Plan, and finally NATO were created largely in response to Soviet threats. There was a public unity within both Europe and America that sustained that strategy. That it went amok, by the way, had nothing to do with Europe or NATO, but everything to do with Asia and the Vietnam War. The Vietnam conflict ultimately was lost, however one might define *defeat*, and a sense of guilt, illegitimacy, and resentment by many Americans and criticism by many Europeans came into vogue. This led to a deep questioning of America's role in the world, and no comprehensive strategy survived.

In 1979, in the aftermath of Vietnam, as head of the Center for Strategic and International Studies (CSIS), I sat down with a congressional study group to focus on recreating a grand strategy. The group got started, but, in spite of all the bright minds coming to testify (Kissinger, Brzezinski, Schlesinger, Luttwak, Blechman), never really blossomed. In retrospect, I think it was because the focus was too much on the United States and too little on our alliances.

My own education on grand strategy was greatly advanced in July 1983, when I went to Europe as ambassador to NATO. I became involved in the most unusual organized alliance in human history. As I reread the treaty, I found a blueprint for a grand strategy. On the frontline of the alliance, I developed an entirely different perspective from the one I had in Washington. Washington, I realized, and its way of thinking about strategic matters were part of the problem!

Within two months of arriving at NATO, I had prepared a lengthy paper for a CSIS Williamsburg Conference on NATO and U.S. Grand Strategy, with the help of my NATO staff. I announced to the conferees that I had discovered the key to the beginning of a grand strategy:

> The thesis of this paper is that the Treaty establishing the North Atlantic Alliance clearly creates a framework and provides needed guidance for such an alliance strategy. If this thesis is correct, then NATO becomes a uniquely valuable strategic asset in a world where coherence and integration are rarely found and where the lack of overall structure fosters wasteful pursuit of conflicting goals. Moreover, if this argument is sound, the challenge to policymakers is to translate the theoretical benefits inherent in NATO into concrete and operational reality. For performance has not matched opportunity.[10]

I went on to argue that, for democratic societies, a grand strategy is characterized by four elements:

1. Grand strategy must be related to society as a whole and must be appropriate to the values of the society and build on its strengths. The first grand strategist, Alexander the Great, understood this well. Indeed, he was a military genius but also a genius at spreading Hellenic culture and values throughout the lands he conquered. The Roman Empire had a grand strategy—*Pax Romana*—that went far beyond the deployment of thirty or so legions required to hold the empire together. It was also a system that made allies, built roads,

fostered maritime commerce, and promoted law, justice, and culture. In the eighth century, Charlemagne tried to recreate the Roman Empire on a Christian model, but his children could not hold together his centralized empire because there was no economic foundation for his grand strategy. The Church, at the height of its unity from the tenth to twelfth centuries, produced its own grand strategy for the princes and potentates of Europe by limitations on conflict—the Truce and Peace of God—along with cultural and religious unity, as reflected in the great cathedrals of Chartres, Rheims, Cologne, and Strasbourg. There was an unparalleled unity of values and aspirations summed up in Gothic architecture. Furthermore, Napoleon had a grand strategy as well, combining brilliant conquest, French revolutionary ideas, and Napoleonic law; Hitler had his strategy of perversions and conquest within his framework of national socialism. The first left only his law; the second only the revulsion of the world.

2. Grand strategy must be multidimensional. In the more than forty years since the end of World War II, the concept of security has broadened to include freedom from vulnerability of all kinds. The 1973 October War in the Middle East and subsequent oil shortages demonstrated the West's weakness. Terrorism and technology penetrate our domestic security. Massive Third World debts make our overextended banks vulnerable. Acid rain and problems of dioxin have pinpointed our openness to ecological deterioration. All of these concerns must be addressed.

3. Grand strategy should not only integrate the various instruments of national policy but must also regulate their use. These policy instruments cannot be used in isolation. A grand strategy provides an "integrated conceptual framework" that defines the relationship among goals and instruments, and among the instruments themselves. Grand strategy also implies setting priorities and allocating resources. To be practical, grand strategy must accept limits, especially in democratic societies. The values, social structures, and political institutions of a society impose limits on the acceptable behavior of its members and its government. This is true internationally, as it is in the domestic arena.

4. Grand strategy must be public strategy. Walter Lippmann, the most influential columnist in the decade following World War II, argued for a "public philosophy"—the idea that sustained credibility and a sense of legitimacy among the public was vital for effective

governance in a democratic society.[11] Today there is an equal need for "public strategy," one that is comprehensible and acceptable to the populace whose support is essential, with a sense of legitimacy as in the 1950s.

Regretfully, I must add that this sense of public strategy and legitimacy is exactly what the bespectacled, pipe-smoking Vice Admiral John Poindexter forgot during his stewardship as national security adviser. In the aftermath of the Libyan raid, disinformation was put out to keep Qaddafi off guard, and as NATO ambassador I was told to give the information to our allies without being informed that it was false. Admiral Poindexter, without remorse, regret, or apology, testified before the Select Investigating Committees that the approval of the diversion of arms-sales funds to the Contras was his decision and his alone, appropriately so. According to Poindexter, the decision should not have gone to the president nor been discussed with the Senate or House Intelligence committees, as required by law. A talented friend of mine, William Casey, also lacked a full appreciation of public accountability and hence too often slighted the checks and balances controlling the agency. These philosophies were the antithesis of an effort to build public strategy backed by public support.

In terms of historical achievement, those who met and signed the North Atlantic Treaty in Washington on that early spring day in April 1949 deserve to be placed just behind the Constitutional Fathers who created the miracle in Philadelphia. They produced a remarkable treaty document representing an enormous contribution to humankind. The treaty not only provided a framework for a grand strategy as I have described it but also defined a relationship among sovereign nations that extends far beyond military matters.

Interestingly enough, Article I sets the alliance in a global as well as a regional context. Article II is a vital yet often overlooked component of the treaty, reflecting the multiple dimensions of NATO's grand strategy.

> The parties will contribute toward the further development of peaceful and friendly international relations by strengthening their free institutions, by bringing about a better understanding of the principles upon which these institutions are founded, and by promoting conditions of stability and well-being. They will seek to eliminate conflict in their

international economic policies and will encourage economic collabora-
tion between any or all of them.[12]

Our Constitution very quickly had its first ten amendments to
bring it to full maturity. So too did the NATO treaty have its so-called
Wise Men's Report by the Committee of Three.[13] The committee was
constituted in 1956, seven years after the signing of the treaty, to
explore "ways and means to improve and extend NATO cooperation in
non-military fields and to develop greater unity within the Atlantic
Community."[14]

The committee went on to say that Article II and Article IV
(which emphasizes consultation), "limited in their terms but with at
least the promise of the grand design of an Atlantic Community, were
included because of the insistent feeling that NATO must become
more than a military alliance . . . that while defense cooperation was
the first and most urgent requirement, this was not enough . . . [and]
that security is today far more than a military matter."[15]

Even the achievement of this fundamental goal—deterrence of
any conflict—is conditioned by nonmilitary factors as much as by
military preparations. The Committee of Three argued the case when
they pointed out that the deterrence role of NATO, based on solidarity and strength, could be discharged only if the political and economic relations among its members were cooperative and close. "An
Alliance in which the members ignore each other's interests or engage
in political or economic conflict, or harbor suspicions of each other,
cannot be effective for deterrence or defense."[16] In other words,
Article V, the core of the treaty to prevent World War III, can be
subverted by quarrelsome allies.

The Wise Men's Group also related other aspects of society to an
alliance grand strategy. It noted, for example, that "progress in [sci-
ence and technology] can be decisive in determining the security of
nations and their position in world affairs."[17] It also called on NATO
countries to promote cultural cooperation because the sense of community binding the people and institutions of the Atlantic nations "will
exist only to the extent that there is a realization of their common
cultural heritage and of the values of their free way of life and
thought."[18]

Finally, there has been concern from the beginning about mobilizing public support for the alliance. Information activities remain the

responsibility of individual NATO members. Since the mid-1950s, however, all member governments have expressed support for more attention to this critical area.

The commitment to collective defense is the core of the strategy. Article V of the treaty states that the signatories agree that "an armed attack against one or more of them in Europe or North America 'shall be considered an attack against them all."[19] The glue of the alliance may be the common interest of its members, but this obligation is the key to its success. Any potential aggressor must assume that, in the event of hostilities, it faces the combined military and political weight of all member nations. In the 1930s this is exactly what Hitler became convinced he would never have to face. It was what Europe lacked in that traumatic summer of 1914 that culminated in the guns of August.

The treaty provides for alliance members to implement its provisions "in accordance with their respective constitutional processes."[20] This was a necessary political provision to obtain ratification, since the U.S. Senate was unwilling to forfeit its Constitutional role in war powers. Thus a specific response by the alliance after an attack is not automatic. Nevertheless, the pledge to collective security, made *in advance* of any conflict, sends an unambiguous signal to adversaries of what to expect, not necessarily in terms of a specific military response but in general involvement. In doing so, it underscores the commitment of the alliance to deter conflict at all times rather than simply to improvise together in a crisis.

In reexamining the treaty and reviewing the early thinking about the alliance, one can only be struck by the breadth of vision of those who committed their nations to this remarkable experiment. Their views were neither narrowly limited to military matters nor one dimensional with regard to future challenges to global security. In the treaty, and in its transformation into a working document, they were able to construct a far more effective framework for a grand strategy than the United States has today.

All of this was an unparalleled achievement that we have not managed to duplicate on a global basis. In the past fifteen years there have been three attempts by the executive branch to come to grips with a grand strategy, at least in some of its dimensions. The first was when President Nixon took office at a time of reevaluation occasioned by Vietnam and of global repositioning with the opening to China. Henry Kissinger, using his own intellectual capabilities and those of a small staff, authored for the president a series of annual reports to Congress that were highly conceptual and strategic in their approach.[21] Such reports did not endure. In the waning years of the Reagan administration, Dr. Fred Ikle—a strategic purist who questioned European nuclear theories with a cold Swiss logic—teamed up with Dr. Albert Wohlstetter to chair a group on the deterrent aspect of strategy, which shall be discussed later.[22] Of more continuing significance, Senator John Warner—himself a student of grand strategy—took a congressional initiative to require the executive branch to issue an annual report on the national security strategy of the United States. While falling short of a truly integrated grand strategy and existing more on paper than in reality, the report signed by President Reagan in January 1988 is a step forward. The Warner initiative hence became a highly significant one in our national attempt at strategy making.[23]

These reports, along with the NATO structure, show that it is possible and practical to have a grand strategy. Many of the pieces of such a strategy already exist, but we must put them together. First, we must examine how the greatest of alliances does and does not work, and study the implications of the lack of such a structure for the rest of the world.

2 How NATO Works
. . . or Does It?

I FIRST arrived at NATO headquarters near Brussels on an uncharacteristically hot, dry day in mid-July 1983. Sprawled along the highway from the Brussels international airport to the city, the Headquarters is marked by a circle of the sixteen flags of the nations making up the North Atlantic alliance.[1] One recent secretary-general called the jumble of office buildings "rather horrid looking," and it certainly is compared to the magnificently gilded sixteenth-century Grand'Place in downtown Brussels. But the labyrinthine structure has its utility and is able to accommodate all of the national missions, each headed by an ambassador, along with the national military delegations.

My first greeting and briefing was given by my deputy chief of mission (DCM), Stephen Ledogar, a former fighter pilot turned Foreign Service officer, with an imposing 6′ 6″ diplomatic presence. Secretary of State George Shultz once called him "the master negotiator," but for me, Ledogar was a master team builder. He was able, through constant care, to keep our mission staff of 100 of Foreign Service, Defense Department, U.S. Information Agency, Federal Emergency Management Agency, and military personnel working together. This was in sharp contrast to the house divided in Washington.[2]

NATO, like the rest of Europe, was about to go on "vacation" for six weeks, and I had arrived just in time for the season's last series of NATO meetings. There was no need to worry about response to a crisis. During holidays standby representatives, diplomatic and military, could meet in council session at any time, day or night, within an hour. It was from that council that my position derived its title: U.S. Permanent Representative on the North Atlantic Council. "Permanent" because the secretary of state or foreign ministers would be there only three or four times a year and only occasionally would the council meet at heads-of-government level in a NATO summit. I would represent the United States the rest of the time. The NATO ambassadors long ago became known in NATO jargon as the "Perm Reps."

One of my many distinguished predecessors, Donald Rumsfeld, who went on to be White House chief of staff and then secretary of defense, always insisted that U.S. ambassador to NATO was "the best job in government." More than any other job in our government, it combines diverse activities of diplomacy and defense and public articulation into one position, and requires regular travel to the countries of the alliance and dozens of military commands and units. The position has nearly always been held by a well-known political appointee with a strong professional background, the most noted being David Bruce, who was revered as the greatest American ambassador of his time. The one appointee drawn directly from the Foreign Service was my immediate predecessor, the multilingual Tapley Bennett. He was as close to Foreign Service "royalty" as one could be, holding the record for ambassadorial postings and with a gracious wife born into diplomatic life.

When I arrived at NATO, Joseph Luns was secretary-general. He was to serve for an unprecedented tour from 1971–1984. Still broad shouldered, once the dashing young man about Europe, he first entered the Dutch cabinet in 1952. As secretary-general, he relied on his years of authority, and his voice was so imposing that one Dutch woman said he was "capable of overruling a thunderstorm." He had charisma, wit, and a dry humor that charmed royalty and disarmed any chief of state. He needed such aplomb, for a secretary-general has to chair meetings of presidents and prime ministers, as well as foreign and defense ministers.

Promptly at 10:15 the next Wednesday, Joseph Luns banged his gavel and looked pleased to welcome me as the new U.S. ambassador. Each Wednesday, the sixteen ambassadors seated themselves around a ring of tables in one of the many NATO conference rooms for a full meeting of the North Atlantic Council. Behind each ambassador sat his DCM and other staff who could crowd around if the ambassador swung his chair back for a quiet consultation. On the table in front of me lay many cables from Washington, cleared by bureaucrats in the State and Defense departments and sometimes other departments, providing what I should say "under instructions." I soon learned that whenever I entered into free-flowing "uninstructed" comments, my backup staff held its breath trying to decide how to report back to Washington.

The first item of regular business is invariably "political subjects," when any ambassador can comment on any world development in or out of NATO's jurisdiction. Following "political subjects," the main agenda items are taken up. These might, for example, relate to the review and approval of reports on negotiations or budgetary matters, reports on preparations for the next NATO Foreign Ministers Meeting, or an announcement by the U.S. ambassador as to the availability of our Geneva arms-control negotiators to meet with the council.

If there is any matter requiring council approval, it has to be done by consensus. In the Warsaw Pact, only one vote counts—that of the Soviet Union. At NATO, one vote—that of the smallest country's representative, say, Luxembourg or Iceland—can block consensus. Of course, any small country would be very careful in doing so. For example, smaller countries not in agreement with the general position taken in communiqués issued after NATO Foreign or Defense Ministers meetings usually add their "footnotes," or reserve their positions, rather than block the document. Some critics of NATO say it cannot truly be effective because of this consensus rule, which pulls NATO down to the least common denominator or to stalemate. But in three and a half years in the U.S. chair, seldom did I see NATO fall to the least common denominator. Rather, the strength of the NATO collegium uplifted the weak.

The NATO Council is unique in the history of the world and in the annals of democratic nations, which too frequently have been incapable of acting collectively in their common interest. This is a collective body which at times experiences sharp individual differences and many quirks, but it has acted effectively to prevent World War III for over forty years. The NATO Council, and the consensus that follows from it, is the heart of the alliance's deterrent.

In the past, the councils and conferences that shaped global politics were ad hoc, short-term affairs designed to readjust European stability after stresses and strains in the state system threatened to tear it apart. The councils of the nineteenth century, and indeed those up to World War II, were based squarely on the nation-state system. The process involved intense jockeying for power and position among competing states. When, in the aftermath of World War II, nations looked upon the tragic postwar world, it was clear that the old way of diplomacy and security had led to disaster. A new order had to be built upon the simple proposition, stated by that heroic World War I nurse Edith Cavell, that "patriotism is not enough." Collective security is essential.

Although NATO differs in many respects from the oft-paralyzed United Nations, it was actually established pursuant to Article 51 of the United Nations Charter. Article 51 specifically authorized "collective self-defense if an armed attack occurs against a member." In deterring war (and continuing to survive) NATO succeeded where the other alliances of the 1950s—such as SEATO and CENTO—did not.

The Council's fundamental purpose is to enable sixteen democracies to work together within a detailed structure as they deal with security and foreign policy issues, as well as generate and apply defense resources to deter war or attempts at coercion short of war. Toward these ends, the Council has created over three hundred subcommittees on politics, economics, defense, mobilization, or armament matters, many made up of governmental experts from NATO capitals. Radiating out from NATO Headquarters are three huge military commands sprawled across Western Europe and the Atlantic.

How and why did this unique structure come about? In March 1948, following the Soviet coup in Czechoslovakia, representatives of Belgium, Luxembourg, France, the Netherlands, and the United Kingdom met in Brussels to establish a mutual-assistance treaty. They created a supreme body known as the Consultative Council of Foreign Ministers, as well as a Defense Ministers Committee. After the imposition of the Berlin blockade, these Brussels treaty members created a military organization, the Western Union Defense Organization, with Field Marshal Montgomery as chairman of the Commanders-in-Chief Committee in Fontainebleau.

Soviet pressures on Norway, in addition to the Berlin blockade, gave further impetus to talks with the United States on the creation of a North Atlantic alliance. Many leading U.S. politicians were opposed to any such action. Their fears ranged from rearming a divided Germany to provoking the Soviet Union. But Harry Truman, George Marshall, and Dean Acheson were able to forge a bipartisan coalition with Republican Arthur Vandenberg, chairman of the Senate Foreign Relations Committee. This gave birth to the Vandenberg Resolution, adopted in June 1948, which recommended "the association of the United States, by constitutional process, with such regional or other collective arrangements as are based on continuous and effective self-help and mutual aid." Diplomatic talks which were subsequently opened culminated in the creation of NATO on April 4, 1949. This was a historic departure, the first such peacetime alliance ever concluded outside of the Americas by the United States in the 160 years since the ratification of the Constitution in 1789.[3]

I was able to celebrate this event some thirty-five years later with the naming of the newly purchased residence for the U.S. ambassador to NATO. This rambling, loaf-shaped, dormered Flemish country house, with a large, cobblestone courtyard at the end of a tree-lined avenue, was surrounded with thirty acres of gardens and lawns, stretching to groves of pines and distant fields. We named the manor house Truman Hall, and the old farmer's house, remodeled for our congressional visitors and others, became the Vandenberg Guest House. One visitor, Senator Robert Dole, furnished us a picture of Arthur Vandenberg, symbolizing the congressional partnership with Harry Truman that had made NATO possible.

Indeed, it was in September 1949 during the Truman administration that the first meeting of the NATO Council of Foreign Ministers took place. At this time, a planning committee on military cooperation was set up. It was initially felt that a simple pledge of support by alliance members would be enough to deter the Soviets, but the Soviet-inspired North Korean invasion of South Korea led many to a different conclusion. Could Western Europe be next? NATO decided to organize for the possibility that it might have to defend itself.

At the September 1950 North Atlantic Council meeting in New York, a forward strategy for the defense of Europe was agreed upon. During the December 1950 NATO Council meeting in Brussels, a Supreme Allied Headquarters was established in Paris, with the famed leader of the liberation of Europe, General Dwight Eisenhower, as Supreme Allied Commander Europe. Soon thereafter, additional

American troops arrived in Europe. Committees composed of representatives of foreign, defense, and finance ministers proliferated; and in May 1951, the decision was made to give all these portfolios to the deputy foreign ministers, who had been meeting in continuous session. In 1952, a permanent Council of Ambassadors was established, and it was agreed that an international appointee would serve as permanent chairman, or secretary-general. Lord Ismay, Winston Churchill's tried and tested wartime chief of staff, was selected.

The original alliance members were Belgium, Canada, Denmark, France, Iceland, Italy, Luxembourg, the Netherlands, Norway, Portugal, the United Kingdom, and the United States. Greece and Turkey joined in 1952, and the Federal Republic of Germany in 1955. The alliance survived the Suez crisis in 1956, but it suffered a major blow when the French withdrew from the military command in 1966. Subsequently, NATO Headquarters moved from Paris to Brussels in 1967.

This explains why military matters relating to NATO's integrated command are not discussed in the full council, but rather in the Defense Planning Committee (DPC), with the same ambassadors around the table minus the French. Reporting to the DPC is the Military Committee, to which allied nations have assigned a very high-ranking military officer. The French keep their ears there, in the form of a "liaison officer" with the rank of three-star general. Another anomaly is that Spain, NATO's newest member, has not become part of the integrated military commands, but unlike France, it has full representation on the Military Committee and the DPC. Indeed, NATO is not a neat alliance.

There have been some very impressive generals in the alliance. When the Supreme Allied Command Europe departed Fontainebleau, France, for its new home at Casteau, near Mons, Belgium, there had already been five Supreme Allied Commanders Europe, or SACEUR. No military man in the Western world has greater attention showered on him than the SACEUR, who is looked upon by some officers as next to the deity Himself. No small wonder, since Dwight Eisenhower, the leader of the crusade to free Europe of Nazi oppression, was the first, bringing enormous prestige and awe to that office.

While I was NATO ambassador, former Army Chief of Staff Bernard Rogers was SACEUR, successor to General Alexander Haig. The intrepid Rogers served from 1979 until June 1987—longer than any predecessor. He was firmly independent, at times even from Secretary of Defense Weinberger and the Joint Chiefs of Staff, and later openly opposed the agreement for the elimination of intermediate-range nuclear weapons, because he saw it as weakening deterrence. The Pentagon always felt Rogers could wear whichever hat he was given, though the one of U.S. Commander in Europe did not always fit the head of the NATO Commander. But when all is said and done, NATO owes General Rogers a debt of thanks for facing the facts and speaking out on the true state of NATO's conventional-defense vulnerabilities. This enabled some of us at NATO Headquarters to rally round and find solutions. It is unfortunate that the publicity over his criticism of the INF Treaty later obscured this important contribution.

In a crisis, the SACEUR has two special roles, which give him a certain primacy in the alliance and which also grant him direct access if need be, to the heads of allied governments. He would be the first, during a time of high East-West tension, to request through the Defense Planning Committee the reinforcement of Europe from across the Atlantic. The request would be modified or endorsed and sent to the U.S. president through the U.S. ambassador to NATO. In theory, six divisions and sixty tactical air squadrons—that is, about 1,500 tactical aircraft costing $50 billion—could arrive in Europe within ten days. Even before that, on his own authority, SACEUR could call back from the United States to Europe the so-called dual-based forces, 100,000 men, if he saw an emergency.

Furthermore, if an invasion came and the battle line were giving way, it would also be SACEUR who would first request permission through the DPC to implement the awesome plan for limited nuclear strikes.[4] The DPC can endorse or modify SACEUR's request and pass it to the two nuclear powers in the integrated command: the United States and the United Kingdom. No commander in human history has had such a daunting responsibility.

The question, however, is not how SACEUR would perform in the hours of real crisis, for his options then would be relatively few. The real test is whether the ambassadors in the Defense Planning Committee in Brussels and key officials in capitals throughout the alliance would make timely decisions under conditions of extreme stress and conflicting political views. Rogers has said that, because of the lack of sustainability in ammunition and other key stocks, in the

event of full-scale engagement, he would have to request using nu
clear weapons within days, not weeks. NATO has allowed conditions
to develop whereby decisions have to be made in a very short period
of time.

SACEUR's huge command runs from the North Cape of Norway
to the shores of North Africa, and from the eastern shore of the Atlantic
through Asian Turkey. Yet in peacetime most of the forces in these areas
remain under national command and are only "chopped" to him—that
is, put under his command in times of crisis. SACEUR also controls a
small, multinational conventional force called ACE Mobile Force,
which can be sent at the first sign of crisis to any threatened part of the
alliance, especially vulnerable areas of the NATO flanks. This maneuver
element makes clear to a potential aggressor that an attack against one
member of the alliance will be treated as an attack against all, whether
on the central front or along the flanks.

Also under SACEUR's direct peacetime command is the NATO
Airborne Warning and Control System (AWACS), which consist of
eighteen Boeing E-3A aircraft principally based in Geilenkirchen,
West Germany. AWACS was the result of a forward-looking collective response to an evolving Soviet threat, and it provides a good
example of how NATO works at its best. By the 1970s, NATO faced
a new problem posed by attacking aircraft with the capability of
operating at very low levels, beneath the detection and tracking
capabilities of ground-based radar. In 1978, the NATO defense ministers agreed to fund a fleet of surveillance planes to meet this new
threat. Thirteen members of the then fifteen-nation alliance joined
together to acquire an advanced surveillance, detection, and com-
mand/control capability and by 1986 delivered the last of the eighteen planes. Flying just inside the border between NATO and the
Warsaw Pact, the aircraft can see deep into the potential enemy's
territory and are a great contribution to the security of NATO's
European territory.

For nearly three hours I flew with a multinational crew from what
in essence is a NATO air base at Geilenkirchen, West Germany.
While the ACE Mobile Force pulls together different national units,
the AWACS force actually brings together individuals from different
countries and trains them into multinational crews. This exceptional
program came together because the allies have put alliance needs for
air defense and political solidarity above purely nationalistic demands.

Joseph Luns, Alexander Haig, as well as former Secretary of Defense Harold Brown deserve great credit for this model initiative.

In 1952, two other major NATO commands were established, the principal one under Supreme Allied Commander Atlantic (SACLANT), headquartered at Norfolk, Virginia. This command extends from the North Pole to the Tropic of Cancer and from the coastal waters of North America to those of Europe and Africa, with the exception of the English Channel. This latter area, extending from the southern North Sea through the English Channel, is under Commander-in-Chief Channel (CINCHAN). The smaller command reflects British naval influence and its recognized right to have a major command regularly assigned to a British admiral. The job of both commands is to guard the sea-lanes and deny them to the enemy. SACLANT's responsibilities are mainly operational, and the majority of forces under the U.S. admiral are American.[5]

Analogous to the role of the ACE Mobile Force have also been created the NATO Standing Naval Force Atlantic—a small, permanent, multinational force of allied frigates—and under CINCHAN, the NATO Standing Naval Force Channel—largely composed of nine countermeasure vessels from several nations. Such cooperative measures and international teamwork show NATO at its very best, as we perm reps witnessed during maneuvers on the high seas.

When I arrived at NATO, the basic problem of the alliance was not in the smoothly run military commands nor on the political side of NATO Headquarters where political and arms-control consultations with the NATO Council were frequent and profound. The real problem was the sprawling headquarters at Evere near Brussels consisting of a plethora of directorates, committees, and boards whose efforts were not coordinated. There were few flows of information and analysis among the different divisions and agencies. Even assistant secretaries-general did not regularly meet to discuss how better to integrate their areas of political and economic cooperation, defense planning, armaments cooperation, command and control, air defense, infrastructure, and logistics. This alliance bound by a treaty, with a blueprint for a grand strategy, was being compartmentalized to death at its own central headquarters.

After several months at NATO I worked with Steve Ledogar to pound out a long analytical cable to Washington about this problem.

My staff labeled it my "disconnect" cable. Steve's precise words hit like bullets on target, and Washington could not miss what was being said. NATO Headquarters could not compel capitals, but only influence them; yet it lacked the comprehensive scope to make the convincing argument for more resources from the alliance members. It was not organized in a way that made the best use of its superior resources.

One of the institutions of the alliance that was rusting was its Military Committee. Indeed, almost no one had ever heard of it outside of NATO circles, due to the glamour that went to the Supreme Allied Headquarters at Mons.[6] I argued that the chairman, always a European officer, should have a higher public profile as a way to de-Americanize the alliance. I also urged that the Military Committee chairman become more involved in NATO Council deliberations: there should be greater interplay between the political and military sides of the NATO house. I never won accolades from SACEUR by suggesting the role of the chairman be upgraded, although it began to happen when the forceful German General Wolfgang Altenberg assumed the position.

I also argued that defense and foreign ministers should overlap more in their work and the gap between the diplomatic and the military be eliminated. During my first December set of NATO ministerial meetings in Brussels, everything was done to get defense ministers out of town before foreign ministers arrived. Had I not briefed George Shultz in the car coming in from the airport, he would have had no sense of what had just taken place at the defense ministers meeting. The two meetings, a few hours apart, were isolated from each other, as if they occurred in two entirely different worlds. Of course, unlike NATO's early days, finance ministers had not come to any meetings since the early 1960s, and therefore never understood NATO problems. The challenge was not to devise a new structure for NATO, but to overhaul the machinery, upgrade to the political level any technical things that were stalemated in order to break bottlenecks, and coordinate the various efforts.

The reform of some of the weaker components of the organization received a remarkable boost with the arrival of Peter Carrington in June 1984. Carrington is an English pragmatist, with a bantamweight fierceness, belied by a rapierlike humor. His career has been distinguished by his attempts at political reform, starting in 1954 when Harold Macmillan, as defense minister, selected the young lord as his parliamentary secretary in an attempt to reorganize the ministry over the opposition of the British army, navy, and air force. Later, Carrington even dared to try to reform the House of Lords, a body highly resistant to change.

At NATO, Carrington often masked his deadly serious reform intentions with whimsey, as if to relax the opposition. But he was shocked at the antiquated equipment of the International Staff and their lack of word processors. He found the NATO Headquarters' crisis-management center, unlike SACEUR's, to be a "relic." He strove hard to increase the quality of political analysis. As might be expected from such a "people" person, who even sought works of art for grim NATO corridors, Carrington also moved to upgrade the quality of ranking personnel appointed by NATO nations for the large International Staff. He began by appointing an ingenious British Foreign Service officer, Brian Fall, as his chef de cabinet.

With his past training and natural genius, Carrington contemplated reform and improvement, neither of which came naturally to NATO. Both required leadership and initiative. He was willing to go against the grain to meet the challenge facing NATO; in other words, to develop a strategy, not for the battlefield, but for organizing NATO's superior resources to make it effective and efficient in organizing deterrence, improvements, and political cohesion. NATO has remarkable machinery, quite unparalleled in the history of statecraft. However, this machinery needs to be used in a more comprehensive and integrated fashion if we hope to win the battle of peacetime preparation. Then we will never have to fight a war. And what is more, NATO can truly implement the grand strategy that its treaty promises.-

3   The Moral Crossroads

W HEN I arrived at NATO in July 1983, the U.S. and Soviet negotiators were arguing in Geneva over deployment of Soviet SS-20 missiles aimed at Europe. The allies had the leverage of possible counterdeployments of U.S. Pershing II and cruise missiles if the Soviets refused to reduce or eliminate their SS-20s. Western Europe, however, was seething with antinuclear emotions. Peace movements demonstrated in all NATO capitals against deployment of Pershing and cruise missiles on European soil. These demonstrators seemed not to care that the Soviets had nuclear weapons poised across the border. In Bonn alone, 300,000 people demonstrated in the streets against the prospect of new U.S. nuclear missiles being placed on German soil. Public consensus over NATO policy had broken down. In the eyes of the demonstrators, nuclear weapons were immoral. To them the deployment of cruise and Pershing missiles was a provocation to the Soviet Union and a sign of U.S. interference in Europe. For many in Europe—as well as in the United States, including the American Catholic bishops and the Ground Zero movement—NATO stood at a moral crossroads.

In the past several years the people in NATO countries have been forced to confront fundamental moral questions regarding the intra-alliance relationship within the East-West struggle. First, those in churches and peace groups have had to come to terms with the role of force, and the threat to use force, against an adversary. Second, world publics have had to debate the proportionate level of force in response to gradations of aggression—conventional or nuclear—including the question of the first use of nuclear weapons. Third, in light of the Pershing II and GLCM deployments, and subsequent withdrawals, they have had to debate how to share equally the burden of nuclear risk. And finally, the public, especially in Europe, has had to deal with the assertion by some of a "moral equivalency" between the two superpowers. This issue that grows more complicated with a robust, articulate Gorbachev projecting peace and goodwill and winning popularity contests with Western leaders.

Whenever I talked with people in the peace movements, I tried, first of all, to get our terms of reference straight. When we consider the moral dimension of public policy issues, we are dealing with ambiguities and seldom with absolutes. In the lives of nations, as distinguished from the lives of people, moral choice is more difficult and ambiguous. This dilemma was identified by the Protestant theologian Reinhold Niebuhr in the title of his classic, *Moral Man and Immoral Society*. In foreign and security policy, only partial solutions are possible; one must constantly strike unsatisfactory balances between compromise and security, between order and progress, and at times, simply between the lesser of two evils.

This ambiguity has vital significance for our understanding of the nature of peace and what is necessary to preserve it. Part of the problem with the "peace" debate and the peace movement is that there is too little discussion of what peace really is, how it has been manifested in history, and how we can attain it. The new Peace Institute authorized by the U.S. Congress should take on that task.

There are two traditional but often forgotten concepts of the nature of peace. These are reflected in the Latin word *pax* and in the Hebrew word *shalom*.[1] *Shalom* connotes a sense of peace that relates to wholeness and health, security and prosperity, and righteousness in their fullest sense. The concept implies not just the pursuit of happiness but the actual achievement of happiness. Peace in the sense of *pax* connotes the peace of the ordered political community that makes living together possible. It has to do with justice, compromise, prudence, and the balance of power—a balance often between order and liberty in the human community.

While distinct, these two definitions of peace are inseparable, and our concept of peace must be an integration of the two. The concept of peace implies much more than the absence of war.

Grounded in a respect for the sanctity of the individual and a sense of obligation to our neighbors, the pursuit of peace is a process. It is an ongoing effort to create conditions within which individuals and societies can flourish, in which there are recognized limitations on the use of force, where checks and balances exist, and in which there is a strong sense of proportion between means and ends.

We must recognize that peace is often the product of a known willingness and capability to defend a society. St. Augustine was one of the first church leaders to struggle with the ethics of war in his mammoth work, City of God. He wrote against the backdrop of the onset of the decline of the Roman Empire. Rome had been invaded by the Goths, a civilization was threatened, and St. Augustine struggled with a theory on the use of force in just defense. To decide to wage war, St. Augustine argued, there had to be competent authority—that is, the authority must lie in the state and not just a self-appointed group of people. Also required was a just cause (an attack on Rome was certainly that) and right intention; cruelty, the desire to hurt, vendettas, or arrogance of victory were not among them. St. Augustine was the first of a stream of scholars, theologians, and international lawyers leading up to the twentieth century who have grappled with these fundamental issues.

The League of Nations Covenant and the United Nations Charter in our century have tackled the question of what constitutes just war, differentiating between defense and aggression. NATO's security policy is based on the "inherent right of individual and collective self-defense," expressed by Article 51 of the U.N. Charter, and thus it has moral legitimacy. Under the North Atlantic Treaty, members agree to refrain from the threat or use of force that would in any way be inconsistent with purposes of the U.N. Charter. Despite this background, some people continue to question the moral legitimacy of the NATO alliance. Polls in the United States and other NATO countries—with the exception of France, which emphasizes self-defense—show that the alliance remains popular and widely accepted, but nevertheless faces a major problem.[2] It is that some people believe NATO is only a military alliance. The image of guns, tanks, aircraft, and nuclear bombs does not inspire the younger generation. It wants something more, something inspirational, with a strong political purpose. In my talks around Europe and America, I have found that many Europeans view NATO as an American imposition on them, and vice versa.

Among those who do accept NATO's purposes, however, are a growing number who question its means and its strategy. An increasing group of influential people, including church leaders, former government officials, political theorists, and philosophers, have challenged the legitimacy of NATO's central strategy of deterrence, especially the doctrine of first use of nuclear weapons in response to a massive Soviet attack with conventional weapons. Even a former U.S. secretary of defense, Robert McNamara, has spoken out against current NATO strategy, the very strategy that he helped formulate.

These attitudes should be of great concern; for to be effective, deterrence must not only be credible to our potential adversary but reassuring to our own people. Without a basic consensus, NATO ultimately will not deter; it will not last. NATO therefore must respond to changing circumstances. As we shall note time and again in this book, military history is a tragic catalogue of failures to adapt realistically to change. What is a lesson of history on the military side is also a lesson of history on the moral side.[3]

Margaret Thatcher has boldly called NATO the greatest peace movement in history. NATO is dedicated to the preservation of peace because we know all too well the abomination of war in this century. It is a defensive alliance and will never fire the first shot. The problem, however, is that the advent of nuclear weapons has only magnified the dread of war. Of course, as we will discuss in more detail later, many Europeans, especially within governments, welcome nuclear weapons as having abolished war for all time. These weapons have created the prospect of death and suffering of such horrific proportions that they believe no one would ever be so insane as to use them. But NATO does have a nuclear strategy, so there is a moral debate. How can we ensure peace and prevent nuclear war, and at what cost? The answers do not rest in absolute pronouncements that are not likely to work, but in establishing a process of real deterrence and stability, to include confidence-building measures and arms control. We will be judged as much by our results as by our intentions.

Our problem, and the basic moral ambiguity we must confront, is that often all of our options are unattractive. There is no perfect choice. All the options involve some element of moral risk and the possibility of pain and suffering for people. Certain theologians have argued that, faced with the prospect of nuclear war, nothing is better than peace at any price, under any circumstance, and that preemptive surrender is in order. I have grave difficulties with this position. Advocates of this option speak as if our only choice in a crisis is between surrender or nuclear war. Clearly, the answer is "neither."

Another alternative offered is simply nonviolent resistance, a policy championed by the heroic Martin Luther King, Jr., and the historic Mahatma Gandhi. Both King and Gandhi were tremendously brave men whose unique form of courage left a lasting imprint on their nations' histories. But Martin Luther King's United States and Gandhi's British-ruled India are far different from today's Soviet Union, Czechoslovakia, Poland, or East Germany, even with *glasnost*.

Another approach for avoiding the nuclear dilemma was offered by Jonathan Schell in his moving book *The Fate of the Earth* published in 1982. At the conclusion of his essay, Schell called for a freeze in deploying nuclear weapons, a 50 percent cut in nuclear arms, eventual elimination of all nuclear and conventional arms, and the replacement of today's system of warring sovereign states with a new political system for resolving international disputes.[4]

Schell's prescriptions for total disarmament, like earlier proposals for universal systems, would be marvelous if they could be achieved. But there is no way to disinvent nuclear weapons. Knowledge cannot be erased. Schell's naïveté is far from unique, and many Europeans decided that President Reagan was a bit naïve as well with his talk about the total elimination of ballistic missiles. I believe that the elimination of all nuclear weapons would indeed make the world a safer place, although many NATO officials would disagree. But this is an absolute solution in a world where absolutes rarely exist. The answer to our nuclear dilemma does not lie in trying to banish all nuclear weapons. As Cardinal O'Connor, a member of the committee that drafted the American Catholic Bishops' Pastoral Letter, commented: "An individual in conscience can say, 'I will in no way involve myself with nuclear weapons.' A state cannot do this."[5]

A very different approach from that of Jonathan Schell was taken in a realistic book entitled *Living with Nuclear Weapons*, prepared by some of America's best thinkers at Harvard University. Derek Bok, president of Harvard, asked these highly experienced and profoundly thoughtful men to "supply the public . . . with an objective account of the basic facts about nuclear arms control" and to provide "a credible body of knowledge and analysis with which to . . . arrive at a thoughtful informed opinion." They succeeded admirably. In this excellent analysis, the Harvard Nuclear Study Group argues: "It is widely assumed that changes in the numbers of weapons in the superpower arsenals—either upward or downward—are the major determinants of the risks of war. Sheer numbers, however, matter far less than factors such as the vulnerability of weapons, the credibility of commitments to allies, and the imbalances in conventional forces."[6]

There is, of course, a basic moral dilemma in nuclear deterrence. In traditional Western just-war doctrine, there are two components involving the ethic of war: the decision to go to war and the conduct of war. In this latter category, two principles are applied: discrimination and proportionality. The threat to take human life in order to preserve it has been a central dilemma since long before the nuclear age. As we have noted, the nature of nuclear weapons and their enormous destructive power threaten the principles of proportionality and discrimination, which are essential ethics of war.

The principle of discrimination in war, for example, was notoriously violated in the night bombing of Dresden during World War II. Dresden was not primarily a military target, and there was indiscriminate killing of the population and needless destruction of a great city. Historians and ethicists still debate the proportionality of dropping the atomic bomb on Japan. Was it necessary for military victory to be so massively indiscriminate? Today, critics of the theory of Mutual Assured Destruction (MAD) charge that it is nothing but a more violent continuation of the indiscriminate strategic bombing doctrine of World War II.[7] Advocates of this form of deterrence argue that assured destruction is so disproportionate for each side that war becomes unthinkable, even conventional war between NATO and the Warsaw Pact, since NATO has threatened to respond to a massive conventional attack with nuclear weapons. This school of thought also holds that making nuclear responses more proportionate and discriminating also makes nuclear war more thinkable, and hence must not be considered. Understandably, these issues can become quite confusing.

In assessing these arguments it is important to draw a distinction between when nuclear weapons will and will not be used. On one hand, the use of nuclear weapons can be considered as one option in a flexible-response strategy that allows for their use at any time including, if necessary, first use. In contrast, one can consider their use only in response to the other side's first use of nuclear weapons. The American Catholic bishops, taking their lead from Pope John Paul II, have accepted this latter concept of deterrence, not as an end in itself but as a temporary requirement. We must recognize that the Catholic bishops, while saying yes to conditional deterrence, clearly said no to first use of nuclear weapons under any circumstances.

Putting aside this debate about first, second, or no use, we have only ourselves to blame for our overreliance on nuclear weapons. As noted earlier, throughout NATO's history alliance members have been unwilling to commit the economic resources necessary to provide the conventional forces that could withstand, and thereby deter, a Soviet attack. As we have seen, NATO initially adopted a nuclear retaliatory strategy because these massive U.S. weapons provided Europe with defense on the cheap. Later, another European rationale came to the fore when Europe was faced with the prospect, raised by U.S. and Soviet negotiators in Geneva and codified in the INF Treaty, of the elimination of all intermediate- and short-range nuclear weapons from Europe. Many prominent Europeans suddenly began to see conventional forces as the villain. They argued that conventional military balances always end up in war, as in World Wars I and II, and that it takes the nuclear threat—a disproportionate one with such an inordinate risk for an aggressor—to end the chance of war. In a later chapter I will explain why I disagree with this view.

Among publics, chemical weapons are as controversial as nuclear ones. During my tenure at NATO, perhaps the most vexing and divisive problem within the NATO Council itself—and indeed, within Congress—was the issue of the modernization of chemical weapons. Even though they are entirely different, NATO doctrine categorized these as weapons of mass destruction, like nuclear weapons. The residual effects of chemical weapons used in the First World War by the Germans in 1915 had left over a million casualties, and many of those who lived suffered hideous effects. NATO doctrine holds out the possibility of a response to a chemical attack with nuclear weapons. As bad as chemical weapons are, a response with nuclear weapons is totally disproportionate. NATO had to find more flexibility.

During the Nixon administration, the United States unilaterally ceased the manufacture of chemical weapons, but the Soviets continued to add to their already massive stockpiles. Over the years, the U.S. chemical stockpiles in Europe and at home succumbed to age, making many of the weapons obsolete and unsafe. In the 1980s, however, the Defense Department was able to develop chemical weapons called "binaries," which are much safer because the two ingredients needed to make the weapons highly toxic are not combined until the weapons are actually unleashed. It was agreed that these weapons would not have to be stockpiled in Europe, but could be flown to Europe in a crisis. A fierce debate ensued in Congress when the administration sought approval to begin manufacturing these new weapons. Senators Nunn, Cohen, Glenn, Roth, and Warner, who had so favored conventional-defense improvements, supported binary production. In effect, they argued, a lack of modern chemical capability created a deterrence loophole that could negate many of the conventional improvements on which NATO was working so hard. Without them, the Soviets could always call our bluff, and if we were not bluffing, we would be faced with the horrible choice of responding with obsolete chemical weapons or nuclear weapons.

In the House of Representatives, opponents introduced a provision to require the NATO Council (technically, it should have been the DPC) to agree in advance of U.S. production to have the weapons forward-deployed in peacetime—something the administration said was unnecessary. I spent weeks either phoning members from Brussels or walking the halls of Congress. Good men can vary widely over issues of proportionality, and I had good friends on the other side. But Europeans resented being drawn into a legislative fight. They wanted the U.S. to manufacture the weapons but didn't want to have to defend them publicly. The divisions on both sides of the Atlantic were deep. At Geneva, meanwhile, the Soviets began to negotiate seriously for the first time, apparently recognizing that the inequality between U.S. and Soviet stockpiles was a focus of real attention.

I believe that the improvement of NATO's conventional forces is not only a military but a clear moral responsibility, and a chemical deterrent must be an integral part of this effort. We have not reached our full capability of executing NATO's strategy of flexible response at the conventional level, and the three-legged deterrent stool remains unbalanced.

Even with major conventional improvements, even if in the 1990s the first-use doctrine were to be discarded, it would be necessary to have nuclear weapons in NATO's arsenal. The United States cannot and will not carry this nuclear burden alone. The French deterrent is for the defense of France. The British deterrent is coordinated with NATO, but it is small. U.S. nuclear weapons placed on foreign soil for "extended deterrence" are a part of sharing the nuclear burden. Our ability to achieve improved conventional defense, arms control, and balanced disarmament is dependent upon allied unity, collective security, and burdensharing in all aspects. The basic Soviet strategy has been to split the alliance and separate the United States from Europe, as the Kremlin tried to do over INF deployment. When the Soviets saw this strategy failing, they moved toward arms-control agreements.

There are some people in Western Europe as well as in the United States who want to throw off their nuclear burden and not be a part of this difficult effort simply by taking their country out of the alliance. Others want to stay in the alliance but not share its risks and burdens. From the beginning of the alliance there have been differences in the burdens and risks. Norway came into the alliance with the provision that it have neither foreign troops nor nuclear weapons on its soil in peacetime because to do so would provoke the Soviet Union. For years the alliance has absorbed that inequity owing to special circumstances, but when the British Labour party advocated a similar policy, most of NATO was deeply alarmed.

Earlier, Archbishop of Canterbury Robert Runcie identified the moral weakness in this stance when he asked, "Is there not a moral inconsistency in seeking to remain within an alliance which accepts the policy of nuclear deterrence while declining to take one's share in the means by which that policy is sustained?"[8]

The British Labour leader Neil Kinnock apparently never quite accepted this. During the course of an informal NATO luncheon, Kinnock assured the Perm Reps that if he were prime minister, the United Kingdom would remain a strong NATO partner despite the end of its own independent deterrent and removal of U.S. nuclear weapons from British soil. The NATO ambassadors, especially those going through the political ordeal of INF deployment, were aghast.

More than just morally questionable, the idea of alliance members choosing when and when not to accept the fruits and duties of membership is dangerous. This is not true collective security and creates the conditions for miscalculation and errors in judgment that could ignite the next conflict. The answer to overreliance on nuclear weapons, and their first use, is the moral imperative to build a strong conventional-force capability. Yet most critics of the former are not willing to pay for the latter.

*   *   *

Another problem facing NATO is the growing perception in Europe of a certain moral equivalence between the two superpowers. Some critics in the West have simplified the issue by criticizing U.S. weapon programs while ignoring the Soviet military buildup, its form of government, and its international conduct. Thus it is easy to talk about unilateral disarmament when one's gaze is averted from the threat. The starting point for wise choice, however, must be a study of the harsh realities of the world and an understanding of what it is the Western alliance is deterring. In his remarkable book *The Terrible Secret,* historian Walter Laqueur outlines the predicament of a world that ignored, and in some cases denied, the enormous tragedy of the Holocaust in Nazi Germany at the very time it was taking place. Information and evidence existed but was rejected by some Christian and Jewish leaders, publishers, journalists, and diplomats. They did not want to believe, so they did not.[9] Laqueur's book is a chilling reminder to those who ignore the reality of today's Soviet Union, even with *glasnost.* We must face the fact that immense power, including an enormous nuclear arsenal, is wielded by people unconstrained by our moral or civil law.

This does not mean that Soviet citizens are necessarily malevolent, or that Gorbachev is not, as both Reagan and Thatcher say, different from past Soviet leaders. But the current Soviet system has been built on insecurity and totalitarian control, all of which have been used to justify exaggerated notions of what security requires. The reforms that Gorbachev has proposed have not yet been turned into a way of life. As Reagan rightly said during his Moscow visit, the challenge is "to institutionalize change and put guarantees on reform."[10] If the Moscow summit enhanced Mikhail Gorbachev, it also enhanced Ronald Reagan as the leader of the democratic alliance. While dealing with security matters, Reagan's daring to address human rights issues from public fora also is a reminder of the different human conditions in the democratic countries of the West and the Communist countries of the East. There is no moral equivalence.

This discussion leads to a second problem: the moral perception in Europe of U.S. leadership of the alliance. Eisenhower and Kennedy were popular presidents in Europe. Johnson was tarnished by the unpopular Vietnam commitment. Nixon was admired for his diplomacy with China and approach to arms control, but he was cut short by Watergate. Ford's brief period benefited from the continuity provided by Kissinger. Carter, a deeply moral man, was often seen as ambivalent. And finally, a very strong Reagan, popular in the United States, was perceived in his first term as a "Rambo" by many Europeans and in his second term ridiculed over the Iran-Contra affair.

The nuclear issue again rears its head in this complex equation: Europeans want the so-called nuclear umbrella, or guarantee, but do not particularly like the guarantor. Reagan's Strategic Defense Initiative (SDI) was his way to break out of both the moral and the military dilemma of Mutual Assured Destruction and develop a nonnuclear defensive system to stop offensive missiles. He even said he was willing to share the system with the Soviet Union. I have had enough personal conversations with the president to know his deep sincerity, even on the latter offer, which disturbed many of his advisers. Yet many Europeans took SDI as provocative to the Soviet Union and Reagan's way of regaining strategic superiority.[11]

The problem of U.S. leadership in Europe—both the desire for it and the resentment of it—will be considered in a later chapter. Whatever the shortcomings or inconsistencies of that leadership, and whatever the shortcomings and inconsistencies of the leadership of other NATO nations, there is no moral equivalence between East and West. Over a decade ago, Jesuits began to debate whether there were just sinful men or also sinful structures. There are indeed political structures that have checks and balances, and there are structures that are monolithic. During the bicentennial of our Constitution in 1987, we celebrated a structure with checks and balances, quite different from the governance in Moscow. In 1989, we celebrate the fortieth anniversary of a remarkable democratic alliance, quite different from the Warsaw Pact.

The alliance and its leaders may not be perfect, but it is magnificent in its values and ideas, and in its ability to preserve the peace. It encompasses both *pax* and *shalom*. Its leaders must be more articulate in expounding these values. Indeed NATO in the nuclear age must restore balance, flexibility, and proportionality to its defense capabilities, in place of an early reliance on the use of nuclear weapons. This is a moral imperative that can provide the best possible basis for broadening our consensus and placing us on a higher moral road.

4 Charlemagne's Children

I REMEMBER the perplexed head of a traveling congressional delegation standing in my office door at NATO Headquarters and chiding: "Ambassador, we have visited all over Europe and NATO is a mess." It was late autumn, 1985. The Treaty Organization, in fact, had never been in better shape. In a historic display of unity, it had deployed missiles in the face of intense Soviet opposition. By contrast the European countries were divided, nationalistic, lacking in labor mobility, and incapable as yet of forming a truly common market.

The problem began with Charlemagne, I explained to him, the great king of the Franks who unified much of Europe in the eighth century and had himself crowned emperor of a new Roman Empire. The economy of the times made it difficult to support centralized rule, and his grandchildren quarreled and split up the empire. It has been a cockpit of conflict and nationalism ever since.

Europe as a political entity does not exist. Only NATO—set up to oppose Soviet expansionism—had managed to bring peace to Charlemagne's ancient empire. This most remarkable achievement in the history of statecraft has not only protected Western Europe against the Soviet Union, but also Western Europe against itself.

Europe is not only Balkanized from the political and cultural point of view but American ambassadors must also deal with the convoluted institutional structures in Europe. For example, at NATO meetings none of the ambassadors were to mention—directly and officially—other institutions, such as the European Community (EC).

Despite the fact that we were only a few miles apart physically, with NATO near the airport at Evere and the EC in downtown Brussels, we were hundreds of miles apart intellectually. Moreover, the Organization for Economic Cooperation and Development (OECD) in Paris, dealing with the economic problems of all industrial democracies, was separate altogether from any security considerations.

In reality, economics and security are interrelated and entwined in the North Atlantic alliance as never before, regardless of diplomatic compartments. The economic and social reasons for Western Europe's coming together are manifold. A unified Western Europe with a gross domestic product (GDP) for European NATO countries of $3.4 trillion, added to $4 trillion for the United States,[1] would represent a huge contribution to deterrence of war or blackmail in the 1990s. Putting just France and Britain or France and Italy together with Germany gives an industrial agglomeration equal to that of the Soviet Union.[2] But how does one establish a solid and cohesive entity within the Western alliance?

How could a better dialogue be started on these great and grave issues overarching NATO, the EC, and the OECD? Might it be possible to get together institutes and other organizations in Europe that rarely talk to each other, to join with American ambassadors in Brussels in creating an unofficial forum, also involving members of the U.S. Congress?

I found willing partners in our ambassador to the European Community, George Vest, our OECD ambassador, Edward Streator, and our ambassador to Belgium, Geoffrey Swaebe. The conference guru was my colleague Michael Moodie. The first meeting, in November 1984, addressed economics and security; the second, in February 1986, dealt with high technology, Western security, and economic growth. Secretary of State George Shultz, a former professor of economics, became a special supporter of this collaborative effort to relate economics and security and also to interface U.S. ambassadors in Europe. With more than four hundred people participating in the two meetings, I got my full share of education from the deliberations:

Item 1: Unemployment emerged as Europe's most pressing policy issue. U.S. unemployment rises and falls cyclically, but Europe's rises during recessions and, if anything, only levels off during periods of expansion. Demographic trends offer a gloomy picture as unemployment among twenty- to twenty-four-year-olds is still growing and female participation in the work force is on the upswing, creating additional pressure on the job market.[3]

Item 2: The welfare state was dragging Europe down. Even for the Federal Republic of Germany, government spending had gone from 37 percent of GNP in 1970 to 47 percent by 1980. The United Kingdom had a similar record. The figure is more than 60 percent for Denmark and the Netherlands.[4]

Item 3: Indolent, timid, and rigid attitudes have contributed to Europe's economic problems. European businesses and governments have emphasized risk aversion rather than risk taking. U.S. investment in research and development was over $107 billion in 1985 alone, compared to $39 billion for the combined R & D spending of West Germany, Britain, France, and Italy.[5] Europe has the potential of being the second largest source of R & D funds in the world, yet it lags well behind the United States.

Item 4: The technology gap between Europe on the one hand, and America and Japan on the other, could undermine the security of all. Europeans continue to make important contributions to science, as measured by such criteria as the number of articles in scientific journals or Nobel Prizes. In fact, more Nobel Prize winners have come out of one college at Cambridge University than from the whole of Japan. Yet this occurs at the same time as European societies are beginning to develop an inferiority complex about high technology. It is with respect to innovation, therefore, that Europe lags behind the United States and Japan. An expanding international marketplace is vital to the success of high-technology industries. Protectionism is not only the enemy of the consumer but of a true common market in Europe, of transatlantic relations, and of NATO.

Item 5: Government procurement in Europe, which often consumes up to 17 percent of the total European GDP,[6] is the most glaring example not only of Europe's nationalism but of the danger of excessive government involvement in economic decision making. Holland, Belgium, and Denmark had about 96.6 percent of their procurement budget go to national companies (although some are subsidiaries of foreign companies), Britain 98.3 percent, Germany 99.7 percent, France 99.91 percent, and Italy 100 percent. So there are only national markets for government procurement in what Europeans proclaim as a "common market."[7]

Item 6: Agricultural subsidies constitute about 70 percent of the EC budget. Former European Community Commissioner Christopher Tugendhat estimates that if agriculture is extracted from the EC's budget, what is left amounts to only about 1.2 percent of the total spending of national governments.[8] With an inefficient agricultural subsidy not only costing the consumer dearly but swallowing up all the European Community's resources, it is no wonder that there is little or nothing left for constructive and innovative programs.

Item 7: Economic problems riddle Europe's defense industrial sector, which is aimed at promoting constructive competition but is in fact filled with government-directed duplication. For example, as I pointed out in my speeches:

- eleven firms in seven alliance countries build antitank weapons
- eighteen firms in seven countries design and produce ground-to-air weapons
- sixteen companies in seven countries work on air-to-ground weapons

No wonder NATO Secretary-General Lord Carrington quipped that if you want a cacophony, you let each musician choose for himself the key, the tempo, and whether to play fortissimo or pianissimo; that if you want operational discord in the armed forces, you build main battle tanks that cannot fire the same shells—as we have done—or different national communications equipment that can't speak to each other—as we have done.[9]

Despite the difficulties in these seven areas, it is possible to be too pessimistic and cynical about Europe and to lose sight of what has happened there in the last forty years. The wars in Europe have ended. Beginning with the daring idea of the European Coal and Steel Community, and then the European Economic Community, Europe has begun to come together, both on its own continent and with regard to international trade and aid.[10]

Europe's political consultation and collective action have faltered in their reactions to terrorism, Moscow's shooting down of the Korean airliner, and the 1981 crisis in Poland. Nevertheless, political cooperation within the EC—what is called PoCo—has made great strides. In June 1985, the European Council meeting in Milan formalized previously informal consultations and required that each member-nation consult before launching individual foreign-policy initiatives.

The European Monetary System, an idea put forth by European Economic Commission President Roy Jenkins in December 1978, has been a huge step forward. As a result of an economic assessment on which all the involved nations agreed, the European countries have begun to align their currencies collectively. The European Currency Unit (ECU) was established as a new form of international money with widespread use in international bond issues. Despite duplication, subsidies, and compartmentalization in European industry, the Tornado military aircraft and the Airbus are successful products of European consortia. While our own shuttle program has been in deep trouble following the Challenger disaster, the Ariane space-rocket project has had a shining success, with eleven launches in eleven months. By 1988, the EC appeared to be on such a dynamic course that Americans began to fear the completion of the European "single market" scheduled for 1992.

Nevertheless, the legacy of Charlemagne's children is clearly felt in Europe, and it is important that any look at grand strategy should recognize and deal with centuries-old diversity if we are to promote new unity.

West Germany

Any chapter on Charlemagne's children and their divisions must focus on Germany, the heart of Europe. The Carolingian realm became the Holy Roman Empire, a grouping of princes and prince-bishops that was, to quote an old adage, neither holy, Roman, nor truly an Empire. The twelve centuries of German history since then have been marked by the division of these most fractious of Charlemagne's heirs. The bloody Thirty Years War ended in 1648 with the Treaty of Westphalia, which recognized over 300 separate German states. This splintering was to the advantage of the great powers of Europe and remained the status quo until Bismarck's policy of "blood and iron" forged German unity. The rise of this new militarist Empire was eventually to bring down the old order of Europe in a first world war and again produce the dismemberment of Germany in the aftermath of a second.

The first Chancellor of the Federal Republic of Germany, Konrad Adenauer, chose close association with the democratic nations of the

West over the goal of reunification. Rearmament, NATO member-
ship, and a historic treaty of friendship with France in 1963 followed
Adenauer's commitment to a "merger with the free populations of the
West." In the early 1960s an economic miracle took place in West
Germany under the "social market" leadership of Ludwig Erhard,
Adenauer's financial wizard and second Chancellor of the Republic.
Today Germany is the third greatest economic power in the West.

Under the prodding of the NATO democracies, West Germany
has also assumed a greater role in the common defense effort, fielding
the largest active armed services in Western Europe, with 495,000
soldiers and mobilizable reserves of 775,000 for all services. At NATO
we worried about demographic trends that will force a major reduction in the size of the German Army in the 1990s. Ironically, the
German Army is the only true NATO army, with all its forces committed to SACEUR's command. Yet a German general has never
commanded one of NATO's two multinational Army Groups. Having
been on maneuvers with German forces, I know firsthand of their
great élan and professionalism.

Today the politics of the West German republic give rise to
concern, particularly when compared to the days of Christian Democratic (CDU) party leadership under Adenauer or Erhard, or even to
the Social Democratic (SPD) leadership of Willy Brandt and Helmut
Schmidt. The 1980s have been a tumultuous decade. The radical
Green party emerged as a political movement and helped pull
Schmidt's SPD to the left, ultimately fracturing the coalition government with the centrist Free Democratic party, led by Foreign Minister Hans Dietrich Genscher. Helmut Kohl's CDU-led government,
a "coalition of the middle" again with the Free Democrats, has had the
strength to manage the tough deployments of Pershing II and cruise
missiles of German soil, but not to restore a compelling vision of
Germany's future in a divided Europe.

The breakdown of German consensus on defense issues is evident
in the Social Democrats' flirtation with the idea that mutual security
with the East might be more practical than alliance security with the
West. In any event, they seemed to argue that it was possible to have
both. The 1987 SPD party platform, entitled "Peace and Security,"
revealed the foundations of the concept of a security partnership with
the Eastern Bloc. The first premise is that nuclear weapons themselves are the threat. Security, they argue, can be assured only with

a potential enemy, not by arming against him. Second, values can be secured only in peace, and the two German states have a common responsibility for ensuring peace and detente. Defense policy must, therefore, be "nonprovocative" and structurally incapable of offense.

If the SPD increasingly turns East rather than West to find its security moorings, all German parties are looking West just enough to consider new security arrangements with France. The shock of the Reagan-Gorbachev 1986 Reykjavik meeting, and the perception by many Europeans that their security concerns were being bypassed, accelerated this effort to expand Franco-German defense cooperation. "Cheeky Sparrow," a 1987 joint exercise of 77,000 French and German troops in southern Germany—80 miles from the Czech border—was an unprecedented step toward closer cooperation between these NATO neighbors. By the autumn of 1987, the two countries had broadened their defense ties to form a Joint Defense Council.

During these unsettled political times in West Germany, a remarkable leadership from this once defeated power has come to the fore in the very headquarters of the alliance: Carrington's successor, Manfred Woerner, as Secretary General; General Wolfgang Altenburg, chairman of the Military Committee; and Henning Wegener, Assistant Secretary General for Political Affairs. This speaks to the pronounced abilities of each, but also to the maturity of the alliance. Perhaps the thorniest problem for each of the three is the issue of the remaining short-range nuclear weapons on German soil, supposedly to be modernized in accordance with a 1983 NATO agreement, the so-called Montebello Decision. West Germany's own decision to comply will take place on the eve of the German general elections in 1990 and under the shadow of Gorbachev's call for a "third zero" of eliminating all remaining nuclear weapons in Europe.

Benelux

Following the example of Prussia in the nineteenth century, it was decided after World War II that a *Zollverein*, or customs union, would be established among Belgium, the Netherlands, and Luxembourg. Accordingly, a common external tariff was adopted in 1948 by these countries, henceforth known as "Benelux."

These three countries certainly cannot be judged by size in terms of their imprint upon history. De Gaulle helped Brussels by deciding to eject NATO Headquarters from Paris. All of Western Europe helped this city of gold-leaf guildhalls by making it the seat of the Common Market. Twenty-five percent of Brussels is now foreign, and it is the closest thing the continent has to a capital of Europe. But the Belgians have given something more than just a physical capital to Europe. They have also provided an array of highly conceptual diplomatic leaders: postwar Prime Minister Henri Spaak; Foreign Ministers Pierre Harmel, Henri Simonet, and Leo Tindemans; and EC Vice-Chairman Etienne Davignon—all of whom have sought through various ways to put Europe back together again.

Belgium has been plagued with its up and downs, in both medieval and modern times. After World War II, however, Belgium's economic restoration became a small miracle, marked in the beginning by its 1958 World's Fair and continued with seemingly unending prosperity in the 1960s. Belgium extended its social-welfare benefits to the point where it nearly went broke in the downturn of the 1970s, leaving as a legacy a tax system that stifled initiative and investment. Economic problems were only exacerbated by the social splits between the French-speaking Walloons in the south and the Dutch-speaking Flemings in the north. One cannot be anything but dismayed at the intensity of this continuing division, impacting on every government decision.

In the 1980s, coalition governments led by Wilfried Martens courageously instituted austerity budgets. Defense spending suffered, however, creating some serious problems for Belgium's armed forces. Following the U.S. example during Vietnam of pulling some troops back from Europe, Belgium brought many of its forces back from Germany so that 56 percent are now in-country. In air defense, it coproduced American F-16s in a deal made at the currency exchange rate of 27 francs to the dollar and was devastated when the rate shot up to 60 francs, leaving not enough money to purchase ammunition. If war were to come tomorrow, shiny new F-16s are available but without sufficient ammunition stocks. A key player in a network of air defense, Belgium, unlike the Netherlands, has been unable to purchase the modern Patriot air-defense missile. Lack of Belgian participation will create a gap in the NATO air-defense belt and, more specifically, in the Belgian corps as it is forward deployed to Germany in time of crisis.

*   *   *

A land of famous painters, philosophers, and sailors, the densely populated Netherlands is a unique country with two-thirds of it beneath sea level, protected only by dunes and dikes. With so few resources at home, Dutch financiers and industrialists have always thought internationally. On an economic high in the 1960s, the Netherlands, under Socialist leadership, extended its benefits with huge costs and high taxes. With the 1970s economic downturn, the nation suffered very high unemployment. A more conservative leadership balanced the budget, cutting defense as well as welfare costs. As with Belgium, Dutch diplomacy was often shaped by the complications of coalition government.

The Netherlands was at the heart of the European peace movement, and Protestantism and Catholicism weigh heavily in party structure. Those taking the lead in conservative fiscal policies often, for religious reasons, had reservations about the deployment of Euromissiles. The Dutch faltering in this area, always the laggard among the "basing" nations, became a pervasive political problem at NATO. Veteran Ambassador Jaap de Hoop Scheffer became a valuable link between the Dutch cabinet and the NATO Council. With his help, as well as that of U.S. Assistant Secretary of State Richard Burt, the divided nation successfully pulled itself through the difficult task of deployment.

The Dutch have a good fighting force and outstanding generals such as the recent chairman of the Military Committee, General Cornelius de Jager. But its corps, like that of the Belgians, is badly maldeployed, with 86 percent based in-country. In its determination to stay with national manufacturing, the Dutch pay twice as much for 155mm artillery rounds and have ammunition shortages in key areas. Unlike the Belgians, the Dutch did manage to purchase the Patriot missile system. The ever-inventive Richard Perle worked out a skillful "offset" scheme whereby the Americans, in return for the Dutch purchase, bought Dutch goods to compensate the balance of trade.

Luxembourg, with its historic grand duke and duchess and its beautiful citadel city high above the river, has an army of less than 1,000. It however houses the increasingly impressive NATO maintenance and supply organization, whose original mission was procurement but which is now being extended for repair and maintenance with a wide range of technical support. Luxembourg is also the site of a huge new complex for the European parliament and also plays host to a different kind of complex in banking, insurance, and communications.

Many of NATO's military problems are related to the economic difficulty of smaller nations that cannot on their own do what is needed. These three small states were the pathway of invasion in the two world wars and, situated as they are in the direct line of any Soviet blitzkrieg, could be again. Simply berating them in general on weak defense performance can be counterproductive. Creative, collective approaches are needed, as we shall discuss in Part Two of this book, "The Strategies."

France

If West Germany is the country in Europe most totally in the alliance, then France in a sense is the least. In fact, while I was American ambassador to NATO, I was constantly asked whether France was a member of NATO. Indeed, her membership is a "special category." The Maid of Orleans, Joan of Arc; the great builder of the Versailles Palace, Louis XIV; or the loner General Charles de Gaulle—they all would have wanted France to be in that "special" category, but it certainly creates problems for others. Indeed, France is a force to be reckoned with in the NATO Council.

In the spring of 1959, de Gaulle withdrew his Mediterranean fleet from the NATO command, using the rationale that it was needed for the Algerian conflict. But he made the shift permanent. He next said that no nuclear weapons would be allowed on French soil unless they were under French command and control. As for nuclear strategy, his views ran directly against the new ideas of flexible response that the U.S. defense secretary was discussing within NATO. Flexible response was fallacious, in his view, because no nuclear war could be kept limited; it would all be strategic. Furthermore, he did not believe in what was to be called "extended deterrence," whereby one nation, the United States, would come with its nuclear weapons to the defense of other nations in a crisis. It was DeGaulle's belief that a nation would use nuclear weapons only in its *own* defense. Consequently, de Gaulle saw France's possession of its own nuclear weapons, the *force de frappe,* as a prerequisite of true independence and security.

In 1966, de Gaulle moved to withdraw France from NATO's integrated command. His principal grievance was that NATO was "an

American organization."[12] In many ways, Gaullism became tantamount to anti-Americanism. On a whole range of issues, from the dollar to détente, de Gaulle took positions that were not only contrary to those of the United States but almost deliberately provocative. French independence for him was not an abstract idea but something to be defined in terms of opposition to the United States. Similarly, European unity was acceptable to de Gaulle only if it involved no reduction of French sovereignty. De Gaulle was a passionate believer in the nation-state, and his Grand Design of a *Europe des patries* was reminiscent of a nineteenth-century continental system led by France, which excluded Britain and, of course, the United States. The one-time student of history had forgotten history and what had led to past French defeats: the lack of an integrated military alliance.

In 1968, de Gaulle's forecast of the disappearance of East-West blocs was shattered. That very year, when de Gaulle lost power in France, Soviet troops and tanks moved into Czechoslovakia, brutally destroying not only the so-called Prague Spring of "communism with a human face" but also de Gaulle's fantasy of a Europe from the Atlantic to the Urals. From then on, de Gaulle cooperated more with the United States, and his successors have continued to do so.

In the wake of the accord eliminating all intermediate-range nuclear weapons in Europe, France has been forced to reevaluate its defense position. In recent years, the French nuclear deterrent forces have consisted of six nuclear-powered ballistic missile submarines, eighteen land-based intermediate-range ballistic missiles, a small force of Mirage bombers equipped with nuclear air-to-surface missiles with a range of from 60 to 200 miles, and about thirty Pluton tactical missiles with a range of about 75 miles. The French, long realizing the need to maintain a modern nuclear force if the country's defenses were to remain credible, are in the midst of an across-the-board nuclear modernization program.

Although nuclear weapons remain the cornerstone of French defense policy, Paris has nonetheless also demonstrated a renewed interest in conventional defense. France's dilemma, however, is similar to that of many other NATO allies: it does not have the resources to do everything it should on the conventional level. In general France's "go-it-alone" approach has led Paris to several expensive national weapons-development programs, such as the Rafale advanced combat fighter and the Leclerc main battle tank, despite stiff competition from both Europe and the United States. Meanwhile, the

French navy has invested a large share of its procurement budget in the construction of the first French nuclear aircraft carrier, the *Charles de Gaulle*, with a price tag of about 13.9 billion francs.[13] Obviously, not all of France's defense purchases are national, and Paris took an important step to shore up its air-defense capabilities when it decided to purchase the U.S. AWACS for airborne reconnaissance.

While French procurement policy remains nationally oriented, an important feature of their recent approach to conventional defense has been an emphasis on cooperation with other European nations, especially Germany. In addition to endorsing a commitment to the defense of West Germany, France and Germany have also established a joint brigade.

Paris has also been a leader in the rejuvenation of the Western European Union (WEU). Prime Minister Jacques Chirac's call for a European defense charter, for example, prompted the WEU to issue a Platform on European Security Interests in October 1987, emphasizing the need "for a more cohesive European defense identity." The platform also expressed the determination of its seven members to "defend any member country at its border,"[14] again implying a French commitment to the forward defense of Germany. For France, this is a tremendous step forward. More than any other nation in Western Europe, France has the power to right the NATO conventional vulnerability and build a stronger Europe that is also more conscious of global responsibilities.

Italy

By the year A.D. 800, Charlemagne was the arbiter of Western Europe and even the Pope depended upon him. It was Charlemagne who reintroduced the Gregorian chant and enforced the Roman liturgy. His legitimacy was further enhanced by being crowned Holy Roman Emperor by the Pope. Italy today, with its Vatican City whence Roman Catholics throughout the world receive spiritual guidance, continues to have a very special place in Europe.

In spite of a range of threats—not just Eurocommunism (now past its peak) but unemployment and economic and political stagnation—Italy has been a leader in efforts to unify Europe. Italy made the first moves toward the Treaty of Rome signed in 1957, which initiated the European Economic Community. It led the way in the first Wise Men's study of NATO to broaden it from a strictly military organization to one with a political and even a cultural dimension. It has been a staunch member of NATO, proud of the Naples location of the NATO commander in chief of the Southern Region forces that include in wartime the U.S. Sixth Fleet; and also, in northern Italy at Verona, the subordinate command of Land Forces South.

In 1985 I stood in the magnificent courtyard of a beautiful palazzo in Verona, at a ceremony equal to that of any Italian city-state to commemorate the thirty-fifth anniversary of the NATO land command headquarters there. Not far away, burrowed into the side of a mountain, is one of NATO's first underground headquarters, built to withstand an atomic attack. Italy was host country for the cruise missiles deployed to counter the SS-20s, and in fact was a leader in moving forward with deployment. During these years, Italy benefited from the decline of the Italian Communist party (PCI), following the death of Enrico Berlinguer, its longtime dynamic leader. The country benefited even more from four years of the stalwart pro-NATO leadership of the Socialist Bettino Craxi, who gave Italy a much-needed period of stability. It was Craxi who, even after stepping down as prime minister in 1987, pushed Italy into sending eight naval vessels to the Persian Gulf for patrol duty in treacherous waters. Italy never wavered in its resolve, despite direct Soviet blandishments. Luigi Barzini wrote of his own people, "Italians think all sacrifices are acceptable if they help the unification of Europe to advance even an imperceptible step forward."[15]

But Italy has a complex—a middle-child syndrome, so to speak. There is, in NATO, for example, a grouping (in fact, a club within the club) of four nations: the United States, the United Kingdom, France, and West Germany. This grouping is brought together under the rubric of Berlin: the three Western occupying powers and the nation claiming West Berlin. Italy does not make that club, although it is one of the seven nations making up the economic summit. It suffers as a result, just barely in or just barely out, fearful that there is a "directorate" that it does not quite make, even though its per capita income now rivals that of the United Kingdom.

The Iberian Peninsula

West Germany, Benelux, France, and Italy were part of the empire of Charlemagne. The countries that surrounded that area make up the rim of NATO. The Iberian Peninsula is part of that rim.

The Pyrenees wall off the Iberian Peninsula, parts of which were long under Moorish rule. Portugal and Spain had possessed vast empires that waxed and waned. In this century, under their respective dictators, Salazar and Franco, both Portugal and Spain stayed out of World War II, although Franco received Hitler's help in the Spanish civil war, one of the most vicious conflicts ever fought in Europe.

Portugal, a dictatorship in an alliance of democracies, was one of the original members of NATO and offered to the United States the use of the Atlantic Azores Islands as a major base. Before the advent of jet aircraft this was an invaluable asset as a transit point. The Azores were used heavily in U.S. supply of Israel during its 1973 war, and today the islands remain important for antisubmarine warfare in the Atlantic. With the revolution in Portugal in April of 1974, there was a deep fear, especially on the part of Secretary of State Kissinger, that Portugal would go Communist. Largely owing to the efforts of Dr. Mario Soares, the Socialist leader and strong anti-Communist, along with other European Socialists, Portugal won the battle against communism. Full democracy has not solved Portugal's economic problems, which place the country at the bottom of NATO in terms of economic development. No country has had its heart more fully in NATO or been more supportive of the United States. Portugal also provides IBERLANT, the NATO maritime command for that region, and a 4,500-man brigade as part of the NATO reserve for possible deployment to northern Italy.

In Spain after the civil war, Franco maintained a repressive state and was openly contemptuous of what he saw as the "un-Spanish" notion of democracy. For this reason, Spain was hardly welcome in NATO. Franco did, however, negotiate the use of four major bases with the United States: three for the air force and a naval facility near Cadiz, later expanded into an invaluable home port for nuclear submarines. The White House always kept these accords as "executive agreements" so that the Senate would not have to ratify a treaty with a dictator, especially one who had cozied up to Hitler and Mussolini.

After Franco's death in 1975, Washington applauded Spain's steps to democracy under King Juan Carlos, although many Spaniards thought Washington had been too close to Franco. They felt that by giving him military and economic aid, the United States had not used its influence to further democracy in Spain. In 1976, the renewal of the bases agreement was upgraded to a Spanish-U.S. Treaty of Friendship and Cooperation, out of which the economically hard-pressed Spain benefited to the tune of $1.2 billion. On May 30, 1982, Spain became NATO's sixteenth member.

When Felipe Gonzalez's Socialist Labor party won a landslide victory in the 1982 general elections, Spanish participation in NATO was frozen until there could be a popular referendum on the membership issue. Although his party had initially opposed membership in NATO, as prime minister, Gonzalez became convinced of its benefits and proceeded to wage an intense campaign for approval. The referendum question that was finally put to the voters, however, supported continued membership only on three conditions: (1) that no nuclear weapons be stationed in Spain; (2) that Spain remain outside NATO's integrated command; and (3) that there be some diminution of the U.S. military presence in Spain. The question, posed this way, carried.

The Spanish developed their own theory of participation in NATO: although they would not be in the integrated command, they would not follow the French model. Rather, they would participate in such bodies as the Defense Planning Committee and the Nuclear Planning Group. General Rogers not only resented Spain's efforts to claim positions on various committees before engaging in any real consultation about terms or obligations but he also disapproved of a situation in which another nation in the alliance received its benefits without being part of the integrated command.

I personally supported the process, however, because it seemed the only way for the Spanish to ease toward military participation. I felt that with education and time they would end up in the commands. Moreover, I also felt that by joining NATO, Spain would be safeguarding its democracy.

As details for NATO participation were sorted out, the time arrived for renewal of the U.S.-Spanish bases agreement, and, coincidentally, it looked like Rogers was right and Abshire was wrong. As mentioned, the Gonzalez referendum included a gradual reduction of U.S. forces in Spain as a condition for NATO membership. Actual control of the four bases had already been placed in Spanish hands, but with the exception of the port at Rota, the U.S. presence was highly visible, especially at Torrejon near Madrid, where the 401st Tactical Air Fighter wing was located. The United States offered to redeploy the air wing elsewhere in Spain. The Spanish rocked the Americans by rejecting the offer. The U.S. NATO ambassador should have been instructed to turn over the issue to the Defense Planning Committee—in effect, making it a NATO and not just a U.S.-Spanish problem. It was not just the United States but NATO that was being hurt, and perhaps this was part of the reason why Spain was rebuffed in its move in 1987 toward membership in the Western European Union. In early 1988, Spain and the United States agreed that the 401st fighter wing would be removed, with ever-faithful Italy offering to accept the burden Spain had rejected. The United States has continuing access to its other facilities in Spain. It is now time to bury our past misunderstandings and encourage ways for Spanish politicians and military leaders to better understand what are the duties and benefits of membership in the grand alliance of democracies.

Greece and Turkey

Following World War II, the first U.S. commitment to Europe, in fact the beginning of the containment policy, came in the form of the 1947 Truman Doctrine, with military and economic aid for Greece and Turkey. The tragedy of the Greek-Turkish quarrel is that both nations have rich cultural heritages to offer the alliance: Greece with its Hellenism and Turkey as a bridge to the Moslem world. Both are also of great strategic importance.

Nowhere have the divisions within NATO approached the ferocity of those between Greece and Turkey on the diplomatic level, whether over Cyprus, the island of Lemnos, the territorial waters around the Aegean, or oil rights. As if the situation were not bad enough, there was an attempted military coup d'etat in Cyprus in July of 1974, followed by a landing of Turkish troops ostensibly to protect the Turkish minority. The enchanted island of Aphrodite had long been a trouble spot. While under British rule, the Greek majority of the island had pressed for *Enosis*, or union, with Greece. Cypriot independence was achieved in 1960, and this was followed by many years of intercommunal violence between the two populations. The 1974 landing led to Turkish control of one-third of the island, accompanied by a population transfer and refugee problem. U.N. forces were interposed between the two sides, but the bitterness has continued to this day and shows no sign of being resolved.

Following the invasion of Cyprus, the military junta in Athens resigned and liberties were restored under Constantine Karamanlis. However, Greece withdrew from the integrated military structure and did not return until October 1980. With a combined armed forces of over 200,000 men and women, its percentage of gross domestic product going to defense (6.1 percent) is the highest in Western Europe. Visiting Athens in 1984, I received a threat briefing in the beautiful marbled room of the Greek joint chiefs of staff. The threat turned out to be not the Warsaw Pact, but Turkey, situated just across the Aegean.

When Greek Socialist leader and former professor of economics at Berkeley Andreas Papandreou came to power in 1981, Greek policy statements carried strong anti-American overtones. Once in power, he called for "phased withdrawal" of U.S. bases and better terms for Greece in NATO and the EC. At one point, Papandreou declared that, compared to the Soviet Union, the United States was the real threat to Greece. Subsequently, relations have mellowed.

The very real contribution of Turkey to deterrence and defense, both within NATO and "out of area," should not be underestimated. With regular armed forces of over 650,000 and almost a million reserves, Turkey brings considerable military power to the alliance. Despite a lack of modern equipment, the fighting quality of the Turkish army is superb—a fact I experienced firsthand during the Korean War by observing Turkish troops serving in my division. Most important, control over the vital Dardanelles, through which Soviet naval forces must pass to reinforce their presence in the Mediterranean, together with Turkey's position astride the flank of a potential Soviet push toward the Persian Gulf, gives this long-neglected member of the alliance a unique strategic role. With current initiatives to expand Turkey's industrial base (including the pursuit of cooperative arms production) and to modernize its armed forces, there is a promising opportunity to strengthen security in NATO's Southern Region, as well as to build upon our long-standing economic and political relations with this important ally.

A strong note of hope has emerged, however: in early 1988, a secretly arranged meeting took place at Davos between Papandreou and Turkish Prime Minister Turgut Ozal. There, the two leaders agreed to some positive steps: annual summits and the installation of an Athens-Ankara hotline.

The Northern Flank

Europe's northern outer ring is very different from the continental region that made up Charlemagne's empire. Icelanders, Norwegians, and probably Danes might not readily describe themselves as European. They are a part of NATO, but also a part of what they call the Nordic balance, with three nations in NATO and two that are not: Sweden and Finland. Norway and Denmark have no foreign troops or nuclear weapons on their soil in peacetime.

With the nearby shadow of Soviet power, the Nordic countries like to think of security in economic, social, and political terms, and have no interest in upsetting the status quo. When Norway and Denmark were considering the NATO option, Sweden actually tried to create an alternative—a regional defense union for Scandinavia without the great powers. While Sweden rejected the NATO option, the United States—to the consternation of the Swedes—made it quite clear that a U.S. military commitment went only to those countries belonging to NATO. But the shadow of NATO does protect Sweden, even if not to the same degree as Norway and Denmark.

The real complication of the balance in the North was perhaps best summed up by a director of long-range planning in Sweden's ministry of defense. "There has never been a balance of power in Northern Europe," he said. "The Soviet Union is the dominating power. Forward basing [of the United States] does not change that."[16] This tends to place the United States in a "provocative" position if it tries to alter what amounts to an imbalance. The Nordic allies do not worry, however, since most of them do not see the Soviets resorting to force. Moreover, one has to believe that the neutrals—Sweden and Finland—would fight if attacked, as Finland did in the winter of 1939–40. Plainly, though, they are without collective security, and this could invite miscalculations in the future.

Norway has a high level of public support for NATO. Its troops are well trained, but are far too few for effective defense. The discovery of oil and gas in the North Sea was a great economic boon to Norway, but it also increased its Atlantic orientation.

Within the alliance, Iceland's strategic location plays a vital role in the North Atlantic. The military base at Keflavík serves as a stepping stone between America and Britain, and as a base to launch airborne warning systems and antisubmarine aircraft. However, the inconsistent political tradition of this island has twice led to calls for the United States to leave Keflavík. Fortunately, these calls were not realized, and despite a series of unpleasant "cod wars" with Britain over fishing rights in the seventies, Iceland has remained a reasonably committed member of the NATO alliance.

Denmark has a far more complicated history that affects its role today. In 1864, it was quickly defeated in the war with Prussia and Austria over Schleswig-Holstein, and it began to develop a new defense theory based on neutrality and nonprovocative defense. This served to keep Denmark out of World War I. Similar theories emanate from Denmark today; "defensive defense" is postulated, as if plain defense was actually provocative. Danish proponents of this concept forget—or else remember too well—that Hitler ruthlessly invaded Denmark in April 1940. Its defense collapsed after only a few hours.

Denmark's role is more complicated mainly because of its coalition government. Conservative and liberal orientations in domestic and foreign policy differ and in a time of crisis it takes a two-thirds vote of the Danish parliament to transfer Danish forces to SACEUR. This worries NATO crisis planners to no end. It is not just Denmark's mobilization and commitment that cause alarm but the fact that NATO procedures require consensus, not just majority vote by the NATO planners. So if the Danish parliament failed to get a two-thirds majority in favor of action, its government would postpone moves agreed on by the rest of NATO.

With all the initiatives of the NATO Nordic nations, it would be tragic indeed to write them off. To begin with, opinion in this area is not uniform, and many staunch political and military people are working hard to keep these nations in the North Atlantic family. It is important that we in the United States appreciate the diversity of Nordic defense thinking. We must act with subtlety and not as a U.S. bull in a Nordic china shop, as one or two high-level defense department officials have done.

The United Kingdom

Unlike the Roman emperors, Charlemagne never conquered Britain, a land where migrations mingled Celtic, Saxon, Danish, and Norman blood. Modern democracy was born in England, and Westminster Palace is rightly known as the Mother of Parliaments. Napoleon once dismissed the British as a "nation of shopkeepers," but Waterloo showed they were something else, too. A combination of their trade patterns, naval power, and military prowess led to the largest empire the world has seen.

"Splendid isolation" was how the British referred to their policy with regard to Europe in the last century. But after the tragedy of two bloody wars, during which the best of two generations of British youth were destroyed, Britain learned her lesson. It moved from splendid isolation to "splendid commitment" to NATO, even though it initially kept its distance from the EC. If there were deep divisions in Britain over joining the Common Market, there was also great unity over its commitment to NATO.

Apart from "standing alone" against Hitler in 1940, Britain's greatest contribution to the world in this century was the dismantling and transformation of its empire into a "commonwealth" of equal nations. Although this action was dictated by forces outside Britain's control, no other European country ceded its empire in the fifties and sixties with such speed and grace. Parallel with this development came the gradual realization that Britain was no longer as useful to its transatlantic ally as it had once been, and that Britain's true place was in Europe.

Two tragedies were to come in British politics. One was the breakdown of the strongly bipartisan foreign policy on NATO and its strategy, similar to what has happened in the Federal Republic of Germany. Euromissile deployment did much to further polarize opinion in Britain. The U.S. nuclear protector had become an object of resentment for many in Britain. The other major problem was Britain's economic decline and a standard of living that threatened to drop below that of Italy. This was a humiliating thing for a nation that once fueled the industrial revolution and on whose empire the sun had never set.

In 1979, this nation in trouble turned to the Conservative party, led by Margaret Thatcher, the "Iron Lady." Like the stubborn Churchill who saved Britain in 1940, the new prime minister was just what was needed, despite the understandable concerns about her lack of sensitivity to the underprivileged, particularly the unemployed. She battled for privatization and made great efforts to roll back an overextended welfare state, efforts now bearing fruit in the form of greatly improved economic performance. Mrs. Thatcher supported her friend Ronald Reagan under the most unpopular conditions in the Strategic Defense Initiative and on the use of U.S. bases in Britain for the raid on Libya. As the longest consecutively serving British prime minister, Margaret Thatcher has achieved a position of unique prestige and leadership within the alliance. Thus it is fitting that she host the first NATO summit with the new U.S. president. But balanced against the new strength of the "special relationship" is Mrs. Thatcher's skepticism toward the idea of European unity. Instead, she sees a future Europe merely in terms of "separate countries working together," and her insistence on the need to retain national sovereignty is much criticized by her European partners.

Meanwhile, on the defense level, the United Kingdom is caught between its other defense commitments and the Trident nuclear submarine program; between the demands on its naval forces, in the Falklands, for example, and for much more important tasks in the North and Norwegian seas; and its commitment of over 56,000 troops in the British Army of the Rhine deployed astride the invasion route on the northern plains of Europe. The choices become especially difficult after a decision to impose a zero defense-budget increase. At NATO, the British ambassador and defense minister can no longer chide lagging nations about not meeting the 3 percent defense increase adopted in 1977, but they can point out that the percentage of Britain's GDP devoted to defense is one of the highest in NATO.

The legacy of Charlemagne's children and neighbors is still clearly felt in Europe. Their lack of unity and the effects it has on issues like trade and economics makes the record of alliance cohesion all the more remarkable. As we have seen, there are positive forces at work in Western Europe. We must develop a common strategy to promote them.

5   To Withdraw or Recommit

T HE 1949 Vandenberg Resolution and the subsequent Treaty of Washington were unprecedented commitments to collective security for the United States. The political organization created by this treaty soon evolved into a mutual defense organization with a military command. American divisions were on the spot in Europe. Two divisions in 1949 increased to four in 1951 with the Korean war, and to six in 1961 with the Berlin crisis.

President Eisenhower did not envision that these divisions would stay in Europe permanently, and controversy has arisen time and time again over their continued presence on European soil. In 1968, with the burden of the Vietnam War, Washington transferred some troops from Europe to the United States, but those troops remained earmarked for duty in Europe. This modified withdrawal helped alleviate manpower problems, reduced defense expenditures, and placated some members of Congress who were against the size of our European troop commitment.

In 1967, the year prior to the Soviet invasion of Czechoslovakia, congressional criticism of the size of the U.S. troop commitment had grown, led in part by Senators Mansfield, Javits, and Symington. There was talk that with the French withdrawal from NATO's military command and new efforts at détente, the alliance might become an anachronism. The Soviet invasion of Czechoslovakia in August 1968 quelled such sentiments, but in 1969 it reappeared when the Canadian government called for a broad review of the necessity of maintaining forces in Western Europe.

The new Nixon administration affirmed its strong commitment to NATO, symbolized by the new president's visit to NATO Headquarters. On Capitol Hill, however, the war of attrition in Vietnam and the revelation of secret commitments in various trouble spots produced skepticism about all foreign commitments, and in the Senate, an examination of all national commitments began. Then it happened.

The day was May 19, 1971. There was a vote on the Senate floor. At issue was the Mansfield amendment to withdraw 150,000 troops from Europe. I sat in the crystal-chandeliered room of the Senate Majority Leader, hospitable Mike Mansfield, while he took a call from his wife. At the time, I was assistant secretary of state for congressional relations, and was in his office on other business about Southeast Asia. I heard him say to his wife, "They are voting again. I do not know how it will go. All I wanted to do is send a signal." His signal to Europe was that our troops should not stay there forever, and his signal to the White House was that it should think about some withdrawals.

Since Mansfield's intention to resurrect his amendment had become known on May 11, the administration had been furiously lobbying against it. President Nixon had given National Security Adviser Henry Kissinger direct coordinating responsibility. Dean Acheson, present at NATO's creation and strongly against the amendment, was easily persuaded to become the spokesman for the Eastern Establishment. This patrician Democrat turned himself into Nixon's chief lobbyist in the successful effort to defeat the amendment. It was remarkable how that group closed ranks over NATO when so many of its illustrious members were by then split over the Vietnam War. Others who phoned senators or lent their names to the effort were John McCloy, McGeorge Bundy, George Ball, Douglas Dillon, Henry Cabot Lodge, Cyrus Vance, General Lucius Clay, Robert Lovett, Robert Murphy, and a number of former NATO commanders and chairmen of the Joint Chiefs of Staff. One might have called it the transatlantic establishment's last stand. They stood well. Mansfield's amendment was beaten 61 to 36.

Mansfield's opponents had received some strange help. In a speech in Soviet Georgia on May 15, Leonid Brezhnev announced his willingness to explore mutual troop reductions in Europe. This cleared the path for the birth of what ultimately became the long-unrealized negotiations on Mutual and Balanced Force Reductions (MBFR). Mansfield's opponents argued that, in light of possible talks, the United States shouldn't give something away and get nothing in return, so the troops should stay as a card to play in achieving a bargain with the Soviets. Despite the Mansfield defeat, however, there was also born the idea that another Mansfield-type amendment would be offered at some time in the future, and that it would pass, pulling U.S. troops out of NATO.

Henry Kissinger was to write in his book, *The White House Years*: "It had been a close call. We had barely avoided the dismantling of twenty-five years of foreign policy on the eve of the conclusive phase of the Strategic Arms Limitation Talks."[1] Kissinger had indeed been the organizer of victory, and he had a right to be proud. It was ironic, then, that the ongoing tensions over the U.S. troop commitment to Europe would so evolve that Kissinger would later write in a *Time* magazine essay on March 5, 1984:

> [I]f Europe should opt for a perpetuation of the present ambivalence or for only a token improvement [in conventional defense], then the U.S. will owe it to the overall requirements of global defense to draw certain conclusions. If Europe by its own decision condemns itself to permanent conventional inferiority, we will have no choice but to opt for a deployment of U.S. forces in Europe that makes strategic and political sense.[2]

Kissinger suggested that over the next five years perhaps up to half of the U.S. forces should be withdrawn. His was a prod to Europeans to do more, or else we would do less.

Kissinger was not the only prominent American who was thinking in these terms. His *Time* essay was generated in part by a conference sponsored by my Center for Strategic and International Studies (CSIS) that took place in Brussels in January 1984 and included noted members of Congress. One of them was destined to be a dramatic actor on the NATO stage during the next few years. I speak of Georgia senator Sam Nunn.

I first knew him when he came to the Senate in 1973 at age 34 from a small south Georgia town hardly involved in global strategy. But already, young Sam was marked as the great-nephew of the one-time revered chairman of the House Armed Services Committee, Carl Vinson. In 1974, as a freshman senator, Nunn testified before our Murphy Commission. Just before he spoke, Commissioner Mike Mansfield told us privately, "Pay attention to him, he will soon be the best mind on defense problems." Several years later, when I was out of government, I brought Nunn onto the advisory board of CSIS, and he intrigued a scholarly audience with a highly conceptual lecture on strategy, in which he placed a premium on out-thinking the potential aggressor.[3]

Nunn is just such a thinker, who has equal command of both concepts and details. It is little wonder that, as Mansfield forecasted, he became respected as the preeminent strategist in the Congress. His intellectual honesty made him so politically fearless, even to the extent of criticizing his fellow Georgian, President Jimmy Carter, on defense issues, that he subsequently became a prime catalyst in moving the Democratic Congress and President forward to a more robust posture.

In January 1983, my Center for Strategic and International Studies (CSIS) had sponsored a conference in Brussels. It was during this conference that I hosted a private luncheon for my house guest, Nunn, with other members of Congress and all the NATO ambassadors including the secretary-general, Joseph Luns. Sam Nunn could be counted a friend of NATO and had opposed any troop-withdrawal amendment. I remember very well his dismay during our lunch that some of the most important ambassadors—and indeed, the secretary-general—appeared to show too little concern about the state of NATO's conventional defense. They had displayed their belief that the problem was not too alarming and that, in any case, Europe could do no better.

The frustrations of Kissinger and Nunn were no greater than my own. I remember a lunch given for me by our minister in London, Edward Streator. Among those present was my old friend, Oxford don and dean of British military historians, Sir Michael Howard. When I brashly announced to the group that NATO needed to be turned around, Michael said, "David, NATO is like a dam. It is there. You don't turn it around." My response was, "The dam leaks." The exchange clarified our differences: aggressive Americans like myself typically want to fix things; Europeans often prefer to live with them.

A similar attitude characterized many American NATO hands: the alliance and flexible response worked, so don't mess with it. My own military staff, and we had some brilliant officers, presented me with a study on NATO strategy that said flexible response was sound and working well. I rejected it and, upon probing, found that most of the officers who had contributed to the report really didn't believe it either. How could they, when Supreme Allied Commander General Bernard Rogers said NATO would run out of ammunition in a matter of days, and when any nuclear escalation would put us at an even greater military disadvantage? The real problem was how to correct this sorry condition. Withdrawing troops was not the answer. This would only foment a transatlantic crisis and realize a fundamental aim of Soviet strategy.

During my first year at NATO I was plagued by a paradox. On the one hand, NATO had won an extraordinary strategic victory. The allies had hung together on the INF deployment of their Euromissiles; the Soviet strategy to divide them had failed. The NATO multilateral and bilateral diplomacy were perfectly handled. After the Soviet negotiators walked out of the conference room in Geneva, the allies began to deploy. The Soviets apparently hoped that hints of a return to the Cold War would shake the allies' resolve. No such thing happened, and the chagrined Soviet negotiators had to return to the table.

On the other hand, this NATO success on nuclear deployments was part of the problem. The nuclear issue so occupied not only NATO Headquarters but, indeed, our State and Defense departments that no one was willing to confront the problems of conventional forces. At the Department of State, Richard Burt and his Bureau for European Affairs were totally absorbed in the one issue—INF deployment—and they were handling it with superb skill. At the Pentagon, the powerful Richard Perle focused his energies elsewhere. He was a tough combatant, with a Florentine bent for political infighting to thwart whatever he saw to be concessions on arms-control agreements by the State Department. Perle had little interest in developing a collective way to improve NATO's conventional forces; he believed in bilateral deals.

I knew full well that, sooner or later, we would be headed toward another transatlantic crisis over the shape of conventional-defense forces and that there had to be a new, major initiative to improve them. But there was a stumbling block; Europe had not come out of its recession. Unemployment ran high and coalition governments were fragile. Europe was in an economic stall. In fact, living standards were dropping in parts of Europe. The success of INF created a sense of having done what had to be done on defense at considerable political cost, and the defense of Europe would have to rest on nuclear, not conventional, capabilities. European politicians realized that nuclear forces did not cost economically depressed Europeans any money, while conventional forces did and were therefore not appreciated.

While Europe's economy was especially bad in 1983–84, the unwillingness of NATO members to spend money on improving conventional defenses had been a fundamental problem since NATO's meeting in Lisbon in 1952. During the early years of the Carter administration there was a valiant effort to force conventional-defense improvements. Ambassador Bob Komer came to the Defense Department first as an assistant to the secretary and then as an under secretary of defense with special responsibility for progress at NATO. Hard driving and imaginative, called "Blow Torch" affectionately by admirers and caustically by critics, Komer showed what one man could do in a generally receptive administration in which the president was willing to participate in two NATO summits. NATO's approval of the Long Term Defense Program (LTDP) was largely the result of Komer's driving effort, supported by Under Secretary Bill Perry and Secretary Harold Brown. Each nation pledged to increase defense expenditures by 3 percent in real terms to finance needed improvements. Improved cooperation on transatlantic armaments was to be part of this effort.

The LTDP fostered new momentum but it foundered, as other efforts had, on the distractions caused by the taking of American hostages in Iran. There was also a congressional setback about this time, when a pro-NATO, pro-armaments cooperation chairman of a defense subcommittee, Dan Daniel, led his group to Europe in the summer of 1978. To the shock of the subcommittee, it found Europeans, from defense ministers on down, interested only in one issue: the United States' buying more weapons in Europe. There was complacency about conventional-defense vulnerabilities and deficiencies, low ammunition reserves, and increasing Soviet superiorities. Again, this was the same ambiguity that Kissinger wrote about. The subcommittee issued a blistering report and terminated its interest in transatlantic arms cooperation.

To make matters worse, when the Reagan administration came to power, it subsumed the LTDP into NATO's regular process. In the Pentagon, the special NATO machinery set up by Komer was dismantled. Armaments cooperation was to be turned over to the private sector, in keeping with the general private-sector philosophy of the

Reagan administration.[4] It was ironic that an administration that appropriately took much credit for a major U.S. defense buildup went the wrong way initially on NATO. With former Supreme Allied Commander Alexander Haig as secretary of state, the Bonn summit of 1982 issued a declaration on improved conventional defense, but it was like a tinkling cymbal and sounding brass. There was no faith in the pronouncement, no strategy for implementation, and Haig was on his last go-round.

In the autumn of 1983 the one window into a new conventional-defense effort appeared to be through armaments cooperation: to take an initiative to make better use of the superior financial, technological, and industrial base of the alliance in the development and production of military equipment. With my staff, I pounded out a cable over forty pages long, soon known as the "monstergram." This was sent to the secretaries of state and defense and the national security adviser. The cable argued that, as 1983 had been the Year of the Missiles, 1984 must become the Year of Conventional-Defense Programs. Alarming trends in the NATO–Warsaw Pact conventional-force balance had become NATO's number one problem. But there was another danger, too; growing congressional frustration at Europe's unwillingness to do something about this inadequacy. Conventional improvements had become an imperative. Without new resources, the first step had to be a broad new initiative in armaments cooperation to make better use of existing resources.

The cable laid out a several-part strategy, beginning with a top-to-bottom approach including a blessing and mandate from the president himself. An interagency committee would be set up on transatlantic armaments cooperation so that the executive branch could speak with one voice and promote one strategy, and so that the civil war in the Defense Department between Richard Perle's policy bureau and Dr. Richard DeLauer's research and engineering people could be brought into harmony. DeLauer favored armaments cooperation, but Perle shied away from such a collective approach. The cable recommended that the president also encourage or mandate a committee or commission on armaments cooperation with members outside of the executive branch, involving Congress, industry, and labor.

I knew very well that such a cable would not change policy. We needed a political strategy sustained by an action network in Washington. My special assistant, Rhodes scholar Dennis Kloske, played the role of a classic cavalry leader reconnoitering the terrain before a battle, to find how flanks could be turned and victories won. Except in this case, the terrain was Washington and the flanks to be turned were people who wanted business as usual. Dennis made friends easily and sparkled with insight on armaments and tactics, but he never forgot the strategic objective of building coalitions for our cause—on and off Capitol Hill. My concern was avoiding the damage that could result from the active opposition of the bureaucracies, which were wedded to the traditional view that a NATO ambassador—or any ambassador—was not to initiate policy.

In November I gave a major speech to the Atlantic Treaty Association in Rome. I sought to broaden the armaments-cooperation issue and to call for what I termed a "resources strategy" for a better return on defense investment. This initiative, with armaments cooperation as a key element, made an impact. At the December 1983 Defense Ministers Meeting, as ministers and ambassadors sat around the great U-shape table that fills NATO's largest conference room, German Defense Minister Manfred Woerner cited the speech and endorsed the call for a NATO resources strategy and improved armaments cooperation. Woerner, forceful and with the direct bearing of a gentleman pilot of the Luftwaffe, was quickly joined by several other defense ministers. Cap Weinberger was impressed and he reread the forty-page monstergram. Since the "policy" section of the Pentagon continued to argue against any high-postured program that would "raise expectations," the compromise was that we would concentrate first on some "early wins" and then move to the broader program. In gaining high-level support for movement on a strategic approach to armaments cooperation, we had won our first battle, and now we aimed to win the campaign. Help came again from Manfred Woerner.

Woerner told me privately that he wanted to introduce something he termed the Conceptual Military Framework. The Pentagon, he complained, had made a series of disconnected initiatives at NATO, with such exotic names as Air Land Battle, Offensive Counter Air, and the Emerging Technologies initiative. These came in addition to work being done by NATO's own military people on problems such as hitting targets deep in the enemy's rear areas. There should be a far more coherent approach, Woerner argued, both to sell programs to parliaments and to improve military performance. A long-term perspective was needed. Woerner asked for my personal support. I was delighted, for I saw it as a centerpiece for developing an overall strategy to better use NATO resources.

When the initiative was made public, the Washington bureaucrats, who thought in numbers and not in concepts, were decidedly unenthusiastic and took any such proposal as a European attempt to avoid spending new money. Nonetheless, the requirement to develop a Conceptual Military Framework was approved at the Defense Ministers Meeting. The Military Committee, plus the three military commands, were each to develop Conceptual Military Frameworks and the Military Committee was to design an all-encompassing one. Meanwhile, many in both the State and Defense departments continued to scoff at the very idea that had emerged from Woerner's truly strategic mind.

The actions of the defense ministers during their December 1983 meeting were not advanced enough to avert a transatlantic crisis, however. We were in a race against time, and we were to lose. Senator Nunn, while encouraged by their recognition of conventional problems and up to date on my activities, was neither fully confident of Pentagon follow-through nor convinced of any major effort on conventional defense from the lethargic capitals of Europe. Quietly he began to sort over drafts for a troop-withdrawal amendment. His was an incentive amendment, not a withdrawal amendment à la Mansfield, just to get some of our troops out. Nunn did not think that way. Rather, as what I would call a resource strategist, he thought in terms of how the superior U.S. investment in NATO was being aborted by allied failures. He cited one glaring example: in a crisis, the United States was to fly 1,500 aircraft costing over $50 billion to Europe, but there were not enough shelters to protect them when they got there.

Nunn's logic regarding withdrawal, similar to Kissinger's, was that lack of European defense investment was condemning us to a "trip wire" strategy, so that the large number of U.S. forces would not make much difference. He proposed removing 90,000 troops over three years. His amendment, however, provided the allies a way to avoid this. Nunn required the allies either to fulfill their 3 percent increases mandated in 1977 or to meet several output requirements. These would help solve problems like the low number of essential facilities and shelters for U.S. reinforcing aircraft and the severe ammunition shortages.

I knew exactly where Senator Nunn stood on his amendment

because of my close relationship with him and because my two staff colleagues Dennis Kloske and Mike Moodie were always in touch with his staff. At our Tuesday luncheon sessions, I began to warn the ambassadors of the dangers of a troop-withdrawal amendment unless we could show more NATO activity. At the same time, I urged Nunn to offer his amendment as a warning but not to call it up for vote. My arguments were twofold: (1) we were getting NATO to take a new look at its conventional-defense problems, and the attitudes of the defense ministers were changing; and (2) Peter Carrington would be arriving in June as the new secretary-general, and it was not right to hang such an amendment around his neck. Nunn answered two arguments with three: if he went forward, he would put on record any letter from me about the changing attitudes on conventional-defense improvements; his amendment was aimed at NATO capitals, and, whether we liked it or not, he might just be helping us; and his amendment would not pass anyway.

When the proposed Nunn amendment was discussed by the Senate's Democratic caucus, it immediately caught on. The White House legislative office estimated it could command more than seventy-five Senate votes, for Republicans were falling into line behind the highly respected Nunn. The White House began to talk about not actively opposing the amendment, so great appeared to be the majority for it. I was a bit desperate.

I went all out to get those senators I knew on the phone. I argued that if this amendment passed in the wake of the INF deployment, of MBFR negotiations, and with the arrival of the new secretary-general, it could be disastrous. When I reached Senator Bill Roth at his home in Delaware on the weekend, he said he'd already agreed to be the Republican cosponsor of the Nunn amendment. He said he'd just returned from the Luxembourg meeting of the North Atlantic Assembly, an organization of NATO parliamentarians. There, European delegates had argued that absolutely nothing more could be done to improve conventional defense. "How can your new program get anywhere with that attitude?" the senator asked.

In dismay, I appealed to the good sense of Senator John Warner, whom I reached on his Virginia farm. Success! He would stay with us and be in touch with Senator Tower, who should lead the floor fight. In the ensuing Senate debate, John Tower, chairman of the Senate Armed Services Committee, was indeed a tower of strength on the

Senate floor. He argued that to pass the amendment would be to "kick our friends in the teeth." Tower pointed out that "nobody [would] regard this as a signal; they [would] regard it as bullying."[5] Senator Nunn replied: "Is it too much to ask your friends and allies to do what they have pledged to do?" Nunn argued that we simply couldn't send American troops to Europe while looking them in the eye and saying, "Fellows, you are going over there and about the time you arrive the allies are going to run out of ammunition."[6] At that point, Senator Bill Cohen spoke up, noting that "when it comes to rattling cages, the Senator from Georgia has already rattled cages" and that he had "already sent a message to the European alliance."[7] Cohen proposed a way out, an alternative amendment that provided for reporting on NATO's progress rather than Nunn's mechanism for automatic troop withdrawal. As the vote margin narrowed, President Reagan himself made the final phone calls and the alternative Cohen amendment passed.

In the shaken capitals of Europe there was relief. However, there was also deep anger on the part of those who, like Manfred Woerner, had known and worked with Sam Nunn over the years. Nunn himself became concerned over this reaction but believed the Europeans did not understand how his amendment differed from Mansfield's. As for the attitude in the Senate, many who had voted against Nunn told him that they would be with him the following year if NATO failed to respond. Nunn would have a clear majority.

Meanwhile, at NATO Headquarters it was time for a changing of the guard. Secretary-General Joseph Luns climbed into his armored Rolls-Royce, flags flying in defiance of terrorists, and departed NATO after over twelve unprecedented years in that post.

Despite his pedigree as the sixth baron and his prestige as former First Lord of the Admiralty, Defence Minister and Foreign Minister, Peter Carrington cared nothing for ceremony—he did not need it—and his first act was to put Luns' cherished Rolls-Royce up for sale. Shortly after his arrival, he asked me to his office to help interpret the warning shot fired at NATO by the United States Senate. Two years earlier Carrington had delivered the annual Alastair Buchan Lecture at the London-based International Institute for Strategic Studies. As Sam Nunn had pointed out to me, Carrington had attacked East-West "megaphone diplomacy" and stressed the importance of the political side of the alliance without addressing conventional defense. Carring-

ton, a consummate politician, put the lecture aside and quickly interpreted the seriousness of this new message. There was in the making
a transatlantic crisis that could destroy the alliance, and Carrington
knew it. He quieted ambassadorial chatter around NATO, such as:
"We will not respond; allies don't threaten each other this way." And
when I first took him to visit Nunn in his Senate office, Carrington
said, "Senator, I am with you. Not your method, mind you, but your
end, your objective." The unconventional British lord and the determined Georgia senator established instant rapport.

I often thought how Peter Carrington shared similar qualities
with former Supreme Allied Commander Dwight Eisenhower. Neither long-range thinkers nor conceptualists, they both had a genius for
the here-and-now, and at getting different people and difficult allies to
work together. Grand strategy almost always involves coalition strategy, and no grand plan has an ounce of a chance of success without the
leadership of an Eisenhower or a Carrington. Indeed, the genius of
Peter Carrington turned the troop-withdrawal threat into a redoubling
of alliance efforts on conventional defense. This was perhaps the most
delicate time in NATO history since the French withdrawal from the
military command, certainly in terms of relations within the alliance.
The problem for Carrington was how to produce concrete results on
improvements, sufficient to prevent passage of another amendment
the following year.

The first test of defense investment following the fight over the
Nunn amendment was what is known in arcane NATO language as the
infrastructure contribution. NATO has one basic common fund, a
large financial pool based on a cost-sharing formula to which allies
contribute in proportional shares. As early as 1950, it became clear
that a common fund was needed for fixed installations, such as military
headquarters, airfields, telecommunications installations, fuel pipelines, and so on. The infrastructure fund is NATO's single most efficient effort. In the summer of 1984, new infrastructure funding was
before the ambassadors for approval. Since the largest contributors are
the United States and Germany, the first step is an agreement between the two principal contributors. Caspar Weinberger and Richard
Perle doggedly tried to drive commitments as high as they could go.
After months of haggling, a compromise was set doubling past efforts.
Moreover, Carrington used his charm with SACEUR to have priorities changed so that the critical facilities identified by Senator Nunn

were funded almost totally. This was the first hard evidence of allied response to Nunn.

In autumn of that same year, one year after our monstergram, Washington began to take a new conventional-defense initiative seriously. As usual, the Pentagon and State Department were at odds, and I was very fearful that Washington would come up with a piecemeal approach. Carrington had earlier commented to me that he *also* believed NATO should concentrate on only one or two key efforts, and do them well. The second problem, a political one, was choosing who should sponsor the new effort. Washington authorities and Carrington wisely recognized the effort should not be "Americanized" and that the Germans had to be persuaded to take the lead. Thus, at an autumn meeting in Washington between President Reagan and Chancellor Kohl, agreement was reached on a "German initiative," backed by the United States, to be introduced in the December 1984 Defense Ministers Meeting in Brussels.

On the eve of the meeting, however, a difficult dispute arose between Manfred Woerner and Richard Perle over the communiqué language mandating the initiative. Woerner wanted language that emphasized harmonizing NATO activities for better use of defense resources, which tracked more along the lines of my thinking, while the Pentagon wanted a statement of more money. The fight got so bitter that talks were broken off and the initiative was all but dead.

I had my staff concoct a last-minute compromise. When the ministers and ambassadors assembled in the large NATO conference room, I handed the compromise language to Cap Weinberger. There would be "more," but it would come from "better use." Luckily, British Defence Minister Michael Heseltine sat next to Cap, who passed the compromise language to him. Both approved. It was then sent around the room to Woerner, who by that time considered the initiative dead. About to speak, Woerner picked up the paper, read it with a nod, and in a flash introduced an initiative that led to the most comprehensive reexamination of NATO conventional defense in its history.[8]

In the follow-up, Peter Carrington showed his genius again in working out a program of seven papers to be developed on various issues ranging from net assessment to planning, logistics, and armaments cooperation. First, he consulted and cajoled the military commanders who became alarmed that NATO's political headquarters was actually thinking on military matters; second, he assured the ambassadors who feared that NATO might be breaking out of "business as usual" into some new structure of defense management as the United States had imposed in the Long Term Defense Program of the 1970s. "No new machinery," Carrington pledged, but suddenly the idling NATO machinery got a large jolt of electricity. The integrated commands and the Military Committee also pushed to completion the mandated Conceptual Military Framework. With typical honesty, Rogers said: "The only question is why we did not have one before."

Later that spring, Senator Nunn was back as my guest at Truman Hall. After briefings at our NATO mission, he was impressed with the coherence of the program to obtain a better return on overall defense investment and wondered aloud why the Pentagon did not have such a framework. He expressed his pleasure on the positive program over lunch with Carrington, who mused that there might be another amendment to keep the pressure on, but a positive one this time. Later that day, Nunn confided that he would set his troop-withdrawal amendment aside that year, but he did not want this known. He wanted to work in secret with his staff and mine on a positive-incentive amendment, while everyone thought he might again move on troop withdrawal.

With Nunn's consent, we opened conversations with Deputy Secretary of Defense William Taft, who became an essential ally as chairman of the new NATO Armaments Cooperation Committee, which was brought into being by our monstergram from Brussels. As finally worked out, the new Nunn amendment would set aside $200 million, which could be spent by the services only if they worked in cooperation with the allies. Allies had to put up their own money, although not on an exact dollar-for-dollar basis. A second part of the amendment set aside $50 million for side-by-side testing of weapons from the U.S. and NATO countries before acquisition.[9] My cavalry officer, Dennis Kloske, became the liaison with Nunn's and Taft's offices as different versions of amendments were fashioned. A bright young Air Force Lieutenant Colonel on my staff, Richard Paschal, gave critical technical and conceptual advice. Two stalwart senators, John Warner and Bill Roth, joined Nunn in sponsoring this monumental step forward for better use of NATO resources. Senator Ted Stevens became the influential advocate on the Appropriations Committee, for he also had visited NATO and concluded that the headquarters "was getting its act together."[10]

Introduced by a dramatic speech complimenting NATO on its progress while excoriating the Defense Department in other areas, the Nunn-Roth-Warner amendment sent a signal to Europe to get its house in order and to meet the American challenge. The amendment also told our Army, Navy, and Air Force that they should think more about overall strategy in the use of their resources. The alliance had come a long way in the year since it stood on the brink of American troop withdrawals. A new can-do attitude was developing.

Throughout Europe, the two amendments became known as the "bad" and "good" Nunn amendments—a split that even their author, the usually poker-faced Sam Nunn, acknowledged with a wry smile. Maybe both were needed, but the first without the second would have been a disaster. The second represented a stroke of sheer creativity seldom seen in the governmental process. This helped to bring new life to NATO and a new sense of direction, as will be discussed in Chapter 16. The second Nunn amendment was an unusual example of congressional and NATO partnership, in the spirit of the Vandenberg Resolution, with the executive branch as a bridge. Over the next several years this partnership flourished. An official Senate advisory group to the Geneva arms-control delegation was established. As delegation chairman, Senator Stevens started the practice of regularly bringing the group to NATO headquarters and member capitals in a symbolic demonstration of what this Alaskan called the "new Senate partnership" with the alliance.

6   Terrorism Strikes NATO

THERE is not a more dramatic example of Europe's incapacity to take collective action on a question of international security than its response to terrorism during 1985–86, a period that culminated in the U.S. raid on Libya. Terrorism obviously was not addressed formally in the NATO treaty, and has emerged only in the last two decades as a major threat to the security of the industrial democracies. It was only a matter of time, however, before terrorist violence struck NATO. During 1985, the year before the retaliatory raid, 170 of 785 terrorist incidents involved Americans or U.S. overseas facilities around the world. Of these attacks, 63 took place in Western Europe; American fatalities amounted to 38 of 825, while injured reached 157 of 1,217 victims worldwide.[1] If our European allies want American troops in Europe, Europeans should make it safe for Americans. Instead, Americans appear to have been singled out for attack. The Reagan administration made antiterrorism a top priority, with Secretaries of State Alexander Haig—himself a target of a bombing when he was SACEUR—and then George Shultz as high-postured spokesmen.

Europeans and Americans in Europe faced two kinds of terrorism: indigenous terrorism by local groups within European countries, and terrorism by groups from outside Europe sponsored by states such as Syria or Libya, including their indirect sponsorship of Palestinian terrorism. Examples of indigenous terrorist groups include the Cellules Communiste Combattantes (CCC), or "Fighting Communist

Cells" in Belgium; Action Directe in France; the Red Brigade in Italy; and the Red Army Faction in Germany. Unlike the state-sponsored terrorist groups that targeted Americans in Europe because of U.S. support for Israel, these groups targeted NATO, the military-industrial complex, and the European establishment. There was a wide exchange of information and coordination among all these groups.

If 1983 was the Year of the Missiles for NATO and 1984 the year the alliance began serious conventional-defense improvement efforts, 1985 became the Year of Terrorism. The storm warnings came in the autumn of 1984, when the Fighting Communist Cells bombed industrial companies in Belgium, some near NATO Headquarters, charging that they were involved in producing U.S. cruise and Pershing II missiles. Terrorism came as a shock to Belgium, which, by and large, had escaped such violence when earlier waves swept Europe. The government was not equipped to deal with it. Prime Minister Wilfried Martens frequently went about with no security. With the Walloon-Flemish ethnic controversies, and with memories of harsh police treatment during the German occupation of the two world wars, Belgians had an understandable antipathy toward strong central police authority. There was a blind hope that terrorists would pass through and not stay in Belgium.

This was not to be the case. On January 15, the Reuters office in Paris received from the Red Army Faction and France's Action Directe a communiqué announcing that they were joining forces in an anti-NATO front in Europe: "Attacks against the multinational structures of NATO, against its bases and its strategies, against its plans and propaganda, constitute the first large mobilization."[2] In the early morning hours of the same day, a car pulled up before the NATO Support Center used by U.S. NATO staff and U.S. military personnel assigned to NATO. The facility included a library, gym, community liaison office, snack bar, small PX, and other personnel services. Two military police guards ran out to investigate. Seconds later, a bomb, hidden in the car, rocked the building. Miraculously, the guards escaped death or serious injury, but the blast caused $500,000 damage to the building and considerable disruption of services to the U.S. NATO community.

For the U.S. NATO delegation, the terrorist war and countert-errorist effort were on. American wives who regularly used the support facility were fighting mad. In the words of the *Brussels Weekly*, "Almost immediately personnel were assessing damage and clearing up. . . . In the early afternoon, reinforcements arrived for the food brigade: Carolyn Abshire and Marcie Ledogar had each loaded up with sandwiches, cokes, and thermos bottles of coffee." The wives of military and Foreign Service personnel organized themselves for clean up and temporary aid. "With this team, we could put Humpty Dumpty back together," one witness said. Gussie Haeffner, who headed the Community Liaison Advisory Council, was asked by an interviewer: "Were you afraid?"

"Not afraid, no," she responded. "Shocked at seeing my office in that condition. And angry. I'll be cautious, I'll be prudent, but I won't be intimidated by terrorists."[3]

All security tightened. Mine suddenly jumped from a single bodyguard who rode with me in my two-and-a-half-ton armored sedan to an additional follow-on car with three armed guards. Truman Hall's thirty acres in the countryside were surrounded by camera-mounted, chain link fencing, making it one of the most secure ambassadorial residences in Europe. But if the ambassador was protected, the rest of the staff was not. All staff members were taught that the most successful terrorist incidents, such as the kidnapping of Brigadier General Dozier in Italy, had succeeded because obvious security precautions had been overlooked. Hence, better education in security procedures had to make up for lack of increased physical protection. My sharp administrative officer, Colonel Hank Reed, solicited suggestions from the entire staff so everyone felt involved in the counterterrorism effort.

The terrorist threat was not just limited to Americans. It was NATO-wide. Terrorism was not new to Lord Carrington, who had been a very stubborn Defence Minister during some of the worst difficulties in Northern Ireland. At NATO he initiated studies of the security of headquarters and other facilities and pushed hard for construction of concrete road barriers and electrically controlled iron gates at the entrance to the NATO complex, as well as for additional security personnel from the Belgian gendarmerie. During our ambassadorial meetings, I stressed that the U.S. Congress would not understand a situation in which a headquarters intended to handle crises that might deter World War III was unable to prevent terrorism within its own gates.

During the following months, the terrorist onslaught continued throughout Europe. In late January, a three-star French general was shot while in a Paris suburb. On February 1, a leading German defense industrialist living near Munich answered his door to find a machine-gun wielding terrorist. Even in faraway Portugal, where the terrorist group FP-25 operated, eight bombs went off at a West German air base. In Athens, at Bobby's Bar near the Hellenikon Air Base, a terrorist's bomb injured seventy U.S. servicemen. In April, the headquarters of the North Atlantic Assembly in Brussels, a parliamentary group of NATO legislators, was hit. Before the year was out, terrorists in Liege tried to kill Jean Gol, the hard-line senior Belgian deputy prime minister in charge of law and order. Gol was determined in his fight and had four hundred troops transferred to the paramilitary gendarmerie for the protection of key targets—something that would have been unthinkable a year earlier. But the terrorists had even broader targets. Over 3,680 miles of NATO pipelines, which in peacetime is used by commercial companies, were inevitably exposed. They became a dramatic target for attack.

By the end of the year, Belgian security finally succeeded in cracking into the CCC, with the arrest of three leaders who had carried out twenty-seven attacks in just over a year.[4] Other European governments also fought back. The most important cooperative counterterrorism organization—the TREVI group (Terrorism, Radicalism and Violence International)—was established under the aegis of the European Community. No outsiders, such as Americans, were allowed—only EC police chiefs. At NATO, the Security Committee included heads of internal security agencies. The French, however, insisted that the committee deal only with technical issues; they, as usual, ruled out any consideration of broader political concerns, including state-sponsored terrorism.

The two worst European offenders in dealing with counterterrorism were France and Greece. Athens had strong ties to the Arab world and was extraordinarily lax on security, including at the Athens airport. Paris was a well-known haven for international terrorists. Not until Jacques Chirac became prime minister did the French attitude begin to improve.

Of course, almost every nation had its *bête noire*: in our discussions, as I urged action on the political as well as the technical level, everybody had it on their minds that the U.S. Congress had not ratified an extradition agreement with the United Kingdom and that private funds from the United States continued to help Irish terrorists.

If 1985 closed with some advances in fighting indigenous European terrorism, Charlemagne's children remained deeply divided over the problem of state terrorism originating from Africa and the Middle East. They had a markedly different view from the Americans, who, in Alexander Haig's style, wanted to "get at the source."

Especially with regard to terrorism imported to Europe, the violence had a more complex face to Europeans than to Americans. To Europeans it was something to be lived with and be protected from rather than "extinguished." Italy, for example, had its share of terrorism, including Libyan, but it was Libya's largest trading partner (about $4 billion annually), with over 8,000 Italians working in Libya in 1985. At that time, Libya even owned a minority percentage in Fiat.[5] As for terrorism based in the Middle East and North Africa, many Europeans felt it was U.S. policy toward the Middle East, its excessive support for Israel, and its failure to effect a Palestinian homeland that had given rise to much of the radical action.

The first dramatic case out of the Middle East to land at NATO's doorstep during my tenure was the 1985 Palestinian terrorist hijacking of an Italian cruise ship, the *Achille Lauro*. World attention was attracted to the two-day ordeal, during which an elderly American Jew, Leon Klinghoffer, was slain in his wheelchair and thrown overboard. The hijackers surrendered in Egypt in exchange for safe conduct to Tunisia, a deal which had been worked out between Italian Prime Minister Bettino Craxi and Yasser Arafat. The Egyptians placed the four terrorists on a plane for Tunisia, including Abu Abbas, who had masterminded the original mission. The plane was intercepted by U.S. Navy Tomcat fighters and forced to land at the Italian-operated NATO base at Sigonella, Sicily. This put the hijackers under Italian jurisdiction. Our government wanted the arrest and extradition of Abbas. Craxi declined, arguing that Abbas was under Egyptian protection and carried an Iraqi diplomatic passport.

At the NATO Foreign Ministers Meeting in early December, the Italian ambassador and I sat in on an exchange between Secretary of State George Shultz and Foreign Minister Giulio Andreotti. Shultz made a withering attack on the Italian decision. I had never heard such strong words in a diplomatic setting. No wonder Shultz was so much against the secret White House policy of supplying arms to Iran in an effort to obtain the release of American hostages. During this period, I was lecturing the NATO Council on the need to work together to defeat terrorism, not to ship arms to Iran or Iraq, and to develop more cooperation among the internal security forces of the nations within the alliance.

Terrorism, and its accompanying diplomatic tensions, increased in and around Europe. In late December of 1985, Palestinian gunmen using grenades and machine guns attacked passengers at the Israeli airline's check-in counter at Rome's airport, and five Americans were slain. That same day there was an attack in the Vienna airport.

On January 7, 1986, the United States broke all remaining economic relations with Libya, ordered all Americans there to leave, and the next day froze Libyan assets in the United States. The administration then launched a political campaign to have allies take similar action. Deputy Secretary John Whitehead was rushed to the European capitals and NATO headquarters to muster support, but met with little success. Italy banned arms sales to Libya, and Canada supported U.S. action, but the responses by the other allies were weak. Margaret Thatcher had a special problem in that she was resisting Commonwealth pressures for sanctions against South Africa. On January 27, the EC foreign ministers put out a halfhearted resolution but with no enforcement powers. As James Markham wrote in the *New York Times*, "it was a classic confrontation between an activist American . . . and Europeans accustomed to coexisting with unpleasant neighbors."[6]

In mid-March, the Reagan administration began naval maneuvers in the Gulf of Sidra. It was the nineteenth such exercise since 1981, as I pointed out to the Perm Reps, when arguing that they should not get too alarmed. This was the eighth time the United States had operated below what Qaddafi had warned was "the line of death" (that is, below 32°03′N). Clashes followed. The maneuvers were ostensibly held to exercise freedom of navigation, but they were plainly designed to send a signal to Qaddafi.

In April things heated up. A bomb exploded at La Belle, a West German discotheque. One American and one Turkish woman were killed and 230 were wounded, including 50 Americans. Three days later a bomb exploded on board a TWA flight to Rome, killing 4 Americans. U.S. officials claimed "absolutely convincing evidence" of Libyan involvement but they failed in their efforts to persuade the allies to expel all Libyan diplomats from their countries. The U.S. ambassador to the United Nations, Vernon Walters, was sent to several European capitals about the time that Italy successfully convened another meeting of EC foreign ministers.

At two o'clock Tuesday morning, on April 15, 1986, U.S. war planes carried out an eleven-minute strike on Libya. Thirteen F-111 bombers based in Great Britain and twelve A-6 attack aircraft from the Sixth Fleet hit five military and intelligence targets, but there was also some damage to foreign embassies, a hospital, and Qadaffi's tent. By 9:00 A.M. Brussels time, I stood before a specially convened meeting of the Perm Reps in Lord Carrington's private conference room, reciting the purpose and nature of the strikes from a newly arrived cable from Washington.

By Wednesday all ambassadors had received instructions for their responses. There was much criticism. When all Perm Reps had presented their criticisms, I had to respond: U.S. military personnel were in Europe to keep a collective commitment against a common adversary. There had to be a collective commitment against terrorism or else, surely, congressional sentiment to withdraw those troops would grow. The 1930s should have taught all of us the price of appeasement and inability of democracies to act together. The same applied to the new scourge, terrorism.

If Perm Reps were trying to hold the alliance together, never was there a more dramatic contrast between European and American public attitudes. Republicans and Democrats united behind the president, while the European public opposed him. While Margaret Thatcher supported the president and allowed him to use F-111 aircraft based in the United Kingdom, the majority of the British public was openly critical of Reagan and Thatcher. In West European eyes, Rambo had done it again. Lord Carrington, in a BBC interview on April 27, said that as a result of the attack, "the situation is as bad between Europe and America as I can remember in the period I have been associated with the Alliance."[7]

I phoned Senator Sam Nunn to gauge both the temperature in the Senate and his own. Nunn said if he were to offer a troop-withdrawal amendment the next day, it would pass the Senate in a moment, and a number of Senators had asked if he planned to do so. The climate was bad. The French ambassador was scurrying around the Senate office building, greatly concerned about the anti-French sentiment that had built up as a result of the French refusal to let the British-based U.S. bombers fly over France on their way to Libya. American critics were saying this was the reason we lost a plane. Ambassador Walters even publicly spoke of French ingratitude and referred to the postwar help the United States had provided to France.

John Whitehead was again dispatched to Europe for consultations, including to the NATO Council. After his presentation, the Perm Reps made their comments, but the one that stood out was that of the wise Italian ambassador, Paolo Fulci: how ironic if an alliance that the Kremlin could not split during the missile deployment was now split by Colonel Qaddafi. The room was hushed.

By then Europeans were doing more than complaining. The EC foreign ministers had their second special meeting in one week and did what they had refused to do in January: they limited the size of Libyan diplomatic missions. The embarrassed French dropped their opposition to discussing terrorism at the summit. The Reagan administration publicly praised the EC ministers for the actions they had taken, and both sides tried to heal the wounds.

There was no way for the United States to invoke the treaty against Libya. Although NATO was a successful organization in its explicit treaty area, in America, NATO got the blame for what happened outside its treaty area. In fact, the treaty area was almost touched at one point. After the U.S. raid, a Libyan patrol boat fired two missiles wildly at a U.S. coast guard station on the Italian island of Lampedusa. If Libya actually attacked the island, which was in the NATO area, Italy and the United States both would have invoked the treaty.[8]

Subsequently, the Reagan administration and the European allies deserved high marks for healing official wounds. The Permanent Council in Brussels has, through their camaraderie, a marvelous capacity for such a task. But if the official wounds were healed, the public attitudes on both sides of the Atlantic remained at odds, awaiting further detonation. The perception of a Europe "filled with terrorism" kept thousands of U.S. tourists out of Europe the following summer, resulting in deep injury to the economies there.

Unfortunately, in 1986, things were to go from bad to worse for the alliance, but the monkey was to be on the American back. I continued to give my updates on terrorism at NATO Council meetings, arguing that no arms be sent to either Iran or Iraq to fuel their ongoing war. From time to time the council also received selective reports from the Military Committee on the conflict that had implications for the energy lifelines of Europe.

By the first of November the autumn colors were gone from the trees on the rolling grounds surrounding Truman Hall, and the rains were frequent. It was the last go-round in this idyllic country setting for my wife and me, for I knew—and had told George Shultz over a year earlier—that I had to return to Washington to reestablish my roots and to plan the future of the policy research center I had helped found. I had recommended as my replacement, ironically as it turned out, two well-known Americans: Robert McFarlane and former Senator John Tower. Both had the connections to keep alive the partnership our mission had established with the Congress, both knew negotiating and defense-policy issues, and both could carry on our public diplomacy campaign. Fate had a different destiny for each of us in a violent maelstrom that would test each of us and the nation.

The weird and unbelievable story broke in a Beirut newspaper: Bud McFarlane and others had made a secret flight to Teheran the previous spring. As press reports mounted, the picture developed of meetings involving negotiations about arms for hostages, a trade facilitated by Middle Eastern arms dealers. As the November days passed at NATO, the stories went from bad to worse. On November 13, the president addressed the nation. He explained his eighteen-month diplomatic initiative, which, of course, had occurred during the period when George Shultz, myself, and others had berated allies for selling arms to Iran and bargaining for the release of hostages.

The speech did not satisfy the Congress or the news media. In Europe, diplomats and politicians began to wonder whether the United States was headed for another Watergate trauma and a politically incapacitated leader of the alliance. On November 19, the president held a press conference—the worst in his career—and came under attack for misstatements. The president ordered Attorney General Edwin Meese to conduct an inquiry into what had transpired. In so doing, Meese found out about the diversion of funds to the Contras, in apparent violation of the Boland amendment. The president established an investigating board headed by Senator John Tower.

The arms-for-hostages bombshell struck not long before I hosted a Thanksgiving Day luncheon for the Perm Reps. At the end of the lunch, I said I had some off-the-record comments. Obviously we had an alarming situation in Washington. I knew the ambassadors' concerns, for so many had asked for my private opinion. I too was shocked at the implications of trading arms for hostages, and now the diversion of funds. But this was not another Watergate. I had served in the first Nixon administration. Nixon, extraordinarily brilliant in the diplomatic field, tragically had tried to cover things up, and this had produced a prolonged crisis of the presidency. I was confident that Reagan would not do that; he would be open and honest. I made my declaration, not knowing the facts. Later, many ambassadors expressed gratitude and praised my confidence. Secretly, I was worried.

Two days before Christmas, I received a surprising call from Donald Regan. It was necessary to separate the Iranian inquiry from the regular agenda of the White House. The president and vice president wanted me to assume the job of Special Counsellor to the President, reporting directly to him for a ninety-day period.

I wanted to think overnight about this request, talk to advisers, and work out a set of terms to be understood in advance as to how I would be allowed to operate and ensure the integrity of my mandate. When the president phoned me the day after Christmas, he stressed how he wanted an open investigation to get the facts out, and in this job I would receive his full support. I told him I accepted his summons because he had restored strength to the presidency in the first two-term administration since Eisenhower. He was the leader of the alliance, and the strength of the alliance depended on his strength.

It is bizarre that the Middle East—that ancient area of conflict that had fostered new forms of violence—would so wound Carter and Reagan, two leaders of the alliance. This new form of warfare, for which alliances were never designed, can paralyze, divide, and test our traditional instruments of diplomacy.

7 The Deterrence Debate

DETERRENCE is a state of mind at a given point in time. It is based on perception, a political and psychological phenomenon rather than a military or technical one. Many in the West think they know exactly what will deter the Soviet leaders, as if they can see into the Soviet mind today or predict that state of mind, say, ten years from now. Many believe that the nuclear weapon is the absolute one, and has produced absolute deterrence for all time. Yet some of those same people lack such certainty when nuclear proliferation in the Third World is discussed. No one, however great an expert, can predict precisely what will deter under various circumstances of crisis and strain.

It is sometimes said that diplomats overly concentrate on what they see as an opponent's intentions, while military people dwell on what they see as the opponent's capabilities. This can sometimes mean that the diplomats become a bit too optimistic, while the military are unduly pessimistic as a result of looking at "worst case" scenarios. However, this phenomenon is widely understood and tolerated. "Intentions versus capabilities" is debated quite openly within our bureaucracies and among our scholars. Unfortunately, particularly within the intelligence communities, allowance is not made for the possible progression to war as a result of miscalculation and misperception, or as a result of a sudden change in calculations or perceptions. The reason no one can absolutely predict behavior is that no one can foresee all circumstances.

We already noted that the Truman administration publicly excluded South Korea from its defense perimeter and withdrew its forces. Yet when North Korea attacked, Harry Truman related that attack to what might happen in Europe, and therefore completely reversed his course. A new perception reversed his intentions. Did North Korea expect such a reversal? Certainly not. On the eve of the Falklands conflict, statements were made that led to similar miscalculations. One might call it "Galtieri's gaffe" after the leader of Argentina's military junta, who needed to create a successful foreign crisis in order to distract Argentine attention from growing domestic problems. He mistakenly calculated that if he seized the Falklands the British surely would not or could not mount a countercampaign from 8,000 miles away without the political and logistical support of the United States. He also erred in believing the Reagan administration would not give assistance to the British side. On the other hand, the British had already miscalculated by assuming that Argentina would not dare undertake a military action against them. Miscalculation and misperception reigned on both sides and contributed to the outbreak of war.

Those who accept the above analysis for conventional war situations argue that nuclear weapons have changed the calculations completely, perhaps forever. I call this the "traditional nuclear wisdom." It argues first that the Kremlin's leaders are not like Hitler or the Japanese clique planning Pearl Harbor. They are Marxist-Leninists; they believe history is on their side. They are cautious; they do not have a timetable; they do not take risks.

Of course, this is exactly what the CIA thought before the Cuban missile crisis, when it estimated that the Soviets would never place nuclear missiles outside the Soviet Union, for they had never done so in Eastern Europe. National Security Adviser McGeorge Bundy strongly endorsed this view, even publicly. Only CIA Director John McCone dissented—and turned out to be correct. Nikita Khrushchev did not calculate the risks as the rational CIA analysts thought the Communist leader should. The precedents relied on to judge the Kremlin's actions did not, after all, hold true.

Second, these experts of traditional nuclear wisdom say that none of the examples of past wars apply, now that nuclear weapons are a part of the equation. There has been so much researched, written, said, and dramatized about nuclear war that no thinking leader would court it. Its horror has in itself become the deterrent.

I believe that this point is only partially valid. One can argue that if the people who began World War I really could have foreseen it as a war of attrition over the next four years—with 30 million casualties—they never would have started it. People now know that in a nuclear war, 30 million people can be killed by only a few nuclear salvos. This has been publicly dramatized in movies, television programs, tracts, and by concerned scientists.

The fundamental fact is that nuclear weapons have been used, and we Americans alone have used them; yet we tend to think we are the world's greatest, most generous, most rational, most moral democracy. Nuclear wisdom will respond that in 1945 there was then no prospect of nuclear retaliation such as both superpowers face today. It is that prospect of retaliation, they argue, that is the sobering new factor that produces ironclad deterrence. But in an age when massive nuclear retaliation is not only possible but probable, this same democracy—along with fifteen other democracies—is prepared to use nuclear weapons first, if necessary, to prevent a defeat by Warsaw Pact conventional forces. Or so says NATO strategy. According to that strategy, under certain circumstances, we ourselves would threaten to initiate nuclear war. According to traditional nuclear wisdom, then, the Soviets would never be so irrational as to initiate war, because they could not be certain it would remain conventional. But this view leaves us in the position of being the irrational ones—the side threatening nuclear war—and the Soviets are the rational ones.

In their willingness to support such a doctrine, our NATO allies in Europe are fond of their own two rationalizations that enable them to hold to the traditional nuclear wisdom. First, they say that if the United States remains strong in its will to initiate first use in the face of an overwhelming conventional attack, it introduces such uncertainty in the mind of the opponent that the opponent will never attack: the risk to his survival outweighs any gain. In essence, we have the absolute weapon.

It is exactly here that a major new military problem intrudes, one that did not exist twenty-five years ago when our strategy was being conceived in a climate of U.S. nuclear superiority. It punctures the traditional nuclear wisdom. Theoretically, NATO has options for limited use of nuclear weapons and does not immediately have to go to a massive retaliatory strike against the Soviet Union. But will these options be credible in the 1990s?

Even today, the problem is that at every level of escalation the Warsaw Pact has just as many if not more weapons than NATO. NATO would be militarily worse off, not better, if it ascended this "escalation ladder." No doubt the reason that the U.S. Joint Chiefs of Staff were able to support the "double-zero" agreement on Euromissiles is that they would not recommend to the president that we would be better off militarily if NATO or the United States used these options.

Second, many European experts retort to Americans: don't take this all so seriously. If our conventional forces are crumbling, and the Supreme Allied Commander Europe is authorized to make selective use of his nuclear weapons, the real purpose would not be military, but political—to send a signal to the Kremlin of our determination, and to ensure that it realizes that the risks to the Soviets outweigh any gain. The Soviets will be rational enough, the argument goes, to see that they have no choice but to withdraw. If this "game of chicken" were ever put into effect, it might indeed become if not Armageddon, then something close to it.

An example of this thinking is evident in NATO exercises. To avoid having to consider the consequences of any such nightmare, a typical scenario ends after NATO makes a very selective use of its nuclear weapons. In this scenario, the Kremlin "gets the message," and then sues for peace. Of course, these ideas predate the Chernobyl nuclear accident and the panic in Western Europe over the fallout. This fallout would be miniscule compared to that following the "selective use" of nuclear weapons. The opposite scenario from that of the Kremlin backing down is not played politically at NATO. It is that the Kremlin sends word over the hotline to Washington: "I got your political message. I am going to double the megatonnage you sent me and send you a political message back." This message is that NATO cannot prevail in a nuclear war.

The fine art of "signaling" has been a rather dangerous game in this century because of the way signals have been misunderstood. The adverse effect of negative signaling has been rather clear—for example, the unintended one sent by Dean Acheson when he drew a Pacific security perimeter that excluded Korea. But positive signaling, during the Johnson presidency in Vietnam, for example, did not work either. In 1965 we sent to Vietnam light rather than heavy divisions to signal a limited commitment, and later used bombing pauses to encourage negotiations. Granted, an initial nuclear release by NATO is hardly a signal that could get lost in the fog of crisis or war. But the Soviet Union has a psychosis bred by attacks from Napoleon to Hitler, combined with a phobia about "encirclement" and a military doctrine that assumes that any limited nuclear exchange could certainly escalate to all-out war. The Soviet leadership might well use NATO's nuclear signal to trigger plans it might have for a major preemptive strike, at a minimum, throughout Europe. They could calculate that once NATO understood this "war fighting" signal, the United States would sue for peace. Moreover, the Soviets could choose to direct a preemptive strike at the United States itself. The Japanese calculated that a preemptive attack on Pearl Harbor would render the United States either unwilling or incapable of pursuing the war.

The fundamental point is that no one knows how nuclear powers will react. No war in this century has turned out exactly as planned. The vulnerability of the traditional nuclear wisdom is that its endgame is the most wildly unstable and irrational situation in human history, filled with unknowns. Plainly, what was once a sound strategy when we had nuclear superiority will be turned on its head by the 1990s. Flexible response, a good strategy, has been seriously weakened, not by the INF treaty, as some charge, but long before that. It's worthwhile to review how this happened.

Part of the original flexibility of flexible response resided in the nuclear superiority we enjoyed at every rung of the "escalatory ladder." McNamara was very wary of the nuclear element of the strategy even then, unlike the incumbent SACEUR, Air Force General Lauris Norstad. McNamara wanted to see the allies build up conventional forces so that consideration of the first use of nuclear weapons would be long delayed.

While the discussion about flexible response and how it applied to NATO was proceeding in the 1960s, another debate was taking place concerning doctrine at the strategic nuclear level. When McNamara became secretary of defense, he inherited the doctrine of massive retaliation. But soon the technological revolution that brought about intercontinental ballistic missiles rendered that policy obsolete; the Soviets could now respond in kind. McNamara initially thought that there was a possibility that nuclear war might be limited, that is, might be terminated before all-out escalation, and so formulated a policy of "controlled response." But a debate ensued, and controlled response was tarred as a war-fighting strategy, not a deterrent strategy. McNamara became convinced that controlled nuclear war was not possible, and settled on the policy of "mutual assured destruction." Assured destruction sought to deter an attack against the United States by threatening unacceptable punishment; that is, in retaliation we would destroy the Soviet Union.

But assured destruction, too, had its critics. Would such a threat seem credible in the face of a limited nuclear strike by the Soviet Union? Did we, in fact, not require more options? As criticism mounted, a new secretary of defense, James Schlesinger, took up the debate, bringing to high office a truly "strategic mind." He had worked on these questions while he was director of strategic studies at RAND and developed a policy of flexibility in nuclear use, requiring the United States to have a wide range of options with which to respond appropriately to any level of Soviet attack. Though elaborated on by subsequent administrations, this idea of proportionality in response has remained central to U.S. strategic doctrine to this day.[1]

Many years after he left office, McNamara came out against first use of nuclear weapons under any circumstances, along with former National Security Adviser McGeorge Bundy, diplomat-historian George Kennan, and nuclear negotiator Gerard Smith. They had an article in *Foreign Affairs* in 1982 in which they argued that dependence on the threat of first use of nuclear weapons had become a crutch for Europeans which helped them avoid doing anything really constructive on the conventional level.[2] Their declaratory solution of publicly stating "no first use" was too drastic and certainly premature, at least in 1982. Even today the specter of possible first use by NATO—regardless of the military irrationality—helps maintain the calculus of uncertainty in the Soviet mind. The threat also complicates Soviet military planning, forcing greater dispersion of Soviet forces. Why, through a unilateral declaratory statement, discard what at least could be used as an extraordinary negotiating card?

But the point is that this calculus of uncertainty cannot last. The irrationality factor will increase year by year, as will the capability of the Soviets to deter NATO's first use. On the military level, smart conventional weapons in the 1990s will increasingly have more utility than those same weapons configured in a nuclear mode. Thus the four critics—wrong indeed in their timing and in unilaterally abandoning first use—made some good points with fundamental long-term applications to nuclear strategy.

If we look at history, what has happened at NATO is not unusual. I call it the rearview mirror syndrome. Military history is one of constantly changing relationships among technology, tactics, and strategy. The nation that doesn't attempt to identify those changes and look ahead rather than through the rearview mirror is doomed. Take, for example, France in 1914 and then in 1939. An esteemed center of military education had been the École de Guerre in Paris. What was being taught there on the eve of World War I about the superiority of the offensive was indeed correct—but for 1814, not 1914. They did not want to disturb their mind-set by looking at the experiences of the last year of the American Civil War, when Grant and Lee used trenches, breastworks, and Gatling guns; or the Russo-Japanese War, where increasing defense protection and firepower forced the conflict into a static confrontation. In the late 1930s the École de Guerre again looked out the rearview mirror, at 1914. It concluded that defense was predominant, hence the glory of their Maginot Line.

Like those on the faculty of the École de Guerre, the tendency of many Europeans, and indeed some U.S. NATO hands, is to believe that because deterrence through the threatened first use of nuclear weapons was successful twenty years ago, it can work eternally. All we need do is believe in it. I call this group the nuclear true believers. They act as if nuclear deterrence in its present form is an article of religious faith and that to question it is heretical or, in some cases, unpatriotic. It is vital that we consider new approaches.[3]

At a September 1979 CSIS-sponsored conference, Henry Kissinger, then out of government, delivered a speech on deterrence that shook Europe and its unquestioned faith in deterrence. He said, "therefore I would say—what I might not say in office—that our European allies should not keep asking us to multiply strategic assurances that we cannot possibly mean or if we do mean, we should not want to execute because if we execute, we risk the destruction of civilization."[4]

I also remember vividly a meeting five years later, in 1984, in the Oval Office when Peter Carrington expressed tactful concern over the questions that were being raised about the credibility of nuclear deterrence, its morality and workability, and the new emphasis on SDI. Reagan responded that our nuclear strategy had been conceived in the days when we had nuclear superiority, but we had lost that superiority. The old way was no longer viable. It is interesting that this was the very same president who before his election had talked about trying to regain nuclear superiority, something that made Carrington and the Europeans shudder as overtly provocative of the Soviets. Even before his election, Reagan gave up such a quest and was left with the doctrine of Mutual Assured Destruction (MAD).

Carrington responded with an anecdote about the First World War. I think it was taken from a famous cartoon of "Old Bill," a British predecessor of G.I. Joe. Two men were in a muddy foxhole. One kept complaining and wanted to leave. His foxhole mate snapped "If you know of a better 'ole, go to it!" The moral to Carrington's story for Reagan was that a new deterrent foxhole had not yet been dug, by SDI or any other means. But there is a problem Carrington did not identify: The sides of the foxhole have eroded, the bottom has been filling up, and the men are exposed to danger, whether they know it or not. Certainly in the 1990s NATO's current deterrent strategy—upon which it depends to prevent World War III—will be exposed and vulnerable.

Today the first victory that must be won within the NATO community is psychological: to get away from the rearview mirror and look forward toward the 1990s. Europeans must be convinced that there are sounder, more proportionate ways to defend Europe. In West Berlin, charismatic John F. Kennedy said that the United States was willing to risk its cities to defend Europe's because it needed European freedom to protect American freedom. But we then enjoyed a 10-to-1 nuclear superiority over the Soviet Union.[5] Distinguished Europeans have muttered to me: "What you are saying is, there's no longer a willingness to risk Chicago for Berlin or Frankfurt or Brussels. The old American will is gone. Your attitude toward Europe has changed. Europe is no longer worth it to you."

This response misses the problem. In the deterrence of war and in war itself, will is important. But success is generally based upon a combination of strong will, good strategy, and effective preparation. Today we cannot trade Chicago for Frankfurt or Berlin. Most of Eurasia and North America would be destroyed by such nuclear exchanges. What is important—and essential in our alliance strategy—is that the Soviets believe they cannot attack Western Europe with impunity, that they cannot make it a nuclear battleground without putting the Soviet Union itself at risk.

The January 1988 "National Security Strategy Report" of the president to the Congress describes deterrence in perhaps less basic but more rounded terms than the Carrington-Reagan dialogue in the Oval Office. Flexible response seeks to deter by confronting an aggressor with three possible responses: first, by direct defense to defeat aggression without escalation, such as defeating a nonnuclear attack with conventional forces only. What NATO has made itself incapable of doing is just this, I fear. Second, by threat of escalation to nuclear weapons, a threat that we have argued is deteriorating in credibility. And third, by the threat of retaliation, which raises "the prospect that an attack will trigger a retaliatory attack on an aggressor's homeland, causing his losses to far exceed his gains. Our deterrence of a Soviet nuclear attack on the United States is based on our resolve to retaliate directly against the Soviet Union."[6] I should stress that this form of deterrence is highly credible and must be kept that way in the 1990s.

If one were to follow the logic of this chapter, it is not, as many Europeans think, Reagan's initiation of the concept of SDI, or moral pronouncements by Reagan or the American Catholic bishops, that is undercutting NATO strategy the most. It is, rather, the underlying technological and strategic trends. If nuclear escalation in the 1990s lacks credibility and military logic, then it is good to move from a strategy of increasingly incredible first use to a strategy of credible denial and retaliation. At both the strategic level of U.S.-based forces and the conventional level of NATO-based forces, this requires a clear defensive capability of denying the success of an attack. This is to say that the separation of deterrence and defense has become too great, and at both levels deterrence must be improved in the 1990s through more realistic defense.

In January 1988, the Commission on Integrated Long-Term Strategy, cochaired by Fred Ikle and Albert Wohlstetter, released its long-awaited report, "Discriminate Deterrence." Among the principles accepted by the commission was that "to help defend our allies and to defend our interests abroad, we cannot rely on threats expected to provoke our own annihilation if carried out." In the European context, the report argues that "the Alliance should threaten to use nuclear weapons not as a link to a wider and more devastating war—although the risk of further escalation would still be there—but mainly as an instrument for denying success to the invading Soviet forces."[7]

A stinging rebuttal came from three highly distinguished Europeans: Sir Michael Howard of Oxford; Karl Kaiser, head of the key policy research center in Bonn; and Francois de Rose, the intellectual former French NATO ambassador. Among other things, this threesome took the language as if it were a call to deter by threat of initiating nuclear war only in Europe. This, they argued, would "erode European confidence in the capability of deterrence to prevent war." On conventional war, they said: "The notion of a grand conventional conflict to defeat Soviet forces has no support in Europe, primarily because the means do not exist but also because it would be likely to produce the kind of annihilation of Europe that Americans fear from nuclear escalation. If, moreover, tactical nuclear weapons were used only 'as an instrument to deny success to the invading Soviet forces,' their nuclear response would undoubtedly result in the nuclear destruction of Central and Western Europe while leaving the aggressor untouched."[8]

But as commissioners Brzezinski, Kissinger, Ikle, and Wohlstetter responded, attempts such as theirs to make deterrence remain credible in the next decades should reassure, not frighten, Europeans. The Americans were speaking of worried European publics, as compared to the governing elites who were happy with the current nuclear strategy. They argued, first, that the Europeans had misread the report in saying they intended to rely only on nuclear forces based in Western Europe to deter attack. Rather, the commissioners were arguing that both Western European and U.S. continental-based weapons should be used in discriminate ways; and second, that suicidal or indiscriminate threats—by French, British, or American strategic forces—weaken deterrence by undermining credibility.[9] Furthermore, the Americans noted that the Europeans appeared to imply that "no possible improvement could enable NATO to stop any Soviet invasion any place in Europe without NATO's using nuclear weapons; and that if NATO did [develop such a conventional capability], NATO could not deter the Soviet use of nuclear weapons. NATO's situation would then be hopeless. But we reject this proposition. The conviction that Europe can have no response that would not lead to its own destruction undermines public support for the alliance."[10] This battle of the op-ed pieces showed the wide divergence between European and American thinking.

What is striking is that in European thinking, deterrence and any real ability to defend have become disconnected. To the Europeans, the U.S. guarantee of the defense of Europe has become tested by our willingness to go to nuclear war even when we are less well off militarily at such levels. Rather than pushing Americans in this direction, Europeans should see that the heart of the U.S. commitment to the defense of Europe came after the Korean invasion, when Harry Truman committed U.S. divisions on the ground in Europe to an integrated command. Article V of the North Atlantic Treaty said that an attack against one shall be taken as an attack against all. But this stipulation allows each nation to go through its constitutional process—meaning that the military commitment of forces to combat is not automatic. If U.S. troops on the ground are attacked, however, the president's constitutional powers as commander in chief are immediately activated. The War Powers Resolution never dared restrict the president's clear power to respond immediately to any such attack. Perhaps the most important item in the Ikle-Wohlstetter report is that Kissinger and Brzezinski, who had talked of troop withdrawals, reversed their position to support a clear commitment to forward defense. But this salient fact was missed by the Europeans.

The reason the U.S. conventional-defense guarantee is so important is that, as we have said earlier, a war is not likely to start at the nuclear level or even with a long-planned grand conventional attack. As in 1914 and 1939, it will probably start with limited moves of conventional forces, no doubt with miscalculation and misperception. This is the basic level where we lack flexibility and where deterrence must therefore be reinforced. A short warning attack cannot be deterred for sure with the threat of nuclear weapons when we are significantly less than equal at lower nuclear levels.

Of course, even in the Cold War crises, when we had nuclear superiority, in the final analysis it was often the conventional forces that counted. Supposedly in 1956, at the time of the Hungarian uprising, we had some ideas of a strategy of "roll back," and we had a solid nuclear superiority, but we were deterred by the vast Soviet conventional superiority. Contrary to popular belief, in the Cuban missile crisis our nuclear superiority was not the reason the Soviets withdrew their missiles. Plainly, it was our conventional-weapons superiority in the area and our multiple conventional options of naval blockade, air strikes against the missile sites, or lastly, a full-scale invasion of the island. Unlike the nuclear options, which Kennedy never threatened except in retaliation to a nuclear first strike from Cuba, these conventional options were usable and planned for if the Soviets did not back down. The conventional option was the decisive and effective one in preserving the status quo and the peace.

Second, our European friends fail to recognize that miscalculation, misperception, unclear alliances, and ineffectual leaders of the democracies were the causes of World Wars I and II. If the allies had united sooner and been willing to fight in concert, there would have been a state of deterrence without nuclear weapons. The nuclear bomb is not the eternal answer, and it is foolish to argue that having the bomb is the only way World Wars I and II could have been prevented. An alliance of democracies committed to what is in Article V of the NATO treaty would have prevented both world wars. It is time to return to reality and go beyond the shibboleth that conventional forces, unlike nuclear ones, cannot deter.

Whether we like it or not, conventional forces will be the decisive element in the power balance in Europe during the 1990s. The growth of Soviet theater nuclear capabilities may deter any first use of nuclear weapons by NATO. But if NATO has failed to anticipate the diplomatic, political, and ultimately military effects of enhanced Soviet theater nuclear capabilities, no amount of last-minute "will," stated in the heat of a crisis but unrelated to reality, will change the situation. Will is needed, but it is needed *now* to prepare for and avert this unhealthy trend. A famous basketball coach once said that all the will to win during a game is to no avail if there has not been the will to train, practice, and prepare for the game.

8 What if War Comes?

IN 1984, several months after SACEUR Bernie Rogers had given the Perm Reps a briefing on the alarming status of NATO's critical deficiencies, we visited the Commander-in-Chief Southern Europe (CINCSOUTH) in Naples. The U.S. admiral commanding NATO's Southern Region gave us a very different impression, one that was less pessimistic than General Rogers'. In fact, CINCSOUTH was fairly satisfied in his estimate of how well NATO would do against the Warsaw Pact if a conflict ever erupted.

How could two military men with access to the same facts differ so markedly in their estimate of how well NATO would do? The answer rests in their assumptions of what kind of attack the Warsaw Pact would launch, where it would be, how much time NATO would have to prepare, and how well NATO would exploit that time. In short, the response depends on the scenario.

When the ambassadors next saw SACEUR, they asked Rogers why this difference existed. After some checking, word came back that the admiral's assessment was based on his assumption that NATO had plenty of warning time, would take advantage of it by fully mobilizing, and that U.S. reinforcements would have been deployed to Europe and would be in place.

Before discussing alternative scenarios and NATO's most troublesome military problems as it looks to the 1990s, some of the facts of the current Warsaw Pact-NATO balance should be kept in mind. Estimating the relative balance of forces between two adversaries like

NATO and the Warsaw Pact is a complicated task.[1] Many factors must be considered, including geography and terrain, numerical comparisons of the force structures of both sides, operational concepts, and comparisons of nonquantitative factors such as readiness and technology.

The geographic location of an attack is a key feature in any scenario. Southern Europe—with the mountains of Italy, Greece, and Turkey, surrounded by water, and with Iberia widely separated from direct contact with Warsaw Pact forces—is not the most fragile sector of NATO. The security of the Central Front, especially along the inner-German border, remains the key sector. Adequate defense in that region depends on not only prior warning time but a fast, smoothly operating NATO response. How well NATO will do in Central Europe, therefore, has a lot to do with the scenario one envisages.

The second critical factor is numbers. Over the last twenty years, manpower levels in active Warsaw Pact forces in Central Europe have stayed relatively stable. So has the number of Warsaw Pact divisions. What has changed dramatically, however, is the amount of equipment and weapons the Soviet Union has deployed in East Germany, Czechoslovakia, and Poland. The Soviet Union has moved in almost four times more weapons than NATO has introduced in the same twenty-year period.[2] As a result, the Warsaw Pact currently enjoys a noticeable superiority over NATO in most weapons categories: an almost 3:1 edge in tanks, combat aircraft, surface-to-air missiles, and attack helicopters; and more than a 3:1 margin in artillery and infantry fighting vehicles. The overall balance is 2.2:1 in the Soviets' favor.[3]

Some critics suggest that these ratios are not sufficient to ensure a Warsaw Pact victory because an attacker needs at least a 3:1 ratio to be certain of success. What these critics often overlook is that superiority is not needed across an entire front, but at the decisive point of attack. In fact, Napoleon, Robert E. Lee, and Heinz Guderian won their spectacular victories not with greater numbers overall but because they were able to marshal the necessary superiority at the place in the battle where it mattered most.

Growing Soviet strengths are matched against key NATO weaknesses, especially shortcomings in deployment, readiness, and sustainability. This is particularly true in northern Germany, where NATO's Northern Army Group—composed of West German, British, Canadian, Dutch, and Belgian forces—confront the most heavily armored and most ready Warsaw Pact troops. This imbalance has been created in part by NATO itself, which has not matched Soviet improvements in forces for that area. Inferior numbers, however, can be offset by better quality, and this has been NATO's traditional approach. NATO continues to enjoy a technological edge over its adversaries and relies on better technology to balance the Warsaw Pact's greater numbers. Tank for tank or airplane for airplane, NATO allies produce better equipment than the Soviets.

NATO's problem is that the Warsaw Pact has been closing that technological gap. Over the last ten years, for example, they have reduced NATO's technological lead in a range of areas from tank armor to submarine design. The Warsaw Pact's latest fourth-generation tank, the T80—with a high-velocity 125mm gun, specialized ceramic composite armor, high speed-to-weight ratio, sophisticated laser range finders, and other characteristics similar to NATO's latest tanks—may only be 70 to 80 percent as good as its NATO counterpart.[4] The same can be said of the most advanced Warsaw Pact aircraft, artillery, attack helicopters, and a range of other systems. But one has to worry whether the NATO equipment is sufficiently better to make up for the serious shortfall in numbers.

The picture that emerges in Central Europe on the Warsaw Pact side is one of a significant combined arms capability deployed forward. The spearhead of that capability is vast amounts of Soviet armor, much as tanks spearheaded the German blitzkrieg attacks in the early days of World War II. In terms of quality, Warsaw Pact forces may not be as good as NATO's, but they provide their commanders with capabilities they never before enjoyed.

Moscow has also been changing the way it thinks about how to use these forces, shifting from "mass" to "speed" to achieve decisive effects. Beginning in the early 1980s, the Soviets have introduced what they call Operational Maneuver Groups (OMGs), for example, patterned after the forces the Germans used so effectively in their blitzkriegs. An OMG is a flexible concept for the Soviets and might be a reinforced division or a corps—all built around a combined-arms concept of armor, assault helicopters, self-propelled artillery, rocket launchers, and mobile air defense. Much like Guderian at Sedan on May 13, 1940, they are aimed at making a breakthrough, and rather than encircling units, they race deep into the NATO rear to attack nuclear delivery systems, command and control centers, and other vulnerable targets.

In the 1950s, Moscow viewed tactical aircraft almost exclusively for air defense. In the 1960s and early 1970s, aircraft were little more than aerial artillery, while nuclear weapons were still preferred for attacking deep targets such as NATO's command and control facilities and airfields. Today, however, the Soviets have a different concept of air operations, one that is much more sophisticated and flexible. That concept dovetails with the growing emphasis on the speed of the ground attack, and it emphasizes a total approach: attack helicopters will provide support for the armored units leading the breakthroughs; tactical aircraft will hit NATO forces as they try to move to their defensive positions; and bombers—increasingly the more sophisticated Backfires—will have command and control headquarters, air bases, and NATO's nuclear capabilities as their primary targets.

NATO's problem, then, is a growing Soviet capability to preempt those things NATO must do to put up a robust defense. In this sense, NATO's problem is a matter of timing; it can be partly corrected if NATO has the time to mobilize reserves, deploy forces forward, prepare terrain, and reinforce from North America. Whether it will have that time is another question. One factor determining how much time will be available is the state of readiness of the respective forces: What percentage of the unit's wartime manpower is actually in the unit? Are they stationed near where they will fight? How well trained are they? Is their equipment in good repair? Relatively speaking, Soviet forces deployed forward in Central Europe are the most ready of its forces.

NATO, on the other hand, confronts some readiness problems, perhaps the most serious of which is the maldeployment of its forces, especially those intended to fight in northern Germany. In peacetime, for example, over 50 percent of NATO's brigades in Central Europe are out of position and/or stationed more than 100 kilometers from their general defensive positions. Approximately 56 percent of the Belgian and 86 percent of the Dutch forces, for example—which are responsible for defending important sectors of the inner-German border—are stationed in their respective home countries.[5] When the United States withdrew some troops from Europe in the 1960s, these two countries figured they could copy our bad example, so a real maldeployment was created in the vulnerable Northern Army Group.

As a result, NATO loses advantages it should inherently enjoy as the defender. The familiarity of the units with their fighting positions is decreased. Units arriving at main battle areas lack time for preparing defenses. Initial defenders who must screen critical areas before maldeployed forces arrive dilute their own effectiveness. Finally, and perhaps most seriously, doing what must be done if NATO is to put up a robust defense—such as moving forces forward—could be perceived as provocative in a crisis, threatening to spark the very conflict the action is designed to deter. As a result, NATO leaders and decision makers in NATO capitals would be reluctant to authorize those measures needed to begin mobilizing the defense efforts.

The problem is not one suggested by some people: that NATO will be caught by surprise. It won't, at least in the sense that the alliance intelligence community will see plenty of indicators that the adversary may be up to something and will inform the political leadership. The issue is how soon that warning will be unambiguous and whether policymakers will act on the warning they are given.[6]

Historically, and certainly in the twentieth century, there is a plethora of examples in which a defender has been unprepared to make the transition from crisis to actual conflict, and the attacker has achieved operational surprise: Belgium in 1914; France in 1940; the United States in 1941, when the Japanese attacked Pearl Harbor; the outbreak of conflict in Korea in 1950; Israel in 1973; or Britain in 1982, over the Falklands. In each of these cases, and many more, there was some evidence of the possibility of an attack. That evidence was either too ambiguous for policymakers to take decisive action, or they found reasons to dismiss it and postpone action.

Obviously, the clearer the warning, the easier it is for policymakers to justify taking the serious steps involved in preparing NATO's defense, such as calling up reserves, moving troops to their defensive positions, and so on. The more ambiguous the warning, the more reluctant policymakers are to take these steps, not wanting to escalate a crisis that could lead to the outbreak of conflict.

How much time does NATO need, and how much time will it have? Three possible scenarios might be considered. The first might be called rapid reinforcement. In this scenario, the Warsaw Pact mobilizes its forces and brings in reinforcements from the Western Military Districts of the Soviet Union to constitute the second echelon of the attack before that attack actually begins. This scenario takes about two weeks, and it is the traditional one for which NATO has planned. With ten days to two weeks to prepare, NATO nations can actually execute the necessary defensive measures. Forces are redeployed to their forward defensive positions, terrain is prepared to inhibit an armored attack, the process of bringing reinforcements of troops and fighter aircraft from North America will have begun, and so on.

Under these circumstances, NATO's defense could be quite robust indeed. Many alliance members have taken important steps that will enhance their performance. The United States, for example, has begun to preposition weapons, ammunition, and other stocks in Europe to supply six reinforcing divisions from the states so it can meet its commitment of ten divisions in Europe in ten days. Shelters and other facilities are being provided so that the 1,000 to 1,200 reinforcing aircraft will have protection when they arrive. Germany has created twelve home brigades that can provide essential support services for troops moving to the front. Similarly, Britain has created eight additional territorial brigades.[7] If NATO has time to mobilize, as it would in the scenario just described, all these assets will come into play. As a result, NATO forces would make it very rough going if the Warsaw Pact decided to attack. It is this kind of scenario that CINC-SOUTH may have had in mind when he told the Perm Reps that the situation was fairly satisfactory.

This does not imply that NATO is ensured of success in this scenario, of course. Soviet reinforcements, in particular, could pose a significant problem. For this reason, the alliance must continue its efforts to deal with this second echelon of Soviet forces. We must push forward on NATO's capability to conduct Follow-on Forces Attack, designed to exploit advanced technology to strike behind the enemy's front lines and delay, disrupt, and destroy Warsaw Pact reinforcements. The technologies involved are in some cases highly exotic, but the program combines advances in reconnaissance, weapons, munitions, and communications to perform this vital task.

A second scenario is one in which the Soviet Union mobilizes all its forces—all 120 divisions.[8] In this situation not only do reinforcements come from the Western Military Districts before an attack, but units from the Moscow, Volga, and Ural Military Districts are introduced into Central Europe as well. These, however, are cadre units, which means they require extensive manpower to be mobilized and trained to fill them out. They are also distant from the European front. Their mobilization and deployment, therefore, takes considerable time, and such blatant military measures would certainly provide NATO with unambiguous warning early enough to implement its defensive measures.

In this scenario, NATO's problem is not readiness; it would have time and it would be ready. Sustaining a cohesive defense for more than a few days, however, would be difficult. Some NATO forces only have a few days' worth of ammunition, and they would find it very difficult indeed to stop the continual waves of Warsaw Pact forces.

In the third scenario, NATO's Indicators and Warning System provides some warning information but it is ambiguous, just as Soviet intentions were toward Poland. The Perm Reps in Brussels debate whether reinforcing Europe will be provocative or will reinforce deterrence and prevent a crisis from escalating. Soviet activities continue, but nations can't agree on what that activity means and mobilization does not begin. Then Perm Reps are told that Soviet reinforcements from the Western Military Districts have arrived in Europe. NATO nations—some reluctantly—agree that this measure suggests hostile intent and mobilization begins. Units in Germany begin to move to their defensive positions. Belgian and Dutch units begin to move forward. The reinforcement plan is approved, and the first troops and aircraft from the United States begin to arrive a few days later.

Then, before Europe is fully reinforced, the Warsaw Pact attacks. They catch some NATO forces in transit. Operational Maneuver Groups exploit gaps created by unprepared defense positions because NATO forces responsible for the area, even if they are on the scene, have not had time to get ready. Roads on which troops are moving forward get clogged by refugees from the early battles hurrying in the other direction. NATO airfields are destroyed, or are attacked with chemical weapons, making it difficult for the reinforcing airplanes to find safe places to land. The defense in northern Germany hasn't had enough time to cohere, and armored breakthroughs in the north threaten the flanks of German and U.S. forces fighting in southern Germany. NATO policymakers confront the choice of defeat or possible use of nuclear weapons.

The geography of NATO's Central Region is a critical feature of this quandary. Allied Forces Central Europe (AFCENT) is broken into the Northern Army Group (NORTHAG) and the Central Army Group (CENTAG). The latter area is far stronger, even though the best avenue of attack against the key city of Frankfurt, only 100 kilometers away, is through the Fulda Gap on the border between East and West Germany. To take Frankfurt would cut Germany in two. The U.S. Fifth Corps holds this vulnerable sector of the line and, along with the Seventh Corps to the south, is at the top of NATO readiness and sustainability. A second avenue of attack is through what is known as the Göttingen Corridor, toward the famous industrial area of Germany, the Ruhr Valley. This sector is held by the crack German Third Corps. Another avenue, less attractive, is farther south, near the city of Hof, but it has many more obstacles and is covered by the U.S. Seventh Corps.

The classical place for the Warsaw Pact to attack is not against the strength of CENTAG but the weakness of NORTHAG, an area more susceptible to blitzkrieg because there are no mountains or large forests. This is where NATO's forces are most maldeployed. There is only one German corps there, and in peacetime it and the British Army of the Rhine (BAOR) to the south are stretched thin. Despite its urban sprawl and wooded areas, the NORTHAG area is most vulnerable because it lacks operational reserves and adequate supplies of ammunition.

The U.S. Third Corps, with its current headquarters at Fort Hood, Texas, is to be the reserve for this area. That is very far away indeed, and if we are ever to cut our troops committed to NATO, the cut should be here and not in Europe. These forces include the First Armored Cavalry Division, the Second Armored Cavalry Division, and the 49th Armored National Guard Division. An additional brigade of U.S. land forces is in Europe. The overall idea is to get six divisions to Europe in ten days, but the question is: When? If the war has started, ports and airfields may not be intact to receive them, and the prepositioned equipment worth billions of dollars could have been destroyed. The inability of these forces to arrive in time could lead to the ultimate failure of NATO's defense.

Two issues that arise in analyses of the overall NATO–Warsaw Pact conventional balance are, first, the role of French forces, and, second, the reliability of the Soviets' allies in Eastern Europe. French forces are indeed often overlooked in terms of the contribution they can make. Paris has demonstrated a growing interest in conventional defense in recent years, despite its insistence on remaining outside

NATO's integrated military command. The French have 50,000 troops stationed in southwestern Germany, including two armored divisions with 400 tanks and one motor rifle division.[9] They have established a Corps Headquarters in Lille, in northwestern France. The 1987 joint Franco-German exercise also demonstrated that Paris is thinking about how its recently created Force d'Action Rapide (Rapid Action Force) might be used to cut off armored penetration across the German border. Unlike the unhappy days when de Gaulle pulled France out of the integrated command, no Soviet today could calculate that France might not join in the defense of Europe.

As for East European forces, their help is key to any success of a Warsaw Pact offensive against NATO. East European forces represent 45 percent of the Pact's conventional forward assets, and they are assigned specific roles in various specific contingencies.[10] Unlike NATO, however, an alliance of free states jointly deploying forces for defensive purposes in peacetime, the Warsaw Pact is a military bloc with membership enforced through Soviet coercion. East Europeans show little respect for the Soviets, and they have little motivation to fight a war with NATO. But it would be rash to overestimate East European unreliability as a factor favorable to NATO. East Europeans have joined the Soviets in military actions against their fellow Warsaw Pact allies in Hungary in 1956 and Czechoslovakia in 1968, and they were poised on Poland's border in 1981. There has been traditionally close contact between Soviet and East European officers, and Moscow has made a concerted effort to integrate them into the overall Soviet command structure. It might be best to assume that these Pact forces will follow the Soviet line of march. If the Soviets, with the smell of victory, are successfully advancing to the west, the Eastern Europeans will be loyal; if they are retreating to the east, or the hostilities become protracted, these allies might well be disloyal. Over the next decade, we may witness an increasing "fault line" develop between the Soviets and their satellites, which could rupture under the stress of crisis, especially a prolonged one.[11]

NATO's responsibilities, of course, extend far beyond Central Europe to Norway in the north and Turkey in the south. These areas are important, not only because developments in these regions could greatly affect what happens in Central Europe, but in their own right as well. Norway and Turkey are the only NATO states that share a

common border with the Soviet Union. NATO's Northern Region also
serves as a gateway to the Atlantic, while its Southern Region not only
constitutes the northern littoral of the critical Mediterranean (with the
exception of Yugoslavia and Albania) but also adjoins the volatile
Middle East and Persian Gulf. In assessing the overall Warsaw Pact-
NATO conventional balance, each of these areas poses additional—but
different—problems for the Atlantic alliance.

In contrast to Central Europe, the problem in the north is not so
much with ground forces as with naval forces. Any Soviet attack across
Scandinavia would have to violate the territory of neutral Finland and
Sweden. I think both countries would fight to defend themselves.
Rather than a difficult ground attack in what could easily be very
inhospitable weather, Moscow might seek to achieve its military objectives in the north, by sea.

The last twenty years have witnessed a remarkable growth in the
Soviets' Northern Fleet, based on the bleak Kola Peninsula, an area
that has some of the most heavy concentrations of military facilities in
the world. During this time, it has not only grown in numbers to more
than 120 submarines and over 70 major surface combatants[12] but the
capability of individual ships has grown immensely with the introduction of the Kiev helicopter carrier, the Kirov battle cruiser, and the
Kara and *Kresta* class destroyers.

The size and capability of the Northern Fleet give Moscow the
capability of creating in the Norwegian Sea what I call a "fleet in
being," using that nineteenth-century naval term for a fleet that can
exercise its will and influence without firing a shot. This fleet becomes
especially potent if it marries with units from the Baltic Fleet, which
has shown a capacity to operate in the Norwegian Sea as well. Under
exercise conditions, the Soviets have demonstrated that they can
mobilize half the Northern Fleet in three days;[13] they can establish a
submarine barrier in the gaps between Greenland, Iceland, and the
United Kingdom in three days; Soviet warships can be in Europe's
Western approaches in eight to ten days.

The first task of these forces is to create a bastion protecting the
strategic nuclear submarines in the far north. The second task is to
form a defensive perimeter to add depth to that protection; the trend
has been for the Soviets to expand that perimeter farther and farther
south. The third job is to deny important access to the allies for their
unobstructed naval operations. Even before a crisis, therefore, under

the guise of exercises, Moscow could deploy its naval forces astride NATO's vital northern sea lines of communication, threatening NATO's ability to reinforce Norway, Denmark, and, ultimately, all of Europe. Successful Soviet amphibious operations against Norway prior to reinforcement could also give them control of key airfields in central Norway, from which they could project air power farther south and even against central Europe. With such military power, the Soviets could exert substantial political leverage against Oslo and Copenhagen in a crisis.[14] To put it bluntly, I am shocked that NATO and indeed our own Navy's maritime strategy have not given more attention to this ability to turn NATO's northern flank before war ever begins.

In the north, as in Central Europe, therefore, time is critical, especially to ensure a NATO naval presence in the Norwegian Sea. Reserves are also vital (to man P3 reconnaissance squadrons, for example), and their availability also depends on NATO's making timely mobilization decisions. The struggle for time will decide the war.

In the Southern Region, NATO's problems are in some respects similar, but in key respects quite different. As in the north, ground forces on both sides are characterized by a lack of readiness. Mobilization is required to give NATO forces time to prepare. Ground operations themselves could be conducted in three separate subregions: eastern Turkey, Thrace, and northern Italy, although significant operations in this last region are unlikely. In eastern Turkey, where the Turks share a common border with the Soviets, and in Thrace, at least initially, the terrain is mountainous and favors the defender. The Turks would have problems sustaining a conflict, however, since they suffer from chronic obsolescence of equipment and they sit at the end of a very long, and rather vulnerable, line of communication. We often forget that it is 4,000 kilometers from Portugal to eastern Turkey.

As in the north, however, ground forces are relatively less important than naval forces. The Mediterranean is central, and NATO still enjoys the tremendous advantage of dominating that inland sea. However, the Soviets have the easier mission of sea denial, which can be conducted to a great extent by land-based aircraft. NATO must perform the more demanding task of sea control. In order to retain its dominance of the Mediterranean, NATO must maintain a viable regional infrastructure. Bases and adequate communications are critical. Basing, however, has become a contentious issue, largely because the

United States continues to face difficult negotiations with four key countries—Portugal, Spain, Greece, and Turkey—that provide facilities for the U.S. Sixth Fleet and other vital U.S. forces in the region. We have already mentioned the thorny basing problems with Spain. Greece has pronounced that the United States must leave if upcoming negotiations do not prove acceptable to the Athens government. Because of budget cuts, U.S. security assistance to Portugal and Turkey has been squeezed, raising resentment in those countries. Another political problem undermining NATO's military effectiveness in the region is the previously noted Greek-Turkish dispute. Its impact is pervasive, from diluting the effectiveness of exercises to preventing the creation of a viable air defense.

Some creative thinking is needed to address the problems of the Southern Region, especially by the states in the region. The problems between Greece and Turkey must be resolved. Italy must decide what role it should play—whether it wants to orient itself toward the Central Region or the Mediterranean—and what the best use of its resources would be in order to play that role. An Italian brigade committed to the Central Front would be both a real and symbolic commitment of extraordinary importance. Spain's entire contribution to the alliance remains the subject of negotiation. Germany has recently made a contribution to NATO's naval presence in the Mediterranean, but this is primarily to demonstrate political solidarity with the United States and other allied forces in the Persian Gulf, and it is not likely to be permanent. France, too, could play an important role; a more significant French presence could alleviate some resource allocation problems, such as where the United States should put its carriers. France has talked of a joint French-Spanish-Italian council to coordinate Mediterranean issues, but as yet it has only been talk.

An overview of the NATO–Warsaw Pact balance provides good and bad news. On one hand, over the last twenty years, NATO has made significant progress in developing its ability to deal with the threat that, in the 1960s, was believed to be most likely: a reinforced Warsaw Pact attack for which NATO, responding to intelligence and warning, had ten to fourteen days to mobilize, redeploy, reinforce, and prepare. On the other hand, for the 1990s, a different threat is emerging: the Warsaw Pact's increasing capability for a potentially decisive shorter-warning attack spearheaded by heavy armor. This blitzkrieg potential is poised opposite NATO's area of greatest weakness, the north German plain. Interestingly, when my net assessment team of Phil Karber, Mike Moodie, and myself touched on this point during our presentation to the Senate Armed Services Committee in January 1988, that normally cool ex-astronaut, Senator John Glenn, literally came out of his chair. He was particularly disturbed when I pointed out that the problem is half the Soviets' fault, owing to their forward deployed armour, but half our fault due to maldeployments. "How could NATO allow this to exist?" he chided. My response was that NATO Defense Ministers do not truly talk through their problems, basing their assumptions on a net assessment as we were doing. They generalize problems, and hence do not develop resource strategies to close off such flagrant vulnerabilities.

There is another alarming trend within NATO that may increasingly contribute to what happens if war comes. This involves what has been termed "structural disarmament"—the alliance spending more and more money to buy less and less equipment, with the result that spiraling costs of small, inefficient production runs threaten either to overwhelm defense budgets or perilously diminish weapons inventories and capabilities. We touched on this term earlier. The term and concept of structural disarmament was coined by Tom Callaghan. Our association goes back to a group created in the early 1970s at CSIS to promote U.S. cooperation with its allies in the development and production of armaments. Callaghan is a prophet crying in the wilderness, warning policymakers of the diminished collective defense and wasted resources by the United States and its allies, stemming from their nationalistic, shortsighted procurement policies. "We are unilaterally disarming ourselves," is the Callaghan cry.

Structural disarmament has created a situation with, for example, four different national main battle tanks in Europe that cannot even fire the same ammunition, or a host of different tactical battlefield-communications systems—American, Dutch, French, German, Belgian, Italian—that cannot speak to each other or even to NATO's own communication system.

As Callaghan has pointed out, European governments have suffered severely at the hands of structural disarmament. The basic reason is that their defense markets, confined by the restrictions on trade with their neighbors, are too small to sustain economically viable production runs. The size of the market determines the price of the unit. Francois Heisbourg, the highly regarded director of London's prestigious International Institute for Strategic Studies, has bemoaned the fact that "it is a paradox that there should be less openness between European countries than between the U.S. and Europe."[15] Moreover, parochial interests have spawned wasteful duplication, as individual European nations try to support their own national industrial capabilities. Competition is not the norm for European defense procurement; protecting national industrial capability, even at excessive cost, is.

Britain's experience with structural disarmament is especially telling. The United Kingdom emerged from World War II with a powerhouse defense-industrial base. Shut out of trading with its allies, Britain was unable to tap the continental-size market it needed to sustain that base. With small production runs, weapons costs rose. Development and production of individual systems was stretched out, bringing lower annual costs but much higher total costs for the life of the programs. Force readiness was slighted; reserve stockpiles were run down. Previously stretched programs were cancelled, including six different interceptor aircraft, two ballistic missile systems, and several aero-engine projects. Disarmament had begun.[16]

The United States was insulated from the pernicious effects of structural disarmament for some time. But today it is hitting home with a vengeance. The Senate Armed Services Committee reported in 1983, for example, that the air force was buying fifty to sixty fewer planes than it needed to keep the force at an acceptable average age. They concluded that the inevitable result was "the steady aging of the force which translates into reduced capability and rising support costs."[17] More generally, according to Callaghan, during the past five years weapons have been produced in the United States at just 50 percent of efficient production capacity. A fourth of the major acquisition programs were produced at a rate below the minimum economic rate for those systems. Half of the twenty largest weapons-systems programs were stretched out.[18]

As in Britain, the impact of stretch-outs has been devastating. The air force estimated, for example, that stretching out the F-15 for just three years in the 1970s cost $2 billion. That money could have bought eighty-three additional airplanes but had to be devoted to overhead instead. Similarly, stretching out procurement of the army's

Patriot air-defense system in the 1980s added $1 billion to the U.S. bill—an amount that could have purchased 1,760 more missiles.[19]

Structural disarmament imposes both economic and military costs. Beyond the reduction in force structure, as Britain learned, readiness is also diminished. So, too, is combat sustainability, as constantly rising procurement costs soak up more and more of the limited resources devoted to defense.

Structural disarmament poses the dual dangers of exacerbating the shortcomings NATO already confronts vis-à-vis the Warsaw Pact and undermining other efforts the alliance might make to bolster its conventional-defense capabilities. No one country can solve NATO's structural-disarmament dilemma. It is a coalition requirement demanding a coalition solution. What NATO might do to rise to this challenge is the subject of a later chapter.

9 U.S. Global Perspectives

A central theme running throughout this book is that the cockpit for World War III is in Europe. But it is more than possible that the next major political crisis or global conflict could be triggered by events outside the NATO area, particularly if destabilizing trends in the Middle East, Latin America, or other Third World areas continue. At a minimum, World War III could begin as an out-of-area conflict that escalates to a direct superpower confrontation. It could occur in the Middle East just as easily as in Europe, and then spill over into the Atlantic theater. By the same token, the Soviets could use NATO conventional-defense vulnerability in the 1990s to constrain U.S. action in a Third World crisis. This is a new emerging danger that has escaped our planners.

The United States is a superpower with global interests and responsibilities, facing global challenges. Among those challenges is its competition with the Soviet Union, which extends beyond Europe—where it is so starkly manifested in military terms—to Asia, Africa, and Latin America. The challenge for the United States stems in large part from problems indigenous to those regions where poverty, overpopulation, corruption, and a host of other ills create conditions of instability. What is destabilizing are unconventional threats within what Halford Mackinder called the "rimlands," which can erode the edges of the Western alliance.[1]

Will the need to focus on the Pacific, where there are new opportunities, or on Latin America, where there are new dangers, force the United States to falter in its commitment to Europe? Will the military threat in Europe come to be seen as less palpable and secondary to threats elsewhere? The daunting task for America is to establish the *right* balance in our policies and priorities toward all these areas: a strategic prize in Europe, a powerfully dynamic Pacific, a volatile Third World. The job is also to see if there are any ingredients of the NATO story that could be applied globally.

Asia and the Pacific

In January 1950, Secretary of State Dean Acheson gave a speech that, in effect, drew a defense perimeter in the Far East that included Japan but not South Korea. Over a year earlier, the Joint Chiefs of Staff had even directed the withdrawal of U.S. forces from the Korean Peninsula.

Knowing they had military superiority over the South, the North Koreans thought they had been given a green light from Washington. With the encouragement of the Soviet Union and China, they attacked. A dumbstruck Harry Truman, busily helping to organize the defense of Europe, suddenly became fearful of the political signal that the lack of U.S. response in Korea would send to those who had designs elsewhere. Truman thought back to times when acts of aggression by the strong against the weak had gone unchecked. He remembered the Japanese in Manchuria and the failure of America to respond, and the resulting Japanese expansion southward. If the U.S. did not respond, Truman believed, the Soviets might well think they also had a green light to move on Western Europe. Out of concern for the future of Europe as well as Asia, he ordered U.S. forces to respond to the North Korean invasion. The Korean crisis was seen as convincing proof of the global interrelationship between deterrence and defense. Whatever P'yŏngyang's belief, they miscalculated, and their misperception brought on war. Unlike the wars in Europe, however, the Korean conflict remained a limited one. There was neither an expansion of the conflict (although Chiang Kai-shek wanted to unleash his armies) nor the use of nuclear weapons.

Although the war in Vietnam was also limited in this sense, that conflict was different altogether, reflecting the general nature of postwar conflicts around the globe. Unlike Korea, the Vietnam conflict did not begin with a dramatic attack by conventional military forces. It started as a war of subversion in the south, based on guerrilla tactics and Maoist theories of unconventional warfare. Not until the 1972 Easter offensive did the war assume a truly conventional character. For the United States, it was a war of gradualism and attrition, the way of Grant rather than Lee, but unlike Grant's war, it ended in defeat and disillusionment.

When South Vietnam collapsed, so did the sense of American invincibility in battle. Doubts were raised about whether we could ever fight effectively in unconventional conflicts. What also collapsed was the idea that the containment doctrine, which had worked so well in responding to the threat in Europe, was applicable to other areas, especially the Pacific.

The biggest problem facing the United States in the Pacific community is the lack of a cohesive framework within which all parties can come to grips with the spectrum of political, economic, and security problems. The Southeast Asia Treaty Organization (SEATO)—the loose counterpart to NATO created to implement containment in Asia—fell apart in the 1970s, another casualty of the Vietnam War. The multilateral security organization of Australia, New Zealand, and the United States (ANZUS) has all but disintegrated in recent years in the face of New Zealand Prime Minister Robert Lange's disassociation from any U.S. policies of nuclear deterrence. There is only one organization in the U.S. government that has enough cohesion to glue together some semblance of a coherent U.S. policy: the United States Pacific Command.

In February 1988, I met with Admiral Ronald Hays, commander in chief, Pacific Command (CINCPAC). From his headquarters' bay window, high on the Aiea Heights overlooking all of Honolulu, I could see a half-dozen warships lying at anchor in Pearl Harbor, ships of the largest U.S. naval force, the Pacific Fleet. Off to the left, several huge military transports lumbered off the runway of Hickam Air Force Base. Adjacent to the runway sat two modern F-15 Eagle jet fighters of the Hawaii National Guard, the only air-defense resource assigned to protect the Hawaiian Islands. I also noted Blackhawk helicopters flying low over the water. They had taken off from Wheeler Field and flown down the same pass Japanese Zero fighters took to bomb the fleet in 1941. These Blackhawks were from the army's Western Command, 25th Infantry Division.

Dominating the office of the commander-in-chief was a huge map of the Pacific. With his command ranging from the Arctic to the Antarctic, from the West Coast of the U.S. to the eastern shore of Africa, this American four-star admiral is the one common link that nations of the Pacific Basin have with the United States.[2]

CINCPAC does not have the burdens or the advantages of a NATO-style multilateral coalition. There is no Pacific Council that corresponds to the North Atlantic Council, no Defense Planning Committee or integrated military structure. Hence, Admiral Hays is not a Supreme Allied Commander Pacific, only Commander in Chief of U.S. Forces. Consequently, U.S. policy in the Pacific is carried out in a distinctly bilateral, one-on-one fashion. CINCPAC's mission is similar to NATO's: to deter the Soviet threat; preserve the peace; and provide security for the U.S., its allies, and other friendly nations within the command's boundaries. Over lunch, Admiral Hays was firm in asserting what a NATO commander certainly cannot say: that he has conventional superiority over the Soviet Union in his theater.

The Pacific Command has set a course to raise the visibility of its mission by reminding Washingtonians and Atlanticists that the world's fastest-growing economies are in the Pacific. U.S. trade with Pacific nations exceeds that with Europe; seven of the world's ten largest banks are in the Pacific; over 60 percent of the world's population lives in the Pacific Command's area of responsibility; and seven of the world's ten largest armed forces are in the Pacific area—over twelve million men and women under arms.[3]

But what is our conceptual framework for promoting security in this vast region? To the extent that we have such a framework at all, it is what might be called the residue of the Nixon Doctrine, which came in the wake of Vietnam failures. The Nixon Doctrine was enunciated by the president in Guam in 1969, when he stated that America's priority is to help nations defend themselves. This was different from the iron-tight containment strategy of the 1950s and very different from the thrust of John Kennedy's inaugural speech about our determination to defend freedom everywhere in the world.[4]

Nixon articulated three key points in that news conference in Guam. First, the United States would not commit ground forces in huge numbers, as we did in Vietnam, in defense of countries with whom we do not have a bilateral defense treaty. Second, the United States would strive to assist nations in the Pacific region to develop internal stability through economic development and internal defense forces, and by membership in an economic coalition to help expand trade throughout the region. Third, the United States would maintain a conventional and nuclear umbrella over the Asian countries and defend them from Soviet aggression. And all this would be done without the benefit of a multilateral coalition.

Ironically, there is a more stable balance in Asia today than in the wake of Nixon's articulation of his doctrine and the turbulent 1970s, when the United States began its withdrawal from Vietnam. At the same time, the treaty organizations have suffered marked deterioration. Conflicts arising in the Pacific are most often local and bilateral, unlike the NATO area, in which the focus is on major East-West blocs. The same description applies to the Asian subcontinent, where India and Pakistan, and India and China, continue to confront each other.

In contrast to the Atlantic region, where threat perceptions may sometimes differ only in terms of degree, in the Pacific, threat perceptions vary widely. Some countries, like Japan and China, have a well-developed fear of Soviet aggression. The South Koreans worry mostly about the huge North Korean threat within miles of their borders. Taiwan is concerned about an invasion by mainland Chinese forces, while Vietnam perceives China as its primary foe. The Philippine government has serious internal problems with a Communist-dominated insurgency. To the south, Australia and Papua New Guinea view Indonesia as a potential threat to their stability and sovereignty. Malaysia and Thailand see the Soviet-backed Vietnamese as their primary threat. Bangladesh—supplied, trained, and supported by China—fears the power of India. Sri Lanka, reeling from the Tamil insurgency, is also wary of Indian domination. And the list goes on.

At present, there is no common threat to evoke a security coalition in the Pacific and Indian oceans. Nor is there a broader multilateral framework that encompasses these disparate elements. Consider the extraordinary diversity of some of the land washed by the Indian Ocean beyond Africa's eastern coast: Mauritius, with a pro-Western orientation; Madagascar, still within the area of the Pacific Command, inclined toward the left but coming around to a more neutral approach; the Seychelles, an island paradise suffering from an overly regulated economy and an overload of Soviet advisers; Sri Lanka, torn by a vicious ethnic war with heavy Indian involvement; India, looming large in southern Asia, beset with internal problems. Although India's considerable military capability is largely focused against the People's Republic of China and Pakistan, it is increasingly able to project force into the Indian Ocean. India has just recently acquired a Soviet attack submarine.

In the Pacific, the contrasts are just as striking. Australia, a solid ANZUS partner with very capable forces, provides great help to the United States in maintaining our Indian Ocean presence and providing leadership in the South Pacific. However, New Zealand, like an ostrich with its head in the sand, seeks to escape the requirements of its security interests. Tremendous damage has been done by its efforts to lead an antinuclear movement in the Pacific region.

The Pacific contains the world's most populous country, the People's Republic of China, with a billion-plus people; and one of the smallest, Tuvalu, near Samoa in the South Pacific, with a mere ten square miles of land and 8,000 inhabitants. The list continues: Oceana, newly independent but fragile, whose security interests focus on economic and internal problems; Brunei, oil-rich, friendly, with limited military capability, yet whose ruler has a broader regional security outlook; Singapore, a success story, pro-Western and very active in regional security; Malaysia, beset with racial problems, yet managing economic growth and with a pro-Western military; Indonesia, a wavering economy with primarily internal security threats; Thailand, our frontline ally in need of military assistance; Cambodia, occupied by Vietnam since 1979; and Vietnam itself, aggressive and dependent on the Soviets.

What does all this variety mean for the Pacific? The more than thirty-four countries and twenty-three island-states make the relationships involved and strategic planning extremely difficult. It complicates trade agreements and virtually precludes a multilateral approach to security. Thus we are forced to proceed with a slew of bilateral relationships without any unifying framework. It is, therefore, essential to establish some clear priorities among these relationships.

The first priority must be Japan, the second largest economic power in the world. It has pledged under its U.S.-inspired constitution not to enter into any arrangements for collective security. Its bilateral treaty with the United States commits the United States to Japan's defense but not the reverse. Therefore, if the Soviets were to attack in Europe but not in the Pacific, and specifically not against

Japan, the United States could not launch counterattacks from Japan. Similarly, if the Soviets attacked elsewhere in the Pacific, the Japanese would have no treaty obligation to permit Americans to use their bases there. The importance of Japan and U.S.-Japanese relations are discussed later, but understanding this unequal treaty relationship is important to any strategic analysis of the Pacific.

America's second Pacific priority must be Korea. Although the Republic of Korea has a mature military capability, it still looks to the United States and the Second Infantry Division to balance and round out its military forces (629,000 on active duty and reserves of almost 5 million).[5] South Korea also depends on U.S. tactical air fighter squadrons, naval presence, and logistical support to blunt attacking North Korean forces. Fortunately, the South Koreans have developed a logical framework for their force buildup with the United States, which requires few U.S. ground forces to be deployed to the peninsula in the event of invasion. Instead of moving large numbers of troop, cargo sorties would be used to deliver ammunition and critical resupply parts to South Korean forces. As in Europe, U.S. deterrent strategy toward North Korea following the Korean War relied on the possible first use of nuclear weapons. Today, however, the south could no doubt be defended by conventional forces alone.

The South Koreans realize, as we do, that the Korean Peninsula is the most dangerous area of the Pacific in certain ways and is becoming more so. Today the North Koreans are forward deployed: they have tunneled up to, and perhaps under, allied lines, reducing the warning time of an attack to twelve hours or less. The North Koreans are deeply jealous of the tremendous prosperity of the South. Kim Il-Sung, the leader of North Korea, has pursued a bankrupt political strategy in this most totalitarian of all Communist countries, elevating his son Kim Chong-Il as the heir apparent to the premiership. This is causing ripples throughout North Korea and in other Communist countries. Economically, North Korea is in desperate straits and this has led to the final element of North Korea's bankruptcy: the military. Without fuel, tanks and armored vehicles are not exercising, aircraft are not flying valuable combat practice sorties, and naval ships are not patrolling. The most ruthlessly trained, hard-as-nails military establishment in the world (with a force of 838,000 on active duty and reserves of perhaps 5 million)[6] is losing its razor-sharp edge. Although it is difficult to imagine a second Korean conflict being more than a limited war, with forward deployment, no warning time, and potential instability in the North, Korea remains an area with great potential for a conflict involving Americans.

The third Pacific priority for the United States must be the Philippines. Although it has historically close ties to the United States, the strategically located Philippines remains involved in the affairs of the group of nations not formally aligned with either Washington or Moscow. Nevertheless, the Philippines hosts two critical U.S. bases—a naval base at Subic Bay and Clark Air Field near Manila. These bases have served as forward outposts for the projection of military power in the Pacific for decades. Clark Air Field hosts almost 10,000 U.S. personnel as well as two fighter squadrons with almost fifty combat aircraft and a tactical airlift wing of sixteen C-130 transports. Subic Bay is one of the key ports used by the seventy ships of the U.S. Seventh Fleet in the western Pacific. The loss of these facilities would be catastrophic not only for the United States but for countries in the region whose security continues to depend on the U.S. presence. In the event that access to these bases is denied, in the present economic climate it is questionable that Congress would appropriate the several billion dollars needed to replicate their capabilities elsewhere.[7]

Many Filipinos, however, do not perceive a Soviet threat to their country. The major security problem for them is the ongoing conflict with Communist guerrillas. Under these circumstances, Filipinos do not always see the value of the U.S. presence, and critics contend that the bases only serve to further U.S. "imperialist" interests.

The Philippines have gone through something of a political miracle in the transition from Marcos to Aquino. I visited Corazon Aquino in June of 1987 and was impressed not only with her but with the great potential of the Philippines—political, economic, and social. Yet these islands, vital to America's regional interests, still face a $26 billion foreign debt and 35,000 insurgents.[8] At the 1988 CSIS Williamsburg Conference, Amos Jordan put forth the idea of creating a consortium of Asian nations to financially support the Philippines. While acting to solve the economic problems of the Philippines, these Asian countries could also emphasize the importance of the U.S. bases to overall Asian security. Clearly, resolving the multiple problems of the Philippines, particularly its economic difficulties, must be a priority not only for Washington but for all free nations in the Pacific. As my friend from West Point, General Ramos, pointed out to me, defeating the ongoing insurgency will depend critically on the success of Filipino efforts toward economic and social reform. Military initiatives alone will not suffice.

   With more imagination than his predecessors, a shrewd Gorbachev launched a new Soviet Pacific policy in his July 1986 Vladivostok speech, which pointed to a reassertion of Soviet interests and power in the Pacific. The speech portrayed the Soviets as a misunderstood power seeking to play a leadership role aimed at a more open and peaceful Pacific area.[9]

   Gorbachev uses the diversity of the Pacific to his advantage. He has a strong working relationship with both North Korea and Vietnam. In May 1985, the Soviets began to supply advanced fighter aircraft to the North Koreans in return for overflight rights and naval anchorages. Moscow gives Vietnam economic assistance in return for military facilities. The Kremlin hopes to broaden its ties with South Korea, achieve inroads into the South Pacific, and consolidate its ties with India. Gorbachev has also moved to improve relations with the People's Republic of China. He has succesfully pressured Vietnam to begin troop withdrawals from Cambodia, withdrawn Soviet troops from Mongolia, and made major concessions on the demarcation along the Sino-Soviet border.[10]

   Militarily, the Soviets have engaged in a considerable buildup in their Far East forces in the last ten years. The Soviet Pacific Fleet is now their largest, with well over three hundred combatants including their Kirov class nuclear-powered, guided missile cruiser. There are over 120 submarines, including the very quiet Akula-class. The Soviet Far East Air Forces include 2,000 combat aircraft—about one-third of their total air power. There have been modernization efforts to upgrade the long-range strike aircraft, with the addition of Bear and Backfire bombers.[11] Since 1986 alone, the Soviet army in the Far East region has increased in size from fifty-three to fifty-seven divisions and its tanks, artillery, and helicopters have been upgraded and modernized.[12]

   The Soviet naval base at Cam Rahn Bay, built by the United States during the Vietnam era, with its superb facilities and secure "lease" rights, continues to be expanded. With the completion of a 4 million gallon fuel-storage facility and another pier, the Soviets have the capability of supporting a strike combat force of ships, submarines, reconnaissance aircraft, and fighters. It also gives them their only warm-water port in the Pacific and their largest facility outside the Soviet Union. The vulnerable Malacca, Sunda, and Lombok straits linking the Indian Ocean and the South China Sea are all within easy striking distance, and through them pass oil tankers to and from the Persian Gulf.

The Soviet reach now extends to the South Pacific, where it has signed a fishing treaty with tiny Kiribati, enabling trawlers to gather useful intelligence on the geography of the area as well as eavesdrop electronically on the U.S. missile test range at Kwajalein Island.

The fulcrum of Soviet Pacific strategy centers on the ports of Vladivostok, base for about 30 percent of the Soviet surface navy, and Petropavlovsk on the Kamchatka Peninsula, the home of Soviet Pacific submarines. The forces at Vladivostok, however, face serious bottle-necks in exiting the Sea of Japan, where there are only three possible routes: La Perouse (Soya) Strait between Sakhalin and Hokkaido, Tsugaru Strait between Hokkaido and Honshu, and Tsushima Strait between Kyushu and Korea. The problem facing the Soviet navy was demonstrated as early as 1905, when the entire Russian fleet was destroyed or captured in the Tsushima Strait during the Russo-Japanese War.

The Persian Gulf

Throughout this book I emphasize the need for a strategic approach and recognize the relationship between economics and security. Nowhere is the confluence of the economic and military elements of security more dramatically illustrated than in the Persian Gulf and the Middle East.

A critical element in maintaining economic security is the protection of energy lifelines, from the Persian Gulf and around the Cape of Good Hope, as well as those vital straits in the Pacific. The Philippines receives 65 percent of its oil from the Gulf, Japan 57 percent, Korea 50 percent, and Europe on average 21 percent. Despite the growing role of overland pipelines for the transport of oil, between 450 and 500 ships and tankers pass through the Strait of Hormuz in a single month.[13]

Although the United States receives only about 15 percent of its oil from the Persian Gulf,[14] the prosperity and safety of our friends and allies requires that we give the Persian Gulf–Indian Ocean region a high priority. There are two basic liabilities, however. Unlike the situation in the Pacific, if the United States projects power at such a distance, it puts itself in a position of conventional inferiority vis-à-vis the Soviets. Second, at least until 1987, the allies had not contributed anything significant to our efforts on their behalf. It should be recalled that until the Labour government in London pulled British forces out of the area "East of Suez," Britain had for a century kept stability in the region. This was a part of the grand containment strategy of the 1950s—a division of labor giving the British responsibility for that area.

Today the United States projects power to the Persian Gulf from both Europe and the Pacific, a formidable task in either case. To sail from the West Coast of the United States to the Persian Gulf takes twenty-five days. It takes thirty hours to fly in a C-141 cargo plane to Diego Garcia, a small British-owned atoll in the Indian Ocean where we have facilities to support our naval forces in the area. Yet Diego Garcia is still 2,500 miles from the Strait of Hormuz. From the Mediterranean it takes about five days to move a carrier through the Suez Canal, obviously a vulnerable target in wartime.[15] Plainly, U.S. forces in the Middle East and Persian Gulf have thin lines of communication.

Meanwhile, the Soviets have access to a variety of facilities on the rim of the Indian Ocean—at Ethiopia's Dhalak Island, Aden and Socotra, as well as in the Seychelles, Mozambique, and Madagascar. They also hold what is called in strategic parlance "internal lines" from Siberia to European Russia.

While the United States has traditionally kept only four ships actively based within the Persian Gulf at Bahrain, at the height of the 1987–88 operation to escort the eleven reflagged Kuwaiti tankers, it deployed forty-eight ships, manned and supported by 25,000 U.S. Navy, Army, and Marine personnel.[16] Although the specific task of escorting tankers might not have been predicted, the general requirement for U.S. forces to deploy in or near the Persian Gulf was anticipated. The navy has consistently argued that the global commitments of the United States—including requirements in the Persian Gulf— demand the strategic mobility and flexibility inherent in naval forces. One of the rationales for the recommissioning of our battleships, at an estimated cost of $470 million,[17] was their possible utility in the region. The U.S. Central Command (CENTCOM), which evolved from the original Rapid Deployment Force of the Carter administration, is the U.S. military instrument in the area and guarantees Western access to the Arabian Peninsula and its vital oil reserves. Overall, CENTCOM's area of responsibility embraces nineteen countries in Southwest Asia, the Middle East, and East Africa. A program for prepositioning U.S. supplies with increased sea and airlift, also begun during the Carter administration, is underway. Yet we have insufficient air and sea transport capabilities to provide adequate strategic mobility.

Ever since the British withdrawal, we have shouldered the burden in the Persian Gulf, even though the United States is less dependent on oil from this region than any of our allies. Inevitably, such a situation raises questions about allied burdensharing. In the wake of the Iraqi attack on the USS *Stark* in May 1987, Secretary Weinberger brought up the issue of help for the Persian Gulf at the spring meeting of NATO defense ministers. He was met with deafening silence.

Over the summer of 1987, however, quiet pressure from the United States and a deterioration of the situation in the Persian Gulf—especially the Iranian-sparked riots in Mecca—prompted the allies to act. By the end of the year, largely under the auspices of the Western European Union rather than NATO, allied naval forces from Britain, France, Italy, Belgium, and the Netherlands contributed thirty-four combat ships, minesweepers, and support vessels.[18] The West German government, citing constitutional limitations on the use of its military, contributed naval forces to the Mediterranean to demonstrate political solidarity with its allies and compensate for the redeployment of other allied forces to the gulf.

Historically, U.S. policy in Southwest Asia has been driven in large part by concerns over the Soviet Union. The Reagan administration assumed the role of reflagging the Kuwaiti ships simply because it knew the Soviets would do it otherwise. Since the days of Catherine the Great, Russia has had a declared interest in the Persian Gulf and its warm-water ports. During the Hitler-Molotov conversations of 1940, there was a famous statement of Soviet ambitions to that effect. President Truman's first confrontation with his erstwhile Soviet ally was sparked by demands that Moscow honor its commitment to remove its forces from northern Iran. President Reagan's mistimed and ill-considered arms-for-hostages initiative with Iran was also motivated in part by concerns over Soviet policy in the area.

Although the experience of the Soviets in Afghanistan is likely to discourage further adventurism in the region, they have developed a military capability that could be used to move south into Iran. U.S. contingency planning should not ignore this capability and should be prepared for any additional escalation of hostilities in the region that might enhance the likelihood of Soviet action. For a move against Iran, Moscow has two options: a buildup north of the border followed by a drive deep into the country; or a move into northern Iran, consolidation of the position, and then a push farther south, perhaps to capture Iran's oilfields. Led from the Southern Military District and drawing from the Turkestan, North Caucasus, and Trans-Caucasus Military Districts, the Soviet Union could marshal some thirty-two divisions and almost 1,000 aircraft. These forces vary, however, in their readiness level. Two or three motorized rifle divisions are said to be fully ready, but several weeks would probably be needed to make all of the region's forces fully prepared for combat.[19] Their past material shortages have largely been resolved, and modern arms—such as the BMP armored vehicles, advanced air-defense systems, and extended-range self-propelled artillery—continue to replace outmoded equipment. The Soviet mix of aircraft favors ground attack missions rather than air defenses, and the introduction of almost four hundred combat helicopters bolsters an air fleet that has been markedly improved since 1979 with the addition of MiG 29s and SU-24s.[20] Whatever form an attack takes, the Soviets would encounter severe operational difficulties in any move into Iran, such as the rudimentary road and rail networks, adverse weather conditions, and mountainous terrain. Despite these obstacles, the U.S. military views Soviet forces as clearly more than adequate to defeat soundly any combination of regional forces.[21] This is one reason why it is likely that sooner or later there will be a restoration of U.S.-Iranian cooperation.

Latin America

The Persian Gulf, the Pacific, and Europe are the three theaters that have witnessed Soviet-U.S. superpower rivalry since the end of World War II. Another is emerging, one that is much closer to the United States but about which many U.S. citizens remain largely unaware: Latin America. Many of the challenges to the United States in the region are nontraditional security problems: drug trafficking, illegal immigration, uncontrolled refugee flows, corruption, and enormous debts. In the face of these challenges, the competition with the Soviet Union is not likely to take a direct form. Rather, the task of the United States is not to allow itself to be so distracted by these difficulties that it undermines its ability to deal with commitments elsewhere in the world where it confronts the Soviet Union directly.

As in the Persian Gulf and the Pacific, there are a number of conflict scenarios in Latin America that have global ramifications. These could involve Nicaragua and Cuba, Mexican instability, and attacks against regional energy production facilities or key transit points such as the Panama Canal. In all of these scenarios, the United States is forced to redirect political attention, and perhaps military resources, away from areas and problems of direct concern to the Kremlin. This area, however, is clearly important strategically to the United States.

For example, the economic importance of this region should not be underestimated. More than 8 percent of U.S. investments worldwide and about 32 percent of U.S. investments in developing countries are located in the countries of the Caribbean Basin. The Caribbean countries are dependent on the United States not only for capital but for a considerable amount of their trade. The Caribbean imports 41 percent of its goods from the United States and exports about 60 percent there. The economic future of Mexico, which is our third largest trading partner, will have a major impact on the American economy. Let us not forget that in terms of energy Mexico has claimed petroleum reserves of 72 billion barrels, probable reserves of about 250 billion barrels, and production in the range of 3.5 million barrels per day.

The security implications of instability in Mexico and the Caribbean region are considerable. In time of war, major reinforcements, about half of NATO's supplies and most of its petroleum, oil and lubricants would be shipped from U.S. ports in the Gulf of Mexico. The security ramifications of the loss of the Panama Canal would be global.[22]

Despite these realities, and the active role of the U.S. Southern Command (SOUTHCOM) in regional security planning and assistance in South and Central America, the U.S. is not used to thinking about the problems to our south in security terms. Mexican instability would, in one fell swoop, present the United States with a border security, domestic law enforcement, and humanitarian problem, and therefore an entirely new type of strategic challenge. As for alliances, the regional structure that does exist—the Organization of American States (OAS)—predates NATO, yet ironically has achieved little of its potential.

The situation is somewhat different in Central America, where Soviet-backed involvement is a key factor. Nicaragua is a dramatic case in point. Farther south, in Panama, U.S. strategic interests in the canal overlap with a brewing domestic crisis and the very real issue of who will control the canal after 1990. Over the longer term, the United States cannot afford to overlook the impact of the Latin American narcotics trade, a nontraditional but very real threat to the fabric and security of the Western nations.

Canada

As a consequence of a long history of fundamentally sound relations, the United States often takes Canada for granted, economically and strategically. Few people are aware of the important, recent agreements between the United States and its northern ally. Fewer still have noticed the clouds on the horizon that may threaten this relationship.

On March 18, 1985, the United States and Canada signed an important Memorandum of Understanding, the key feature of which spelled out a program to upgrade the outdated Distant Early Warning (DEW) radar system as part of a broader effort to modernize North America's air defenses. The new system consists of a chain of fifty-two ground radar stations across the northern Atlantic, the Canadian Arctic, and the Labrador coast.[23] The reaffirmation of the U.S.-Canadian Defense Production and Development Sharing Agreements, envisioning an overall balance in defense and trade as well as strengthened defense-industrial capabilities in both countries, was another important step taken by the Mulroney government. A third was the renewal of the North American Air Defense Command (NORAD). In the nondefense area, the recent U.S.-Canadian Free Trade Agreement has many implications, not just for U.S.-Canadian relations but for U.S. economic relations with other allies as well.

The current mood in Canada, which cuts across the political spectrum, suggests that the defense of North America should be given priority over other NATO obligations. Despite the long-standing calls by the New Democratic party for Canadian withdrawal from NATO and NORAD, the majority of Canadians do not want to abandon the alliance or bilateral defense efforts. A healthy 81 percent of the people recently polled by the *Toronto Star* supported continued membership.[24] Yet there are a number of disturbing trends that suggest Canada's role in the alliance may be changing. Canadians are increasingly worried about the threat to their homeland from Soviet naval activities and from new technologies such as cruise missiles, which have opened the Arctic in particular as a new zone of potential military operations. This is particularly troubling at a time when the alliance is striving to bolster its conventional-defense capability in Europe.

Throughout the Trudeau years, from 1968 through 1984, the focus of the government was on cutting military spending, supporting peacekeeping and civil operations, and maintaining a low profile on the European front. Brian Mulroney's Progressive Conservative party came to power committed to a strong political and financial commitment to restore Canada's military capability. It conducted the first major review of Canadian defense policy since 1971, the conclusions of which were published as a White Paper on Defense in June 1987. The paper outlined the government's decision to consolidate Canadian forces committed to Europe by relinquishing the commitment of Canada's Air Sea Transportable (CAST) brigade and two fighter squadrons to reinforce Norway and permanently attaching them to the country's brigade now in Germany. More important, the paper gave great weight to homeland and home-seas defense. This was particularly evident in the decision to purchase up to twelve nuclear-powered attack submarines at a cost of about $400 million each. Overall, the government proposed to increase Canada's defense spending by 2 percent each year in real terms for the next fifteen years.[25]

Canada's mainstream opposition Liberal party criticized the government's decision because of the expense of the program, the questionable rationale for the nuclear submarines, and the political implications for Canada as a nonnuclear country. On the other hand, it argued with the government on the need to bolster local defense while maintaining ties with NATO.

The Mulroney government's policies on defense have also generated expressions of concern from NATO allies. Some critics note the relative modesty of the overall effort, pointing out that the proposed

2 percent increase falls short of the 3 percent goal to which NATO governments have long been committed. Others express concern that the government will not be able to sustain even the proposed level of spending at the expense of domestic needs. Still others have worried that if the Mulroney government were to lose the next election and its successors were to cancel the proposed program, NATO would lose both reinforcements for Norway and the planned defense program. The most serious concern, however, arises from Canada's new defense priorities, in particular the expensive submarine program. More pressing needs are seen to exist in the areas of equipment modernization, joint U.S.-Canadian upgrading of the NORAD system, and the purchase of additional ships for transatlantic convoy duties.

Although Canada's NATO commitment is strong, the New Democratic party could change this. It could draw attention to the commitment, highlighting its inconsistencies with the general thrust of national policy. Under such circumstances, it is unclear whether popular support for Canadian membership in NATO could be sustained. Even if a majority of Canadians continue to support membership, what would the relationship between Canada and the other NATO allies be if Canada seems intent on retrenching and unwilling to bear the burdens and risks of alliance membership? Any future Canadian government will surely find management of its relationship with its allies an ongoing challenge.

In sum, the global burdens facing the United States are staggering, with the result that we have a gap between our capabilities and our commitments, especially in the Indian Ocean–Persian Gulf region. Furthermore, our principal allies in Europe live in one strategic world, those in Asia in another, while the United States, with its global responsibilities, is forced to live in a third. The NATO alliance clearly plays a crucial role in preventing World War III, but deterrence must be global as well as regional. What is needed is a long-range conceptual framework that reconciles our global challenges and balances competing interests and responsibilities. But, in a period of severe prospective budget cuts, such a framework is nowhere to be seen.

10 The Power Balancers: Japan and China

IF the unity of Europe is critical to a successful grand strategy to prevent World War III, the roles of Japan and China are equally crucial. Each now carries weight in the global power balance, and their geopolitical potential is staggering. Think of what it would mean to U.S. grand strategy if Japan moved to neutrality or gave her technology freely to the Soviet Union, or if China again tilted toward the Soviet Union. Neither seems possible now, but the starkness of such thoughts is sobering. Any analysis of the elements of a strategy to prevent World War III would be incomplete without consideration of these two Asian powers.

Japan: Economic Superpower

Today, Japan is *the* other economic superpower. Some, like Professor Ezra Vogel of Harvard University, have even referred to Japan as number one.[1] Critics have responded by citing the fragility of Japan's export-driven economy and the vulnerability inherent in Japan's overdependence on energy imports and related sea lines of communication. Yet Japan withstood both the oil and currency shocks of recent years. When the U.S. stock market collapsed in October 1987—with repercussions in all other markets—the Japanese stock market was the most resilient. Japan has become the world's largest creditor nation. In the list of the world's largest financial institutions—insurance companies, banks, and brokerage houses—Japanese firms have replaced U.S. ones. Japan has a better-educated population—with a 99 percent level of literacy—and has more engineers than the United States. It has the highest level of savings—four times that of the United States and twice that of Europe. Its economy roughly equals the combined economies of the largest three European NATO countries—West Germany, France, and Britain—and exceeds that of the Soviet Union.

During my June 1987 trip to Japan, I encountered acute concern and much debate about where Japan stood and where it was going. It was a time of uneasiness. In the United States, the trade bill loomed on the horizon and negative reaction to the Toshiba technology sale to the Soviet Union was at a peak. Aside from pressure from the United States, the Japanese had problems of their own. The rise in the yen was having a tremendous impact on corporate profits, yet it was not helping to reduce the U.S. trade deficit.

In our meeting, Prime Minister Yasuhiro Nakasone was as impressive as ever; the outward symbol of a new world role for Japan. He expressed great concern that the "zero option" for intermediate-range missiles was being applied only to Europe. It was a great achievement that a month later a global agreement was reached. It showed us as much about the political adroitness of Gorbachev to reduce the threat perception in Japan as it did about the skill of our negotiators.

I knew this would be my last meeting with Nakasone as prime minister. Of the three leaders who were in position to succeed him in office, I had met the open, affable Foreign Minister Shintaro Abe—most like Nakasone in demeanor—and the wise and skillful Finance Minister Kiichi Miyazawa numerous times before. This was my first time, however, with Noboru Takeshita, so very different in appearance and leadership style from that of Nakasone. He is a traditional Japanese leader, moving only from strong consensus, careful to maintain harmony at all times.

I had a constant theme in all four meetings: how could our democracies think in the long term and comprehensively? We were threatened by our compartmentalization and shortsightedness in the United States, our protectionism. I pointed out how in the last four years we had been able to get NATO to think long range. How could we do this in the relationship between the two economic superpowers? Takeshita became electrified over this discussion of long-range analysis, strategic comprehensive approaches, and contingency planning. While he had been chief cabinet secretary—a position not un-like our chief of staff—he had tried to encourage long-range thinking but said it was not sustained. He has another chance now as prime minister.

By all odds, Japan more than any other modern nation has been able to develop and pursue a grand strategy. Made up of small islands lacking most basic resources, Japan has had to develop ways to do more with less—to think smarter rather than richer. Japan has em-barked on a comprehensive strategy a number of times during its history. The first such strategic reassessment and initiative, following over two hundred years of isolation, came in 1868. With a determi-nation to modernize Japan, the Meiji leaders set about constructing a strong educational system, building business and large corporate structures, improving military and maritime science, and developing a bureaucracy for the central government. They sent groups abroad to learn and master the different Western systems. The best systems were then selected and adjusted for the Japanese culture before being introduced into the society.

Regrettably, an emerging sense of international military compe-tition led to a system that gave priority to military power. The first target was China. The war over control of Korea marked the beginning of the meteoric geopolitical rise of Japan and the confused geopolitical decline of China. Japan brought itself into the modern world by defeating a demoralized China, then little more than a "paper dragon." China recognized Korea's independence—which meant Japanese control—and ceded Formosa to Japan. When the island-empire Britain aban-doned "splendid isolation," it was to conclude an alliance in 1902 with this new rising island-power that was aimed very much at Russia. In 1904, this small but vibrant and newly industrialized nation made a lightning attack on Russia. A great Western power had been defeated by an Asian power, and Japan was now on the road to empire.

By 1930, an aggressive military faction was determined to con-quer Manchuria. Japanese grand strategy firmed up, Manchuria was turned into an industrial empire and North China increasingly came under Japanese control. In 1937, when full war with China came, Japan moved south. The statesmen who had produced the great Meiji Restoration had passed on, and such aggressive groups as the Control Faction bent on militant expansion were on the rise and were influ-enced by European fascism.

In response to Japanese aggression in China, the United States gradually introduced sanctions. In 1940, the sale to Japan of scrap metals and high-octane gasoline was prohibited. In 1941, when Japanese troops pushed into southern Indochina, President Roosevelt froze all Japanese assets in the United States. Britain and the Netherlands followed suit. The United States sanctions soon began to take a toll on Japan, standing in the way of Japan's strategy for securing the natural resources that it had always lacked.[2]

Soon after Prince Konoye fell from power and was replaced by General Hideki Tojo, the military planned its attack on the United States, British, and Dutch possessions. Japan's militant leaders—like those of ancient Assyria and unlike those in Rome—devised a strategy that vastly overcommitted the country on the periphery and incited bitter resentment in conquered populations. In their war strategy, the Japanese relied heavily on Germany and the willingness of the gods to smile on a Japan that was bold and courageous. The genuine economic needs of the islands could have been met by investment, development, and trade by its Zaibatsu (huge family-run trusts), but Japan had suffered terribly from the Depression and felt extremely vulnerable to commercial sanctions. It wanted to have direct control over its resources and military potential. Self-sufficiency, not trade, was seen as the answer.

If pre-World War II Japan had gone to one extreme, its grand strategy of reconstruction after the devastating war took it in another direction altogether: toward trade and commerce. The Japanese held on to that aspect most intrinsic in their character: the will to adapt to changed circumstances and survive. Japan had for centuries been a hybrid culture, studying the work, ideas, and technology of foreigners and assimilating them into Japanese society. Japan again set out to borrow from and imitate others, often improving the final product or concept. The homogeneity of the people gave Japan the strength to reconstruct. The war had left a fear—and a willingness to sacrifice— that unified the Japanese. They were desperate for stability and they found it in collectivity, most often at work. The passion for social and economic security, combined with a perpetual unease about the future, created a tremendous work ethic. Enormous sacrifices were made for the education and the job that would mean security for life. The company put rice on the table and enabled the children to go to school. This security blanket produced a loyalty second to none. The result was a renewed unity of purpose essential to the formulation of a new grand strategy.[3]

Foreigners who perceived this cohesiveness began to refer to Japan as "Japan Inc." This term was often used to refer to the way in which the whole country became for a time like one company. Led by highly educated and extremely skilled bureaucrats, government and business worked together to promote common interests. The Ministry of International Trade and Industry (MITI) provided "administrative guidance" for this economic recovery of Japan, manipulating the market to promote economic growth. Exports were the miracle drug—the cure-all—upon which the strategy focused. MITI protected and subsidized those infant industries that were deemed necessary to Japan's survival.[4] Industrial development was facilitated by laws that were devised for that express purpose. Capital investment and R & D funding were coordinated by the economic agencies in a way unknown in the United States or Europe. Economic development was the priority and balanced social development, including concern for quality of life and the welfare of the consumer, fell by the wayside. Japan combined what was until the advent of the Third World's newly industrialized countries, or NICs, a unique combination of high labor productivity with low labor costs. The competition was felt in the United States, where our mature industries were being threatened by cheaper and often superior products.[5]

Although many aspects of Japanese culture contributed to the "Japanese miracle," high-caliber Japanese management and worker training, as well as a successful process of industrial automation, played a vital role in Japan's success. When I toured Toyota City with my wise old friend Dr. Eiji Toyoda, I was overwhelmed by the degree to which the plant had been automated, and I could sense the high morale among the workers. Clearly, Japan has moved from imitation to technological innovation. Indeed, one study concluded that Japan has outpaced America in this area.[6] Japanese innovation is to a large extent the result of intense competition and worker creativity. Another friend, Akio Morita, chairman of Sony, has repeatedly emphasized the importance of the quality of life within the corporation and the need to motivate workers into thinking creatively.[7]

The successful postwar industrialization has brought with it a number of challenges to Japan's future. With a current account surplus of close to $100 billion—3.7 percent of GNP—and long-term capital outflows of some $140 billion,[8] Japan has created tremendous friction in its trade relations. The thrift mentality—constantly saving for another rainy day rather than enjoying now the fruits of one's labor—results in economic imbalances and abnormally low consumption, which makes ameliorating these frictions ever more difficult.

The Japanese agricultural system also creates economic imbalances. My talented young assistant, Jay Collins, who took time from his studies at Waseda University to work on a rice farm, would never let me forget the impact the Japanese farmer has had on Japan's economy. The subsidization of Japanese agriculture takes a toll on the whole economy. Land prices have become so distorted that real estate in Tokyo often sells for several million dollars an acre, and Japan, in terms of property value, is now worth more than the United States. What is often characterized as an isolated agricultural problem directly affects housing, savings, disposable income, and consumption of consumer goods. While American consumers spend only 12 percent of their income on food, Japanese consumers spend 40 percent.[9] Rice-farming households make up only 12 percent of the population, yet the undue weight of the rural vote in the Japanese electoral system, its financial importance to the Liberal Democratic party, and the strength of the "rice caucus" firmly protect the farmers from change.[10]

Despite the rigidity of the agricultural system, Japan has changed markedly during the forty years of postwar recovery. Japan is facing a new era. The economic miracle of Japan's postwar economy and the essence of the society behind it are now being challenged. The often talked about "Japan Inc." is breaking up. Japan has achieved and far surpassed its postwar goals faster than anyone dreamed possible. Cultural cohesion in Japan is breaking down and the younger generation is searching for a different approach to problems. Power has grown more and more diffuse. In particular, bureaucratic power has been diminished and businesses have become more independent. Overall, the private sector is much less willing to follow blindly the government's lead in deciding Japan's future.

The uninformed observer may often see unity in the Japanese Diet. Yet this perceived unity is only a result of intense behind-the-scenes bargaining. Factional disputes are seldom made public but should not be underestimated. Nakasone had vision and a leadership quality that were distinctly Western. He moved forward and encouraged Japan to follow. With Prime Minister Takeshita at the helm, and his traditional Japanese ability to build consensus, Japan will have to decide what its next steps will be. The old goals and objectives that guided Japan so well for so long are now outdated. New long-range objectives must be devised.

One of the most difficult decisions confronting Japan in the 1990s will be the level of its defense spending, one of the most controversial issues in Japan. Not only is there strong domestic fear of military buildup, but most Asian nations greatly fear a remilitarized Japan. However, Japan has already edged beyond its self-imposed limit by spending more than 1 percent of GNP on defense. Owing to currency revaluation and a 5.2 percent increase planned for fiscal year 1988, the dollar value of Japan's defense budget will approach $30 billion. If pensions are included, as they are in NATO, the Japanese defense budget reaches $45 billion, the third largest in the world.[11]

Japanese forces do not need to embrace additional missions, but they do need to achieve the objectives laid out in the most recent five-year defense plan. For example, in January 1983, Japan committed itself to defend its air and sea lanes within 1,000 miles of the Japanese territory,[12] a mission that cannot now be accomplished without the help of U.S. forces. Not unlike NATO forces, Japanese forces also lack the necessary interoperability for joint and combined operations with U.S. forces. Japan's defense suffers from some of the same problems the United States confronts. Investments tend to flow toward more visibly prestigious planes, tanks, and ships, instead of into sustainability, maintenance, infrastructure, or command and control. Interservice rivalry makes the army the dominant service, reflected in its size: seventeen divisions, two of which are armored.

Today Japan's Self-Defense Forces lack the capability defined by their title. They cannot defend Japan against sea- or airborne attacks to the degree outlined in the Mutual Security Treaty with the United States. There are weaknesses in air defenses and the capability to conduct joint operations. There is also a lack of war reserves. Budgetary constraints delay the correction of numerous deficiencies in modern equipment and restrict spending in many other vital areas.

The Ground Self-Defense Force is making some progress. Conversion of the basic American HAWK air-defense missile to the "improved" (I) HAWK and introduction of the domestic Tan-Sam

missile system are underway. More firepower and mobility improvements have begun with the purchase of attack helicopters, transport
helicopters, and new self-propelled artillery. Planned development of
the SSM-1 ground-launched antishipping missile will also bolster the
ability to counter amphibious attacks. For the Maritime Self-Defense
Force, the Japanese are considering enhanced satellite communications, a new patrol aircraft program, and development and production
of a new ASW helicopter. For the Air Self-Defense Force, AWACS
and tanker studies are being completed and could very well lead to
acquisitions in the coming years. The Japanese should continue to
develop and improve their air defense, C3, and maritime surveillance
capabilities. Domestic programs to improve interoperability must
have priority.

A no-cost, yet politically difficult measure for improved security
is greater Japanese-Korean cooperation. One possible starting point is
Korean-Japanese joint air-defense cooperation. Currently, Soviet aircraft take off from Vladivostok and fly down the air "seam" (boundary)
between Japan and South Korea. Although the United States, Japan,
and Korea scramble air-defense fighters against those intruders, they
do so independently. The United States has not helped the problem
by dividing its air forces in Korea and Japan, creating the Seventh Air
Force to support Korea and the Fifth Air Force to cover Japan. Japan
and Korea, led by the United States, can use their defense intercept
zone as a beginning for wider cooperation, thereby presenting the
Soviets with a united, well-coordinated deterrent. This important area
of cooperation could lead to breakthroughs in other areas, supporting
efforts on the economic and technological fronts.

The United States should also take steps to encourage Japan to
increase its capability of denying the Soviets transit through the Soya,
Tsugaru, and Tsushima straits. More than three hundred Soviet warships transit these straits each year.[13] In any war, U.S. and Japanese
forces could mine or interdict the straits, but powerful land-based
Soviet air forces make this an extremely dangerous operation. In fact,
the Soviets clearly see northern Japan, and certainly Hokkaido, as
within their security perimeter.

In this context, the Japanese-Russian dispute over Japan's former
Northern Territories assumes major significance. In a questionable
legal move, the allies at Yalta agreed to award southern Sakhalin and
the Kurile Islands to the U.S.S.R. in return for a Soviet declaration of

war on Japan. More than other factors, this military occupation raises the specter of a Soviet threat for the Japanese people.

So what would be a clever tack for Moscow to take? In one scenario, Gorbachev offers to return the Northern Territories to Japan in exchange for a reduction of U.S. forces there and the demilitarization of northern Japan. Such a deal forces the United States to give up its F-16 fighters and the P-3 long-range submarine-hunter aircraft based in Misawa. Congress then insists, in the name of burdensharing, that the Japanese build new bases or threatens to withdraw U.S. forces. The consensus-building mechanism of the Japanese government might not move fast enough for an overeager, "budget-cutting," or protectionist Congress. Gorbachev then starts to discuss technology, trade, and Japanese industrial initiatives to develop the Siberian frontier. If he can reduce the perception of a military threat in northeastern Asia, he can encourage Japan to be the key in unlocking the resources of Soviet Asia, the development of which is essential if Gorbachev is to improve the Soviet economy.

The return of the Northern Territories by Gorbachev is only one of several contingencies that could vastly change Japanese public perception of the Soviets and shake the fragile defense consensus. At a time of major reevaluations in the economic and security arenas on both sides of the Pacific, Japan will be forced to make some difficult decisions. Japan's economic power has catapulted it into the international arena, yet it remains to be seen how large a role Japan will assume in global politics. At the same time the potential—and in fact, the need—for Japan to play a leadership role among the industrialized nations is tremendous. The United States and Japan must work together in developing a comprehensive cooperative strategy if we are to overcome the problems of the 1990s.

The People's Republic of China

Like Japan, China has emerged as a world power. While Japan's global position has resulted from overwhelming economic, financial, and technological strength, China's position results largely from its imposing size, its growing ability to harness its human resources, and its geostrategic position in the world. The Ikle-Wohlstetter report forecasts that, "over the next 20 years, the Chinese economy may well grow faster than those of the United States, Europe, or the Soviet

Union. . . . By 2010, China may . . . well become a superpower in military terms."[14] Plainly, China can have a direct impact on the ability of the West to prevent World War III. An understanding of the Chinese historical experience is essential to managing the relationship with China.

The Chinese have traditionally viewed themselves as the center of the world. It was this perspective that led the Chinese to play foreigners, or "barbarians," off against each other in order to achieve their historic objectives. In the last century, the objective was mere survival. A decadent China was constantly concerned about imperialist Western powers trying to slice the Chinese melon into parts. "Unequal treaties" had been imposed on China, first in 1842 by the British, and later by the Soviets. In its own version of balance of power politics, China practiced "barbarian management," seeking to create a rift between the Americans and the British, or the Americans and the Japanese.

Given their long tradition of manipulating the balance of power, it was not surprising that with a break in Sino-Soviet relations, the Chinese quickly sought a counterweight to the Soviet Union. Over a period of ten years (1958–68), Sino-Soviet relations had dramatically deteriorated. Not only had Khrushchev failed to adequately support the PRC during the Quemoy crisis and during the 1960s, but he had withdrawn Soviet advisers from China. Soviet troops then began to build up along the border, eventually accumulating up to forty modernized divisions. The Chenpao conflict on the Ussuri River in March 1969 and the sporadic Soviet-Chinese clashes that followed along the 4,000-mile border made it clear to the Chinese that the Soviet Union posed a very real threat.

Chou En-lai shared America's concern about Soviet expansionary objectives. As Kissinger pointed out, "what the Chinese wanted was not vacuous benevolence, or even the practical steps that had been the essence of the previous dialogue such as recognition, United Nations membership, claims, and exchanges. They wanted strategic reassurance, some easing of the nightmare of hostile encirclement."[15] This feeling of encirclement was nothing new to the Chinese. Since 900 B.C., they have gone to extraordinary lengths in meeting the various threats, particularly from the north. Indeed, they employed a million people to build a wall 1,800 miles long to protect them from this threat. This same perception led the Chinese into the Korean

War, where U.S. and Chinese troops fought head to head for the only time in history.[16]

Fear of encirclement related to China's southwestern border as well. Problems in Tibet and clashes with India were not uncommon. Indochina and Vietnam posed constant threats, and Vietnamese-Soviet cooperation only intensified those fears. Here again, China began to perceive the utility of having an "American card" to play off against the Soviets.

To a significant degree, our ability to deter the Soviet Union and promote global stability is dependent upon the effective management of the delicate triangular relationship among the Soviet Union, the United States, and China. While an entente between the Soviet Union and China would run against U.S. interests, any conflict between the two is likely to pull us into a dangerous global crisis. This was clearly recognized in August 1969, when the shrewd global strategist Richard Nixon told his National Security Council that the United States could not sit back and watch the Soviets defeat the Chinese. Indeed, on August 18, 1969, a State Department expert on Soviet affairs dined with a Soviet official, who asked him what the U.S. reaction would be to a Soviet attack on China's nuclear facilities. The Nixon rapprochement with China had not yet occurred, but when the conversation was reported, both Kissinger and Nixon acknowledged "the strategic necessity of supporting China." On August 28, *Pravda* warned China about any further border provocations and appealed to the world to recognize the Chinese danger, adding "no continent will be left out if a war flares under the present conditions, with the existing present-day technology, with the availability of lethal weapons and up-to-date means of delivery."[17] The Chinese leadership urged their people to prepare for war.

Under Secretary of State Elliot Richardson gave the administration's response in a luncheon speech on September 5: "We could not fail to be deeply concerned . . . with an escalation of their quarrel into a massive break of international security and peace." By the end of September, the crisis cooled and the Chinese encouraged Prime Minister Kosygin to visit Peking. Negotiations were soon reopened and President Nixon worried briefly that an actual rapprochement might take place.

What is important to recognize here is that for the United States either extreme in the Sino-Soviet relationship—undiluted hostility or

cordial amicability—would not be in its interest. Some U.S. authorities at times have referred to China as NATO's seventeenth member
because it forces Moscow to concentrate on issues outside of Europe.
That goes a bit far. However, any movement toward entente between
the Soviets and China that might release a significant proportion of the
forty Soviet divisions now deployed along the Sino-Soviet border
would be a strategic disaster for both the Pacific and for the West. It
must not be forgotten that, while the friendship of Nazi Germany and
the Soviet Union in 1939 did not last long, it was long enough to give
impetus to the outbreak of war.

Much like the Chinese, Nixon was able to look beyond Vietnam
and beyond narrow ideological considerations to the strategic importance of the U.S.-China relationship. The genesis of his China strategy
began in 1967, when he said that "there is no place on this small planet
for a billion of its potentially most able people to live in angry
isolation."[18]

The Chinese leaders revered Nixon, with his anti-Soviet moorings and his desire for an "opening," but they deeply doubted President Carter's ability and desire to contain the Soviets. Secretary of
State Cyrus Vance's conception of the Soviet Union ran counter to that
of the Chinese. However, President Carter's National Security Adviser, Zbigniew Brzezinski, understood that an American "paper tiger"
was of little use to the P.R.C. As can be seen from Carter's instructions to Brzezinski in May of 1978, both men believed parallel, long-
term strategic concerns existed between the United States and China;
both countries opposed global hegemony. In other words, the two
nations sought to contain the Soviet Union.[19]

Brzezinski, like Kissinger before him, felt that our dealings with
China forced the Soviets to take us seriously. As Brzezinski watched
Soviet adventurism in Africa and the Middle East, the conventional-
force buildup in Europe and Asia, he looked to China for leverage in
a triangular grand strategy.

In the 1990s, the United States must devise a strategy that will use
the leverage of this triangular relationship to its greatest advantage. As
China moves forward on reforms, the twin components of economic
considerations and maintenance of stability must be built into our grand
strategy. China has the ability to build and deliver nuclear weapons,
produce high-speed computers, and orbit communications satellites.
China's population grows by twenty-three people every minute.[20]

China has come a long way since the Great Leap Forward of 1958, during which 25 to 30 million people died of starvation. Deng Xiaoping's "socialism with Chinese characteristics" moved away from the tightly controlled and planned centralized economy, reversing Mao's policy of national self-reliance and quintupling foreign trade since 1979. Deng abolished rural communes and watched grain production increase from 300 to 400 million tons from 1978 to 1984, an increase equal to the total gain from 1949 to 1978.[21] Growth has been consistent at around 8 percent, six times the rate of Eastern Europe. The new general secretary, Zhao Ziyang, claims that within the next three years the state-controlled sector will account for only 30 percent of the economy.[22]

Despite the enormous progress made by Deng, Zhao has much further to go. There is much to be done with regard to price and wage controls, labor contracts, and finance. China has hardly begun to address the energy and transportation problems that will confront it as reform moves forward. As the Chinese population continues to be exposed to a greater number and variety of consumer goods, expectations will rise, placing considerable demands on Chinese leadership. Having left behind the goal of income equality in exchange for the priority placed on rapid growth, the Chinese must overcome the "iron rice bowl mentality" of a fixed salary guaranteed for life. If China is to achieve a truly open-door economy, it will eventually have to move beyond "the present airlock of administrative intermediation and separate price systems, which insulate the domestic economy from the world outside."[23]

Deng has established the underpinnings for the continuation of reform after his death. The 13th Party Congress provided a coherent and powerful ideological base upon which to continue the reforms. The congress affirmed that China is currently in the "first stage of socialism," defined as a "stage in which elements of capitalism, such as private ownership and entrepreneurial endeavors, can legitimately coexist for a time with elements of socialism such as state ownership and central planning."[24] Years ago, in the context of competition with the Soviet Union, Mao claimed that China had reached pure communism. Now, Zhao has said that the first stage of communism could last for at least a hundred years.

Another issue that further complicates U.S.-Chinese relations is the Taiwan problem. Truman's order of June 27, 1950, moving the

Seventh Fleet into the Formosa Strait indefinitely, forestalled what
had been the feared invasion of Formosa from the mainland. Representative of the Chinese ability to think in the truly long term, Mao
told Kissinger in 1973 that the problem of Taiwan could be solved after
a hundred years. The United States and China made up their minds to
normalize in light of strategic concerns, despite their disagreements
over Taiwan. Without the common threat of the Soviet Union and
similar geopolitical objectives, Taiwan would have been a major stumbling block and there would have been little incentive to move.
Strategically, the Chinese needed a strong United States to counter
the Soviet Union, and as long as the United States was willing and able
to contain the Soviets, ideology was not an issue. The resolution of the
Taiwan problem could wait.

The U.S. position on Taiwan was essentially the same in 1979 as
it had been ten years earlier. Nixon's original negotiating points were
used by Carter. From 1969 to 1979, the Chinese maintained their
basic principles, and most language in the original Shanghai communiqué of 1972 was used in the normalization communiqué of 1978.
Minor adjustments were made in order to appease the public on both
sides of the Pacific, but the real problem of Taiwan was left for future
generations.

I happened to be in Taiwan in February 1979, at the time of U.S.
"normalization" with the People's Republic of China—a sad moment
in Taipei. This small island had been the most productive recipient of
our aid program and had produced spectacular developments in agriculture and industry. As I saw their agricultural research and their
ultramodern shipbuilding and steel production, I thought it unreal
that such an advanced country of 20 million people was being "de-
recognized" around the world.

When I returned to Taiwan in 1987, it was evident that dramatic
steps had been taken toward democratization and trade liberalization.
After thirty-seven years of essentially one-party rule, the opposition
group, the Democratic Progressive party (DPP), is being allowed to
play an increasingly significant role. I met with the then-presidential
heir apparent, now president, Lee Teng-hui. This former professor of
economics with his doctorate from Cornell stressed the need for the
government to play a greater role by investing in the economic infrastructure, transportation, health, and the environment as well as provide additional entrepreneurial incentives. Plainly, Taiwan has a fresh

face for the 1990s, and even by 1988 a plethora of political reforms were in the making.

If a word of caution is necessary about "the power balancers," it is that neither should be taken for granted. Japan, the economic superpower, is a magnificent democracy that, like West Germany, has adopted a U.S.-style constitution. Japan's long-range interests clearly coincide with those of the United States and Europe. Yet if we fail to adequately manage our relations with the Japanese, our relationship could deteriorate and our interests diverge. In the 1990s, U.S.-Japanese strategic perspectives—and indeed our common prosperity—will rise or fall together.

It is in the long-term interest of the United States to maintain strong ties with China, despite the fact that it is communist and far from democratic. China is clearly progressing in a favorable direction, on the verge of absorbing Hong Kong and trying to build ties to an increasingly democratic Taiwan. U.S. strategy should support the movement toward economic and political reform at a pace that can be sustained and will not inhibit stability in China. Although progress continues, as Eugene Lawson said, Chinese "reform has a momentum of its own; to stop is to go back."[25]

A major thaw in Sino-Soviet relations is highly possible and the stage has already been set. Gorbachev has skillfully met all the Chinese criteria for a rapprochement: he resolved the border dispute along the Ussuri River; he pulled back forces from Mongolia; and he withdrew from Afghanistan and prompted Vietnam to withdraw from Cambodia.

In 1987, Deng Xiaoping said that if the Soviet Union would push Vietnam into withdrawing from Kampuchea, he would go "anywhere to meet Mr. Gorbachev."[26] With this in mind, Sino-Soviet summitry may begin.

One would hope that there could never again be an upheaval like the Cultural Revolution, or a geopolitical shift toward the Soviet Union that would allow Moscow to move its divisions away from the Chinese border into strategic reserve for potential use against NATO or the Middle East. Yet, grand strategy must account for the possibility of such disturbing contingencies while continuing to build upon the positive history of recent years.

11 Gorbachev's Superpower

As we try to formulate our grand strategy, we should seek to better understand the patterns of Soviet history as they affect the West. We must remind ourselves what the Soviets have said about war and peace, how they have built their grand strategy, and how they compensate for their deep-seated insecurities. General Secretary Gorbachev speaks of the need to fill in the "blank spots" of Soviet history, [1] although those missing pages of history contain information that could undermine the entire system. Yet he is compelled to examine those pages of history in order to avoid a fatal economic crisis before the turn of the century.

As one fills out these blank spots, what appear to be the patterns for which we must account in our own grand strategy?

First, Soviet history is one of cycles of reform and reaction. Lenin's New Economic Policy (NEP) and Khrushchev's cultural humanism did not survive; maybe Gorbachev's *glasnost* and *perestroika* will. Certainly, with rising popular expectations and the information revolution, new societal forces have been irreversibly unleashed. History suggests that reactionary leadership at the top remains a possibility if the Communist Party appears threatened. Furthermore, even a more liberal regime at the top does not inevitably mean a uniformly more liberal policy abroad. Indeed, the humanitarian reformer Khrushchev tried to put missiles in Cuba. For these reasons, our grand strategy must allow for contingencies.

Second, Soviet transitions of power—Lenin to Stalin to Malenkov

148

to Khrushchev to Brezhnev to Andropov to Chernenko to Gorbachev—are the result of Byzantine intrigue. Outcomes can seldom be predicted by the West, or perhaps even within the Soviet Union. Furthermore, leaders often use one rationale in coming to power—to wit, the "moderate" Stalin—and then adopt a different one later. A victor can turn on his comrades with viciousness. The winner generally sets out to eliminate his rivals, as Gorbachev has so brilliantly done. There is indeed greater restraint, no longer murder, less frequent resort to exile, but the overall pattern has not changed. Thus the transition of power, unlike the power to rule, is unstable, unpredictable.

Third, there is constant tension between governance of the Soviet Union and dominance of Eastern Europe. Enlightenment in the Soviet Union can translate to the satellites, which can result in revolt. The Soviets react with repression. Then there is reaction within the Soviet power system against the ruler who produced the enlightenment. It is a vicious circle. The only way out is a clear decision to give up the absolute control of Eastern Europe, and let it go in the direction of Titoism. But this raises profound military questions as well. A common strand that seems to run through Soviet reactions to Eastern Europe is acting decisively when the rule of the Party is threatened, as was the case in Czechoslovakia. Soviet leaders have tolerated considerable diversity in Eastern Europe on a number of subjects— Hungary on economic organization, Rumania on foreign policy—but when the rule of the Party is threatened, they have acted. As we look toward the year 2000, Gorbachev faces a dilemma perhaps unparalleled in Soviet history.

Fourth, the Soviets at times can be brilliant diplomatists. Stalin, a monster at home, got the best of things in the Grand Alliance by playing Roosevelt against Churchill. Unlike that of the West, Stalin's diplomacy was always related to his larger, long-term strategy. Brezhnev, despite his smarter tailoring, hardly possessed such brilliance. But Gorbachev has constantly surprised the West with his diplomacy. He is an absolute master by any standard for any age. Stalin and Andropov demonstrated how the same individual could be both devastatingly congenial and utterly ruthless. A smiling Gorbachev is said by President Gromyko to have "teeth of steel." In the West, politicians run for office and do indeed have to be political tacticians. But in the Soviet Union, it is deception and maneuver—strategic attributes—that characterize the substance of leadership politics. As one high-ranking Soviet defector says: "If Machiavelli were alive and living in Moscow today, he would be a student, not a professor."[2] Maybe this is why Soviet leaders have often outdone the West diplomatically, from Yalta to Reykjavík.

Soviet, and indeed Russian, history is a story of aggressive policies driven by a sense of insecurity, whether in reaction to Napoleon or Hitler marching toward Moscow, or Allied forces in Siberia after World War I. The communist system is at its heart insecure; it must, as Lenin warned, control information; it must repress "counterrevolutionaries." The Soviet psyche suffers from such an inferiority-superiority complex that it would take a master psychiatrist to analyze it. But there is another basic problem of divided personalities: the insecure indigenous Soviet system. Only half of it is Russian. The other Slavs—Ukrainians and Byelorussians— constitute nations with their own distinct histories, cultures, and languages. Georgia and Armenia enjoyed independence for many centuries. Estonia, Latvia, and Lithuania—strongly Roman Catholic —were forcibly incorporated into the Soviet Union only in 1940. Peoples of Turco-Tartar, Finno-Ugrian, Caucasian, and Mongolian origins continue to cultivate their heritages. The Muslim birthrate is exceeding the Great Russian. There is certainly no danger of civil war as confronted Lenin, but there is indeed a problem of serious civil discord if *glasnost* truly catches on among these nationalities. The unrest in Armenia suggests how dramatically the policy of *glasnost* can destabilize the Soviet state.

In view of these complexities, Lenin's achievement is all the more monumental. As Mikhail Gorbachev was to put it in his early November 1987 speech to celebrate the seventieth anniversary of the creation of the Soviet state, "At the dawn of the 20th century, Vladimir Ilyich Lenin put himself at the head of a close-knit group of comrades and set out to organize a proletarian party of the new type in Russia. It was this great party of Lenin that roused the nation, its best and most devoted forces, for an assault on the old world."[3] Lenin's successors from Stalin to Gorbachev would change that world even more. As an academic friend of mine, Professor Hugh Seton Watson, said, communism is a theory that claims to explain everything: "philosophy, religion, history, economics, and society." It is a vocation "whose devotees accept its discipline in every part of their private and professional lives." But it is also "a science of conspiracy, a technique of wrecking and subversion." It is a revolutionary movement, "a political force which operates in a social environment, which recruits its members from various classes of society, and marshals its armies against various political opponents."[4]

In a sense, communism was meant to be an integrated strategy, a strategy first to justify itself, and then to marshal power and people to change the world. By 1988, this philosophy was in crisis. Nonetheless, as a method for organizing power, communism allowed both the Soviet Union and China to establish strong and unshakable centralized party rule.

Today, whatever his problems, Gorbachev rules over a superpower—a vast empire not only of his own polyglot nation but also of Eastern Europe. Indeed, it's a power that could have real political influence over Western Europe in the 1990s. The achievement is stunning. Before World War I, Imperial Russia was one of several European powers. Now she without her satellites is more powerful militarily than the other European powers put together.

Lenin found power lying in the streets during the Russian Revolution, the power of a nation broken by war and denigrated by a royal leadership that lacked compassion and courage. With the seizure of power, Lenin and his followers firmly installed an all-powerful party, abolishing freedom of the press, outlawing strikes, forming the secret police—the *Cheka*—and crushing any and all opposition. If one-party rule, backed by brute force and terrorism, was increasingly secure, economic failure was massive. The masses stayed hungry. In March 1921, Lenin inaugurated his New Economic Policy (NEP), something that reformist Gorbachev places great stock in today to give legitimacy to his own innovative measures. "These days,"said Gorbachev in the anniversary speech, "we turn ever more often to the last works of Lenin, to Lenin's new economic policy, and strive to extract from it all the valuable elements we require today."[5]

Much has and is being done nowadays to disconnect Stalin's bitter heritage from Lenin. This is a wise approach for Gorbachev as he works out his rationale for change and builds his own legitimacy. But it is not possible to separate the two, if one looks at history objectively. Lenin's system made Stalin possible. Initially, Stalin portrayed himself as a moderate, but over the years he eliminated his rivals in a brutal struggle for power: Trotsky, who controlled the army and wanted revolution; Zinoviev, Leningrad Party boss; Kamenev; and Bukharin.

Stalin also set out to liquidate the Kulaks, the most prosperous peasant farmers. Over 10 million were killed—some shot, some exiled, some sent to camps. There sprang up what Aleksandr Solzhenitsyn made famous in his book *The Gulag Archipelago*: huge territorial islands of prisoners spread across the Soviet Union.[6] These crimes against humanity were little known in the West, where liberal writers heaped praise on the "progressive" Soviet Union. U.S. Ambassador Davies even told Washington the show trials were genuine.

Stalin's blackest international crime lay ahead, in the year 1939. Hitler, fearing French and British approaches to Stalin, negotiated a nonaggression pact with a secret protocol that divided Eastern Europe into spheres of influence, including the partition of Poland. Once Stalin had made safe Hitler's invasion of Poland on September 1, and grabbed his part of it, he had a free hand to take the Baltic republics—Latvia, Lithuania, and Estonia—and to attack Finland when it refused to capitulate.

Despite a vague and general fear of German aggression, Stalin rejected all warnings of an imminent German attack, making no specific plans to meet it when it came on June 11, 1941. For the next year and a half, until the Battle of Stalingrad in the winter of 1942–43, the Soviets suffered defeat. Then, for more than a year, Stalin called upon his people to fight, not for the Communist Party, but for Russia.

Owing to his disasters, Stalin joined the so-called Grand Alliance of the Soviet Union, Britain, and the United States. In that alliance, Stalin played his political hand brilliantly. He sized up all parties and personalities, understanding the equations of power and how to manipulate Churchill and Roosevelt. Stalin became known in the Western press as "Uncle Joe," a kindly image.

Stalin's biographer Professor Adam Ulam of Harvard calls Stalin's greatest wartime victory not Stalingrad but Teheran, his first meeting with Franklin Roosevelt in November 1943.[7] Roosevelt was confident in his charm and was committed to developing trust and support for a United Nations. Stalin was confident in his grand strategy, which had territorial aims far beyond the war and the Grand Alliance. He aimed to separate Roosevelt from a suspicious Churchill, who might try to restrict his postwar role. Roosevelt came away from the meeting convinced that Stalin would be a good ally and partner. It is quite remarkable what Stalin got out of his two partners in the Grand Alliance. When he made concessions at Yalta on the principle of free elections in Poland, it was against the backdrop of Roosevelt saying, on February 5, that "he did not believe that American troops would stay in Europe much more than two years. . . . He could obtain support in Congress and throughout the country for any reasonable measures designed to safeguard the future of peace, but he did not believe that this would extend to the maintenance of an appreciable American force in Europe."[8] One could argue that this statement was something of a green light for Stalin, if he were patient. Roosevelt did not back Churchill's demand for international supervision of the election, and Roosevelt refused to coordinate positions with the British in advance.

Stalin's strategy had been successful. Only after Yalta did it break down, with Stalin's refusal to follow through in March with genuine free elections. Roosevelt, almost on his death bed, was deeply disillusioned. The new president, a blunt-talking Harry Truman, summoned Soviet Ambassador Molotov. "I gave it to him straight," Truman later wrote. "I let him have it. It was the straight one two to the jaw." The stunned Molotov retorted he had never been talked to like that in his life. Truman snapped back, "Carry out your agreements and you won't get talked to like that."[9]

Stalin, a master grand strategist during the war, now wanted too much too fast. As a ruthless man of power, he did not accept Marxist doctrine, which would have dictated that his actions move slowly and await history; this man of steel went fast and made history. Western leaders realized this. At a December 1945, no-holds-barred conference of foreign ministers, British Foreign Secretary Ernest Bevin and U.S. Secretary of State James Byrnes criticized Molotov's arguments and implied that the Soviet Union was oppressing small countries as had Hitler. On March 5, 1946, Winston Churchill, as the West's most distinguished statesman now out of office, made his famous speech at Fulton, Missouri: "From Stettin in the Baltic to Trieste in the Adriatic, an iron curtain has descended across the continent."[10]

Ulam notes with profound insight that it was the U.S. initiative of the Marshall Plan that rocked Stalin and appeared to challenge the foundations of his empire. He was not confused about the American motivation behind what Churchill termed among the "most unsordid acts" of history, nor was he concerned that this plan in execution might restore the economies of Western Europe and make them infertile ground for the spread of communism. It was the extension of this offer to the Soviet Union and its new satellites that shook him. The Czechs and Poles responded too positively. Even the stunned Stalin hesitated and the Politburo debated. "If there is one session of the Politburo for which the minutes could be procured, we should opt, in preference to the more blood-and-thunder ones, for the session which debated this extraordinary American offer," writes Ulam.[11]

There was much to gain economically. But Stalin apparently began to see the proposal as a trap. He had just barely restored order and discipline to his society after the brief but dangerous euphoria in the weeks following VE day, when Russians had demanded new freedoms and prosperity. Could he now lean on the capitalists, acknowledging to them and his own people that he needed their help? When the Marshall Plan became law in April 1948, Uncle Joe Stalin, who through the war years had been able to manipulate the Grand Alliance very much to his benefit, began to feel his isolation and his social and political weaknesses.

At the beginning of 1949, Stalin set up his own feeble counterpart of the Marshall Plan: the Council for Mutual Economic Assistance, or COMECON. COMECON became the opposite of the American plan—which subsidized Europe—with a tyranny requiring the selling of Soviet goods at inflated prices and the purchase of commodities from satellites at below-market prices. Meanwhile, on Stalin's European flank, Titoism was emerging as a problem, and on his Asian flank, Chinese Communist power had consolidated itself, bringing both good and bad news to Stalin. He feared Peking, too, might go the way of Tito; ironically, he more than the Americans might have pushed harder for two Chinese states on the mainland. If an ill Stalin in these last years suspected those around him were enemies, so he feared the same internationally. He even brooded over the "international Zionist conspiracy." Unwittingly, Stalin transformed what he considered to be an economic threat into a military alliance.

The Cold War that Stalin had begun was generating results from Washington, but they were in the economic realm. The 1948 Soviet coup in Czechoslovakia and the June blockade of access to the western sectors of Berlin changed all that. In retrospect, we know that Stalin, the brilliant grand strategist during the war, had launched an initiative that badly backfired. The Berlin blockade convinced the West Germans that neutrality was not an option in the face of Soviet conduct. Stalin had also brought pressure to bear on Norway to enter into a security pact; and the Norwegian government had appealed to the United States and Canada to join in collective security measures in Europe. In June an aroused U.S. Senate passed the Vandenberg Resolution, which in effect changed the direction of U.S. foreign policy toward collective security with European democracies. The Treaty of Washington creating NATO was signed on April 4, 1949.

In Gorbachev's "pages of history," he still argues that NATO is an offensive alliance because it came first and the Warsaw Pact is a defensive one because it came in response. I do not for a moment think this shrewd Soviet believes that. The credit for the creation of NATO belongs to many people—great statesmen in the West like British Foreign Minister Ernest Bevin, Senator Arthur Vandenberg, Secretary of State Dean Acheson, and Harry Truman. But first credit goes to Joseph Stalin. Stalin's coup in Czechoslovakia and his Berlin blockade succeeded in moving the United States from its indirect economic response of the Marshall Plan to the direct military response of the NATO alliance. Gorbachev's brilliant diplomatic reversals of 1987–88 would indicate the strategic and diplomatic advantages he sees in reducing—in fact, in trying to abolish—the perception of the threat from the East. The Stalin of the war years and the Grand Alliance was far more crafty than the Stalin who gave birth to NATO. But let it be remembered that one man, in different circumstances, was capable of both; and one man was capable of moving from one stance to the other, driven in part by age and suspicion and in part by the needs of the system over which he ruled.

The year 1953 was pivotal. Stalin was succeeded by Georgy Malenkov and a period of collective leadership. An armistice was agreed to in Korea, based on stalemate and no rollback. Despite the deployment of tanks to quell riots in East Germany there was some change and relaxation in the Soviet Union: an official amnesty, albeit limited; some de-Stalinization, very much in the pattern of Soviet history during the initiation of the NEP and the Khrushchev enlightenment.

Khrushchev brought a new style to the Kremlin. An improviser, innovator, and public relations man, he was determined to reform and revive agriculture and achieve spectacular economic growth that would outdo America. During the Suez crisis and the Hungarian uprising, he loudly threatened the West with his missiles, although, in retrospect, it was more like the threats of the Wizard of Oz, with smoke and mirrors. Actually, Khrushchev economized and reduced the size of his army from almost 6 million to just over 3 million men. In May of 1955, he proposed dramatic conventional-forces disarmament. By 1957, nuclear weapons were to be destroyed. The Khrushchev political offensive reminds us of Gorbachev's in 1986–87. The latter case is different in a number of ways: a less suspicious West, real and dramatic concessions by Gorbachev, and a negotiating process at Geneva that involved genuine bargaining.

At the historic "Big Four" Geneva Conference in the summer of 1955, Eisenhower dramatically unveiled his "open skies" plan in which the U.S. and U.S.S.R. would exchange blueprints of their military establishments and allow each other to photograph them from the sky. Ironically, this propaganda coup for the allies was used by the Soviets to create a climate that made it more difficult for NATO to feel the sense of danger. Disunifying forces in the alliance—the Suez crisis, colonial issues, and a range of differences with de Gaulle—began to dominate.

The lesson was not that the Geneva Conference should have been avoided. It was that there was not a grand strategy for the West to use it effectively. In short, the allies, especially the Americans, came to see such fora in piecemeal terms, as events in themselves. Mr. Khrushchev and the Soviets saw these events as way stations to further their policy.

Soviet grand strategy has had remarkable flexibility in moving quickly from threats to conciliation, from arms buildup and nuclear saber-rattling to sweeping arms control proposals. The mouthpiece for a new initiative was to be the Polish foreign minister, Adam Repacki, in 1957, calling for a "nuclear free zone" in Europe—that is, Poland, Czechoslovakia, and East and West Germany. The United States immediately rejected the plan, but its core idea survived. It was resurrected increasingly in 1986–87 among European opposition parties as the "double-zero" agreement of 1987 gained momentum, and there were calls by Gorbachev for even a "third zero" eliminating the remaining short-range battlefield weapons. We should also add that in 1959, Khrushchev proposed such a nuclear free zone in the Pacific, something that New Zealand endorsed in 1986.

Little did the allies know the weak position from which Khrushchev was operating. Since Khrushchev's interrelated strategy of nuclear disarmament aimed at Germany and China, Berlin pressures, and Moscow-Peking relations had fallen apart, he began to look in new strategic directions. Fidel Castro's Cuba and John Kennedy's Bay of Pigs fiasco came in handy.

When Raul Castro visited Moscow in July of 1962, planning began for the movement of Soviet intermediate-range missiles to Cuba. Even now no one knows precisely what the Soviet objectives were. What is certain is that a Communist leader entered into a major gamble by placing missiles in Cuba.

What lessons of the Cuban missile crisis should we learn? First, Communist leaders, certainly Khrushchev, are not like Hitler, but under certain circumstances they have in the past, and can in the future, carry out what we would describe as high-risk policies. Therefore, their Marxism has no inevitable constraint in such cases. Second, they can miscalculate, as Khrushchev did in a huge way. When both sides miscalculate, as both the Soviets and the Americans did prior to the Cuban missile crisis, there is a danger of war. Simply put, things can get out of hand. Third, even a more liberal Communist leader—as Khrushchev certainly was compared to Stalin—can under certain circumstances mount higher-risk aggressive strategies to exploit opportunities. These pages of Soviet history must not be lost, but studied well in the West, as Gorbachev restudies his own.

The period following the ejection of Khrushchev in 1964—the beginning of the Brezhnev-Kosygin era—was one of consolidation and repeal of reforms at home and caution abroad. Leadership style moved from Khrushchev's baggy suits and startling innovations to one devoid of any innovation or indeed much intellect. Of course, it very much suited Soviet needs that the United States under President Johnson became bogged down in a major land war in Asia. Brezhnev was the beneficiary of the increasing disaffection of France in the NATO alliance over the U.S. policy in Vietnam and over NATO nuclear policy. This was not a brilliant period of Soviet grand strategy; it was simply that the West was devoid of strategy altogether.

This prompted the new U.S. president, Richard Nixon, to join with Henry Kissinger in developing a grand strategy to reorder the global power balance. They planned to achieve this by doing what had not been done during the previous decade: exploiting the Sino-Soviet split. The strategy was to develop a rapport with China, get U.S. troops out of Vietnam, and strike the 1972 accords with the Soviet Union. For a Soviet Union in deep economic trouble, credits and technology from the West were urgently needed. It was a period of détente and linkage, but here the Soviets soon felt deprived of part of the deal, owing to Senator Jackson's amendment developed with Congressman Vanick. This made "most favored nation" trade status conditional upon the emigration of Soviet Jews. If Brezhnev felt deprived of part of the agreement, many in the Congress felt deceived as the Soviets supported Marxist forces in Angola and then threatened to move airborne divisions to the Middle East at the climax of the 1973 war.

When détente reached its height, the Soviet Union was ruled by a *troika*. The next was characterized by maneuvering among an aging group of potential successors, first between Andrei Kirilenko and Constantin Chernenko, and then between Chernenko and Andropov. Yuri Andropov was certainly one of the key architects of the Afghanistan invasion in 1979, in the course of which the SALT II agreement was lost. He was also a driving force behind the further reversal of the Khrushchev thaw.

Andropov had plotted as successfully against the ailing Brezhnev as a ruthless Stalin had against Lenin in his last year. On November 10, 1982, Brezhnev died. Sixty-eight-year-old Andropov was more of a one-man show than the colorless Brezhnev had ever been. As Soviet ambassador, Andropov had masterminded the suppression of the Hungarian uprising, and later as head of the KGB, he became a skillful suppressor of dissidents and Jews. With this sinister background, there was a campaign to liberalize his image as someone who indeed liked American jazz and had a good command of English.

But his real character was more apparent in the Polish crisis, where he was deeply involved as head of the KGB. At the time of the strike in the Gdansk shipyards in the summer of 1980, the Kremlin felt things were rapidly getting out of hand. Lech Walesa and his trade unions gained recognition. There were public demands for reform, free elections, and the end of censorship. The revolutionary situation was doubly dangerous. To begin with, Poland had far more independence than other Eastern European countries, with the Catholic Church—along with a Polish pope since 1978—playing a critical role. Second, Poland stood squarely astride the Soviet's military communications to East Germany. The Soviets therefore accelerated maneuvers in Poland. By early December, five Soviet divisions appeared ready to invade. If they had done so, and the Polish armed forces of 317,500 plus some 500,000 reserves had fought back,[12] the Soviets would have had three vulnerable fronts at once: Poland, Afghanistan, and China. Rather than invade, there was a military coup in the person of General Jaruzelski. Conditions in Poland only pointed up the fundamental crisis, which remained the catastrophic state of the Soviet economy and the basic failure of the system to perform adequately. Andropov pushed out Brezhnev's crowd and brought a new group to the front, including Nikolai Ryzhkov, now the prime minister, and Yegor Ligachev, now the number two man in the Party—and Gorbachev, then Party boss in Stavropol.

When Andropov died in February of 1984, the brief period of Chernenko rule did little to encourage the perception of a vigorous Soviet leadership. The selection of Mikhail Gorbachev, the young fifty-four-year-old favorite of Andropov, no doubt was a reflection of the desperation over the ailing economy as well as the failure of the Soviet drive to split NATO over the INF deployment, after the walkout of the Soviet negotiators.

By the time of his triumphant arrival in Washington on December 7, 1987, Mikhail Gorbachev had dazzled the world with his style, public diplomacy, and negotiating skill. His strategic reversal on the missile issue will go down in history as comparable to the Nixon-Kissinger reversal on China. In his examination of the pages of history, Gorbachev surely realized how Stalin created NATO, how Khrushchev's boasts about Sputnik triggered Kennedy's buildup, how the Cuban missile crisis galvanized America, and how the SS-20 deployment provided NATO a moment of brilliant achievement.

Gorbachev obviously realized the mistake and moved from acceptance of the Reagan-Perle "zero option" to a "second zero option" of, in effect, unilaterally eliminating SS-23s and SS-12s—a category in which the United States already was at zero. He tried to move with Reagan from a 50 to a 100 percent reduction of strategic missiles and all nuclear weapons, and for drastic conventional-weapons reductions, even unequal ones. Of course, there were other motivations behind his reversals. Denuclearization of Europe had long been a Soviet objective going back to the Repacki plan.[13] More important, the Soviet economy had to be reordered and there had to be relief from the military burden.

In June 1987, the plenum of the Central Committee approved an eleven-point program for *perestroika*—economic restructuring—including programs to make Soviet industrial enterprises self-financing, to broaden the quality-control system, and to increase output. There were new rules to expand the number of cooperatives that operate outside the control of the Soviet state and to allow state and agricultural farms to market more of their products directly to the public. At the 1988 Special Party Conference, Gorbachev appealed for dramatic changes in Soviet governmental structures, calling for new parliamentary bodies led by a President. As Sovietologist Stephen R. Sestanovich has put it, "Gorbachev is not only stirring the pot, he seems to want to redesign it while it cooks."[14]

But for Gorbachev it is an uphill battle, with heavy subsidization and the need to reform the pricing system, the backwardness of the industrial plant, the huge black-market economy, and bureaucratic opposition. *Glasnost*—public openness—is Gorbachev's way of marshaling public support behind his efforts and showing the flaws in the people and policies that have impeded Soviet development.

Perhaps the most fundamental change is that Gorbachev has succeeded remarkably in replacing many of an older generation of Communists with those committed to *perestroika* and *glasnost*. By the time Gorbachev came to America for the treaty signing, nine members of the Politburo had been dropped and 40 percent of the 300-strong Central Committee had been replaced.[15] The military leadership had also been shaken up. But Gorbachev still treads a slippery path with conservatives like KGB chief Viktor Chebrikov and Party ideologist Yegor Ligachev. Added to this is the delicate balance in handling the implications of *perestroika* and *glasnost* in Eastern Europe.

But despite such vulnerabilities, Gorbachev correctly says that *perestroika* is not a whim on the part of some individuals. Rather, the current push for reform represents nothing less than an attempt at a second Russian revolution. It is, Gorbachev says, an "unprecedented endeavor" at "new political thinking." Such developments as a fifty percent drop in the economic growth rate, economic stagnation, rising alcoholism, and a credibility gap with the Soviet people admittedly "threaten the very future of the nation" and have narrowed Soviet policy options by eliminating previously workable alternatives.[16] Although some argue that we are witnessing an admission of the failure of socialism, Gorbachev strongly asserts that his reforms are in accordance with "socialist change." He is thus caught in a major contradiction between the desire for reform and the necessity to preserve Soviet legitimacy.

The plot thickens when one considers that although *glasnost* was introduced to rally support for reforms, there is also a rallying of sentiment against reform. For example, the decision to delay price reform until 1991, or later, reflects domestic resistance to an end to food subsidies. The inefficient and entrenched bureaucrats do not want to see Soviet enterprise put on a profit-and-loss basis.

The real problem is that after three and a half years in power, Gorbachev has not been able to match new political thinking with new progress in economic performance. Indeed, 1987 showed the lowest growth rate since the late 1970s—output in seven of ten industrial branches was down. Agricultural production went down 3 percent and production of consumer durables was off by 2 percent, while drunkenness and moonshine production were up. It does not seem possible that the Soviet economy will meet the five-year plan set by Gorbachev in 1986.[17] Gorbachev's response has been to maintain mobile warfare against the system, coming up with initiatives to attack on new fronts.

An important consequence to Gorbachev's new political thinking was the immediate effect it produced on Western opinion. As reflected on Western television and radio, in newspapers and journals, Gorbachev's reform is often taken as a fait accompli. Increasingly, the "new" Soviet state is no longer perceived as a menace. As people on both sides of the Atlantic argue that the Cold War is over and future security can be found in new arrangements with the East, the rationale behind NATO appears to be losing its force. Mikhail Gorbachev, with his peace program abroad and *glasnost* program at home, has created stunning new perceptions throughout the West.

Whereas Gorbachev may fail on the domestic front, he may attain longstanding goals abroad—even though that was not his prime objective in *perestroika*. If Stalin created NATO, Gorbachev just might dismember it. Indeed, the cruel pattern of Soviet history, as with Russian history before it, is that liberalization fails, but foreign policy succeeds; attempts to ameliorate the lives of the masses fail, but the power of the state grows; reformers become successful statesmen externally even as they fail internally. Even Stalin set out in 1929 to make the Soviet Union prosperous, but his five-year plans only made it powerful. The problem with trying to forecast the Soviet future is that Soviet history has been filled with zigzags of reform and reaction, reversals and unpredictability in leadership. The decade ahead seems to portend, if anything, an even more uncertain world.

Finally, despite Gorbachev's reverent deference to Leninism, adverse trends and now popularized demands for change have led to a questioning of the legitimacy of the Soviet system. Lenin is the father of this failed system. Though not the monster that Stalin was, he made those monstrosities possible. When will the Soviet leadership fill this blank spot of history and face up to the stark truth? If they do, what further crises might this set off? As the noted Soviet dissident Vladimir Bukovsky commented to me, we may not witness another 1917 revolution, but rather another 1905 scenario, when discontented people marched on the Winter Palace demanding a response the ruler was unwilling or unable to give. Could there be marches in Eastern Europe as well? The potential for loss of control remains in many areas. By all accounts, strategists in the West will be presented not merely with continuing zigzags, but also with greater unpredictability than in the past. There will be more opportunity for miscalculation not only on the part of the West, but also on the part of the East, which knows not even its own future.

PART II
THE STRATEGIES

The Grand Strategy

MAINTAINING peace and well-being, pax and shalom, requires a cohesive grand strategy. We cannot afford to be a house divided. That is by far the most important lesson to be drawn from our experience of conflict and competition in Europe and around the globe.

To make the best use of our resources and develop the strength and the influence to achieve our objectives, a grand strategy must harmonize our objectives with our means, equilibrating political, social, and economic considerations as well as military ones. Given our democratic system, strategy must be morally defensible and enjoy the support of the public. Our strategy must be consistent, understood by our allies, and have their widespread support. Strategy should restore our freedom of action, rather than restrict it. In the following chapters I explore how we can build such a grand strategy and develop a more comprehensive approach to security.

I am often struck by the resemblance of the strategist to the artist. Grand strategy, like art, is composed of several elements. And just as the artist must take into account form, color, tone, texture, design, and technique, the strategist must incorporate the diverse dimensions of statecraft into his design. Grand strategy must include consideration of public understanding and approval; it must consider the realities of deterrence; it must reflect the limits of available resources to support national goals; it must be cognizant of technology and the role it plays in shaping strategy; and it must be a product of effective, organized government. By "public strategy" I mean a strategy

understandable to our peoples. It must be consistent with informed
public debate, and meet with public support, both domestically and
globally. That is not to say that grand strategy can be held hostage to
the latest popularity poll. But, over time, a grand strategy that ignores
or fails to gain the support of the public and its representatives is a
strategy doomed to failure.

More than ever in our nuclear age, grand strategy must be at-
tentive to the everchanging realities of deterrence. Although our
effort to deter aggression must include nuclear weapons, I believe we
should give greater importance to the role of conventional forces.
Indeed, the overreliance on the "first use" of nuclear weapons is in
some ways responsible for the situation we will face in Europe in the
1990s: an instability brought about by the disequilibrium between a
mass of Soviet tank armies in forward-deployed positions and NATO's
inability to deploy its resources effectively.

To be sure, conflict and conflict avoidance are but part of the total
interaction of nations. And even within this subset of national actions,
the military instrument is not the only tool that nations can or should
wield to achieve security. Indeed, a grand strategy that is blind to the
benefits of negotiation in furthering national goals is lacking in perspective. But a negotiation strategy must be internally coherent—for
example, negotiations on conventional armed forces must be consistent with negotiations on nuclear forces. It must also be consistent
with military strategy and encompass the entire range of military
threats to security. Negotiating strategy must be formed with a view
toward public understanding and aspirations—for today, as never
before, negotiations are waged in public media as doggedly as they are
at the conference tables in Vienna or Geneva.

Effective grand strategy has always demanded a sensitivity to the
role of technological innovation. But as the pace of technological
advance literally explodes around us, we need to ensure that we
control technology and are not controlled by it. A legitimate strategy
will harness technological innovation so it can work in concert with
broader national goals. In this regard, we need to pay greater attention to the international dimension of technology—to be sensitive to
the ways that we can benefit from technological advances of our allies
and be alert to ways to pursue cooperative research and development.
A given technology might make a certain strategy possible, or even so
attractive as to make it all but inevitable, but we must be careful to

guard against undue reliance on technology. Technology has always been a strong suit in the arsenal of the West, going back to the age of exploration and beyond, and grand strategy must harness these strengths.

A resources strategy implies the investment and application of financial and technical resources at the right place and at the right time, with a clear sense of priorities. The cost of military forces has become so high that no grand strategy is sustainable if it fails to allocate resources efficiently and effectively. Hard choices are being made in our own budgetary process and in the finance ministries of all our allies. The competition for scarcer resources will not disappear soon. The pie is no longer infinitely expandable. Domestic spending, long on the rise, is relatively more immune to cuts than is defense spending. The only effective answer is to harness the enormous resources available to the democracies so as to work in concert. We must, in short, find ways of doing more with what we have—of thinking smarter, not richer.

An economic strategy encompasses free trade exchange-rate stability, multilateral cooperation, and debt management. Unless we make the commitment to shore up the weaknesses in our domestic economic foundation, U.S. national security will be threatened not from external military forces but from internal economic ones. A strategy for the economic superpowers—the United States and Japan—should give special consideration to a relationship in which greater cooperation can produce real prosperity in the future.

The grand strategy of a global power must incorporate the elements of organization and leadership. In organizing for strategy, we must recognize complex and largely reactive bureaucracies. We must harmonize the various elements in government responsible for national security and marshal their considerable talents in support of a coordinated strategic planning process. I believe the most effective way to accomplish this is to separate the National Security Advisor's function into two separate endeavors: retain a traditional adviser responsible for ongoing operations and coordination, and create a cabinet-level presidential counselor responsible for overall strategy. Such an individual, a presidential grand strategist, would be responsible for the true integration of politics, defense, and economics—the essential legs of any national policy. He would place the events of the day in the context of a long range grand strategy and vice versa.

Finally, as we seek to organize ourselves better for strategy making, it is essential to be clear about our objectives and to establish priorities among them. It is the argument of this book that the first objective of a grand strategy must be to prevent World War III. If we do not have such an effective strategy, under a particular set of unstable circumstances we could return to the type of situation that existed in 1914, the kind of uncertain conditions that can precipitate a world war, although nobody planned it.

The second objective of a grand strategy must be to prevent Soviet coercion of our allies, short of war. Our strategy must inhibit coercion in its many forms, in Europe and around the world. It should ensure that through a combination of our resources, technology, and negotiating strategies, the short-warning, blitzkrieg capability of the Soviets is ended—both as a threat to Western Europe and as a lever during Third World crises.

The third objective must be to ensure economic strength and growth and maintain an open and free trading system. Our military power and our political influence cannot be maintained without commensurate economic capabilities. Gorbachev's problem is that the Soviet Union is a military superpower without being an economic one. We also need to better analyze the relationship between economic and military strength.

The fourth objective is to encourage global stability. There is a word of warning, however. The objectives must discipline the means, but the means must also discipline the objectives. Strategy demands priorities and, in the Third World, this requires making a distinction between vital and important interests and recognizing the corresponding costs. In dealing with the Third World, more often than not our strategy should follow what Liddell Hart termed the "strategy of the indirect approach," where efforts are not over-Americanized.[1] If history tells us anything, it is that to squander our strength all over the world is surely the way to national decline.

Finally, the rise or decline of the United States as it approaches the year 2000 is not a function of deterministic forces. Rather, it depends on our ability to develop the strategy, organization, and leadership that I put forth in Part II.

12 Political Strategy

A FUNDAMENTAL principle of classical strategy is unity of effort. In their practice of the art of war, the great generals of history divided their opponents and defeated them one at a time. Napoleon Bonaparte was a master of this strategy and almost the whole of Europe fell before him.

Napoleon met his final defeat on the rolling farmlands near Waterloo, on the other side of that enchanting forest of tall beech trees that borders Truman Hall. Napoleon ultimately failed in his plan to divide and defeat separately the two armies arrayed against him: the combined allied forces—British, Dutch, and Belgian—led by the Duke of Wellington and the Prussians led by Marshal Blücher. Napoleon first attacked the allied vanguard to the west, then repulsed the German forces to the east expecting Blücher to flee toward Germany, each army looking after its own national interest. But Blücher did not behave that way. Instead of retreating east, he marched northwest, to join Wellington, leaving the route to his native Germany exposed. Together they defeated the greatest military leader of the time. Had the allies united from the beginning, instead of waging separate battles and negotiating separate peace agreements, Napoleon's conquests would have been impossible.

Our grammar school courses in ancient history taught us that the Greek city-states never quite managed to stand together in the face of a Macedonia intent on conquest. I have already described the disunity and ambiguities among the democratic alliance powers that led up to the two world wars. These examples from military history demonstrate that the political strategy of an alliance is in a sense even more important than its military strategy. It is precisely the absence of political unity, much more than a lack of military capacity, that has brought about the wars of which we speak.

Today our political strategy must operate on two levels: first, the maintenance of unity in our relations with friends and allies—the West-West level; and second, the pursuit of dialogue and negotiations with the Soviet Union—the East-West dimension. Indeed, these two aspects of a political strategy are entwined, since the East-West relationship will often be the focus of West-West debate.

Classical Soviet strategy has been to divide Europe, within itself and from America, even though Gorbachev now disclaims such a strategy. With the legacy of Charlemagne's children and George Washington's descendants, Western allies are not automatically united. It has always been difficult for democracies to stand together, especially over an extended period of time. Marxist theory, of course, posits that the decadent democracies, filled with class conflicts, will inevitably fall apart. Paradoxically, it will be more difficult for the West to maintain such unity in the face of an apparently nonthreatening Gorbachev than a clearly threatening Stalin.

Over time, unity can never be sustained merely by a military alliance. Huge commands, tank armies on land, frigates at sea, and jets screaming across the skies are not enough, and they can be too much for a burdened population if these weapons of war have no perceived role in preserving the peace. Once NATO created its military commands, the inherent tension between the alliance's political and military dimensions emerged. There was danger that the political aspect would be lost in the morass of tanks and airplanes.

Yet this huge alliance has always been capable of innovation to improve its political strategy, even when it seemed to be stuck in the mud or on some slippery slope to disaster. The alliance was most divided in 1956, when the United States split from Britain and France over the Suez crisis. In its wake came the Wise Men's Report, commissioned by several NATO ministers, which greatly broadened NATO's scope.

A decade later, in 1967, Pierre Harmel, the foreign minister of Belgium, initiated the report that bears his name. This report helped cope with the crisis precipitated by French withdrawal from the military command and de Gaulle's rush towards détente. De Gaulle had truly split the alliance at its military heart, and the timely Harmel Report defined the fundamental approach that was to guide NATO's efforts for the next two decades and balance NATO's policies between détente and defense.

In place of de Gaulle's inference that a military alliance was no longer needed, the report noted that NATO's fundamental task is to "maintain adequate military strength and political solidarity to deter aggression and other forms of pressure and to defend the territory of member countries if aggression should occur." It described the need for a suitable military capability to ensure the balance of forces in Europe and to create a climate of stability and confidence.

The report then addressed NATO's second task: "to pursue the search for progress toward a more stable relationship in which underlying political issues can be solved. Military security and a policy of détente are not contradictory but complementary."[1] Indeed, this was the essence of de Gaulle's more far-reaching formulation: "from détente to entente and cooperation."

For Europeans and Americans, however, the very word *détente* took on different connotations. In the United States, support for the word itself and the approach it connoted reached its peak when Nixon and Kissinger concluded the 1972 Accords and the first Strategic Arms Limitation Treaty (SALT I) with Moscow. Détente, however, came under massive political attack from critics such as the Committee on the Present Danger, created by citizens with governmental experience who felt that the United States was being lulled into letting down its guard. During the 1976 presidential primary campaign, candidate Reagan attacked President Ford on this score, and a defensive Ford announced that he had struck the word *détente* from his vocabulary. For Americans of the Reagan school, the negative connotations of the word lived on, and Reagan's term of preference once in office became "constructive dialogue."

At the December 1983 Foreign Ministers Meeting, Leo Tindemans, the Belgian foreign minister, proposed that the perm reps study what had happened in the ups and downs of East-West relations since the Harmel Report of 1967. They would report to the foreign ministers in late May with their findings and recommendations. There would be a stormy period ahead, and Tindemans wanted to ensure that there was a common NATO line and effort, especially since the

Soviets would now be inviting individual ministers to Moscow in an effort to split the alliance.

The real work on this four-month study was done by what is known at NATO Headquarters as the Senior Political Committee. My political counselor on this committee was Robert Frowick, a Foreign Service officer who lived and breathed alliance politics, relished NATO's political give and take, and fought over every word, sometimes upping the ante so as to get a better compromise. Frowick successfully argued the need to examine the East-West balance realistically and over the long term. We needed to recognize the implications of the Soviet military buildup, their willingness to exploit any apparent NATO weaknesses, and their practice of using either pressure, as in Poland, or outright military intervention, as in Afghanistan. I might add that all representatives agreed it was very important to analyze the ferment taking place within Eastern Europe and its profound meaning for the Western alliance.

This East-West study of some forty pages was the backdrop of the Spring 1984 Foreign Ministers Meeting in Washington. These meetings, known as the "Ministerial," were divided between an open plenary session in Washington and, on the request of Secretary Shultz, an informal, "super-restricted" session at Wye Plantation outside of Washington where only the foreign ministers and ambassadors from each nation would be present. On our side, that made me the hand-cramped notetaker for about six hours. Wye was deluged with rain and despite the fact that the helicopter with Secretary-General Luns and other notables could not get off the ground, the "Ministerial" did. The ministers used the study as the basis for issuing a memorable Statement on East-West Relations.

This was an excellent political strategy document. The basic premises of the Harmel Report were reinforced, but there was also a new emphasis: that realism, strength, and cohesion come first, and a more stable relationship between East and West based on dialogue and cooperation would follow. The document went on to say that this could "only be fruitful if each party is confident of its security. . . ."[2] The point for our political strategy making is this: our diplomatic efforts with the Soviets, including arms control, cannot be truly successful without NATO's first shoring up its defense posture and maintaining political cohesion. Alliance dialogue and defense are both necessary and interdependent, but they are not equal. Adequate military strength along with political cohesion are fundamental pre-requisites for building a more stable East-West relationship.

The Washington Statement, little reported in the press, represented a basis of understanding for launching a constructive East-West dialogue in the latter 1980s. It gave NATO a unified political strategy at a time when it faced the grim and unpopular task of deploying cruise and Pershing II missiles. At the same time, it opened up new ways of reinvigorating the East-West dialogue. The groundwork was laid for the dramatic increase in East-West dialogue that began in 1985—from the Shultz-Gromyko breakthrough talks that January, and the subsequent launching of the Geneva nuclear and space talks, to President Reagan's November summit with the new general secretary, Gorbachev.

As I noted, Tindemans' purpose in launching the study that gave birth to the Washington Statement was to keep the allies together on policy toward the East. His accent on unity was to pay off. An open and persuasive Vice President George Bush visited the NATO council and alliance capitals. When President Reagan followed up his Geneva talks with Gorbachev by meeting with allied leaders at Brussels, veteran Italian Foreign Minister Andreotti was to declare that the alliance's consultative process had never been so good. Alliance political consultations were at a high point—a compliment to Joseph Luns and Leo Tindemans, to Richard Burt with his Special Consultative Group, and, above all, to the Reagan administration for maintaining unprecedentedly close communications with the five NATO nations in deploying the Euromissiles in the face of political opposition. The two-track strategy of negotiations and deployment had to be harmonized, and it was handled with great skill on both sides of the alliance. NATO's political strategy was working. In subsequent chapters, I will explain why the surprising nature of the Reagan-Gorbachev Reykjavík summit so upset this truly brilliant period in NATO political strategy.

Lord Carrington arrived at NATO a month after the 1984 Washington meeting. His first love was the political process. "After all," he was fond of saying, "NATO *is* a political alliance." However, I do not believe that Carrington, in his desire to reinforce NATO as a political alliance, fully appreciated what had just been accomplished in what I call "Harmel Revisited." Carrington is not someone given to political theories or abstract thought. There were also doubts by some in the

U.S. Defense Department and even Atlanticists in Europe as to whether Carrington would be able to keep the U.S. connection healthy. In the Conservative party, he was classified as a "wet," that is, a bit liberal, and more pro-European than pro-American, as compared to Margaret Thatcher, who nevertheless had a deep affection for the charming Peter Carrington.

The overriding objective of Carrington's mentor, Prime Minister Harold Macmillan, had been to take the United Kingdom into Europe. As Defence Minister in the 1970s, Carrington gave a priority to Europe rather than to British global commitments. No doubt this European orientation influenced his approach to the Falkland Islands war, which brought about his resignation as foreign secretary in 1982. In an uncomplimentary biography that appeared just as Carrington became secretary-general, Patrick Cosgrave[3] forecast deep problems resulting from Carrington's European tilt. Cosgrave's forecast turned out to be quite wrong, and this became clear through Carrington's energetic reaction to the Nunn amendment and his careful posture during the Libyan raid.

In his initial year, Carrington was much more worried than I about a possible U.S. backlash from upgrading the Western European Union (WEU) or other such European institutions. Only after the shock of the Reykjavík negotiations did he begin to take more seriously the urgent need for a more cohesive European defense identity in the revitalization of the WEU. If Carrington tried to be impartial, he had a fundamental understanding: the alliance could not lose the United States, either its president or its Congress. Regardless of what mistakes the U.S. president or Congress might make, Carrington saw the American commitment as central to NATO's political strategy.

The thorniest question of all was the Strategic Defense Initiative (SDI). In congratulating the Atlantic alliance on consultations, Andreotti politely overlooked the introduction of SDI by President Reagan in March 1983. SDI had been introduced without any prior consultation with the allies. I quipped that Europeans should not be put off by lack of alliance consultation on SDI since the president had not even consulted members of his own administration. It was not just SDI that bothered Europeans, but the implication in the president's pronouncement that Mutual Assured Destruction (MAD)—a key to NATO's concept of nuclear deterrence—was out of date and even immoral. During the Kennedy and Carter administrations, there were suspicions in Europe that these liberal Democrats were at heart soft on nuclear weapons. But never in their wildest dreams would they have suspected concern over such morality from a Republican hawk like Reagan.

What did this new initiative mean to NATO strategy? At the 1985 Lisbon Foreign Ministers Meeting, there were rumblings among some European ministers about the need for formal consultations on "NATO strategy," in particular the effects of SDI on the strategy of flexible response. I had instructions from Washington to block any such initiative, and I faithfully did so for over a year. I argued, first, that SDI was a research program and we did not know whether it would work; and, second, hypocritically, that allies certainly did not want to see any questioning of flexible response. In the next ministerial go-round, a logical George Shultz began to think that an examination of NATO strategy would be wise. I had to whisper to him that Washington—the NSC, the Pentagon, even his department—wanted to avoid it. There was a basic, publicly unstated reason. Washington, the Pentagon in particular, had not thoroughly studied SDI's implications on strategy. We had not yet done our homework and such a study might prove embarrassing.

That this work had not been done was not due to a lack of ability and talent. Some brilliant strategic minds served within the administration: Paul Nitze, guru of strategic planning since the dawn of the nuclear age; Dr. Fred Ikle, long-time RAND Corporation analyst; intellectually restless Richard Perle; and a range of bright military officers. It was a tragedy that there was not the capacity within our compartmentalized NSC process to bring together such minds into an effective team. They could have defined the way ahead and joined the United States in genuine dialogue with the Europeans through the NATO Council, the DPC, and the Military Committees.

The lack of systematic strategic analysis was to cost the United States dearly, and this cost came to the fore in the devastating aftermath of the October 1986 Reykjavík summit. In the week prior to the summit, I had followed instructions and assured my fellow ambassadors that Reykjavík was, in reality, a meeting to talk about a meeting. Midway through the summit I received a call from Reykjavík with an update on what was transpiring there: proposals for 50 percent strategic missile reductions, maybe eventually 100 percent, and for the zero agreement on INF and so forth. The focus was not on a future summit after all, but on a deep cut in strategic weapons. I phoned Carrington with this bombshell and, when he finally adjusted, I phoned back to announce that SDI had been a sticking point and the summit had fallen apart. Gorbachev and his spokesmen charged that the meeting had broken down because of U.S. intransigence on SDI.

Meanwhile, President Reagan, the eternal optimist, publicly claimed the many successes of the meeting and the desire to continue to talk. However, the morning newscast and newspaper headlines all over Europe bought the Gorbachev line, in contrast to Reagan's, and reported the meeting as a failure—even a "fiasco," putting blame squarely on Reagan. Stories circulated about a serious breakdown in superpower relations, and there was an atmosphere of dismay even at NATO Headquarters.

Early on a Monday morning, October 14, I met with George Shultz, who had flown in to brief a hastily summoned group of NATO foreign ministers on the outcome of the meeting. Possessed of a remarkable physical stamina, Shultz was again fully composed, after the obvious dejection he had shown earlier on television from Reykjavík. He told me that we had not capitulated to Soviet demands just to get an agreement, as "some" national security advisers and secretaries of state had done in the past.

At the NATO Council briefing, Shultz was solid, methodical, and unruffled. After a round of comments and questions by all ministers, Carrington pulled a tour de force in the propaganda war with the Soviets. The difficult French always insisted that no communiqué be issued after such political consultations. Carrington got around their flank by saying that, "with the approval of the Council," he would do a bit of his own summing up. He did just that minutes later for the press. He expressed the warm appreciation of the Council to President Reagan for his efforts at Reykjavík and to George Shultz for his briefing, and he called for follow-up discussions in other negotiating fora. Slapping hard at the Soviet position of linkage, he pointedly said, "We also felt that the opportunity to make progress in some areas should not be made hostage to difficulties in other unrelated ones."

At their own press conferences, NATO foreign ministers refused to describe the summit as a failure, and none criticized Reagan. Before the meeting West German Foreign Minister Genscher had told the press that Reykjavík's failure could lead to a major setback in East-

West relations. Now he changed his emphasis. In the European press, these remarks turned the tide.

Within two days, this show of NATO unity had forced an adroit Gorbachev to change his tune, cease blaming the Americans, and join in talk about the successes of Reykjavík. Gorbachev said that he was keeping the door open for a follow-up. Obviously, the Soviet Union was deeply frustrated at its inability to exploit divisions in the Atlantic alliance after the Reykjavík summit.

Meanwhile, on the eve of the Defense Ministers Meeting in Gleneagles, Scotland, dissention was resurfacing. My own nuclear policy advisers John Reichart and Robert Watters worked until the early morning hours to convince the NATO communiqué-drafting group to accept the language that Weinberger felt Reagan needed. Carrington was supportive throughout, with the result that an even stronger pro-American declaration emerged.

Behind this rally-round, however, the Europeans were beginning to seethe with the recognition that first SDI and then the hasty Reykjavík meeting were undercutting both NATO's military and political strategies. An increasing number of ministers were determined to study the military implications. Their security was at stake, including their concept of what constituted nuclear deterrence, and the Americans seemed to be negotiating over their heads. After much haggling and negotiation, it was finally agreed that the Military Committee, not the DPC or the NATO Council, would do an assessment that would appear to be routine, with little publicity.

We were truly reaching a watershed in NATO consultations. NATO's unity was preserved only by Carrington's deft helmsmanship in high seas, and the former First Lord of the Admiralty deserved another medal for valor. But Gorbachev was playing a clever game. He had been outdone by Ronald Reagan at the first Geneva meeting, in personality and certainly in public reaction. On the Reykjavík go-round, Gorbachev had laid a trap to lure the unprepared Americans into a sweeping renegotiation for which he was totally prepared. As Europeans really studied what had happened they began to tell me with tongue in check that they had finally swung around to my view and become believers in SDI. They felt that Reagan's intransigence had saved them from eliminating the nuclear weapons they had deployed with such political sweat and blood.

In a hardly charitable line, Christopher Bertram, for eight years head of the London-based International Institute for Strategic Studies, wrote, "The realization is gaining ground that a Western Europe that wants to be taken seriously politically will have to address not just the problems of the common economy but that of common security as well." Together with the European consensus against the Reagan administration's recklessness in Reykjavík, this was "beginning to concentrate European minds." He went on to say that if there is one common implication in the challenges now confronting the alliance, "it is the need for a more concerted European effort, conceptual as well as material."[4]

What happened over the ensuing months was that the big European powers began to split over nuclear negotiating strategy. The British and the French felt any talk by Reagan about returning to zero all strategic nuclear missiles was devastating, since ultimately this could lead to the loss of their deterrent. The Germans had no such problems, but resented being left with short-range battlefield nuclear weapons that could hit only Germany. The lack of an in-depth NATO strategy study was increasingly evident in an alliance in nuclear disarray. What Brezhnev had not achieved by brandishing SS-20 missiles—divisions in the alliance—a far more skilled Gorbachev was achieving through his clever negotiating strategy.

Again, however, the NATO machinery and a deft Peter Carrington partially put Humpty-Dumpty back together again. Whatever private concerns they may have harbored about the way things had been done in Iceland, ministers as politicians began to recognize the unparalled feat of eliminating all SS-20 missiles, that after all, this was to be the end objective of the two track decision and that European support was important for Senate ratification. NATO then issued communiqué after communiqué giving ringing endorsements to help in ratification. The March 1988 NATO summit communiqué said: "The recently concluded INF agreement between the U.S. and the Soviet Union is a milestone in our efforts to achieve a more secure peace and lower levels of arms."[5]

Christopher Bertram, however, had put his finger on what post-Reykjavík truly meant: the need for a more independent Europe. But the question was how to develop a political strategy that would enable Europe to truly become a second pillar.

So many Americans argued that withdrawing some U.S. forces would help to foster that European identity. My assessment in this book of the challenges of the 1990s makes clear why I reject this notion of encouragement through withdrawal. Our political strategy, I believe, must call for a recommitment to Europe. The two-pillar concept of transatlantic alliance must become the keystone of our political strategy, and it must be based upon mutual commitment and mutual security.

The first priority of the new president of the United States in 1989 should be to fully support a two-pillar approach within the alliance. This should be done in the form of a joint resolution of the Congress. As President Reagan wisely said at CSIS in December 1987: "the Alliance must become more and more an alliance among equals—indeed, an alliance between two continents."[6] Certainly the new president should join in a NATO summit soon after his inauguration. But a work program and an action plan are needed. The deputy foreign and defense ministers, along with the military chiefs of staff, should be put to work in regular NATO Council meetings to work out better formulas for consultation on strategy.

Are there other reforms that should be considered in creating a West-West political strategy? I reject a one-time Kissinger suggestion that NATO's secretary-general should be an American in return for a European SACEUR. Plainly, everything possible should be done to avoid the "over-Americanization" of the leadership of the alliance. I believe a U.S. secretary-general would do more harm than good. However, I would encourage the idea of a European SACEUR if the French were willing to return to the integrated command. The link to the U.S. nuclear chain of command could be through a U.S. deputy or chief of staff. Wherever possible, NATO-based committees, such as the Special Consultative Group that was chaired by Richard Burt, or the High Level Group chaired by Richard Perle, should be given European leadership. The European chairman of the Military Committee has become more visible recently, and this is an important step forward. But it is essential that such moves be made without any U.S. disengagement of troops, ideas, or people.

The U.S. presence has helped prevent war and Americans can greatly encourage European initiatives toward unity. I believe we must commit ourselves to NATO at the highest level. The new president should raise his NATO ambassador to cabinet rank, as is done with the U.N. ambassador, and have a person of that stature always at

NATO. That ambassador's clout with the State and Defense departments, with the NSC, and even more important, with the Congress would be enhanced, and the Europeans would know it. Such imaginative measures are absolutely essential as NATO makes its transition to a two-pillared alliance. We mustn't play the game of those whose strategy is to separate the United States from Europe, or indeed foster an America that is hovering on the brink of withdrawal from Europe.

As part of the effort to build a strong European pillar of NATO, the defense-related institutions of Europe should be upgraded and reinvigorated. The Western European Union is clearly first among these. Formed under the 1948 Brussels Treaty, its importance was soon allowed to lapse. During the modernization of INF in the early 1980s, however, the WEU was partially revitalized. It is generally perceived that the exclusion of Norway, Denmark, Turkey, and Greece is an advantage: Norway and Denmark do not allow nuclear weapons on their soil; Denmark has become a so-called footnote nation, which does not take positions in NATO communiqués commensurate with its allies; and Turkey and Greece are beset by quarrels. For these reasons, the WEU's expansion should be very deliberate. At the same time, its liaison with NATO should be increased, as its present secretary-general and great Atlanticist, Alfred Cahen, has tried to do. Toward this end, the WEU Perm Reps would be better located in Brussels, as compared to London, where they are today, and, indeed, might be the same ambassadors serving at NATO.

Ultimately, a political strategy for creating a healthy, two-pillared alliance requires both creativity on the part of individual nations and also a collective commitment. There must be harmony between America and Europe, but it is equally important that harmony exist *within* Europe. It is up to the Europeans themselves to bring about a degree of political cooperation among themselves. The European Community is composed of twelve very separate nations, and few people wish for a United States of Europe modeled after America. Nevertheless, it is not too much to hope that there can be progress toward political unity in Europe, in the same way as the Common Market was established. There is, however, opposition to the idea. Convinced "Europeans" like Roy Jenkins fight a losing battle in a country like Britain, which has always been reluctant to get involved in close political cooperation with its European neighbors. Mrs. Thatcher's government is no exception in this respect, and it is essential that the traditional hostility to the idea be overcome. The greatest single thing that would enhance deterrence and ensure the prevention of World War III is a unified Europe with a GNP greater than the Soviets and comparable to that of the United States.

West-West political strategy must also encompass partnership with parliaments and the U.S. Congress, otherwise this two-pillared unity cannot come about or be sustained. The North Atlantic Assembly is the only interparliamentary consultative body in which elected representatives of the United States, Canada, and their Western allies meet regularly to discuss issues of collective deterrence, defense, and international cooperation. The assembly seeks to provide dialogue and mutual education of legislators and also to have direct influence on public and parliamentary opinion. By far the biggest problem has been that U.S. congressional delegations have not been broadly representative of the full Congress. On the European side, delegate quality varies: toward the top are Norway, Germany, Spain, and—interestingly enough—France, where the Chirac government had the chairman of the Defense Committee attend, and where the former Socialist defense ministers are also active.

The brightest spot of all is a new study—Senator Charles Mathias's last legacy as president of the assembly—entitled "NATO in the 1990s: Towards a New Transatlantic Bargain."[7] The chairman of this study is the Republican senator from Delaware, Bill Roth, whose farsighted interest in government procurement and allied cooperation has made a deep mark in Congress.

The study of a panel of fourteen parliamentarians calls for a new political mandate to be adopted at a 1989 meeting of NATO heads of government, building on the Harmel Report and "a real West European pillar in the alliance." It has some refreshingly practical and forward-looking recommendations, such as to develop "routine meetings of the military Chiefs of Staff of West European NATO governments and establish a computerized communications network linking planning staffs in European defense ministries to foster more thorough military cooperation at the European level."[8]

We have outlined West-West political strategy within NATO. Now we turn to West-East political strategy for NATO. It must be kept in mind that most West-East diplomacy is conducted bilaterally. NATO's role is limited to encouraging as much West-West cooperation as possible. It is, therefore, all the more remarkable when NATO steps beyond these normal bounds. Few issues have been more difficult to approach than the ongoing East-West dialogue on human rights, the prospects for liberalization in the Soviet Union, and the role that U.S. and allied policy should play in promoting movement in these areas. How are these sensitive issues to be incorporated into our East-West political strategy?

Henry Kissinger's first book, based on his Harvard dissertation, dealt with the nineteenth-century diplomatic triumph at the Congress of Vienna, which fostered the Concert of Europe. Stability and maintaining the status quo—not human rights and democracy— were the aim. However, this became the foundation for peace in Europe. Kissinger aimed to build such a structure with the 1972 Washington-Moscow Accord. He always felt that the Jackson-Vanik amendment, along with Watergate, undermined the accords and linkages established at the 1972 Moscow summit. That human rights amendment made the granting of "most favored nation" trade status for the Soviet Union dependent upon increased emigration of Soviet Jews. This was the first major dramatic foray, an ad hoc one, of the Congress into the domain of political strategy on human rights. Congress acted on its own, cutting across Henry Kissinger's concert with the Soviet Union, which left such diplomatic initiatives to "quiet diplomacy." No complete strategy—truly integrated and balanced—can emerge from such ad hoc initiatives, regardless of their individual value. But the amendment did focus attention on the need for our strategy to deal with "people" issues as well as security and economic ones.

Despite congressional diplomatic method, the amendment did have an effect. Soviet Jewish emigration rose to 35,000 by 1973.[9] However, the Soviets placed an "exit tax" on such emigration. More generally, the Soviet Union in these détente years of 1972–73 was filled with certain glaring human rights abuses, stomping out rabbinical education, repressing the Anabaptists in the Ukraine and the Roman Catholics in Lithuania, and intimidating even world figures such as Nobel Laureate Aleksandr Solzhenitsyn and nuclear scientist Andrey Sakharov.

In 1974, my membership on the Murphy Commission brought me to Moscow, where I was to review how our embassies were operating. Our Moscow political counselor, Warren Zimmerman, gave a dinner party at his apartment. He invited some of the younger members of the Central Committee. Before I left the United States, Senator Jackson had phoned me and said that, as someone recently out of government but in close touch with the White House and the Congress, I was in an ideal position to raise the issue of denied emigration for the Panov couple of the Kirov Ballet Company.

I discovered, however, that there were bigger fish to fry. Just before dinner, Zimmerman took me aside. He explained that Solzhenitsyn had just been arrested a couple of blocks away and the Soviets weren't aware that we knew about it. He asked me to let him know right away if I heard them make any reference to it. In my conversation with one very engaging Central Committee member, he asked why the West was upset about a few dissidents, whereas 35,000 Jews had emigrated. Where was the balanced perspective? Some people in Congress must simply be against an accord between our two countries and prefer the Cold War instead.

"You are not talking about a few minor dissidents," I replied, "but about world-renowned writers and artists, known to the liberal press in America. Your policies have succeeded in creating this ruckus and generating criticism even more from Western liberals than conservatives. Take the Panov case. A senator phoned me just before I left Washington to ask that I raise it. Why spoil your record on the 35,000 who have departed with an exit tax, and by these other denials? Ironically, Russian writers and performers are at the top of world recognition. Did you know that Aleksandr Solzhenitsyn's book is now at the top of the best-seller list of the *New York Times*?"

There was a dead silence.

The next day our chargé in Moscow (we were between ambassadors), "Spike" Dubs, held a small lunch for me with the ubiquitous Dr. Georgi Arbatov and his strategic specialist. Over cocktails, Dubs said to Arbatov: "I have just heard that Solzhenitsyn is to be stripped of his citizenship and expelled. Solzhenitsyn does not want to leave his beloved Mother Russia. That is pretty severe—what was done to Trotsky—to take away his citizenship."

"Oh," Arbatov rolled his eyes, "I can think of things far worse than that." He was referring, I guess, to Siberia. "Solzhenitsyn wanted his Calvary. We denied him martyrdom. He will now go to the West. He will be *your* political problem."

The dramatic ouster of Aleksandr Solzhenitsyn captured the imagination and indignation of the West and inflamed East-West attitudes all the more. When President Ford turned down a meeting with the Russian writer at the White House, Ford was widely criticized in the Congress by far more people than Senator Jackson. Arbatov's forecast had come true. This political blunder put Ford and Kissinger on the defensive during the Republican primary with Governor Reagan and in the campaign with Governor Jimmy Carter.

If the 1972 Moscow Accords did not effectively help in developing an East-West political strategy that incorporated human rights, another multinational summit certainly did. It is quite ironic that in these tumultuous political days, when human rights and détente spurred such domestic debate in the United States, there took place a remarkable summit in Helsinki. After two long years of negotiations at the Conference on Security and Cooperation in Europe (CSCE), there was a summit of thirty-five heads of government to review and sign the conference's final document. There was a debate within the Ford administration about whether the president should attend what critics branded a "Second Yalta" or, even worse, a final legitimizing of Soviet rule over Eastern Europe. A defensive White House began to emphasize that the meeting's final document would not be a treaty but a nonbinding agreement.

The whole scene—indeed, the entire game plan—was deeply ironic. From the 1950s onward, the Soviet game indeed had been to have a conference on "European security" without the United States. The so-called neutral and nonaligned countries of Europe (Finland, Sweden, Austria, Ireland, Liechtenstein, Malta, Monaco, San Marino, Holy See, Switzerland, Yugoslavia) were to be included. But the European members of NATO were not duped into contributing to the basic strategy of separating Western Europe from the United States and Canada. They insisted that the North Americans be included. They also demanded that the status of Berlin be legitimized because the Soviets had insisted since the Berlin crisis of the early 1960s that the city was an integral part of East Germany.

Leonid Brezhnev was so anxious finally to have this conference that he gave in on these two demands. His strategy was to push what he called at the 24th Party Congress in 1971 his Party's "peace program." His aim was "to proceed from the final recognition of the territorial changes that took place in Europe as a result of the Second World War." He wanted this summit conference as a feather in his cap before the 25th Party Congress planned for early 1976. He would then be the Soviet leader that ratified the existence of what amounted to the Soviet Empire. That was just the point on which Scoop Jackson, Ronald Reagan, Jimmy Carter, and the right wing were focusing; and President Ford, who had decided to drop the word *détente* from his vocabulary, was understandably sheepish about attending. Presidential candidate Ronald Reagan on July 25, 1975, said of the proposed accords, "I am against it, and I think all Americans should be against it."[10]

The bullish West Europeans deeply wanted the conference and developed a more coordinated and comprehensive political strategy than the confused United States. Early on, the Soviets paid a price—the Berlin agreement— for the CSCE process and the Helsinki meeting. For them and others, the Soviet insistence on language about the inviolability of frontiers and "non-intervention in internal affairs of other nations"—code words for Soviet hegemony over Eastern Europe—was a fact of military power anyway. Moreover, they thought this might be more than balanced by the opening of frontiers, that historic Iron Curtain. If present borders were "stabilized," at least in the suspicious Soviet mind, they could be opened to an increasing flow of human exchanges and varied communications. This could all lead toward freer movement of people, ideas, and information. Such was the dream, the hope, the vision of many Western Europeans in a divided Europe.

There were three parts, or so-called baskets, to the Helsinki Agreement. The first basket related to "security in Europe," including military measures to build mutual confidence between the two sides and other aspects of security and disarmament. Out of this basket came the Stockholm Conference on Disarmament in Europe, discussed in the chapter on negotiations. The second basket related to cooperation in the fields of economics, science and technology, and the environment. The all-important third basket—humanitarian cooperation—was added at the insistence of the Western European nations, Finland, and interestingly enough, Yugoslavia. There were provisions on family reunification and visits, binational marriages, increased cultural and educational exchanges, and improved working conditions.

As the so-called Helsinki process developed over the coming years, the position of the NATO countries was coordinated at NATO

Headquarters, with NATO ambassadors meeting together with representatives to the CSCE. A clear political strategy emerged, and it came to be termed "balance in the Helsinki process." The Soviets constantly wanted to stress the first basket, "security," where they could float new but one-sided arms-control proposals and downgrade or sweep under the rug the embarrassing provisions of the third basket, which they had signed and apparently hoped everyone would forget. However, "Helsinki watches" sprang up, even in Communist countries, to monitor each government's compliance with all aspects of the agreement. The U.S. Congress officially set up its own commission to report on compliance.

This systematization of human rights discussions illustrates how far U.S. diplomacy with the Soviets has progressed since the early 1970s. George Shultz goes to Moscow and includes a visit with Dr. Sakharov, in contrast to a Ford White House that was afraid to receive Solzhenitsyn. President Reagan meets with dissidents at his Moscow summit. The Soviets do not break off negotiations. At every bilateral summit of Reagan and Gorbachev and at meetings of foreign ministers, human rights are on the agenda. Plainly, it has been made a systematic part of U.S. bilateral diplomacy and NATO multistate diplomacy in ways scarcely imagined in the early 1970s. President Ronald Reagan, on May 27, 1988, speaking in Helsinki on his way to the Moscow summit, put it very well: the thirteen-year-old Helsinki process had succeeded in setting "new standards of conduct" in human rights and international security. It "grapples with the full range of our underlying differences and deals with East-West relations as an interrelated whole."[11]

Between the Harmel doctrine as revised by the Perm Reps in 1984 and the CSCE Helsinki process, the West has finally developed a rather extraordinary political strategy. This strategy is certainly responsible in part for the political change taking place within the Soviet Union and Eastern Europe today. We have been doing some things quite right.

13 Public Strategy

AN effective public strategy for the United States, the industrial democracies, and Third World democracies must be constructed on the truth.

This, of course, flies in the face of traditional diplomacy, about which it was once quipped by a British diplomat that "an ambassador is an honest man sent abroad to lie for his country." Traditional diplomacy was at its peak, following the bloodletting of the French Revolution and the upheaval of the Napoleonic wars. Stability, rather than truth or freedom, was given highest priority. This is the customary excuse for those keeping silent in the face of human rights abuses.

Today, the nineteenth century method of secrecy is difficult even in totalitarian societies, so great is the power of mass communications in an information age. Especially in democracies, political strategy must be not only understood but endorsed by political leaders and their constituents. Short, decisive actions in the fields of diplomacy or the military are still possible without initial broad support. But over the long haul, majority public support, if not consensus, is needed.

At the heart of the construction of a public strategy must be the element of credibility. No short-term Madison Avenue approach can make up for it in the long term. Policies must be explained and communicated with all the advantages available, as Roosevelt did with his remarkable radio style or Reagan with his television manner. But long-term policies must have credibility and legitimacy. Communication is the key to achieving this, because we must have a coherent strategy to communicate that truth and that legitmacy.

Access to information is at the heart of public strategy. As part of the Helsinki Agreement, the signatories pledged themselves to make information more fully available, even though the Soviets tried to hedge their specific commitments on this point. Free access to information goes to the heart of the censorship problem. Robert Frowick was the State Department backup negotiator for the U.S. delegation and was constantly pushing for recognition of the rights of international broadcasting. We won. The Soviets conceded in language, and the Helsinki Final Act recognized the importance of mutual dissemination of information and "the essential and influential role of the press, radio, television, cinema, and news agencies and of the journalists working in these fields."[1] When East-West relations worsened in the early 1980s, the Soviets resumed the Communist practice of jamming broadcasts by the Voice of America (VOA) and certain other radio stations. But the international reach of Cable News Network (CNN), and other efforts emanating from Italy and elsewhere are indicative of the momentum building in the private sector. It will soon take a quantum jump with the advent of European direct broadcast satellites whose "footprints" blur national and political boundaries.

As the first chairman of the U.S. Board for International Broadcasting, I had learned to appreciate the extraordinary role of international broadcasting and eventually wrote a small book on the subject.[2] BBC External Service, Radio Canada International, Deutsche Welle, and Voice of America were all stations that broadcast the news and the best of their nation's culture to Eastern Europe and elsewhere. Radio Liberty's broadcasting to the Soviet Union and Radio Free Europe's broadcasting to Eastern Europe were different: they were, in effect, surrogate home services that—through external research and information as well as access to collections of *samizdat*, or underground literature—were able to broadcast back to these countries what was truly happening there. The British Broadcasting Corporation (BBC) External Service and Deutsche Welle (DW), which are independent of the governments that fund them, also have a role in this area, though a more limited one. The cumulative effect, however, of these external broadcasting stations on listening audiences starved for credible information is enormous.

As for Radio Liberty (RL) and Radio Free Europe (RFE), the CIA had set up and secretly funded these two stations in the 1950s. For the 1950s, when the radios needed to be hurriedly set up, this was a necessary covert operation, but it stayed covert too long. As the CIA connection became suspected in the early 1970s, Senator Clifford Case questioned their secret funding and abruptly introduced a bill requiring open funding. Senator Bill Fulbright called the stations "relics of the Cold War," advocated that they be abolished, and introduced a bill that appropriated only enough funding to close them down. A fierce battle ensued in the Congress. In the Senate-House Conference, antagonisms became so great that pro-RFE/RL chairman of the House Committee, "Doc" Morgan, and his House conferees refused to meet again with Fulbright.

As assistant secretary of state for congressional relations at the time, I called on Senate Majority Leader Mike Mansfield. I knew he had deep reservations about the two stations and that it was wrong, indeed tragic, that the CIA funding was continued so long in secret. But it wasn't right to have them die because of the impossible Senate-House problem and personality conflicts.

The majority leader agreed and asked Carl Marcy (chief of staff of the Senate Foreign Relations Committee) to start working to get a compromise paper. It worked. Morgan accepted a compromise plan and legislation was passed. The stations were placed under the State Department for a year while an outside panel of experts studied the future of the stations. Despite his opposition, Mike Mansfield's sense of fairness had saved them.

President Eisenhower's brother, Dr. Milton Eisenhower, was appointed chairman of the panel. Its principal recommendation was to set up a public oversight board modeled after that of the BBC. Their report[3] also validated the radio stations' vital role as a surrogate home service for the closed countries of the communist bloc. Radio Free Europe had done so well with some of its research and analysis that its economist on Poland had predicted the country's meat shortage before the Polish government did. Survey research showed that in the course of a month about half the adult population of Eastern Europe listened to the news, commentary, and programs of RFE, and perhaps 30 to 35 million Soviet citizens listened to Radio Liberty in the course of a month.[4] I began to call them "Radio Human Rights" and even suggested they be renamed.

Later, President Ford asked me to become the first chairman of the new Board for International Broadcasting. I was forced to think through the subject of "public strategy," at least in the areas of international broadcasting. As chairman, I visited not only the RFE and RL operations in Munich but all of their external facilities. I became enthralled by what all this meant as a new dimension of diplomacy: people-to-people diplomacy. The radio stations were counteracting the censorship, indoctrination, and propaganda of communist governments, as well as the inbred suspicion of the "capitalists" supposedly out to destroy them.

In his book *1984*, George Orwell described how the Thought Police and the Ministry of Truth would not only suppress any intellectual opposition but also transform human beings into computerlike, programmed, easily manipulated creatures. An expert MIT professor, Ithiel del Sola Pool, said that the full realization of *1984* had been prevented largely because of international communications and, above all, because of international radio.[5]

As board chairman I testified four times a year before different congressional committees. One well-meaning congressman would always ask me, "How are your propaganda stations doing?" I would recite again our litany: truth is our weapon. Unlike Dr. Goebbels in Hitler's Third Reich, or Radio Peace and Progress out of Moscow, RFE, RL, VOA, and BBC External Service do not need to slant the news. The highest standards of journalism are our objective, for it is this which gives these stations so much more credibility in Communist Europe than the local state-controlled stations.

The importance of these radio stations is not limited to our people-to-people diplomacy; they are also an intimate element of our national security.[6] Solzhenitsyn, in his Nobel Prize lecture, said aptly, "blocking of information makes international signatures and treaties unreal; within the zone of stunned silence any treaty can easily be reinterpreted at will."[7] These radio stations can also be crucial in crisis management, so that the peoples of the Soviet Union and Eastern Europe are not driven to a state of fear and manipulated by the communist apparatus. In short, for a range of reasons, international broadcasting is a key dimension of our public strategy.

The Western radio stations must be upgraded, refurbished, and better coordinated. In fact, U.S. international communications policy must become more coherent and comprehensive. An indefatigable leader determined to reach this goal is the extraordinarily effective congressman from South Florida, Dante Fascell, now the chairman of the House Foreign Affairs Committee. In 1976, in the wake of considerable Soviet backsliding, he led Congress to create a U.S. commission to monitor and encourage compliance with all the provisions of the Helsinki Final Act. A grand strategist of communications policy, he has called for a presidential council on international communications and information policy to serve as an advisory group, not only to the president but to Congress and the private sector as well.[8] In the executive branch, Zbigniew Brzezinski was the most knowledgeable champion of international broadcasting and he was able to greatly interest President Carter in the subject. Truly, the rescue and reformation of RFE and RL, as well as VOA, have been exemplary efforts that have cut across party and ideological lines.

Only part of our public strategy, however, deals with the other superpower, its people, and the countries under its hegemony. The other part must deal with non-Communist world public opinion and particularly the battleground of ideas in Western Europe. In early 1983 I was asked to go as ambassador into the European arena where philosophers, ideologues, theologians, and politicians had drawn each others' intellectual blood for centuries. This was the stormy year of the Euromissile deployment, and the Kremlin was seeking to split European opinion.

Soon after my arrival I was blessed with an inquisitive and imaginative public affairs adviser, Stan Burnett, who went on to the top career position as counselor at the United States Information Agency. He collaborated with Mike Moodie to plot our public strategy for all of Europe. Mike was to initiate a program of bringing together at NATO the defense intellectual and political science elites—the heads of the various think tanks throughout Europe. We would work with other missions to initiate conferences interrelating economic and security affairs; we would reach out even to religious groups and the peace movement; we would start our own pamphlet series making the case for NATO and do this in conjunction with the Atlantic Council in Washington so they would have U.S. distribution as well;[9] we would initiate speeches all over Europe calling for improvements in conventional defense and armaments cooperation. We would reach agreement with the public affairs officers at our embassies in the NATO area on a common set of public affairs goals on security issues and start a vigorous program of regional work that would include sending small groups of European journalists to Washington for two-week programs on topics such as SDI and the conventional-weapons balance. A new consensus had to be built in an alliance all too split over nuclear questions.

This entire effort was funded as a part of the U.S. Information Service program for Europe. We had to make up for what NATO, as an international organization, could not do. NATO itself labored under a severe handicap: information policy was designated a national, not a collective, responsibility. The French wanted to keep it that way because they did not want to be too "collective." In spite of the handicap, Peter Carrington became a one-man show in communicating the goals and principles of the alliance, much in demand throughout Europe and in America, on the *Today* show, at the universities of South Carolina and Texas, before the Los Angeles and Boston World Affairs councils. His speeches were thoughtful—greatly understated compared to mine—and always fresh and spliced with Carrington humor.

Part of the problem of public strategy making in the alliance stemmed from the leader of the alliance himself and his relationship to the leader of the Kremlin. When Ronald Reagan enjoyed his highest public standing in the United States—at the time of the 1983 Grenada invasion—he suffered his greatest criticism in Europe. *U.S. News and World Report* wrote on December 1, 1986, that the fight against terrorism was regarded in Washington as the "Third World War," with Europe a bunch of softies. With this background, the Iran-Contra caper came as a devastating blow to U.S. leadership, especially when we consider Ed Luttwak's injunction that a grand strategy need not be brilliant but must be consistent. Polls showed the problem: one voter in three in the United Kingdom regarded the United States and the Soviet Union as "an equal threat to world peace"; one in five, mostly young, said the United States was the greater threat.

The *New York Times* was to write: "Mikhail Gorbachev once again turned the arms control tables on the United States. Just as he has done before, Mr. Gorbachev took what had begun as an American proposal, repackaged it and presented it as a Kremlin initiative, enhancing his reputation as a peacemaker and a man prepared to take bold steps to slow the arms race." The *Times* said once again that Washington was caught by surprise by a new Soviet arms-control offer. The White House spokesman hastily called a press conference to note that the idea of the "zero option" was first proposed by President Reagan in 1981, not by the Soviets.[10] But a USIA survey noted that most people in France, Britain, and West Germany believed it was a Gorbachev initiative.[11]

There is no question that part of this perception came from the internal disagreements and fights over policy within the administration and the Congress. Indeed, basic unity on negotiating strategy is essential for an effective public strategy; a house divided can neither stand nor keep outsiders from noticing the cracks, and it cannot maintain that first principle of public strategy: credibility.

Our form of government, with the president and the Congress, itself creates friction. Automatically we have a division, a possible discord that does not exist in parliamentary systems. The balkanization within both the Congress and the executive branch intensifies divisions. The antidote to this is better long-range strategies in each dimension we have discussed, all of which contribute to an effective public strategy.

There is a second requirement: there must be input from the head of the United States Information Agency (USIA). He should be a cabinet member to ensure that public strategy receives strong billing. He must be able to speak up and not be cowed by the Oval Office. He must be the keeper of the public conscience for the president and the spokesman for consistency in grand strategy. This elevated USIA director should also chair the International Communication Council proposed by Congressman Fascell.

We must also look toward the vast new areas of opportunity that are now emerging for the dissemination of information. Charles Wick, after something of a slow beginning at USIA, has been a real innovator in these areas. Direct-satellite television broadcasts and the extension of cable television systems, particularly in Europe, already allow viewers in many areas to share in what amounts to virtually common access to programs and information across borders reaching into Eastern Europe as well. If our public strategy is to remain relevant in the face of rapid change, increasing emphasis must be given to programs such as World Vision, a recent USIA initiative to place news about U.S. events and policies on television networks worldwide.

At the level of direct public access to information internationally, as opposed to information directed at Western elites, the bulk of this flow will be via independent commercial efforts. Indeed, the privatization of communications is a growing trend worldwide. While the practice of jamming oscillates with the political barometer, progress on the principle of outlawing it continues. In a 1984 milestone negotiation, Washington's preeminent communications lawyer, Leonard Marks, persuaded the 100-year-old International Telecommunications Union (ITU)—the United Nation's communications traffic cop—to adopt a resolution condemning jamming, and for the first time the Soviets made no objection. One consequence is that a good part of our public strategy depends on the relationship between national and multinational institutions and the press.

As the Soviet Union under Gorbachev pushes its own expansion of communications, the ability of the state to exercise control over communications, both internally and externally, may well decline. Under current plans, the number of telephones in the Soviet Union is likely to more than double over the next decade. Despite official efforts, there will very likely be a progressive erosion of government controls, with implications for the broader political and social environment in the Soviet Union, and especially the prospects for a greater flow of information between East and West.[12] This too will present new challenges and opportunities for public strategy.

For many years, we have been involved in various cultural and scientific exchange efforts. On balance these programs have been a useful component of public strategy toward the East. Exchanges have also had substantial intelligence value for both sides, although the inherently open nature of our society has meant that the Soviet Union and more recently China can derive much more from this process.[13] In this regard the nature of Soviet priorities can be judged from Moscow's enthusiasm for technical and scientific exchanges. We, by contrast, have sent them a far greater number of people in the humanities and social sciences. Future initiatives in this field need to be aimed at broader exchanges, on a quid pro quo basis.

Finally, in the Third World, we may well face further challenges for public strategy, especially in relation to East-West competition. The period of decolonization following World War II and continuing through the 1960s was a time during which the leadership in the newly independent countries of Africa and Asia was confronted with competing Western and Soviet, or Chinese, models for economic and political development. By the 1970s and 1980s, this competition had been resolved on terms largely favorable to the West. The economic and political stagnation of the Brezhnev years had cast a pall over the attractiveness of the Marxist road to development. Should a dynamic Gorbachev with his high international profile succeed in bringing sweeping reform to the Soviet system, the battle over paths to development and stability in the Third World could be joined again. In meeting this challenge, an essential task of public strategy will be to communicate effectively the value of Western political and economic institutions.

Our public strategy must have both shorter- and longer-term dimensions. Certain distinctions between the two must be drawn. While the difference is important, fragmentation is as much the enemy of a coherent strategy in this area as in others.

Prior to the Second World War, the United States did not consider it necessary to project overseas the policies of the government or the cultural achievements of the nation. When the United States entered the war in 1941, it suddenly became acutely aware that information programs were vital to the conduct of war. Various psychological operations were created, the most important of which was the Voice of America. This is an example of the short term. Unlike other countries such as Britain and Canada, the United States did not have a governmental or semigovernmental national radio, and therefore it could not turn to an established organization to create an overseas service.

At the end of the war, the international information and cultural programs set up during the war were transferred to the State Department, where they stayed for eight years. In 1953, John Foster Dulles took over as secretary of state. It was the height of the McCarthy period, and quite a few members of the State Department were accused of Communist sympathies, including Voice of America staffers and librarians. In this atmosphere it was decided to separate operations from policy, and the United States Information Agency was created outside the State Department to conduct information and cultural activities overseas. But two things were to cast a shadow on the 1953 organization. A nonoperational part of the program (the explanation and advocacy of foreign policy) was taken out of the State Department while an operational part (the exchange-of-persons program) was retained.

In 1973, two advisory commissions—one serving USIA and the other the exchange program in the State Department—asked for an independent inquiry into the status of all information and cultural programs. They asked if my Center for Strategic and International Studies could house such an inquiry. I agreed, and we asked Dr. Frank Stanton, then president of CBS, to chair the study with a panel of distinguished experts, and Walter Roberts, a solid professional, as staff director. The panel recommended rectification of the organization that had prevailed since 1953. It proposed that, as in all other countries of the world, the agency which makes foreign policy should also explain it. Conversely, the panel recommended that the exchange-of-persons program be combined with all other informational and cultural activities. Another proposal was that, as in the case of the BBC, the international radio operation—that is, the Voice of America—be set up as a separate entity.

Opposition to the Stanton recommendations arose within USIA, and the secretary of state during the Nixon-Ford transition did not wish to push the proposals through. The Carter administration, however, accepted one of the Stanton panel recommendations and transferred the cultural exchange program from the State Department to USIA. This was a big step forward. But since the panel did not at the same time transfer to the State Department the advocacy of foreign policy, it put the USIA in a difficult position. The recommendations had to combine the highly political function of foreign policy advocacy with the cultural function of portraying American society.

We should recall some clear strategic thinking about public affairs done in Washington in the years immediately following the Second World War. Washington saw clearly that both educational and cultural affairs and information programs had to be part of a coherent strategy, even if each had its own special integrity to be preserved. The public affairs work that accompanied the Marshall Plan in countries such as France and Britain was soundly conceived and effective. But what was most striking was the clear effort to make allies out of enemies in the former Axis countries.

In the Federal Republic of Germany, in the years 1950 and 1951, the United States had 1,200 full-time public affairs operatives and twenty-five U.S. information centers to carry out that public strategy. The annual budget for this operation (for West Germany alone) was more than $50 million dollars. Those are 1950 dollars. The effort in Japan was of comparable size.[14] Today there are twenty-seven Americans doing this work in the Federal Republic. We are still in the process of reducing our effort and closing posts in Germany, Japan, and Italy.[15] We have come a regrettably long way from the days of a clear strategic mission and the resources to support it. These trends must be reversed if we are to have an effective public strategy for a great power.

Although the USIA has been scrupulous in not politicizing its cultural programs, the danger always exists. Many people see organizational fragmentation as the solution despite the fact that, in its life under the USIA roof, the feared corruption of educational and cultural affairs has not taken place. Most Western democracies like France, Britain, and West Germany clearly delineate between the political information branches located in the various foreign offices and their cultural programs, which are usually somewhat removed from the government, like the British Council, Alliance Française, and the Goethe Institute.

The long-term impact of cultural exchange programs on youth can be extraordinary. Here is an area for magnificent cooperation between U.S. public and private sectors. Both have funded the American Field Service and Youth for Understanding (YFU). For years I served as a trustee and, for a period, as a vice-chairman of the board for YFU, which now operates exchange programs in twenty-seven countries including the United States. Teenagers stay with host families while spending a year in school or during the summer months. Among their most successful programs are in countries with cultures like Japan, where, as of 1988, nearly a thousand teenagers have been in the exchange.[16] Japanese companies like Toyota and Nissan have been leaders in contributing financially to these programs.

We live in the information age. Diplomatic relations with other countries are no longer conducted exclusively by diplomats talking with foreign *officials*. Today diplomacy involves not only relations between governments but, with increasing importance, relations with the *people* of other countries. It is no longer enough to explain a government's policies to the various foreign offices. Today it is equally important to explain and advocate our policies to the peoples of other countries. How U.S. actions and intentions are viewed may influence or even determine the policies of other countries and thus the success of our own. In the long term, our exchange programs with the coming generations are absolutely critical, for culture and values must be a fundamental part of any enduring grand strategy.

14 Deterrence Strategy

THE basic problem in the formulation of an effective deterrence strategy for the 1990s is that some people, like me, see deterrence as dynamic, while others see it as static. The latter view deterrence as something achieved by the nuclear bomb for all time, provided Americans are willing to use it.

My first requirement for a deterrence strategy is that the United States maintain effective strategic forces. In this regard, any START agreement offers a special challenge to our mix of land-, air-, and sea-based systems. Nuclear weapons in an age of superpower parity cannot deter all forms of conflict, and extended deterrence based on the first use of nuclear weapons is of declining credibility. But those same nuclear weapons still deter the use of other nuclear weapons. In fact, that form of deterrence is exactly what the Soviets are practicing on us as we approach the 1990s: making our first use of nuclear weapons neither credible nor rational. For us to deter the Soviets from using nuclear weapons in a crisis, our nuclear triad must stay strong, invulnerable, and balanced.

Second, we must recognize that since the Soviets do not believe in the theory of Mutual Assured Destruction, we have been playing a one-sided game throughout the 1970s and 1980s. The Soviets reject vulnerability; they are playing a different game. They believe in a strategy not only of retaliation but also of denial. For the United States to be in a position where we could be threatened at the strategic level is dangerous for us, but it is much more dangerous for our allies. The nuclear threat has the best chance of working when used as a form of blackmail to force us out of Europe.

Third, conventional forces must be improved. Conventional vulnerabilities must be eliminated, and direct forward defense must be made possible or NATO should give up that doctrine. NATO's flexible response must be restored at the lowest, most fundamental level. Though the West will never be able to match the Warsaw Pact man for man and tank for tank, NATO's conventional deterrent capability can be improved significantly. What's needed is a collective will to redirect investment and make better use of our superior resources.

There are several short-term, relatively low-cost measures to improve NATO's conventional forces. At a heads of government NATO meeting, a mandate should be given as follows:

First, NATO must meet its own goals for critical ammunition stockpiles. The alliance is committed to achieving thirty days' worth of critical munitions, but NATO's across-the-board average is only ten days! To allow the Supreme Allied Commander more flexibility to distribute critical ammunition, I have recommended the creation of a new War Reserve Stockpile of common ammunition to which all NATO members would contribute. In addition to building stocks, the alliance can improve the security of ammunition storage sites and seek greater French cooperation in logistical support.

Second, NATO should study the advisability of the creation of an Enhanced Ready Covering Force from NATO's existing forward-deployed units, especially to shore up the NORTHAG area. In the 1990s environment, when two weeks' mobilization and reinforcement of NATO's defenses cannot be taken for granted, units that can be deployed to covering positions in the first hours of a crisis and promise a robust initial defense will blunt the danger of preemptive attack. Interoperable equipment, higher states of readiness, and synchronized reactive command and support will be vital ingredients in this new response capability. This force should be directly under SACEUR and, unlike most NATO forces, should be 100 percent ready in terms of manpower, equipment, and stocks. It should be a multinational command, configured primarily with anti-armor units. NATO should fund these force improvements from a joint fund, similar to the collective solution that led to AWACS in the 1970s. This command covering force would be a huge step forward in increasing the flexibility of our response and also would give us new leverage in our negotiations on control of conventional arms. It should pass to SACEUR's control at the first stage, "military vigilance" in a time of tension, and not be entangled in delayed DPC decision making.

Third, NATO should implement some terrain preparation on its side of the inner-German border. Despite the political sensitivity of terrain-enhancement measures (nondiplomats call them barriers), the fact that they are significant force multipliers should spur NATO to action. I am not suggesting that the alliance dig up Germany to the Rhine to make tank traps. Sensors to aid in target acquisition could enhance NATO's preparation for defense; other options include the cheap and simple construction of hills, gradients, and other barriers that would slow an armored advance.

NATO badly needs a mobile reserve to complement what now amounts to a linear defense. Shortly after becoming prime minister, Winston Churchill flew to France, where the French forces were in full retreat. The French commander-in-chief briefed him from a large map. Churchill recalled the ominous experience:

> When he stopped there was considerable silence. I then asked "Where is the strategic reserve?" . . . General Gamelin turned to me and, with a shake of the head and a shrug, said "*Aucune* [none]."
>
> There was another long pause. . . . I was dumbfounded. . . . It had never occurred to me that any commanders having to defend five hundred miles of engaged front would have left themselves unprovided with a mass of maneuver. No one can defend with certainty so wide a front; but when the enemy has committed himself to a major thrust which breaks the line, one can always have, one *must* always have, a mass of divisions which marches up in vehement counter-attack at the moment when the first fury of the offensive has spent its force.[1]

If Winston Churchill, former regimental commander and military historian, could inspect NATO and its plans today, I believe he would make the same comment. The French are to be complimented on setting up a corps headquarters at Lille in northern France near the Belgian border and aiming to develop helicopter divisions that could be moved forward as a reserve for the NATO Northern Army Group. Part of their effort is only on the drawing board. What SACEUR needs is a fully deployable corps—a mass of maneuvers—that can be thrown at the breakthrough areas to cut off the Soviet Operational Maneuver Groups. If the French would take a sector of the line in southern Germany, a U.S. corps could constitute this element.

Beyond the Enhanced Covering Force concept, there are more radical options available to remedy the relative weakness of NORTHAG (as compared to the relative strength in the CENTAG sector). The German Third Corps could be moved from CENTAG, now on an unlikely axis of attack, to the southern flank of NORTHAG. The Belgians (with no change of Kaserns) could then assume a sector on CENTAG's northern flank.

Any enhanced covering force or redeployments should not be seen as an end-all to our defense problems, however. There is a danger, of running out not only of ammunition but also of manpower before the arrival of the U.S. reinforcing divisions. All nations should do more to develop "mobilizable reserves," forces that are available within the first two weeks to cover gaps that occur in the line, especially during the period before six additional divisions have arrived in Europe. The Germans, for example, have hundreds of thousands of unassigned reserves that could be so organized.

The next consideration is a capability to attack the enemy's rear and interdict his lines of communication. Soon after General Rogers became SACEUR, he began to develop a tactical concept known as Follow-on Forces Attack (FOFA). The assumption of FOFA is that even if NATO's conventional forward forces are able to withstand the initial attacking forces of the Warsaw Pact in the critical central region of West Germany, they most probably will be overwhelmed by reinforcing echelons. Therefore these Pact second-echelon forces should be interdicted early so that they never reach the front. FOFA's aim is to hit at the many choke points, river crossings, and formations in the enemy rear—and to hit moving as well as fixed targets. Until recently there was little prospect of obtaining the right combination of sensors and weapons systems—so-called smart weapons—to locate and hit these moving targets. Now these are being harnessed.

Throughout military history, military institutions have been slow in translating technologies into armaments and effective tactical concepts. In 1940, the Germans and French had the same technologies, but only the former translated them into combined-arms concepts that produced victory on the battlefield. General Rogers deserves the highest credit for developing and having NATO's Defense Planning Committee approve a long-term planning guideline that bucked this adverse trend and got NATO moving in this innovative direction. The

Warsaw Pact generals were greatly impressed, too, and it is necessary to follow through on this initiative.

Crisis Management

In addition to the likelihood that NATO will lack sufficient time to make deliberate decisions, the decline of the efficacy of extended deterrence and first use, and the rise of the importance of conventional forces, create another new situation that has not been adequately recognized at NATO. Reliance on nuclear escalation has, until recently, prevented consideration of what I call the horizontal dimension of deterrence—crisis management, mobilization, and reinforcement—as compared to the vertical dimensions of nuclear escalation. As noted in Chapter 8 concerning the East-West balance, whenever a NATO ambassador asks a NATO commander how he would fare if war came, almost invariably the commander counters that it depends upon how early the Defense Planning Committee and heads of government act to mobilize NATO for the crisis. Whether Western Europe stands or falls will hang on a timely decision to mobilize.

There must be a thorough examination of this shockingly neglected aspect of deterrence. The Soviets have the capability of launching an attack weeks sooner than they could have in the 1960s, when our plans for the reinforcement of Europe were developed, but NATO's crisis-management machinery has hardly improved in the last twenty years. NATO's crisis management is grounded in an alert system that has several phases above normal peacetime readiness: military vigilance, simple alert, reinforced alert, and general alert. Each must be unanimously approved by the Defense Planning Committee of Perm Reps, which can only occur after the Perm Reps have received instructions from their capitals.

It is increasingly clear that the Soviets are attempting to develop a blitzkrieg-type capability that would be decisive before the United States could reinforce Europe. Vital reinforcement can take place only if NATO can manage a crisis effectively and act decisively. Whether, how soon, and under what circumstances Europe will be reinforced could be fatally delayed while Perm Reps debate the consequences of such action. Will reinforcements of Europe be seen by the Soviets as provocative and prompt them to initiate World War III? Will reinforcements act as a deterrent and prevent World War III? The Soviets might offer a cooling-off period for negotiation, which would complicate the decision to reinforce. They could mobilize, back down for a period, mobilize, and back down again. Such action would make it difficult for democracies to respond. These fundamental issues are not part of a conceptual framework of crisis management and diplomacy.

To be fair, NATO is not wholly negligent on this issue. The ambassadors who make up the Defense Planning Committee do participate in key exercises held over a two-year cycle. But these exercises tend to be based on scenarios for the 1960s, and not the 1990s.[2] In 1986, my U.S. mission to NATO tried, on its own, to come to grips with the issue of crisis management. My ideal ally was down the hall in another wing at NATO Headquarters: U.S. four-star general Jack Merritt. As head of the Army War College, he encouraged a probing examination of what went wrong in Vietnam. As staff director for the Joint Chiefs of Staff, he continued to develop such innovative approaches.

Our two staffs went to work on improving our own "net assessments" and examining how a war might really be fought in the 1990s and the problems the United States would face in reinforcing Europe. Another ally in this effort, Dr. Fred Ikle, got the Pentagon behind this reexamination. Early in the Reagan administration, Ikle made a unique contribution to crisis management by introducing the concept of "ambiguous warning" to describe the likely situation NATO would encounter. At the Spring 1987 Defense Ministers Meeting, a review of NATO's entire effort to reinforce Europe in a crisis was mandated. This review, however, only scratches the surface. It is important to define crisis management in broad terms and add the dimension of crisis diplomacy. Crisis diplomacy involves not only the political consultation process within the alliance, but also, perhaps more critically, the problem of communication with the Kremlin. Crisis management and crisis diplomacy must be married to a strategy worked out well in advance but flexible enough to meet evolving situations. The Cuban missile crisis could not compare in complexity to a major NATO–Warsaw Pact crisis.

In the direct Washington-to-Moscow channel, certain progress has been made, beginning with the hotline agreed to in the wake of the Cuban missile crisis, upgraded first in 1971 with a satellite communications system, then in 1984 with a facsimile transmission link, and in 1987 with the U.S.-U.S.S.R. agreement to establish Nuclear Risk Reduction Centers, with a twenty-four-hour watch to carry out functions that contribute to reduced danger of nuclear war.

The very words *crisis management*, of course, are a bit misleading. The problem facing decision makers will never be clear cut; all events will be shrouded in confusion and uncertainty, even in the best of circumstances. Chances for miscalculations and misperceptions run high. Carl von Clausewitz wrote of the "fog of war," a vivid description of the confusion that occurs in battle because a general cannot possibly see all that is going on. If a crisis occurs in Europe in the 1990s, the fog will be as great, but electrified by the fear that thermonuclear war could break out. If nuclear fear were to seize Europe, the Soviets would have a tremendous advantage. They could propagandize the West at will, charging that the United States is about to bring nuclear war to Europe.

A fundamental part of Soviet strategy in peacetime carries over to crisis and wartime. It is the classical lesson practiced by all master strategists, from Alexander the Great to Napoleon: divide and conquer. The NATO mind-set is so worried about nuclear escalation that it neglects the problem of how the alliance could be split by the exercise of the political leverage inherent in Warsaw Pact conventional forces: the Soviet Northern Fleet under exercise conditions could seal off the Norwegian Sea and block the reinforcement of Norway, isolate Denmark, and then, on the verge of hostilities or just afterwards, the Kremlin could offer both isolated countries "sanctuary"; Warsaw Pact forces, with a potential for a blitzkrieg success before Europe can be reinforced by the United States, could offer West Germany "sanctuary" in exchange for neutrality; Greece might be neutralized by offering it support against Turkey. If the Soviets can bring sufficient pressure to bear on these fault lines in the NATO alliance, the cohesion of the alliance could be lost before the first battle has begun.

As disconcerting as the lack of contingency planning is, the vulnerability of the physical facilities at NATO Headquarters is equally disturbing. We have described how the crisis-management mechanism resides in the DPC of fifteen ambassadors (remember, France is not represented in this body), supported by the Military Committee, the situation room, and the International Staff, all at NATO Headquarters. Lord Carrington has brought the situation room up to a reasonable standard. But the entire NATO Headquarters, sprawled alongside the highway leading to the Brussels international airport, is fully exposed to attack by Soviet Special Forces—*Spetznaz*—and attack by stand-off weapons. SACEUR, located 60 kilometers south of NATO Headquarters, has nearly completed a new underground, hardened headquarters. Other NATO military commands have such facilities, some since the 1950s.

Incredibly, there is no such facility for NATO Headquarters, which is to be the very center for managing a crisis that may lead to World War III. The idea of "hardening" was rejected some years ago, at the same time the building of new, permanent facilities for NATO was rejected. The U.S. government opposed such hardening for two reasons. The first was lack of money (although there was money for hundreds of shiny new F-16 fighters and Tornados, main battle tanks, and aircraft carriers). It also wanted to avoid the perception among the European public that NATO was "digging in" for a war. Neither reason is valid if NATO is to view seriously its headquarters as a crisis-management center. Preparations for crisis management and diplomacy must be made and presented publicly, not as isolated ad hoc measures but as part of a new framework for reinforcing deterrence and preventing war.

Maritime Strategy

For the United States and its allies, strong naval forces supported by a coherent maritime strategy are as important a contribution to deterrence as strong ground and air forces in central Europe. The alliance depends critically on seaborne reinforcement and resupply in times of crisis and war. If we cannot deliver the goods, either because we do not have the capability with adequate numbers of cargo ships, or because we cannot protect them effectively due to naval forces being dangerously run down, any hope for success in Europe is lost. If there is no hope that conventional forces will be successful, they make no contribution to deterrence.

Strong maritime capabilities contribute to deterrence in a broader global context as well. Because the United States is a maritime nation, a strong navy and merchant marine manifest a serious intent on the part of the United States to protect its global interests. Even if the U.S. Navy and its allies control the Norwegian Sea, NATO's maritime situation confronts another serious problem: the decline in merchant shipping assets to provide necessary sealift. Merchant shipping does not have the glamour of sophisticated warships, but NATO's ultimate success depends critically on having enough cargo ships of the right kind at the right place and at the right time. NATO nations must do everything they can to revitalize their merchant shipping, despite intense and often unfair competition from Third World and Warsaw Pact states.

Effective maritime capabilities, of course, must be underpinned by a coherent maritime strategy. John Lehman, as a dynamic secretary of the navy, and Admiral James Watkins, as a conceptualist chief of naval operations, put forth arguments for the global maritime role in deterring the Soviets, even in Europe. This was certified in the president's 1987 National Security Statement: "Maritime superiority enables us to capitalize on Soviet geographic vulnerabilities and to pose a global threat to the Soviet's interests. . . . Essential to our wartime strategy, maritime superiority plays equally vital roles in peacetime. Mobile maritime forces, easily deployed in time of crisis, are a traditional symbol of our nation's will and capability to defend its vital interests."[3]

Ironically, it is the U.S. Navy's possible maldeployment for an early projection to go to the Norwegian Sea—in the face of a prepositioned Soviet "fleet in being" there—that offers the first test of global deterrence in a major superpower crisis. The issue is not whether NATO naval forces would prevail over the Soviet navy in the event of conflict. There is no doubt that U.S. and allied forces would emerge victorious. The issue is how much time it would take, which in turn depends on whether allied forces are deployed to the Norwegian Sea early in a crisis. If U.S. carrier task forces have to fight their way into the Norwegian Sea, it could take as long as two weeks. By that time, the central front could be lost.

There are some compensations for a lack of local deterrence in the Norwegian Sea. If in a prewar crisis the Soviets exercised in the Norwegian Sea, the Seventh Fleet could exercise in the northwestern Pacific, near the Sea of Okhotsk and near the Soviet submarine bastion. This directly threatens the Soviet homeland and their nuclear strike forces.

There are dangers here for everyone. The U.S. fleet is vulnerable to air, missile, and submarine attacks. They cannot expect help from the U.S. Air Force because the closest airpower is Misawa, Japan, with single-engine, short-range F-16s. Furthermore, long-range bombers from the Strategic Air Command are thousands of miles away in Guam. On the other hand, a bold move against the unbuffered border of the Soviet Union could, although not necessarily would, cause Soviet planners to rethink their Norwegian Sea or other scenarios. The U.S. Pacific Fleet is a viable threat to the Soviet homeland and against Soviet submarine ballistic missiles.

A final word on our deterrent strategy for the 1990s. Europeans comfort themselves by saying that it is the uncertainty of NATO action that contributes to the calculus of deterrence: the Soviets are deterred because they just can't be sure how we might use our nuclear weapons in a crisis. From the 1950s through the 1980s, this form of deterrence worked. Then, the balance began to change. When the uncertainties become greater than the certainties, we end up in a game of bluff, and the risk of miscalculation and misperception runs high. If present trends continue, this could be the climate in the 1990s. We can easily avoid this, however, by making real efforts to restore balance and flexibility to our deterrence strategy, and by making a short-warning blitzkrieg attack on NATO obselete.

15 Negotiating Strategy

THE United States must pursue arms-control agreements governed by a strategy that goes beyond achieving narrow objectives for specific negotiations at hand. We have never had an overall negotiations strategy. From America's arms-control experience over the last twenty-five years,[1] however, we can now piece together such a strategy that should shape the U.S. approach to negotiations:

- For the U.S., equal outcome is an essential ingredient if arms-control initiatives are to enjoy broad public and political support.
- Linkage between arms control and other Soviet behavior is a political reality.
- Negotiation from strength is necessary to achieve results.
- The security interests of allies must be incorporated.
- Adequate verfication is the sine qua non of a politically supportable agreement as well as a militarily sound one.
- Stability is the fundamental objective—stability in deterrence, arms control, and crisis management.

The question of equality of outcome first seriously arose with the 1972 SALT I agreements. These agreements had two major elements. First, the ABM treaty allowed only two sites in each country to defend against ballistic missiles. It was based on the assumption, at least on the U.S. side, that strategic defense was simply not then technologically feasible. Second, an interim agreement froze the number of offensive nuclear missiles on both sides. In doing so, however, it codified Soviet superiority over the United States in the number of missiles—an unequal outcome. Americans believed they maintained superiority in other areas, such as warhead accuracy, and that it was in our long-term interest to break the momentum of the Soviet buildup. The U.S. plan was to move from an interim to a final agreement limiting strategic forces at a later time.

There was a clear downside to this approach. As Henry Kissinger wrote, "We traded the defense for the offensive limitations."[2] The United States led the Soviet Union in technologies for defending against ballistic missiles (ABM). Critics quickly pointed out that the ABM agreement introduced parity in the area in which the United States had an advantage, yet at the same time, the interim agreement codified the Soviet superiority in offensive systems, Moscow's area of relative advantage.

For this reason, Washington's Senator Henry Jackson became a powerful critic of the agreement. Something like young Abe Lincoln's opponent, Stephen Douglas, this little giant was a very dogged, smart debater who painstakingly marshaled his arguments and could disagree without being personally disagreeable—a quality that helped him a great deal in the Senate club. Supported by his resourceful staffers but very much in command, Senator Jackson developed a surprise move: to offer an amendment from the Senate floor to give direction to the next negotiation. If amended, he would not oppose the agreement, but never again did he want to see "subparity."

Jackson skillfully sought to promote support for his amendment by staying in touch with the administration so that the president might finally endorse it, at the same time wooing Republicans by saying he was not going against the president. Jackson's principal points of contact with the administration for reviewing drafts of the amendment were John Lehman, who coordinated Congressional matters on Henry Kissinger's NSC staff at the White House, and me at the State Department. John Lehman had honed his competitiveness on the Cambridge rowing team and had an intellect of equal prowess. He did not quite share the same zest for the interim agreement as did other NSC staffers. He was also very close to Senator Jackson's two key staffers, Dorothy Fosdick and especially Richard Perle. In the end, a rather ambiguous endorsement for the amendment emerged from the White House.

During the Senate debate, Jackson argued that "in insisting on equality in any treaty to emerge from SALT II, I am certain I am speaking for the good sense of the overwhelming majority of the American public. We should support the principle of equality on which the ABM treaty is based by applying it to offensive systems as well." The amendment passed 55 to 35.

Ironically, "Scoop" Jackson, through his insistence on equal forces, did more than any other American to set the course of America's future negotiating strategy. Even after Jackson's death, his determined aide, Richard Perle, along with veteran negotiator, Russian-speaking Lt. Gen. Edward Rowney, ensured that Jackson's legacy would continue.

The Jackson amendment stated that "the Congress recognizes the difficulty of maintaining a stable strategic balance in a period of rapidly developing technology." Jackson felt our retaliatory forces would become increasingly vulnerable if trends were not reversed by a SALT II agreement, and that the Soviet Union did not subscribe to the theory of Mutual Assured Destruction (MAD) in the first place. This was a very different view from that of Senator Fulbright and others who questioned what difference it made if the United States and the Soviet Union had 10,000 or more warheads, when 300 warheads could destroy both the Soviet Union and the United States.[3]

The Jackson principle of equality was first applied to strategic arms at Vladivostok in 1974, when President Ford and General Secretary Brezhnev reached a provisional agreement on a common ceiling of 2,400 intercontinental ballistic missile launchers, submarine-launched ballistic missiles, and long-range bombers, and a sublimit of 1,320 on multiple-warhead missiles that could hit many targets at a time. The limits were set at high levels, permitting the Soviets to reduce only about 100 strategic launchers and allowing the Americans to build up to those limits.

Jackson's influence continued into the Carter administration, which pushed for deep cuts to bring the Vladivostok figure down to 2,000 launchers overall. A basic Jackson criticism of SALT I had been that it mandated no deep cuts. Cyrus Vance, the new secretary of state, made a trip to Moscow in March 1977 to discuss reductions. Unfortunately, the new position had already been leaked to the press in advance. Vance was met by a resounding silence, and no Soviet counteroffer was made.

Zbigniew Brzezinski, the highly intellectual national security adviser, commissioned Harvard professor Samuel Huntington to undertake a review of the relative military strengths of the two superpowers. His conclusions were reflected in Presidential Review Memorandum 10 and a new presidential doctrine in August 1977 calling for a strategic posture of "essential equivalence" in the military field. This criterion, a bit broader than Senator Jackson's "parity," referred to a condition in which Soviet numerical advantages in one area of strategic nuclear forces would offset U.S. relative advantages in other areas.

Thus, Jackson's legacy of equality of outcome in arms-control negotiations has remained a fundamental tenet of subsequent administrations. It strongly influenced the outcome of the INF negotitions—equality at zero—as well as the Reagan administration's strategic arms negotiating positions.

However, other tenets have entered the arms-control negotiation forum. Also during the late 1970s, there emerged a fierce debate within the Carter administration with regard to the concept of linkage. Should arms control be linked to other areas of Soviet conduct, or should it stand on its own?

In the late summer and autumn of 1977, intelligence sources indicated increasing Soviet involvement and Soviet-sponsored Cuban military presence in the strategic Horn of Africa. In view of this behavior, some people argued that concluding an arms-control treaty with Moscow violated the spirit of the earlier Kissinger concept of linkage between arms control and moderated Kremlin behavior. Opponents of that concept, however, argued that controlling the nuclear arms race was of such significance to humankind that it should be independent of other East-West questions.

The Carter administration was divided. Vance was arguing privately that references to linkage would jeopardize the ratification of SALT II, and Brzezinski was saying failure to warn the Soviets and make some response would jeopardize SALT II ratification. Brzezinski wanted to send a carrier task force to the region as a symbol of our displeasure at Soviet involvement, whereas a State Department assistant secretary argued, "The best protection against invasion of Somalia would be world opinion."[4] Brzezinski did not carry the day, but he was politically correct in his conclusion: "SALT lies buried on the sands of the Ogaden."

When SALT II came up for ratification, a political debate raged over the spotting of a "Soviet brigade" in Cuba. Ultimately, it was not clear whether these forces were newly arrived in Cuba, but the debate raised further questions about conducting arms-control business with a Moscow engaged in foreign "adventures." There was no ambiguity when, in the Christmas season of 1979, intelligence indicated that Soviet troops were being airlifted into Afghanistan. This was the final nail in the coffin for SALT II. The linkage issue proved fatal to SALT II despite sustained effort by many to separate nuclear arms control from other areas of U.S.-Soviet relations. A U.S. negotiating strategy has to take account of the political reality of linkage.

Another issue highlighted by the SALT II debate is the impact of arms-control agreements on our allies, specifically, on extended deterrence—what allies call the American nuclear umbrella. For the United States, the strategic equation is not just related to U.S. deterrence of a nuclear strike or blackmail based on nuclear capability. It also involves extending nuclear deterrence to our allies in order to deter aggression against them. West German Chancellor Helmut Schmidt became especially concerned about extended deterrence when, in the mid-1970s, the Soviets began deploying SS-20 missiles in the western Soviet Union specifically designed to hit targets in Western Europe. Schmidt warned of unexpected consequences of SALT II for Europe: "SALT neutralizes strategic nuclear capabilities. In Europe this magnifies the significance of the disparities between East and West in nuclear tactical and conventional weapons."[5] However, neither NATO, Washington, nor Schmidt had any comprehensive negotiating strategy to address this fundamental dilemma.

It was during this same month that NATO defense ministers created the High Level Group (HLG) and gave it the task of deciding what weapons were needed to maintain deterrence. Neither the Carter nor the Reagan administration—and especially Richard Perle—was convinced that European concerns were justified or that new weapons were needed. However, the European perception was that if Western Europe were attacked, an American response would be more certain if modern, longer-range U.S. nuclear weapons were in place on European soil.

In the HLG's discussions, a series of guidelines emerged. The first was that the new deterrent be ground based; therefore, sea-launched cruise missiles were rejected because they would not have the symbolic value of being stationed on the continent. After careful analysis, ground-launched cruise missiles and the Pershing II ballistic missiles were selected.[6]

The second guideline emphasized that deterrence did not require NATO to match the Soviets weapon for weapon. Matching the Soviets could lead the Europeans to believe that the United States was preparing to confine a nuclear war to Europe.

Another important guideline was that risk associated with deployment should be shared by a number of nations. Politically, the West German people would not agree to become NATO's nuclear battleground, with the remainder of the allies buffered. Therefore Germany accepted both Pershing II and cruise missiles on the understanding that the United Kingdom, Holland, Belgium, and Italy also agree to deploy the cruise missiles.

The final and most fundamental guideline was a "two-track" strategy: negotiate with the Soviets to do away with the SS-20s; failing that, deploy 108 Pershing II launchers in West Germany and 464 cruise missiles in the five nations. In this way, the alliance politically prepared the groundwork for establishing, in public, the principle that it was prepared only to negotiate from strength. In a different way, it was a reaffirmation of the Harmel doctrine.

It was often said by many at NATO Headquarters that NATO should not have embarked on this two-track approach. They felt it would have been better simply to "modernize" quietly. This represented self-delusion; the European publics would never have accepted such an approach. Nuclear deployments would no longer be left to the elites. Concern about verification, which the Reagan administration brought with it when it came to office, also helps explain how the INF issue was ultimately resolved.

At the National Press Club on November 18, 1981, Ronald Reagan unveiled his first arms-control proposal, the "zero option": "The United States is prepared to cancel its deployment of Pershing II and ground-launched cruise missiles if the Soviets will dismantle their SS-20, SS-4, and SS-5 missiles."[7] While many factors bore on the genesis of the "zero option," the argument that it was the only adequately verifiable outcome was a critical contribution to the decision in the face of a divided administration. Some in Europe and America believed that the Soviets would not negotiate on this basis. Richard

Burt in the State Department, for example, was skeptical of Soviet accommodation but felt it was essential to have a sound negotiating strategy that could keep the alliance united during the long negotiations. None of this particularly impressed Richard Perle. Paul Nitze believed negotiations were possible under certain circumstances, but even while at Geneva, he constantly had to contend with the results of bureaucratic battles between the "two Richards." Nitze, by the way, was revered throughout the alliance, as the inspiring *eminence grise* of arms negotiations.

In July 1982, Paul Nitze, in an effort to break the deadlock in the INF negotiations, took his famous "walk in the woods" with Yuli Kvitsinsky. Nitze and Kvitsinsky discussed a possible point of leverage: the failing Leonid Brezhnev might want a summit with Reagan before he died. Nitze wanted to convince Kvitsinsky that the SS-20 program was in neither their political nor military interest. Nitze knew how much the Soviets wanted to eliminate the possibility that NATO would actually deploy the Pershing II missile, which could reach the Soviet heartland within minutes. Nitze's trial balloon would permit the Soviets to retain seventy-five SS-20s (each with three warheads) in Europe. NATO would be allowed seventy-five cruise missile launchers (each with four single-warhead missiles). The Pershing II missile would not be deployed.

Nitze's exercise in creative diplomacy was viewed with deep skepticism and some alarm in Washington. He had no bureaucratic support, and Weinberger and Perle closed ranks behind the "zero option." Nitze responded that it was inconceivable that the Soviets would ever accept the "zero option." The president, quite stubbornly, sided with Weinberger and Perle, telling Nitze: "Well, Paul, you just tell the Soviets that you are working for one tough son-of-a-bitch."[8]

The Soviets were not buying either the walk in the woods or the "zero option." In an effort to get the negotiations moving, Richard Burt designed the so-called interim solution, which allowed three hundred warheads on each side while permitting Pershing II deployment. It was to be a first step on the way to zero, but the proposal got nowhere. As the date for deploying the INF missiles approached, the Soviets dramatically walked out of the negotiations in late 1983.

Negotiations resumed after NATO deployed its INF forces and continued in fits and starts for four more years. Due to his wife's illness, Paul Nitze returned to the State Department as special adviser to President Reagan and George Shultz. In Geneva the new head of our negotiating team was Max Kampelman, a shrewd, articulate former professor and early associate of Hubert Humphrey. Kampelman had won his spurs, and even Soviet admiration, as U.S. negotiator at the Madrid "Round" of the CSCE talks. The INF negotiator, Maynard Glitman, was one who represented the best in Foreign Service professionalism.

By early 1987, the new Soviet leader, Mikhail Gorbachev, recognized he could not shake allied unity and agreed to the zero proposal. Indeed, he stunned the West by proposing the elimination of short-range missiles in Europe as well as the longer-range systems covered by the U.S. proposal. Interestingly, the debate in Congress over the INF Treaty signed at the December 1987 Washington summit focused almost wholly on aspects of verification, thus giving legitimacy to the principle of adequate verification as a sine qua non for a publicly, politically supportable arms-control agreement.

Most recently, the final principle of U.S. negotiations strategy and perhaps its most important—stability—has emerged in the context of conventional arms talks.

In early 1986, Soviet General Secretary Gorbachev made a series of dramatic moves to jump beyond the stalemated thirteen-year-old Mutual and Balanced Force Reductions (MBFR) talks in Vienna, which had produced no movement on reducing forces in Central Europe. On April 18, he offered to negotiate conventional-force reductions "from the Atlantic to the Urals." That offer overturned thirty years of Soviet policy, which had refused to entertain any thought of talks on control of conventional arms that included portions of the Soviet Union but no U.S. territory. His offer was repeated and expanded by the Warsaw Pact in its Budapest Appeal of June 1986.

The Gorbachev proposal crystallized a growing sense in NATO that something had to be done in the area of conventional arms control. That sense had been fostered by MBFR's years of failure, the moderately successful conclusion of the talks in Stockholm to design confidence-building measures between East and West, and the prospect of the start of the Vienna meeting to review the Helsinki accords.

At the Halifax NATO Foreign Ministers meeting in June 1986, the French, Belgians, and British initiated a counter-initiative to the Budapest Appeal intended to force NATO to devise "bold new steps" in conventional arms control. A High Level Task Force (HLTF) was created to formulate a common approach for alliance arms control. It was placed under the patient chairmanship of NATO's deputy secretary-general, the slim, good-natured, and commonsense Italian Marcello Guidi. The major problem was a serious procedural disagreement between the French and the Americans, the latter often led by my DCM, Steve Ledogar, who later became our ambassador to MBFR and negotiator for the prospective talks designed to replace those endless negotiations.

Finally, after much bickering over words, the group produced a declaration on the conventional military balance, endorsed by the NATO foreign ministers in December 1986. I was so proud of this realistic document that I carried it with me as a showpiece when testifying before Congress. As Senator Nunn often noted, many NATO diplomats always wanted to play down the real problems in the military balance for fear of creating alarm or of fostering the idea that they should contribute more money to correct shortcomings in conventional arms. This declaration, however, showed that its authors were now under no illusion about its first objective: "strengthening stability and security in the whole of Europe, through increased openness and establishment of a verifiable, comprehensive and stable balance of conventional forces at lower levels. . . . While maintaining effective deterrence involving both nuclear and conventional forces, we seek to establish a stable relationship of conventional forces in Europe."[9]

The ministers said bluntly that there had to be a recognition of the current facts. They took the Soviets to task for implying that the present military situation was "stable and balanced. It is not. On the contrary it is marked by asymmetries and disparities from region to region." NATO defined its goal of stability as "the elimination of the capability for surprise attack or for the initiation of large-scale offensive action."[10] Thus the principle of stability was firmly established.

Why such a concern over stability in Central Europe? One thesis of this book is that World War III could be a war by miscalculation, a war that springs from mistaken judgments in crises created by instability of the kind that can emerge from a European conventional-weapons imbalance. Any strategy intended to prevent World War III must address this central element of instability and attack it from several angles. It is for this reason that conventional-force improvements and arms control must go hand in hand. The forthcoming conventional-arms control talks, now officially named "the Conventional Stability Talks," will represent a stern test for the United States as to whether it truly applies the "principles" that even allies have established to guide arms-control strategy.

How might we apply those other arms-control principles to this new and most important area of negotiation? Our first principle, equality of outcome, is fundamental to long-term military stability in Central Europe and appears to have emerged as a formal NATO position even prior to the onset of the negotiations. Already NATO and the Warsaw Pact have agreed that the new talks must seek to eliminate the "asymmetries" in the balance. From the NATO perspective, this has translated to a preliminary position stressing an outcome of equal ceilings on conventional forces in Europe—at or somewhat below current NATO force levels. NATO has yet to unfold in any detail how it conceives "equality" in concrete terms, but a focus on tanks and artillery—that is, those forces precisely the most capable of carrying out shorter-warning attacks—seems assured.

Of course, the degree to which this is achievable depends in part on how the Soviet Union defines its goals in the negotiations. The Soviets have indicated, for example, that they are worried by "asymmetries" they perceive NATO enjoys. One such area is advanced tactical aircraft. Another is mobilization capability. There is also speculation that Moscow might entertain an agreement that trades reductions on its side for limitations on the development of advanced Western technology. NATO is justly wary of proposals that might restrict its capabilities in these areas. The question remains, therefore, what NATO could or should be willing to pay to achieve the kinds of asymmetrical reductions necessary to bring NATO and Warsaw Pact forces to equal levels. Thus far, NATO nations have found it extremely difficult to make up their collective mind.

This lack of agreement raises the issue of NATO's leverage in any forthcoming conventional negotiations. Can it negotiate from strength? Analyses of the current situation argue that the minimum cuts necessary to achieve a "stable" balance of forces in Europe from the Atlantic to the Urals are on the order of five for the Soviets and one for us.[11] What incentive does the Warsaw Pact have to engage in such cuts? NATO is not inclined to negotiate in the areas of interest to Moscow, so it has little to put on the table. It is clear, therefore, as in the INF case, that NATO must give itself leverage in the forthcoming talks through the pursuit of a conventional-defense improvements program and creative use of its high technology as outlined in a later chapter. The potential for leverage is there, but unfortunately the March 1988 NATO heads of government summit devised no plan to exploit it. It did not truly apply the Harmel doctrine, as had been done in the missile negotiations. The principle of negotiating from strength must be followed as was done in the case of INF.

While force reductions might be the preferred means of establishing conventional stability, an important contribution can also be made by confidence-building measures to lower the chances of a surprise attack. Confidence-building measures—such as permitting observers at military maneuvers, or perhaps permanent stationing at military garrisons or key rail-transfer points—are not a panacea, but they might bridge the gap until more substantive negotiations are concluded. At the very least, they could ameliorate public pressures for some movement in the conventional-arms control issue.

An important first step in developing useful confidence-building measures was the Conference on Confidence and Security Building Measures and Disarmament in Europe (CDE), held in Stockholm from 1983 to 1986. As our Stockholm negotiator, Ambassador James Goodby, put it: "The Stockholm Conference is different from 'classical' arms control negotiations in that it addresses not the capabilities of war, the numbers of weapons and troops, but rather the most likely causes of war: flawed judgments or miscalculations stemming from fears of sudden attack and uncertainty about military intentions of our adversary." The CDE established a set of concrete measures to increase openness and predictability of military activities in Europe. The thirty-five participating nations agreed, for example, to prior notification of all military activities over a threshold of 13,000 troops or 300 tanks. The accord also provided for on-site air and ground inspections for verification—the first time the Soviets had agreed to such measures in their own territory.

As a follow-up to the Stockholm Conference, limits on the Warsaw Pact's short-warning attack capability could be achieved through several varieties of confidence-building measures: (1) increased "transparency," which would include exchange of information about location of forces and their organization; (2) stronger constraint measures in size, duration, and sequence of exercises and other military activities;

and (3) closing of loopholes in the September 1986 Stockholm agreement regarding limitations on out-of-garrison activities and improved observation measures.[12]

A final word should be said about our individual negotiators because, ultimately, people count. I remember with pride one Council meeting, as I introduced our Geneva negotiators Max Kampelman, John Tower, and Maynard Glitman—and then watched for three hours their superlative briefing on the status of the negotiations and their exchange with Council members. As an aside to me, that very same European ambassador who once, over scotch, complained about the divisiveness in Washington being played out across Europe, said with a wink, "Your negotiators have really got what it takes." These were the best of days in the Council, as Peter Carrington wryly smiled at the performance.

Have we a coherent negotiations strategy? The answer must be no, but the elements for such a strategy have taken shape. These elements—equality of outcome, the political reality of linkage between arms control and other issues, the need for leverage, a recognition of allied needs, adequate verification, and perhaps most important, stability as the goal—must take priority in the approach to negotiations. The important requirement is to develop a long-term arms-control conceptual framework for what constitutes true stability, and all negotiating positions—ours and theirs—should be studied against this stringent standard. The challenge to future policymakers rests in relating these elements in a way that makes arms-control negotiations an integrated component of a grand strategy to prevent World War III. To achieve this objective, the United States must develop a long-term conceptual arms-control framework that encompasses conventional and nuclear elements.[13] As Senator Jackson appreciated, arms control by bits and pieces poses great dangers.

16 Resources Strategy

NATO has two and a half times the population, one and a half times the GNP, superior technology, and about the same military investment, yet it is being outproduced in most military areas by the Warsaw Pact. If one includes Japan, the West's collective GNP rises to over three times that of the Pact.[1]

It was this dilemma that led me in my 1983 speech to the Atlantic Treaty Association to call for a NATO peace time resources strategy. Rather than simply throwing money and technology at the problem, we needed to establish priorities for our financial and technical resources. NATO had to modernize its defenses, but individual nations, with competing domestic economic and social demands, already felt stretched. Therefore, it had to make existing resources go further. With a chaotic investment strategy, with no coherent economic or financial objectives for marshaling its superior resources, the alliance was clearly at risk. It was essential to establish an alliance framework so that national efforts could be channeled in a common direction to achieve a far more credible defense, as "the whole is greater than the sum of the parts."

The major challenge to NATO today, as in 1983, is to develop an effective peacetime strategy to manage its resources, reverse structural disarmament, and reinforce deterrence and defense. Meeting that challenge offers the only chance, first, of restoring the public consensus on defense spending; second, of improving the conventional element of the NATO deterrent; and third, of avoiding another transatlantic crisis stemming from some action such as a congressional troop-withdrawal amendment.

Since 1977, the United States has pressured the Europeans to spend at least 3 percent more a year. The Europeans also talked about better output for their defense spending but paid little attention to how that could be achieved and shied away from establishing any real priorities for NATO. Both sides had lost sight of the classic concept of strategy as a way to marshal, manage, and harmonize resources for the achievement of specific goals.

As I have noted, beginning in 1984, the alliance began to come to grips with the need to bolster its conventional defense and to recognize the need for a peacetime resources strategy. Some may not use my terminology, but the concept has surfaced continually as an important element in the defense ministerial communiqués of the last two years. Moreover, NATO has moved quickly to put the framework for such a strategy in place. Over the past four years, in particular, it has been engaged in an intensive effort to achieve a better understanding of where it is and where it needs to go.

The goal of NATO's resources strategy is simple: to improve its conventional defense effectiveness—basically, to get more for its money. NATO's peacetime resources strategy should not be viewed as a stereotyped scheme like the Schlieffen Plan or the U.S. Industrial Mobilization Plan of 1940. It is above all a state of mind and method, an attitude and approach that examines creatively all trade-offs, multiplier effects, and investment advantages and incentives. It emphasizes long-range, integrative thinking and the relationships between factors—for example, tactics, technology, and logistics—that are generally treated separately. Finally, it stresses raising key issues to the political level where hard choices and difficult trade-offs must be made.

A Dynamic Net Assessment

To determine its military objectives, the alliance must first determine how it stacks up against the potential adversary, where its vulnerabilities and strengths lie. Thus, a dynamic estimate of the military balance becomes the basic element of my resources strategy.

At the 1963 Defense Ministers Meeting, under the influence of

U.S. Defense Secretary Robert McNamara, the NATO Council was instructed to study, with the help of the Military Committee, the interrelated questions of strategy, force requirements, and available resources. When this important new effort was finished in 1966, and what was called a NATO Force Plan for 1966–70 was adopted, it was recognized that this needed to be an ongoing process. Thus new NATO "force goals" were adopted every two years. A "military appreciation" document attempted to identify not only all military factors likely to affect NATO and Warsaw Pact forces, but technological and demographic developments as well. The problem I found upon my arrival at NATO was that the political side of the house—the ambassadors, certainly the foreign ministers—were not reading and studying these NATO documents. Based on a variety of existing NATO assessments, the allies—on the ambassadorial and ministerial level—must develop a collective estimate of the threat. NATO's assessment must not play down the magnitude of the problem, as has been done in the past.

At the conventional-defense level, NATO's problem is not that it is universally weak but that its strength is uneven. There continue to be several critical weaknesses in its conventional forces as well as critical shortages. Warning time has been reduced. Soviet tactics are changing and are being modeled on blitzkrieg concepts of deep penetration. At NATO, I found the military all agreed that the gap between NATO and the Warsaw Pact was widening. As I have already discussed, NATO's ability to implement its strategy of flexible response is increasingly in jeopardy at the conventional level.

In 1984, I had the Pentagon's longtime "net assessment" man, Andrew Marshall, and Major General Edward Atkeson, an army expert on the balance of forces, come to NATO to discuss ways to better coordinate these elements at NATO.[2] I also worked frequently with Phil Karber on a similar effort. After I was out of government, in the spring of 1987, we collaborated with Mike Moodie to develop an unclassified appraisal we could take around Europe and to the U.S. Congress. Long before I left NATO, Cap Weinberger and I recommended to Lord Carrington that a NATO classified net assessment be developed and taken to the capitals to be discussed with cabinets and prime ministers. General Altenburg, the able chairman of the Military Committee, has picked up the call for a NATO assessment, but the alliance machinery has yet to respond. This is a major challenge for the new NATO secretary-general, Manfred Woerner. I find it ironic that the finance ministers in the so-called Group of Seven start with the presentation of an economic appraisal and then have a free-for-all discussion. This never happens with NATO defense ministers, so it is no wonder that NATO capitals do not understand.

Crucial Deficiencies Determined

A net assessment points up critical deficiencies in NATO forces. A major part of NATO's efforts in the Conventional Defense Improvements effort of 1984 was to determine its critical deficiencies in very specific terms. Among the most serious problems identified in 1985 were the following:

- NATO's shortfall in standing ground forces provides the alliance with only a limited ability to prevent a breakthrough. This shortcoming exacerbates alliance dependence on adequate warning and the question of how the alliance will respond to ambiguous warnings.
- There are too many differences in the levels of training, equipment, manning, and availability of mobilizable reserve forces. Some are simply not adequate to the task. Nor does NATO have effective means to defeat, disrupt, or destroy the enemy's reserves.
- There are serious deficiencies in the numbers of suitable aircraft, modern munitions, and support systems for effective, offensive counter-air operations. A favorable air situation depends on early reinforcement, and NATO has not had sufficient infrastructure to receive the airplanes and support coming from the United States. Furthermore, NATO would find it difficult to distinguish between friendly and hostile aircraft.
- The overall military capabilities of Portugal, Greece, and Turkey are seriously deficient.
- In the maritime area, antisubmarine warfare, anti-air warfare, and mine countermeasures must be improved.
- Stocks of simple but essential supplies such as ammunition and petrol are insufficient.

A unique and politically sensitive problem is chemical warfare. At the last minute, the West German foreign minister blocked this issue from inclusion in a list of conventional weapons shortcomings. In the absence of a comprehensive and verifiable ban on chemical weapons, which NATO was fully committed to seeking, the alliance needed not only good defensive chemical capabilities but also an effective deterrent. Today NATO would have to consider a nuclear response to a chemical attack. At a time when all of NATO's efforts are designed to push back as far as possible the moment at which nuclear weapons would be called for, this situation is unacceptable. Many members of the U.S. Congress, seeking to restore some flexibility in this area, have come to favor binary munitions production by the United States. Because our allies are not amenable to peacetime deployment of binary weapons in Central Europe, NATO has been forced to make provisions for these weapons in reinforcement planning.

In Carrington's Conventional Defense Improvements effort in the spring of 1985, NATO achieved consensus on these areas as needing immediate attention. (Only the chemical weapons issue was swept under the table.) The question was, what would NATO do about them? Already there have been some concrete results. Infrastructure funding was doubled. That decision will enable NATO to take care of 90 percent of the minimum operational requirement and 70 percent of the shelters needed to protect aircraft reinforcements coming from North America.[3] The ministers agreed to expand critical ammunition stocks. Secretary of Defense Weinberger and Defense Minister Woerner agreed to develop a system for distinguishing friendly aircraft from enemy ones in order to avoid shooting down our own planes.

The Conceptual Military Framework

Fundamental to NATO's peacetime resources strategy is a central concept of what must be done and how to achieve its goals. In the past, NATO has planned five to eight years ahead. Consequently, when creative ideas emerged, when new technologies became available and novel operational concepts were advanced, NATO was not equipped to capitalize on their potential. West German Defense Minister Manfred Woerner expressed his frustration with this problem when he felt barraged by a host of new ideas—Air Land Battle, Follow-on Forces Attack (FOFA), Emerging Technologies (ET), and others—and needed to know how they related to what NATO was already doing. Clearly, the alliance required a better intellectual and conceptual framework to guide its thinking, direct its planning, and discipline its resources management. Woerner, therefore, proposed the development of a Conceptual Military Framework.

As I noted earlier many in the Pentagon, and indeed some British, tended to question anything with the word *conceptual* in it. As one British general said to me, "It might be an escape from reality" or "It might produce a stereotype doctrine." In defining my resources strategy I was careful never to start with the Conceptual Military Framework (CMF), but, rather, with the discussions of military appreciation, net assessment, and critical deficiencies. After defining our strengths and vulnerabilities, the CMF established objectives and priorities and proposed the best ways for us to use our resources. It was important to review short and long-term trade-offs.

NATO's defense ministers charged the Military Committee, together with the major commanders, to respond to Minister Woerner's challenge. The committee and then Supreme Allied Commander General Bernard Rogers did so with a bold, innovative approach looking fifteen to twenty years into the future. Their Conceptual Military Framework is designed to discipline NATO's military thinking, tactics, and technologies to the battlefield of the 1990s and beyond.

More specifically, the Conceptual Military Framework defined the tasks required of alliance forces. Task definition—and agreement by ministers as to their priorities—provides the base from which NATO's efforts to maximize the impact of alliance resources can begin. Individual nations each year can be given a report card, on not only how each is performing on its part of CDI but also their required contribution to CMF tasks. Those agreed tasks are:

1. Defeat of the lead echelon of the attacking force
2. Capability to attack follow-on forces
3. Winning the air battle
4. Sea control
5. Protection of maritime power
6. Protection of allied shipping
7. Safeguarding rear areas

Later, crisis management was added to these tasks—indeed, a most important step forward.

Goals, Priorities, and Planning

The first three elements of my resources strategy lead to the fourth element: better planning. Armies, navies, and air forces in the sixteen alliance countries each have their own strategies and priorities; on top of this, each defense ministry has its own plans. No wonder there is a problem for genuine integrated planning, something that had been championed for over a decade by my defense adviser, Dr. Larry Legere.

Efforts to improve NATO planning were intensified at the Spring 1985 Defense Ministers Meeting in Brussels. Ministers were presented with a NATO Executive Work Group (EWG) report containing extensive recommendations for remedying deficiencies and, equally important, for strengthening NATO's defense planning. Lord Carrington, in conjunction with Assistant Secretary-General Robin Beard, also began to urge that a new process be introduced on long-range armaments planning that would go hand-in-hand with the force planning process. The Carrington-Beard initiative met with much opposition from nations fearing loss of decision-making power. But the persistence of these two, along with Beard's successor, Mack Mattingly, eventually won out on a NATO armaments planning system. This case again illustrates that progress in the alliance only too often comes from the drive and determination of two or three men who never give up.

Of course, the ultimate aim of better planning is to coordinate the priorities and goals of the various defense ministries to ensure a strong, unified effort. If Sam Nunn's troop-withdrawal amendment was an effort to wake up the capitals of the alliance, this is an attempt to get everybody not only awake but in step. In our own Pentagon, the effort especially paid off through the involvement of its number two man, Deputy Secretary William Taft, in NATO's resources problem. Because he also chairs the Pentagon's Defense Resources Board, which manages the allocation of resources in our own military establishment, an especially important planning link was created.

This linkage was a first for the Pentagon, and Taft carried out his new role so aggressively that, to my initial dismay but ultimate approval, he asked for my right arm, Dennis Kloske, to become his executive for this work. Taft also participated in our new initiative for Council meetings of Deputy Defense Ministers, in which the French vigorously joined, to discuss better use of defense resources at a higher political level. The reinforced Council was used to drive forward the cooperative research and development programs initiated under the "good" Nunn amendment. Taft, the scion of a prominent American political family and the youngest Deputy Secretary in history, deserves great credit for being more active than any previous Deputy Secretary of Defense on NATO matters.

Coalition Solutions for Coalition Problems

As an alliance, NATO must think about planning, working, and, if necessary, fighting as a coalition. Of course, NATO would prefer not to fight but to deter. Deterrence, however, is also a coalition requirement. A brilliant example of what a coalition approach can accomplish is the NATO Airborne Warning and Control System (AWACS). The planning, programming, budgeting, provisioning, training, and commanding of each individual nation does not add up to an effective coalition. Rather, such a coalition is a result of the allies making a collective effort so that the whole becomes greater than the sum of the parts.

I often cite to Congress, as another important example of coalition solutions, a cooperative weapons system developed as a model for reversing structural disarmament. The Multiple Launch Rocket System (MLRS) is a cost-effective "growth" system: an accurate long-range missile capable of dispensing rockets, mines, "smart" weapons, and submunitions. Under the so-called Nunn Cooperative Program, the United States will pay 40 percent of the cost and the Europeans 60 percent. Both get a common, more effective battlefield system at less cost.

While joint funding might be the best approach for the large expenditures like AWACS, other approaches should not be ruled out to meet other needs. We could, for example, collaborate on production. The consolidated European production of the infrared imaging Maverick and the MLRS could become an excellent example of this. Another example could be a European initiative to develop a modern automated facility for the production of ammunition, maybe in a country with lower labor costs like Portugal, Spain, or Turkey. Ammunition shortages remain NATO's greatest deficiency. Although NATO has made some progress on this issue, if the Europeans pooled their resources, exploiting advances in robotics and other technologies, they could greatly increase their efficiency and enhance their wartime production capability and mobilization potential.

Another approach toward coalition solutions is specialization. NATO already has specialization to a certain degree in the maritime field, where the United States and Britain provide blue-water capabilities and other allies concentrate on shallow-water tasks in the British Channel and North Sea. Under budgetary pressures, however, the alliance may be moving toward a kind of de facto specialization as allies individually decide that they can no longer afford to assume particular roles or missions. Rather than specialization by default, NATO must self-consciously examine possibilities for specialization in order to exploit each ally's comparative advantage.

Technology Management

The following chapter discusses technology strategy in general. Here we will stress the importance of sharing technology within the West and protecting our technology from the East.

NATO has neither protected its technology adequately nor shared it effectively; witness the Toshiba-Kongsberg case involving Japan and Norway. The flow to the East of vital Western technology that aids the Soviets in their military buildup in turn forces NATO to take more expensive measures in response. That is hardly an effective use of resources. The costs of technology transfer to Western security are truly staggering. Data obtained by the Soviets on the F-18 fighters saved them perhaps five years of development time and $55 million in research costs.[4] The recent sale of advanced submarine-propeller manufacturing equipment by Toshiba-Kongsberg will allow the Soviet navy to leapfrog seven to ten years of Western research. For about $20 million, the Soviets will drive us to spend tens of billions of dollars on antisubmarine warfare over the next decade and a half.[5]

In the face of an aggressive Eastern block strategy to steal, buy, and divert Western technology, the United States and its allies have been unable to formulate a coherent policy to control the damage. While Washington complains that the West's informal Coordinating Committee (COCOM) is too lax in its role as technology watchdog, our European allies scoff at our list of "critical technologies" (200,000 different items)[6] that may not be exported to the East. At the same time, it is important to realize that the United States will pay a price if an overemphasis on protection prevents allies from sharing technology. The side of the Pentagon that advocates protection from Communist nations has been prevailing over the side of the Pentagon and elements in the State Department that advocate sharing with allies. What is needed in the Defense Department is an assistant secretary who will manage the functions of trade, assistance, and protection, so that these areas are coordinated under a uniform policy. Severely restricting technology sharing when that technology is not the latest state of the art reduces the rate at which the West can incorporate beneficial technology into operational systems on the battlefield. Since our superior technology is our ace-in-the-hole with the Soviets, it is imperative that we harmonize technology protection and technology sharing.

The job, however, does not end there. NATO must also exploit new technologies more effectively. First, relatively mature technology must be introduced into the battlefield. Dennis Kloske took the lead in developing a long-term framework permitting the release of Hughes radar technology to the European Fighter Aircraft consortium. This same framework can be used for other programs.

Arms Cooperation

The armaments cooperation efforts of the 1970s focused on the two-way street, the balance of defense trade between Europe and America, which has long favored the U.S. This would not work for the 1980s because the overall trade deficit reached $170 billion by 1987.[7] Members of Congress had to be convinced that armaments cooperation was not simply a move for Europeans to sell us more weapons, but was a way to obtain a better return on defense investment for all alliance partners. The concept of a resources strategy fulfilled this need, and I used it extensively in briefing visiting Congressional delegations. We built momentum.

From February 1986 to October 1987, over twelve Memoranda of Understanding (MOUs) with our allies were signed to pursue cooperative programs. One such program is a warhead with an automatic target seeker (called a fire-and-forget weapon) to be fired from 155mm artillery. Twelve NATO nations have signed on. Another example, for NATO air forces, is a weapon that can be fired while the plane is standing off a safe distance from the target but which has a modular system with options for payload, guidance system, and propulsion to be selectively mixed and matched to respond to hard, soft, fixed, or moving targets. Seven nations signed up for the program. A third example is an advanced, high-capacity, secure, and Electronic Counter Measure resistant information distribution system for both data and voice. This multifunctional information distribution system provides a capability of interconnecting scattered sources and users, both airborne and surface, and gives their identification and position. The program, to which nine nations signed Statement of Intent, will complement NATO's target-tracking capability, the AWACS. The future of these remarkable efforts remains dependent upon congressional funding as well as European funding, and on working toward partnership for better return on investment and lower unit costs.[8]

European Resource Management

The last element of a resources strategy involves the interrelationship of economics and security and the need for a genuine two-pillared NATO alliance. In short, Europeans must take more initiative in building a defense-industrial complex.

After I had started a public campaign of speeches around Europe demanding that priority be given to a resources strategy, the new chairman of the Independent European Program Group (IEPG) sought a meeting with me at NATO. Jan van Houwelingen was a stocky, genial Dutchman in the religious wing of the Christian Democratic Appeal party (*Christen Democratish Appel*), which gave birth to an antinuclear stance and uncertain commitment to the Euromissile deployment. Some of the old NATO and Pentagon hands were skeptical of this group and rather unhappy to see van Houwelingen in such a key position. I had never met him before, but as I sat across the table from him, I was impressed with his deep sincerity. Unlike many with a moral concern about nuclear weapons, he wanted to work his way out of the dilemma through improved conventional-defense efforts. Behind his modest and mild demeanor, I found a grim determination to make something truly important out of this largely stagnant organization formed in 1976.

Van Houwelingen proposed that instead of many Memoranda of Understanding between individual European countries and the United States, there be one collective MOU. The twelve to fourteen "two-way streets" to the United States, which kept Europe from pooling its resources, would become a single transatlantic highway. Van Houwelingen was a breath of fresh air. Before trying to get the Pentagon on board, he set out to discover what the chances were that the Europeans would act in such a collective manner. His idea was unfortunately rejected by the larger European powers. Britain, for example, was very comfortable at that time with the present system under which it had almost balanced its transatlantic trade. Britain had its "special relationship" with the United States and that helped the technology-sharing problem as well. Ironically, we were able to get Pentagon support for the van Houwelingen initiative. At a subsequent Defense Ministers meeting, Secretary Weinberger made the offer of our willingness to participate in an "umbrella MOU." Plainly, the big European powers did not want to open the umbrella.

Despite the reluctance of the major European powers, van Houwelingen was very successful in giving greater visibility and influence to the IEPG. For example, during his tenure IEPG began to meet for the first time with the full complement of defense ministers. Moreover, in November 1985, he got the support of IEPG defense ministers to form a study team "to submit concrete proposals for improving the competitiveness of the European defense equipment industry." In December 1986, IEPG received the report entitled "Toward a Stronger Europe." It had a great sense of urgency, was very critical of Europe, and offered a way ahead. Real cost growth of European weapons was increasing about 5 percent a year—defense budgets were not.[9] If Americans had this problem, the Europeans were far worse off because of fragmented markets, which led to smaller volume of productivity with the predictable result of higher unit costs. The United States was concerned about burden sharing. One way to better share that burden was for Europe to be able to do more by being more efficient. The report commended the U.S. administration for supporting such efforts even though it recognized "the challenge which will result for U.S. industry."

The report portrayed Europe at a crossroads. If Europe could get itself organized, it would be able "to cooperate in sophisticated programs with the United States," as well as introduce its own products into the U.S. market. Even the jobs of the 1 million people employed by Europe's defense industries would be protected—not, I might add, by protectionism but by competition and market forces. If this kind of organization were not forthcoming, however, by the turn of the century, Europe would be relegated to a subordinate position.

The report noted that Europe's technology base is "encouragingly competitive," but fragmented markets mean that this potential is not being realized. The report noted that the challenge to European defense industries is to "so arrange their activities to improve the cost ratio of R & D to production so that unit costs are reduced to a competitive level. The internal European markets for armaments, although only 40 percent the size of that of the United States, would nevertheless provide adequate scope to improve satisfactorily the cost ratios," were it not for market fragmentation. "A further challenge for the future will be to strengthen Europe's technological base through the coordination of research programmes across Europe and the elimination of unnecessary duplication."[10]

The report, controversial to many nationalistic Europeans, called for "a proportion of existing national defense research funds [to] be diverted to establish a common budget," to go hand-in-hand with a "common research program."[11] Regrettably, this recommendation was too much for the defense ministers to stomach. Much more cross-boundary trading was needed. The bottom line, said the report, was that genuine European-wide competition and not market distortion was needed. The panel called for a defense-industry advisory group and also for a small but permanent IEPG staff of some twenty persons to translate "will into action," with a director general who could also speak to the United States on behalf of Europe. The mild-mannered Dutchman had surprised the bureaucrats who opposed change, and had set off a process to get Europe organized. Fortunately, the industrious Spaniard Eduardo Serra was to succeed him and maintain momentum.

Of even greater concern for not only a NATO but an allied resources strategy relates to those huge sums expended, for example, on fighter aircraft. Japan was convinced to drop the independent production of its own fighter, as did Israel. West Europe is now locked into several such fighters for the 1990s and beyond, one by the French, another by the British, German, and Spanish consortium, and the Swedish Grippen. The so-called European Fighter Aircraft will each cost $55 to $60 million, as compared to a U.S. Hornet 2000, available perhaps as early as 1995 at $25 to $28 million, or an F-16 Agile Falcon at $15.5 million. It is, of course, understandable that Europeans want to preserve their aviation industries, but it would be better in the long run for the allied nations to collaborate with the United States on a fighter for beyond the year 2000. Modern planes, whose costs have skyrocketed so that there is no money for ammunition or air defense, make little sense as structural disarmament marches on. It should be kept in mind that the total cost of these five aircraft for the alliance will be between $60 and $70 billion![12] Ironically, these huge programs are not discussed on a collective basis at NATO. Carrington's call for armaments planning should encompass these massive investment costs, however difficult it might be for sovereignty sensitivities.

17 Technology Strategy

THE arms-control process over the last several years has been driven by the Soviet fear of America's superior technological capability, as evidenced by the Strategic Defense Initiative (SDI). Plainly, the strategic trump card of the United States and its allies vis-à-vis the Warsaw Pact is superior technology. Technology, however, is a strategic potential. An overall technology strategy is needed before its benefits can be realized. Here, as elsewhere, what is needed is a long-term, integrated approach—one that appreciates that we are dealing not so much with emerging as with "merging" technologies.

A coherent, integrated technology strategy faces formidable obstacles in its formulation and implementation. In large military institutions there is almost always resistance to technological and tactical change. With its stress on tradition and continuity, the desire and, indeed, the need to regulate and codify, the military establishment reinforces a disinclination toward change and technological innovation. Historically, some otherwise quite outstanding military leaders have failed to recognize the dynamic interaction between technology and tactics. A famed British naval admiral, John Jervis, condemned his prime minister, William Pitt, as the greatest of fools for trying to force the torpedo on His Majesty's navy. Prior to World War I, in 1910, young General Foch ridiculed the use of aircraft in war. General Lord Kitchener dismissed the tank as a toy as late as 1915. In both world wars, British and U.S. navies initially resisted using the convoy system for the protection of merchant shipping.

It is true that our modern military is the product of a technological age far different from that of Jarvis or Kitchener. Ours is a society where change is commonplace. Nevertheless, our armed services are run by highly skilled managers under great pressure to make the most of existing assets, and their perspectives are inevitably short term. Civilian defense bureaucracies also tend to resist change. I experienced this firsthand while NATO ambassador. The Strategic Defense Initiative was set up to operate outside of the Pentagon bureaucracy for this very reason. By the same token, as NATO ambassador, I found that same Pentagon bureaucracy in the "policy" area attempting to block our proposals for systematically looking at the conventional-defense applications and by-products from the billions of dollars being invested in SDI.

In the spring of 1985, I ran several seminars on SDI for the benefit of Europeans who were upset over the implication that it would separate the United States from Europe. I had a distinguished group of American panel members, which included Dr. James Fletcher, Dr. Fred Seitz, and General James Abrahamson, the SDI director. I do not have a technical background, to say the least, but through our discussions I became greatly impressed with the benefits to our conventional defense that could be derived from the basic SDI investment. Battle management in space was not a replica of battle management over Europe, but the same investment in information technologies could serve both. Rail guns for space defense and European defense would not be the same, but both come from investments in kinetic energy. Sensor technologies and robotics are also used for both. One can imagine the effect of unmanned aircraft or even tanks. The comprehensive "fault-tolerant" data-processing systems being developed for SDI also offer great promise for the new generation of sophisticated conventional weapons that rely on computer control. Dr. James Fletcher, former (and now again) head of NASA, had at the president's behest headed the initial panel on the feasibility of what became known as the Strategic Defense Initiative.

"Why," I finally asked him, "did your panel not look at the conventional applications of these technologies?" It made military sense, it made investment sense, and it made legislative sense where we had in effect a conventional-defense coalition of members of Congress who were skeptical about SDI and could show Europeans more directly that the defense of Europe had not been forgotten.

When he responded that that hadn't been their mandate—which was to see if we could shoot down ballistic missiles—I proposed a second panel, one more centered at NATO to review the conventional aspect.

Dr. Fletcher, Dr. Seitz, Gen. Abrahamson, and Dr. Henri Durand (the NATO science adviser) all enthusiastically agreed. Come Monday morning, my staff was banging out another cable to Washington. I decided it should arrive just as Weinberger was stepping onto his plane for the next NATO Defense Ministers Meeting. Since Cap would read the cable in flight, the Washington bureaucracy would not have time to think up any negative reasons to block the initiative. When he stepped off his plane in Brussels, he was so enthusiastic about the cable that, in the car together, he said, "Let's talk to Carrington."

I knew the State Department would deeply resent such a unilateral move and would never forgive me. In asking him to wait until I could get the State Department on board, I made a fatal mistake. For one solid year a deputy assistant secretary of the Defense Department, not the State Department, would drag his feet, hinder, obstruct, and bureaucratize to derail this effort. He argued that it might let Europeans in the back door to SDI technologies. He also said that we could not be absolutely sure what battlefield uses could occur, so we should not create undue expectations through such an effort.

Meanwhile, the Hill had become increasingly polarized on SDI, and a disgusted Senator Nunn took $350 million from the SDI program and put it into a Balanced Technology Initiative (BTI) for conventional defense. Plainly, "merging" technologies cannot be compartmentalized but should be employed broadly to obtain both better tactical and strategic defense. It is not just the British admiral or prime minister of two centuries ago who can block technological applications, but key actors in our time as well.

Another major impediment for an effective technology strategy is the tendency for bureaucracies and outside experts to rely on panacea weapons or doctrines. The problem is that a weapon or doctrine may indeed play a dominant role for a time but may also be undercut by changes in technology and the operational environment. The blind application of yesterday's technological and strategic lessons will rarely lead to success, and will often result in disaster. The problem with the

Maginot Line as a response to the World War I "lesson" regarding the power of the offensive was not the failure to apply technology to operational concepts but a failure to see emerging new threats and opportunities. The line could have served very well as a defensive shield in conjunction with a mobile reserve—a counterattacking force—that could have cut off the German thrust into Belgium. Although they possessed technology equal or superior to that of the Germans, the French were trapped in a defensive attitude, the legacy of Verdun, which blinded them to the new opportunities for mobility. Today in Europe, there are those who so accept nuclear weapons as absolute that they see no need for any other real defense effort.[1]

There is hope, however, because history also tells us of those military leaders and institutions that have thought in a creative manner about technology, weapons, and doctrine. Often the real innovators are to be found at the lower levels: the colonels, captains, and brigadiers. Figures such as the historian-general J. F. C. Fuller, Billy Mitchell, and the young Colonel de Gaulle were innovative and controversial, and they suffered for it. An exception to the pattern of institutional rigidity was the development by the United States of an extraordinary combined-arms capability for amphibious operations even before World War II. Many critics at the time recalled the Gallipoli experience of the previous war and described the effort as impossible.

Today the challenge of promoting an interface between technology and strategy is perhaps more important than at any point in the past. What new operational and strategic thinking will accompany, for example, the development of Stealth technology for aircraft and cruise missiles? Important, too, is the capacity for flexibility and adaptability—preferably the ability to anticipate, but at a minimum the ability to react quickly. The Israelis may not have anticipated the threat posed by precision-guided weapons to tank operations in the 1973 war. They were able, however, to devise tactical countermeasures in relatively short order, with profound implications for the outcome of that conflict.

A technological lead is no guarantee of a military edge if innovation is not translated into battlefield effectiveness. The Wehrmacht in May–June 1940 was the product of new operational concepts, not just new weapons. The British had invented the tank and Americans dive-bombing, but it was the Germans who first employed both to decisive effect. An essential element in their success was the development of a command and communications structure that allowed the coordination of armor and air power, a combination that has dominated the European battlefield since 1939.

Are we repeating a past error with today's technologies, many of which—like the tank in the 1920s—lack an organizational home and institutional support? Modern air forces resist the adoption of cruise missiles and remotely piloted vehicles that could assume some of their most demanding and highest-cost missions, such as reconnaissance and interdiction. They also worry that such systems could ultimately replace their dearly beloved manned aircraft. The technologies that will provide the ability to see and destroy targets well over the horizon in support of NATO's Follow-on Forces Attack concept may not be fully exploited, nor have we fully explored the broader strategic implications of such technologies. We need force multipliers, but are we prepared to break out of comfortable habits and be innovative?

An area with great potential is that of Stealth, or low-observable technology. This is a revolutionary area with potential application across our force structure—not just for the fighter and bomber aircraft already being developed, but possibly for land vehicles and even ships. Moreover, Stealth exploits a major Soviet vulnerability: the key role of radar-based air defense in safeguarding Soviet and Warsaw Pact territory and covering offensive operations. Perhaps more than any other technology, Stealth will depend for its utility on the development of new, highly innovative operational concepts.[2]

An important aspect of the reluctance to innovate has been a frequent failure to anticipate the effect of technological change on the shifting balance between offensive and defensive power on the battlefield. This is a process of continual and reciprocal change, with success going to the side that can see the swing away from the prevailing operational environment and then manage the necessary changes in a coherent, constructive way.

Just prior to World War I, the European military establishment was taken completely aback by the revolution in favor of defense by modern artillery, the machine gun, and barbed wire. This defensive trend was supported by the rise of "mobilization warfare"—the harnessing of railroads and all other aspects of modern industrial societies—in which the productive power of war economies would outstrip the offensive capacity of armies in the field.[3] Within twenty years, however, the mechanization of warfare and the growth of air-power would restore mobility and again tilt the balance in favor of the offensive. But many so-called military experts did not understand what was happening.

Anticipating where the balance will lie between offensive and defensive power in any future conventional battlefield—in Europe and elsewhere—is of great importance. It influences the potential duration of a conflict and the possibility of escalating to nuclear weapons. For these same reasons it also shapes perceptions about deterrence. Of course, our military planners and engineers must try to shape that balance to our favor—one that gives stability to our defense.

The current trends in weapons technology can help us forecast what that balance might be. "Smart" and "brilliant" munitions guide themselves. Tremendous advances in detection, targeting, command, control, and communications will increase the ability to attack targets at great range. This may well create an environment in which the ability to bring firepower to bear on an armored attacker outstrips the mobility of forces on the battlefield. Factors such as terrain and weight of armor impose limits on mobility that modern tank-heavy forces are rapidly reaching. Advances related to firepower, by contrast, enjoy far fewer constraints. Moreover, as the 1973 Middle East War and the Falklands conflict confirmed, the logistic burden of modern warfare, with its high rates of attrition and consumption, is likely to be immense. Historically, the confluence of these factors has led to wars of attrition in which the ability to restore freedom of action rested on innovation and on superior leadership and morale. It is essential that we promote the intellectual flexibility required for an ongoing and objective assessment of this dynamic offense-defense balance.

The current controversy over SDI is really a rediscovery of the traditional debate about the proper role of offense and defense, stirred by the potential of new technologies. It may be too soon to offer conclusive judgments as to the nature, practicality, and wisdom of deploying a system for defense against ballistic missiles. It is not irrelevant, however, that the Soviet Union has been actively engaged in research on strategic defenses since the 1960s and has spent a good deal more for research on key technologies such as lasers, directed energy, and the related field of antisatellite systems. In terms of the balance between offensive and defensive forces, the Soviets have more or less divided their resources evenly between the two.

With regard to conventional defense, while NATO has been moving to build a capacity for a more "active" defense using FOFA technologies, there have also been calls for "passive" defense, making greater use of barriers including sophisticated sensors, mines, and liquid explosives. The best tactics are often found in a combination of offensive and defensive capabilities. There are measures in this area—some relatively low cost—that could greatly enhance the effective use of terrain in Western Europe for forward defense. During his tenure as under secretary of defense, Fred Ikle tried heroically to persuade the Germans to be more receptive to this option.

A word of warning is in order as we discuss the offensive-defensive balance. At the level of conventional strategy, as opposed to tactics and operations, offense and defense are not "counterbalancing" postures.[4] Experience shows that a strategically defensive stance can be maintained for some time, but it seldom ends the conflict. Maintaining the capacity for maneuver and counterattack to retake any territory overrun is not incompatible with the notion of a defensive alliance.

In the formulation of a technology strategy, management is crucial. Technological and tactical changes in warfare were once long in coming, with progress measured in centuries. During the industrial revolution, major developments occurred over decades; today in the age of electronics and microcomputers, significant change can be measured in years. Today, delays of a few years may be destabilizing. Errors that were once easily and cheaply remedied can now impose disastrously high costs, wasting national resources. Will our ability to manage technological change improve to keep pace with our technological potential?

The British and American technological surge in World War II succeeded largely because of the priority it received at the very highest levels, together with the marriage of managerial ability and extraordinary scientific talent. The 1940 offensive of 3,000 German aircraft against Britain was defeated in substantial part by that very small group of men who had developed radar five years earlier. The decryption of German communications and the development of sea-scanning radar played a great role in the defeat of the submarine threat in the Atlantic. Similarly, the ability to read Japanese signals made possible the pivotal American victory at Midway. At its peak, the Manhattan Project, the climactic achievement of a broader success story, involved some 120,000 persons and $2 billion in the effort to produce a practical atomic weapon.

How should we formulate a technology strategy? How can we make the most effective use of our resources if we focus our technological efforts on maximizing our strategic flexibility, our capacity for the discriminate use of force, and our enemy's weaknesses? A first step is to build on what NATO has already accomplished; a second step is to support and expand what is being carried out in the Pentagon under the aegis of the Competitive Strategies project.

In many respects the ongoing NATO experience provides a valuable model for relating technological initiatives to strategic needs. In the 1980s, the Atlantic alliance, facing the prospect of increasing resource constraints, was presented with the acute challenge of managing the relationship between technological change and the orchestration of doctrine and strategy. It was clear that, more than ever before, technology would make a difference in the competitive positions of the Warsaw Pact and NATO. The question was, and continues to be, which of the two alliances will develop and apply it most effectively? While the NATO allies are generally superior in the laboratories, the Warsaw Pact under Soviet direction is generally faster and more uniform in its ability to transform technological advances into deployed systems. Of course, they have been aided tremendously by the leakage of advanced technology from the West.

During the 1980s, it became evident that the Warsaw Pact was steadily closing the technological gap across the spectrum of conventional systems. A new breed of Soviet military leaders was quick to recognize the importance of the new weapons. As Marshall N. V. Orgarkov said in 1984, "rapid changes in the development of conventional means of destruction and the emergence . . . of automated reconnaissance and strike complexes, long-range high-accuracy terminally guided combat systems, unmanned flying machines, and qualitatively new electronic control systems . . . make it possible to sharply increase the destructive potential of conventional weapons, bringing them closer to weapons of mass destruction. . . ."[5] The new Soviet emphasis is particularly threatening since NATO has long relied on the superior quality of its forces to offset the numerical superiority of the Warsaw Pact.

There were four milestones in NATO's quest for a common approach to exploiting new and emerging technologies. First, there was General Bernard Rogers' concept of Follow-on Forces Attack (FOFA), mentioned earlier. NATO lacks depth behind its major fronts and cannot readily trade space for time. The forward deployment and maneuver orientation of Warsaw Pact forces makes them capable of launching offensive penetrations with little warning. Rogers saw the absolute necessity of slowing down the advance of Warsaw Pact forces by attacking key fixed targets, such as command centers, but also "forces in motion"—all with great precision and at considerable distance from the front. All of these were called the "follow-on forces." Rogers was, by a new nomenclature, advocating a time-honored principle of war of trying to interdict the attacker and hit his more vulnerable rear. The result was a guiding tactical concept (FOFA) that can harness technology to armaments in an effective manner.

It was the advent of new technologies for detection, guidance, attack, and coordination of these elements that offered the opportunity to accomplish his design. The key areas of technological advance include microelectronics and a variety of optical, radar, infrared, and laser sensors. Added to this are the new weapons and advanced data-processing systems that will make possible the location and destruction of mobile and stationary targets up to 300 kilometers behind the front line of battle.[6] The idea is to give to the land battle the surveillance and coordination functions that the Airborne Warning and Control System brings to air warfare. In the munitions field, "smart" and even more autonomous "brilliant" antitank weapons can be delivered in great numbers to the target area by missile. Other advanced weapons are being developed specifically for the destruction of Warsaw Pact airfields, command centers, and other high-value targets. These might previously have required nuclear attack, a fact that takes on even greater importance in the post-INF treaty period.[7]

Would the resources needed to develop and deploy these technologies be forthcoming? Part of the answer was in the second milestone, Caspar Weinberger's Emerging Technologies (ET) program, developed by William Hoehn in the Pentagon, who later joined Senator Nunn's staff. This was the Pentagon half of the Rogers concept. It aimed at the accelerated development of new technologies that could enhance our ability to defend against Warsaw Pact first-echelon forces, bolster NATO's air defenses, and improve the prospects for the interdiction of follow-on forces, as well as our capacity for C3I (command, control, communications, and intelligence).

Whether these new technologies can be translated into operational capabilities in the NATO context will be determined in part by the third milestone, the Conceptual Military Framework. A fourth milestone was the declared effort by the alliance to move toward genuine armaments cooperation among the sixteen members of NATO, disciplined by the operational concepts described above. Notably the alliance began to explore cooperative efforts in the context of a broader alliance defense-resources strategy so that the ET program would not be seen by Europeans as a "Buy American" thrust. Both of these milestones are described in the previous chapter as essential elements of a resources strategy.

These significant milestones have been accompanied by a number of stimulating actions by Congress, which recognizes the need to promote cooperative efforts on technologies for conventional defense. As noted in Chapter 5, in 1985, the NATO Cooperative Research and Development Program was initiated by Sam Nunn to stimulate cooperation on development of defense equipment and munitions and to promote related efforts on material production.

The Nunn program, quite properly, was aimed at getting more from the superior collective resources of the Atlantic alliance while working to reduce NATO's reliance on nuclear weapons by strengthening conventional defenses. In other words, a technology strategy was being developed to reduce NATO's excessive and disproportionate reliance on nuclear weapons. To further this objective, two additional congressional initiatives were launched in 1987: in the House of Representatives' Armed Services Committee, a strong consensus formed behind the Conventional Defense Initiative (CDI), aimed at side-by-side testing and evaluation of existing allied weapons systems and equipment in ten mandated areas; and the Senate sponsored the Balanced Technology Initiative (BTI) to provide support for the development of promising new technologies in a range of areas, including "smart" weapons, surveillance, data processing and communications, armor and anti-armor systems, high-power microwaves, and "special" technologies (for example, superconductors, tactical missile interception, and cruise missile guidance). The CDI and BTI programs are intended as complementary efforts that respond to the challenge of bolstering non-nuclear capabilities and more specifically blunt the Soviet blitzkrieg capability.[8] Dr. Ronald Kerber, deputy under secretary of defense for research and advanced technologies, and his special assistant, Dr. William Snowden, took it upon themselves to develop an architecture for the BTI program, thus making it another valuable piece in an allied-technology strategy.

The West has the advantage of a whole new technological surge, but countries could go broke pursuing each and every technological possibility. One must remember what the tactical and operational requirements of the battlefield are.[9] We have made great strides in this direction through a range of fortunate initiatives in the Congress, at the Pentagon, and at NATO, despite those who would obstruct innovation and the full use of merging technologies.

An overall concept for technology and tactics fortunately bloomed in 1988. It became known as the Competitive Strategies project, which was initiated by Secretary Weinberger at the suggestion of Andrew Marshall and Professor Graham Allison of Harvard University. The project was carried out by an ever-active Dennis Kloske. Frank Carlucci has given it the highest priority. We will never be able to match the Warsaw Pact on a quantitative level, nor can we be as confident as in the past that our qualitative edge will allow us to prevail in the event of war. What we can do, however, is consider how to use our considerable strengths to exploit enduring areas of weakness in Soviet strategy and technology—in short, the pursuit of a high-leverage approach.

The Competitive Strategies project is looking at ways to counter Soviet operational concepts for attack on the central front in Europe. The proposed solutions stress the use of stand-off missiles and surveillance capabilities that allow us to see and attack targets in rear areas, with the objective of disrupting or shattering the Soviet offensive timetable. Intelligence-gathering cruise missiles and unmanned aircraft will be an important part of this effort. In addition, continuing consideration must be given to modernizing existing nuclear and dual-capable systems, as allowed under the INF Treaty.[10]

It was appropriate that the Competitive Strategies effort initially be targeted at the European theater because the NATO mechanisms are in place to manage it there. The next and vitally important step should be to apply this approach globally. As part of this process of thinking competitively, we must also consider the opportunities and constraints that both conventional and nuclear arms-control initiatives may raise.

Another word of warning is in order. One of the strategic questions that has yet to be adequately explored concerns the limits to high-technology solutions—or, more properly, the mix of high- and low-technology systems—in relation to conventional-defense improvement. Certain missions will clearly demand expensive, elegant systems, but their cost will almost certainly preclude deploying them in large numbers. Given the very high rates of munitions consumption during the 1973 Middle East War, it is possible that a conventional conflict with the Soviet Union that lasts more than thirty days may involve the use of munitions that would have been familiar to soldiers in World War II. The question of duration is a critical and politically sensitive one for the alliance. It is likely to become even more so as the balance between nuclear and conventional deterrence continues to evolve. What is clear is that technological initiatives cannot be viewed in isolation from issues of readiness and sustainability.

This, too, is a traditional dilemma that may be characterized as "armament in width versus armament in depth." The choice is between building specialized, highly capable systems without a great deal of sustainability versus a larger number of less-specialized systems with substantial reserves of ammunition and so on.

Today the ongoing nuclear competition has had the effect of driving conflict away from direct superpower clashes. Instead, there has been conventional and unconventional conflict with and between the superpowers' friends and allies, and peacetime competition in nuclear weapons technology within the strategic balance. Even Leonid Brezhnev, not widely known for his powers of imagination and insight, reminded us that "the center of gravity in the competition between the two systems"—the United States and the Soviet Union—is now to be found precisely in the fields of science and technology.[11] This is precisely what worries a more clever Gorbachev.

The strategic balance in the nuclear age has become more important than ever as a political phenomenon. Technological developments in warheads and delivery systems can have diplomatic dimensions more immediate than military ones. Maintaining a deterrent requires the effective adaptation of new technologies to tactics and strategy, so that risks—or the perception of risks—can be manipulated in a way that precludes the actual use of force.

The last element in developing a technology strategy is to exploit technology for truly verifiable arms-control agreements as well as crisis management. New technologies can promote strategic stability through improved intelligence and warning, reducing the possibility of a conventional or nuclear surprise attack. Clearly, this is important to the alliance. A related imperative is the enhancement of our space-based capabilities for surveillance and communications, and the improvement of our ability to protect and reconstitute these vital systems in the event of attack.[12] The space-based systems associated with SDI would mean the existence of a large number of platforms suitable for conventional surveillance and communications tasks.

Our creativity in the field of technology is our greatest asset, as the Soviets well know. But it cannot be productive on its own. Rather, an integrated, long-term approach to the management of technological change is essential. In developing a grand strategy, we must view technology policy in the broadest possible context and encourage innovation at all levels. The effective management of technology can serve not only to improve deterrence and defense but also to promote political cohesion among the allies, and future effective arms control.

18 Third World Strategy

MASTER strategist Frederick the Great noted that disaster stems from trying to defend everywhere, for a country ends up effectively defending nowhere. Such a strung-out, linear defense is the very negation of strategy. Without clear priorities as to interests in the heterogeneous Third World, the United States risks overstretching its resources.

The United States has never come to terms with force as an instrument of foreign policy in the Third World. The history of the Cold War shows that there are times when it is a grave mistake to make accommodating gestures before a truly aggressive opponent, but the history of Third World conflicts also shows the danger of blind confrontation. As Professor Jerry Hough has written, "The United States has seldom, in fact, been willing to use enough force to destroy the adversary. As a result, it has applied too little force to be success-ful, but enough to permit the hardliners in a hostile regime to identify themselves with local nationalism and even achieve a victory over the American colossus." He cites the original intervention in the Russian civil war, the Bay of Pigs invasion, and involvement in Nicaragua as examples.[1] The cumulative effect of overengagement plays into Soviet hands by leading toward exhaustion, if not militarily, then politically. Major setbacks for the United States, in Angola, Ethiopia, and Nica-ragua, all came in the wake of our exhausting, domestically wrenching overcommitment in Vietnam. A relatively modest amount of covert aid might have produced a different outcome in Angola, but we will never know because a Vietnam-weary Congress would not support it.

The Soviets in their global strategy have been far wiser than us. They have followed a strategy of the indirect approach: use of proxies, agents, broadcasts, limited aid, and arms supplies. Of course they also operate under different rules of the game. The Soviets do focus on target countries, but for the most part they operate with flexibility and are able to cut forces without loss of face and without creating credibility traps as we did for ourselves in Vietnam. They are often able to move into and influence the power structure, while tactical expediency can often supplant ideological consideration. Theirs is a low-risk, low-investment, low-prestige approach—often indirect.[2] The exception to Soviet success abroad is Afghanistan, where they abandoned the strategy of the indirect approach.

Given the potential traps that exist in an unconstrained U.S. approach to Third World security issues, our policymakers must be guided by a strategy of selectivity defined by certain fundamental principles. These principles may seem obvious to many, but our historical record suggests that we have proceeded too often without bearing them in mind.

The first principle for our Third World strategy must be a clear definition of U.S. interests and of our commitment. "Vital interest" has been one of the most overused phrases in our vocabulary. If *vital* means "essential to our survival," then not all our interests are vital. Nor are they equal. The war in Vietnam provides a good example of our inability to distinguish vital and lesser interests. This unhappy experience of what began as a low-intensity conflict and ended as a conventional war offers a sobering beginning for a discussion of how to formulate a Third World strategy. In 1964, the U.S. Senate, with only two dissenting votes, passed the Tonkin Gulf Resolution, which stated unabashedly: "The United States regards as vital to its national interests and to world peace the maintenance of international peace and security in Southeast Asia."[3]

Few political leaders had fully recognized and thought through the implications of "vital" interests. Subsequently, over a half-million Americans were committed to an indecisive land war in Asia. Four or five years later, the Congress concluded that the government did not have a workable strategy for success in Vietnam and that the vital interest of the United States had become, in fact, to end the war or, failing that, to end America's direct participation in it. Vital interests and commitments need not only to be defined at the outset but reevaluated with time.

This leads to my second principle for a Third World strategy: constant readjustment of means to ends and of approach to objectives. This means maintaining a sense of proportion. The decision makers who refused to commit U.S. forces to Southeast Asia in 1954 understood this far better than those who committed U.S. forces to the area in the 1960s. It is worth spending a moment on the Eisenhower approach. In his attempt to keep in mind what I call a "strategic sense of proportion" regarding Vietnam, Eisenhower developed precise criteria for U.S. intervention: (1) the French had to pledge independence for the Indochina states, so that there would not be a situation of colonialism, but popular support of the indigenous peoples instead; (2) there had to be a concert of powers, beginning with these local Asiatic peoples but including Western powers; (3) our forces must not move in and have French forces pull out so that we had to take over; (4) there must be congressional consultation and support; and (5) any U.S. intervention must be so constituted as to be militarily effective.[4]

Eisenhower's objective was clearly more than just resolving the conflict in Southeast Asia; it was to do so on terms that would give the United States the political high ground to sustain its action. Given this precise objective, Eisenhower's approach was carefully tailored. Three decades later, in 1984, Caspar Weinberger compiled six explicit criteria for U.S. intervention in general. Weinberger said that the United States should only commit combat forces overseas (1) in support of vital interests, (2) if the commitment is wholehearted and reflects an intention to win, (3) to support clearly defined political and military objectives, (4) if we are willing to reassess continually the relationship between our objective and our involved forces, (5) in the face of reasonable assurance of support by the Congress and the people, and (6) as a last resort.[5]

In response, Secretary of State George Shultz stressed that there was no such thing as guaranteed public support in advance for a military action. This airing of differences came in the wake of the withdrawal of our "peacekeeping" force in Lebanon, a withdrawal that Shultz opposed. It is true that public support can follow a successful short-lived military action, but initial congressional reaction can influence that public support. This principle of proportionality involves continuous review of ends and means, and the purpose of the intervention and the reasons for sustaining it should remain clear.

The third principle of a Third World strategy is an understanding of the proper role of credibility and how it is best served. Just as a rigid view of "vital" interests has often led us to be poor strategists, so has the ill-defined goal of "maintaining our credibility." While the credibility argument is much used in favor either of intervention or of increasing a commitment, few people really understand what that argument implies. Credibility comes on one hand from a sense of legitimacy and on the other from a perception of the capability to be successful. There are different kinds of credibility and their interrelationships are important.

- Credibility to an adversary means creating in an adversary's mind a belief that we will initiate and sustain action if our national interests warrant it.
- Credibility with our allies means fostering their belief that we are willing and able to use our power in their interest.
- Credibility on the domestic front entails establishing with the American public a belief in the worthiness of government policies and the methods and costs of achieving them.
- In cases of intervention, credibility with the indigenous people involves securing their acceptance of the means and goals of our action.

Vietnam was a drastic misapplication of the principle of maintaining credibility. As a result, the United States lost credibility on all fronts: with the American people, with its allies, and with international opinion. Maintaining credibility became an end in itself and not, as it must be, a necessary means to accomplish other objectives. The Kennedy-Johnson strategy created a U.S. involvement entirely out of proportion to its original limited interests. The Soviets ultimately gained an important naval base, but we still have conventional superiority in the Pacific. By striving so hard for credibility in a single place, however, we weakened and discredited our military capability to act elsewhere, we set off inflation at home, and we undermined the economic capacity to sustain a forward defense posture. We pulled some troops back from Europe—a truly vital area—and set a precedent for the Belgians and Dutch to move into their present maldeployed situations. The Vietnam strategy also raised questions about our commitment to Japan.

The U.S. commitment of marines in Lebanon is another interesting case. Geoffrey Kemp, on the NSC staff at the time, points out the nature of the internal debate in Washington in February 1984, as to whether to pull out the marines once they had been committed. Opponents of withdrawal argued that the action would send a signal to the rest of the Arab world that the United States could not be trusted. Yet within a month, the United States was responding to Saudi concerns about the tanker war in the gulf, and there was no credibility crisis from friendly countries in the area.[6] In this case a credibility crisis might well have developed—certainly at home—had the United States stayed committed to a political situation in which it had no initiative and was vulnerable to rising casualties.

My fourth principle of a Third World strategy is to follow as far as possible the indirect approach. It is important both politically and militarily that the United States not "Americanize" operations, whereby our logistics and tactics supplant indigenous efforts. We have seen how NATO, through the NATO Council and DPC, serves as a brake on this occurring in Europe. In other areas of the world, the temptation to take over is even greater and is unrestrained by similar institutions. There must be limits on U.S. involvement if there is to be legitimacy with the indigenous population.

The United States has applied its genius for mass production to fighting wars. Emphasis on massive firepower and "kill ratios"—killing so many more of the enemy than they kill of your own troops so that eventually you must win—have been applications of America's "management" approach. In Vietnam, this produced the worst of all worlds: a strategy of attrition, piecemeal commitment, increasing Americanization.

Contrast the U.S. direct ground actions in Vietnam in the early 1960s with our indirect actions in northern Laos in support of the courageous Meo tribesmen. While the Vietnam war required a massive commitment of forces, the Laotian war involved a small number of Americans at a peak cost of less than $200 million a year. More important, it never affected American prestige, and it allowed for a situation from which the United States could easily disengage. The reasons for the indirect approach in Laos are somewhat happenstance:

the Geneva Accords disallowed military-assistance missions, and Congress blocked conventional U.S. military activities there.[7]

In 1972, as assistant secretary of state, I visited Vietnam, where we had 500,000 people committed; then I went to Cambodia, and finally I flew north to spend the day with General Vang Pao, commander of the Meo tribesmen in northern Laos. Perched on the rim of the Plain of Jars, I was impressed with the highly successful, low-level war fought with the help of a small number of U.S. civilian advisers. The enemy was stalemated, and the operation was never Americanized.

I later dined with one of our foremost admirals, our Commander-in-Chief Pacific, Jack McCain. He said, "Damn it, Dave, now that you are in the State Department, you've got to visit that war in Laos. I can't get in there [because of the Geneva Accords of 1962]. You are an old infantry man who spent time at Fort Benning. You know we need to get in there with a military mission and shape that place up."

"Absolutely wrong, Jack. That is just what we do not need. The war is being fought in just the right way—with our support but their methods." In contrast, when the defense in South Vietnam collapsed, Vang Pao was still fighting and we had to persuade him to evacuate, before his forces were isolated.

The recent example of an operation supported in just the right way was Afghanistan. First, there was a committed local resistance. Second, there was no Americanization of the operation because the political situation disallowed it. Third, success was in no small part achieved by the U.S. contribution of the shoulder-fired Stinger anti-aircraft weapon—exactly the right weapon for that war. Fourth, there was strong bipartisan congressional support.

The fifth principle of a Third World strategy is that whenever we commit forces we should always operate with a special advantage and with competence. The British Empire, in the days of the so-called *Pax Britannica*, helped maintain a century of peace by using its superior fleet, as both a political and a military instrument. It avoided operations on land insofar as possible. When forced to fight on land, the British attempted quick "in-and-out" operations. The Libyan raid and the Grenada landing during the Reagan administration are two examples of similar applications of force. Regardless of political ambiguities, the Lebanon landing in 1958 and the Dominican operation in 1964 are two other examples of successful operations. It is essential that any commitment not be piecemeal or inadequate to the task. The failed Bay of Pigs invasion of 1961 confirms the risks associated with half-hearted commitments. Finally, states with more advanced conventional forces have difficulty using ground forces successfully in areas of extreme nationalism. In the Middle East alone, this has been true of the U.S. in Lebanon, the Soviets in Afghanistan, and the Israelis in Lebanon.

The sixth principle of my Third World strategy is that of properly organizing for special actions in the Third World. Our failed 1980 attempt to rescue the hostages in Iran, the terrorist violence at the Rome and Vienna airports five years later, and the massacre of U.S. Marines in Beirut in 1983 were all events that focused attention on special military operations. A coordinated American response to the challenges of terrorism, insurgency, and the broad spectrum of so-called low-intensity conflict is needed, but military planning for such contingencies has been slow and difficult.

One reaction to the failed Iran hostage rescue operation was to claim that more money was needed for special operations. But Edward Luttwak argued that lack of money was not the problem, that our special forces already had abundant resources. This was certainly true compared to countries such as Britain, France, and Israel, which according to one study have conducted 160 special operations by covert infiltration.[8] Luttwak said that we have attempted high-tech answers to the challenge, such as the world's most expensive night intruders (low-observable delivery aircraft) or nuclear submarines. What we lack is a unity of effort, skills, human intelligence, and willingness to take risks.

Especially in Congress, dissatisfaction with Pentagon planning for limited contingencies was widespread by the mid-1980s. In January 1986, Senator Sam Nunn voiced this concern when he declared that "we are only slightly more prepared to carry out the Iranian hostage rescue mission today than we were when it failed." Congressional initiatives soon followed, and the 1987 Defense Authorization Bill created the position of Assistant Secretary of Defense for Special Operations and Low Intensity Conflict. In one of the most fruitless struggles between Congress and the Pentagon in recent memory, this leadership post, created to facilitate special-operations planning and oversee service-resource activities, has remained vacant since passage of the legislation.

Some progress has been made in forging a coherent policy for low-intensity operations, however. A new unified U.S. Special Operations Command has been formed, with 35,000 active and reserve service men and women, a $2.5 billion budget, and its own assistant secretary of defense. The command includes units such as the army's Special Forces and Rangers, the navy's SEAL units, and the air force's 23rd Air Force Special Operations component and the counterterrorist Delta Force.[9] The commander-in-chief of the Special Operations Command is charged with developing special-operations strategy, doctrine, and tactics. He also has a unique role in developing and acquiring related equipment and materiel.

A further step in the development of a coordinated policy for limited operations was the creation in June 1987 of the Low Intensity Conflict Board of the NSC, chaired by the national security adviser. This senior group, including the secretaries of state and defense, should go a long way in focusing the efforts of the executive branch on special-operations policy. To some extent, however, difficulties in policy coordination reflect a tension between, on the one hand, the missions of special-operations forces and the proponents of the broader concept of low-intensity conflict and, on the other hand, the capability of supporting insurgencies and counterinsurgencies with an array of political, economic, and military instruments.

The basic problem vis-à-vis the Third World is not financial resources, but properly assembling the assets on hand. To handle fast interventions, more light divisions or carriers are not needed; rather, highly trained task-force groups should be forward deployed and matched with airlift.[10] In the Pacific, for example, one way to achieve ready forces is to organize the 25th Division in Hawaii into light-infantry task forces, without the normal division logistical and support tail. Airlift, now maldeployed in the United States, should be forward deployed; or the Hawaii National Guard should be reconfigured to airlift units.

The indirect approach is often required when such things as security assistance or effective covert operations become more important than hardware. Yet for fiscal year 1987, Congress cut 11 percent, or $1.6 billion, from the administration's request for foreign assistance. This was less than 1 percent of the $282 billion appropriated for our defense budget, and one wonders if it is the best allocation of resources. Twenty percent was cut from security assistance. Since sixty-five percent of these funds go to Israel and Egypt, our Third World strategy is without strong global resources. Security assistance is one area for which the Luttwak comment is not applicable: Congress clearly needs to do much more on security assistance.

The final principle of a Third World strategy is that of fostering sustained political support, without which any action is doomed to failure. In any protracted military operation, support from the American people and Congress is essential. In 1954, President Eisenhower valued the judgments of Senators Russell, George, Saltonstall, and Johnson, for the experience they represented and the weight they carried with other members of Congress. At the height of the Dien Bien Phu crisis, Eisenhower had Secretary Dulles invite eight congressional leaders to the State Department for frank consultations that included revealing Operation Vulture, the contingency plan for air strikes to save the French garrison.

There were no such effective consultations in the 1960s. In contrast, the institutionalized and highly publicized committee hearings of the latter part of the decade, especially those of the Foreign Relations Committee, became more of a public debate, with each side trying to win points with the national audience rather than informing and advising the other.

In 1970, I became assistant secretary of state only ten days before our surprise incursion into Cambodia. There was no congressional consultation and the public anger of members of Congress was a prime factor in sparking campus demonstrations. In contrast, before the incursion into Laos, we were able to persuade the White House to consult with Congress so that the purpose of the operation was understood and there would not be criticism while it was going on. Support from a working majority of Congress is the key to sustaining a military operation. The basic problem of operations in Central America has been an absence of this political consensus among Congress, the president, and the public.

The Middle East and Central America are two areas of special interest for the United States that remain essentially outside the superpower relationship and our relations with our industrial democratic allies. U.S. diplomacy here must have three special priorities: (1) involve the Europeans more in maintaining the security of the Persian Gulf; (2) push for a settlement of the Arab-Israeli conflict; and

(3) develop security and stability in the pivotal area bordering the United States.

The Middle East has a major impact on the industrialized world. Religious, economic, and security considerations converge to make a potential tinderbox for World War III. Moreover, the region has a major impact beyond its own borders. So much of the split between European NATO and the United States, for instance, relates to differences concerning the Arab-Israeli situation. Our European allies feel that we have pursued a one-sided policy in the region, ignoring the rights of the Palestinians and failing to put pressure on Israel to make concessions on the occupied West Bank and Gaza.

Despite these differences, the next U.S. president should convince the nations of the Western European Union to play a continuing role in the Persian Gulf area. This helps avoid Americanizing the operation. Furthermore, the Western Europeans themselves should understand that doing so could placate Congress, which is increasingly irate over shouldering a global security burden. The WEU has freedom for such action; it was under the WEU umbrella that Belgium and the Netherlands made limited naval commitments in the Persian Gulf in 1987. One reason a European role has not been better examined is that during the latter days of the Carter administration there was concern about a possible massive Soviet move into Iran. Since that time, there has been no anticipatory focus or doctrine for the kinds of events experienced in 1987—the Iran-Iraq war, reflagging, mine sweeping —to which Europeans could contribute.

The new president must also give high priority to resolving the Arab-Israeli conflict. George Shultz's 1988 diplomatic initiatives are to be commended for recognizing this challenge. But such diplomacy can only be pursued in conjunction with American domestic support. Indeed, Israel faces genuine threats to its security, but neither the majority of the Jewish community in the United States nor the majority of Israelis want to see Israel become the Sparta of the Middle East. Israel is being deprived of the true benefits of its people's talents and of the religious and ethical ideals that should make them world leaders.

In 1977, I visited Israeli Defense Minister Ezer Weizman, an excellent strategist. He told me that despite all the problems, if he could get the military of the surrounding countries together with good maps, but without the politicians, they could work out the true security requirements of everyone. The elements of the Weizman plan included Israeli evacuation of the West Bank; security arrangements for Israel, especially in the Jordan Valley; and the establishment of an autonomous Palestinian entity. At a lecture at the Shiloah Institute, I proposed that the United States offer a security guarantee if those elements were met. Weizman's points remain key features of any effort to bring peace to the region.

Settlement of the Arab-Israeli conflict would ensure a moderate Egypt as a link between Africa and the Middle East. It would lead to unparalleled prosperity for Israel and the possibility of cooperative projects on key resource issues, such as water supplies, with nearby Arab countries. It would provide longer-term stability for Jordan and a hope of a more viable Lebanon. It could heal a rift, deeper than what is generally imagined, between the United States and NATO Europe. It could give better coordination on international terrorism and, indeed, go some way toward ending this problem. It could eliminate this region as a trigger for World War III.

To our south, Central America poses special challenges for U.S. foreign policy—in particular, the countries of Nicaragua and Mexico. The best approach has come from the National Bipartisan Commission on Central America, chaired by Henry Kissinger. The special challenge of Nicaragua is not that it is or soon will be a Soviet military or missile base. The commission said, in January 1984, that before it became a serious threat in that dimension, "the crises would have reached proportions not containable in Central American dimensions."[11] As with the Cuban missile crisis, the United States has overwhelming conventional-forces superiority. The problem is that "Nicaragua's mainland location makes it a crucial steppingstone to provide arms to insurgency in Central America." Our absolute objective—one around which Congress must unite—is, as the commission says, to ensure that "no military forces, bases or advisers of non-Central American countries" are permitted. U.S. policy suffers not from a lack of military resources but from political consensus. There is a resource dimension, however: the United States must follow through on the kind of Central American economic-aid program the commission has called for.

The Cuban economy, like those of other Marxist Third World countries, is a shambles—at a time when the Soviet Union itself has serious economic problems. Over time, strategic opportunities should be sought to detach Cuba from the Soviet Union.

Finally, it is important to understand that Mexico is not so much the gateway to Latin America as it is the entrance to the United States. We are the destination of many of its people and most of its trade. The Hispanic population in the southwestern United States will alter the politics of the region. Indeed, recent demographic projections reveal the impact this area will have on future national policy trends. By the year 2010, three states—Texas, Florida, and California—will control nearly 30 percent of the House of Representatives.[12] Beginning with drugs and illegal immigrants, our problems with Mexico are complex. Their resolution requires a sustained political commitment on both sides. Here the Third World borders the United States, and challenges to our policy and security have regional and global implications.

Our strategy for Mexico must be both economic and political, and it ought to address two fundamental priorities. First, economic trade arrangements should be integrated to serve the mutual interests of Mexico and the United States. For instance, it is important to facilitate credit availability to our southern neighbor within the context of sound Mexican fiscal policies. Second, we must initiate mutual economic-development strategies to stabilize the region and promote cooperative management of potentially destablizing trends. This cooperative approach, in contrast to disruptive mutual recriminations, is essential if the United States is to be successful in its war on drugs.

In dealing with a highly diverse and volatile Third World, we must evaluate ends and means, set priorities, develop consensus at home, and involve allies abroad, acting indirectly where possible. Only then will our strategy have the coherence and effectiveness necessary to bolster America's credibility in the Third World.

19 Economic Strategy

T HERE can be no effective grand strategy without having within it the strong link of an economic strategy. More than ever before, America's security is dependent upon a strong economy. Without a strategy to ensure that we remain strong in this area, we place in jeopardy our relative economic position in the world as well as our ability to defend ourselves. It is essential that any economic program for America encompass and interrelate trade policy, exchange-rate policy, multilateral cooperation, and domestic considerations.

In the past, the direct relation between the ability to produce—economic prosperity—and our national security and international standing was taken for granted. As we look ahead to the 1990s, however, we are constrained by limited resources and must reevaluate our ability to honor global commitments. This examination of resources and commitments must be done in concert with a reappraisal—however agonizing—of how to balance the budget and eliminate the trade deficit. Rarely have Americans thought in terms of a strategy for limited resources in the economic as well as the military field, and a sustained effort is long overdue.

America's ability to devise and manage an economic strategy has been increasingly hampered by developments in the global economic system. The first of these is interdependence where America's economy is directly affected by trade, exchange rates, investments, growth, and inflation around the world. In an interdependent world, the global economic system is only as strong as its weakest link. America has become vulnerable because we have lost what all grand strategists seek to maintain: freedom of action. "Domestic" economic policies of developed and developing nations have a direct impact on the state of the global economy, and the size of the Third World debt has called into question who has the leverage over whom. A debt moratorium by a number of debtor nations could set off a crisis that could lead to the collapse of our banking system. Such interdependence makes for a very complex economic system, and the interrelationships among economic variables have made the discriminate use of policy tools extremely difficult.

A second development that complicates economic strategy making has to do with time. It has become as much of an enemy as a friend. Reaction time in a crisis has been shortened dramatically, and advances in global communication make the containment or isolation of a crisis nearly impossible. Twenty-four-hour-a-day currency-exchange markets mean that crises can occur regardless of the time of day. It is no longer feasible to develop a strategy for the management of a crisis once it has begun. We must develop ways to anticipate crises and avoid them. The effects of interdependence and the pace at which a crisis spreads were never so evident as during the stock market plunge in October 1987. The Dow Jones Industrial Average of New York Stock Exchange shares dropped 23 percent, destroying over $500 billion in assets. Within hours of the New York Stock Exchange's closing bell, prices on the Tokyo exchange had dropped 14 percent, wiping out $400 billion in capital wealth. Australian shares fell 25 percent. Hong Kong's exchange simply shut its doors. In a matter of days, an estimated $1.6 trillion in global stock-market value had been lost.[1]

Third, Balkanization of economic policy throughout the executive and legislative branches of government precludes a coherent strategy. Every department, agency, and committee in government with a mandate relating to economics has its own approach. In Congress, the decline of bipartisanship, the decentralization of power, the rise of single-issue groups, and the tendency to make policy by amendment all detract from our ability to think and act strategically in the economic arena. One of the most glaring examples is the Omnibus Trade Bill that was worked on by a cumbersome Senate and House committee during 1987 and well into 1988. Even in its later form, the bill was far from a coherent piece of legislation. Yet one should not expect coherence in legislation written in a piecemeal fashion by hundreds of staffers in both the House and Senate. Literally hundreds of amendments were added to the dozens of separate bills making up a document of over a thousand pages. The Senate bill alone was put together by eight committees and had over 160 amendments tacked on to it.[2]

If we are to overcome these obstacles, we must establish clear priorities. First, any economic strategy must strive to make the most efficient use of our resources: human, capital, and technological. As we look to the president, it will be essential that he maintain public confidence in our economic future. Within the first year of this new administration, the president needs to develop a strategy and build a partnership with Congress. If he does not act quickly, the window of opportunity may well close and the house become divided again. Despite the problems we face, confidence can be built and maintained as long as the president has a clear sense of direction and strong strategic priorities. A comprehensive strategy does not mean doing everything at once. It means setting priorities but seeing those priorities in an overall whole.

A Global Economic Strategy

A continuing priority for the new administration must be the liberal trade regime. One of the greatest national security threats that will face the new administration is protectionism. It could be the fatal step down the road to a major depression in the 1990s. Let's suppose sweeping protectionist trade legislation is passed. Congress then forces major reductions in U.S. imports from Japan. A protectionist European community immediately follows suit by raising tariffs and lowering quotas on U.S. and Japanese goods. The dollar drops sharply. The Japanese, feeling betrayed and having lost confidence in America and the dollar, slow the pace of their dollar-dominated financial asset purchases, especially U.S. Treasury issues. U.S. interest rates start to rise, asset values collapse, and the exchange value of the dollar plummets until world financial markets are in chaos.

If an economic conference were called in the hope that joint action would restore order to international finance, the United States could not play its traditional leadership role. Its president, bound by retaliatory legislation and handicapped politically, would lack the flexibility to negotiate and bargain. The liberal trade regime would deteriorate so rapidly that world leaders could not reverse the situation. The ensuing trade war would smother growth and employment. Interest rates would reach double digits, and prices would soar. Economic nationalism would hit a peak. Without growth in the industrialized countries, the Third World's support markets would falter. Inflation and currency depreciation would make most Third World countries too risky for new loans. Instability would erode confidence, and direct investment in developing countries would come to a halt. Latin American countries might well declare a moratorium on paying back all Western loans. The rest of the Third World could follow suit. Small and medium-size U.S. banks would be the first to go. And with them would go confidence in the entire financial system. Stock markets would crash throughout the world.[3]

Our global economic strategy must recognize that the United States depends on trade. Although it's happening slowly, the trade balance is improving. In terms of volume, the trade deficit has narrowed and will eventually be reduced in current dollar terms. The non-oil trade balance is improving as fast as it deteriorated in the early 1980s. We must remember, however, that the trade imbalance has become a structural problem, both internally and externally: the economies of most surplus countries have adjusted toward export orientation, while U.S. companies have pulled out of markets, reorienting toward imports. Imbalances are imbedded in our economies and will not disappear overnight. In fact, the enormous imbalances in the global economy that have taken some five years to create may take even longer to correct.[4]

The European goal of a single common market by 1992 will have a major impact on global trade. This impact could be sharply positive or negative, depending on the effectiveness of the new administration and its strategy for dealing with a European pillar. The importance of interrelating and integrating our economic and security policies toward Europe will become a formidable task as economic and security pressures conflict.

The ambitious programs involved in European integration will be achieved only with considerable difficulty. A European Commission study estimates that the removal of all trade barriers will create between 2 and 5 million jobs, result in a 6 percent cumulative drop in consumer prices over five or six years, and allow aggregate cost savings of 2 percent of GDP.[5] However, great attention must be given to the worker-adjustment process, internal policy and coordination, enforcement of antitrust laws, and adverse impact on weaker regions of the European Community. Unless the issues of public procurement and the strength of the European Monetary System are adequately addressed, the move toward European integration may unravel.

America's economic strategy should encourage Europe to move toward its goal of a single internal market, while adamantly opposing any movement toward protectionism. Competition is at the heart of the greater efficiency and higher living standards envisioned by the European Commission. While European ministers acknowledge this to be true within Europe, they hesitate to acknowledge that it is just as true for trade with the rest of the world. Without truly international competition the single-market goal may very well backfire.

Moving beyond U.S.-European trade, America's economic strategy must also aim at updating and broadening the mandate of the General Agreement on Tariffs and Trade (GATT). GATT was originally conceived as an interim agreement pending the establishment of the International Trade Organization, which Congress never approved. GATT has been extremely successful in accomplishing its original purpose: the reduction of worldwide tariffs to relatively low levels. Today, however, international trade continues to be inhibited, not by tariffs, but by nontariff trade barriers such as quotas, voluntary export restraints, and orderly marketing agreements.

We need to strengthen GATT by making it legally binding, improving dispute-settlement mechanisms, and developing a surveillance procedure for periodic review of trade policies. GATT needs to take bold steps to deal with agriculture, which has until now only been imperfectly covered. Agricultural subsidies and restrictions have created global economic imbalances and staggering surpluses that cost consumers millions of dollars a year.[6]

GATT, as it was conceived forty years ago, did not need to deal with such problems as intellectual property rights and the service industry. Now, however, unless it can deal successfully with these areas it will loose the credibility it so badly needs. The 1982 Greenberg Study on GATT and the service industry led Ambassador Bill Brock to push to have that important issue placed on the GATT agenda. In the 1990s, without a broader mandate and greater authority, GATT will become meaningless.[7]

Should the current round of GATT fail, the trading system may well deteriorate into a series of regional and bilateral agreements. The free trade agreement that has been negotiated with Canada is a positive step forward and gives a necessary priority to the free flow of goods and services in North America. Future agreements may also prove wise, especially with our major trading partners such as Japan and Mexico. However, to resort to a whole series of bilateral agreements could place multilateralism in jeopardy. Should the United States begin negotiating bilateral agreements with its major trading partners, we would likely place other countries at a disadvantage, as well as consume an extraordinary amount of time and resources.

A related element of our global economic strategy must be exchange-rate stability. It is the foundation upon which to build a free-trade system. Exchange-rate objectives set by policymakers have little meaning unless multilateral economic-policy adjustments are coordinated. This means, for example, maintaining the appropriate interest rate differential to support the dollar. The understanding reached at the Louvre accord in 1987 has been criticized for sacrificing national flexibility in making internal economic policy. The British have not joined the European Monetary System, which seeks to regulate the volatility of European currencies, because of the implications for internal economic-policy control. Without broad collective agreements on exchange rates and implementation of the necessary domestic economic policy to support them, however, extreme and often unnecessary volatility will continue to disrupt free trade.

Trade and exchange rates cannot be addressed in isolation from Third World debt. The indebtedness of and economic stagnation in developing countries is more than a problem for America. It is a threat to the entire economic order, and the problem is getting worse, not better. By 1988, the less developed countries (LDC) debt had reached $1.9 trillion.[8] The International Monetary Fund (IMF) and the World Bank have worked hard to ensure that new capital and credit continue to flow to developing countries. Both institutions realize that refinancing old loans alone will not lead to greater economic development and balanced growth in the Third World. With the important role of the World Bank in the structural adjustment of developing countries, decreased U.S. support for the World Bank would send the wrong signal to the world about the importance of addressing the problems of debt and development.

The debt crisis is taking a toll on the U.S. economy. The United

States has had to absorb an inordinate quantity of exports from developing countries. At the same time, LDC debt-service burdens squeeze the amount of U.S. goods these developing countries can import. Without a greater combined effort by the member countries of the Organization for Economic Cooperation and Development (OECD) to solve the problems of the Third World, our future may be threatened. The direction of resources must be reversed so that they are flowing into the developing countries instead of out.

At the same time, our economic strategy must encompass the newly industrialized countries (NICs). These countries have become a part of the international economic system, and their actions have an extensive impact on the economies of the developed countries. Each, however, has different problems and deficiencies. Korea is among the largest of the debtor nations. Taiwan and Korea have massive trade surpluses—Taiwan's current account surplus is 20 percent of GNP and Korea's is 8 percent—and while they have been progressively reducing their trade barriers, those barriers remain substantial. Hong Kong and Singapore, on the other hand, are strong believers in free trade. It must be kept in mind that these countries are pivotal for us geopolitically.[9]

In order for our economic strategy to be effective, it must be related to the other components of strategy and coordinated with our allies. An economic crisis may have tremendous consequences for our global security. Presently there is no ongoing forum where allies can pull together and coordinate the myriad of political, technological, economic, and security concerns.

The week of the stock market's Black Monday, October 19, 1987, I discussed the crisis with Edmond de Rothschild at a lunch at his noble Château de Pregny in Geneva. We talked about the speed at which things had collapsed and our ability to react quickly and effectively. His family symbolized the rise of nineteenth-century capitalism in Europe and had survived economic depression and war. Was anything new needed for the system? I reflected on the crisis-management system at NATO and how it needed to be improved. But at least, in the event of a military crisis, representatives from sixteen nations have the consultative framework to react immediately. The G-7 and the OECD have made real progress in collaborating in the financial and macroeconomic areas, yet even they are dealing with only one piece of the pie. Rothschild talked about the role that personal leadership, perceptions, and public confidence play in times of crisis. Black Monday has shown how fast confidence can deteriorate and how impossible it is to view economic problems as though they were isolated to one country. Without a framework in which a crisis can be discussed in all its dimensions, the next crisis, if ever it occurs, may go far beyond the damage of the October plunge. If such a crisis is to be contained, we need to have enhanced crisis-management capability.

The Summit Seven was a positive development, but these meetings become ceremonial at the top level. When at Williamsburg the seven leaders said that global security was indivisible, it was a step forward; and when at Tokyo there was a pronouncement on terrorism, it was another step forward. Even though these meetings have begun to address broad security considerations, the so-called sherpas who prepare them are not enough. At the minimum, the Summit Seven needs to have regular meetings of political directors to discuss broad economic and security cooperation. The meetings should be reinforced by officials from the finance ministries and other agencies, depending upon the agenda. The directors should be given a broad mandate, allowing them to talk about a broad range of concerns.

This strengthening of the Summit Seven would have numerous advantages. First, it would move the topics of the summits away from short-term crisis management to long-range problems and cooperation. It would force nations to consult in a multilateral forum on a regular basis, just like the Special Consultative Group or the High Level Group at NATO. As with NATO, once the framework is set up there is no excuse for not consulting. In addition, it would force the United States to have greater policy coordination within its own government. The representative would receive instructions from Washington, which would necessitate a unified American position.[10]

A Domestic Economic Strategy

The United States has moved from producing nearly 50 percent of the world's goods and services after World War II to about 20 percent today. In five years, we have shifted from a creditor nation to the world's leading debtor nation. Can we still give the world economic leadership? Plainly, the answer depends upon whether we will put our own house in order.

In the long pull, the military strength of a nation cannot outlast its economic strength and productivity. In fact, as the new president devises an economic strategy, the United States will need to address its major domestic problems or it will lack the credibility to deal effectively in a multilateral framework. Without a domestic policy that reflects the realities of the global economy, we will damage not only ourselves but the entire economic system and eventually injure our security and our ability to deter war.

In shoring up the U.S. economic foundation, the first step must be to restore our capital position. The United States is a nation swimming in debt, with astronomical trade and budget deficits. The accruing national debt could reach $2,825 trillion by fiscal year 1989. According to White House calculations, by 1989 the net interest on the national debt will be larger than the federal deficit itself. [11]

The United States has not developed an economic strategy to correct the consumer orientation of our economy and promote greater savings. Rather than borrowing to invest in high-yield activities, such as developing new technology that would raise living standards over the long run, we borrow to consume. Present-day consumption beyond our means is subsidized by foreigners, and we will have to reduce our consumption in order to pay this back.

It is odd that, with the growing recognition of this problem, our current tax law promotes consumption. The absence of inflation adjustment for capital gains, interest, and depreciation; the disallowance of dividend deductibility; and the often double taxation of dividends actually discourage long-term investment. During the Reagan administration, one of the primary economic goals was to control inflation. In the future, however, we must move beyond inflation control to develop a more balanced relationship between spending and production, thereby encouraging saving.

Although the United States has made progress recently on competitiveness, we have a long way to go to compensate for the lag in the growth of labor productivity and capital formation. Insufficient capital and R & D investments, poor labor-management relations, excessive government regulation, and the predominance of short-term thinking have resulted in a weakened competitive position. Many companies have already improved their competitiveness and productivity by emphasizing a "total quality approach" as well as better labor-management relations. [12]

Greater investment in human resources will also increase our competitiveness and help restore our industrial strength. As we look at a viable strategy for our economic security, we must ask ourselves why Japan, with half the population of the United States, has more scientists and engineers? Why does Japan invest, on average, twice as much capital per worker per year than the United States? As a percent of GNP, Japan invests more in manufacturing plants and equipment than the United States. Why has the United States not given education the priority it needs? America's children suffer from unacceptably high illiteracy rates and relatively poor science and math skills. In "A Nation at Risk," the Commission on Excellence in Education wrote of our deteriorating educational foundation. Thirteen percent of our seventeen-year-olds are functionally illiterate. The illiteracy rate among minorities is 40 percent, and approximately 3,000 students drop out of high school every day.[13] Another inseparable problem is the hardship of those who suffer from the adverse effects of a free trade system. There were some 11 million displaced workers between 1981–86. By helping those people to adjust and find new jobs, we would considerably reduce the political pressure that causes protectionism. In a rapidly changing global economy, the United States, more so than most OECD countries, lacks an adequate adjustment program.[14]

A somewhat different element of our economic strategy relates to lowering our vulnerability to strategic mineral-supply interruptions. "The ability to mobilize and increase wartime production depends in part on the availability of critical raw materials. These materials must be indigenous to the country, stockpiled, or available over secure lines of communications in time of war," notes a Joint Chiefs of Staff study.[15] Without securing access, stockpiling assets, or substituting other materials where possible, the United States is vulnerable if a crisis should cause an unexpected surge in demand. In contrast, the Soviet Union, with its abundance of strategic raw materials and policy of autarchy, would be virtually unaffected if critical reserves were suddenly cut.

The United States imports strategic raw materials from many countries. However, most striking is the level in imports of metal ores and gemstones from southern Africa, where the strategically located Republic of South Africa dominates control of these minerals. From 1980 to 1983, South Africa supplied the United States with 61 percent of its cobalt (mostly mined in Zaire and Zambia), 55 percent of its chromium, 49 percent of its platinum, 44 percent of its vanadium, and

39 percent of its manganese—metals most widely used in making steel and lightweight metal alloys for high-performance military aircraft.[16] For nearly all of these raw materials, the Soviet Union would be the next largest supplier.

One option is to develop a strategic reserve of critical raw materials. Although stockpiling incurs high short-term costs, it greatly reduces our vulnerability. Another option is to spread the risk over several foreign sources. Like a financial arbitrageur, the United States may be able to reduce its "portfolio risk" by drawing from diverse sources and becoming less heavily dependent on a single supplier.

Like arms cooperation, resources designated for strategic raw-material acquisition, storage, and development may be more efficiently allocated through joint alliance measures. In the last few years, a number of NATO countries and Japan have expressed genuine interest in acquiring a visible but small stockpile to help coordinate an international strategic stockpile policy. Joint measures such as these would substantially reduce our dependence on single-source raw materials.[17]

Another element of our economic strategy relates to energy. The supply and cost of energy are key strategic factors for the superpowers, for the military alliances, and for the Third World. The energy crises of 1973 and 1979 changed the political landscape in the Middle East, and there is potential for another energy crisis in the 1990s. U.S. oil production is in decline, and its energy industries are depressed.

If oil prices do not rise, U.S. oil import dependency would increase from its present 40 percent to over 60 percent in the 1990s, even without major Mideast disruptions.[18] Canada, Mexico, and Venezuela are America's largest suppliers, and about 15 percent of our oil comes from the Persian Gulf. Yet even today, a disruption of Mideast oil would have far-reaching repercussions, not only for us, but for other countries who import oil from this volatile region.[19]

We must also increase our strategic petroleum reserve from its current level of 545 million barrels of oil in the ground—emergency supply to last 120 days if all sources were shut off—to 750 million barrels.[20] Even more important, production capacity must be strengthened throughout the energy industry, though the mechanism to do this remains extremely contentious. Contingency planning among the industrial democracies also needs to be reviewed.

Economic Superpower Strategy—United States and Japan

The biggest challenge facing the economic strategist is to build a cooperative spirit between the United States and Japan. If they were ever to go to war in the economic arena, global security and deterrence would deteriorate. The United States and Japan must develop a cooperative long-range strategy that recognizes our common interests.

Such strategy making requires us to take a much broader approach to U.S.-Japanese relations. It is no longer rational to approach U.S.-Japanese relations from the narrow confines of merchandise trade and defense spending. Rarely do we look at the relationship in its entirety, integrating our trade, finance, technology, Third World development, and defense policies. The compartmentalization and fragmentation of U.S. policy toward Japan stands in the way of any real cooperation with this great power. Take, for example, the process on Capitol Hill, where dozens of committees on both sides of Congress address a single aspect of our relationship, whether it be agriculture or defense. The legislative assistants who have truly taken on the Japanese relationship as a whole are few and far between.

The problem is even greater in the executive branch, where no department or agency attempts to make sense of the relationship as a whole. The departments of State, Defense, Commerce, Treasury, and Agriculture, and the U.S. Trade Representative are each involved in Japan policy, yet their policies are often divergent. Large portions of our policy toward Japan are being set by congressional amendments. As George Packard expressed so well, "today a welter of intergovernmental working groups, task forces and coordinating bodies share bits of the action, but no one department or agency can be said to be in charge."[21]

The media on both sides have contributed to this fractionalization by focusing largely on aspects of the relationship where there is evident friction and that are the most politically sensitive. Agricultural Minister Takashi Sato emphasized to me how much the press has dramatized often minor issues in the totality of the relationship, but that are the most emotional for both the Japanese and American publics. Seldom are the major cooperative efforts or complementary interests given the attention they deserve. Press coverage of the five congressmen who stood on Capitol Hill smashing Toshiba radios after Toshiba had sold sensitive Western technology to the Soviets provides an excellent example. Japanese who supported firm action against Toshiba resented this performance played repeatedly on their televisions.

In seeking to assemble a strategy, it is necessary to acknowledge the political pressures and realities that exist on both sides. Japan does not live in a political vacuum any more than we do. As we look at questions of burden sharing, and the roles of the United States and Japan in maintaining economic and military security, we must consider capabilities and trade-offs so that each country can focus on its comparative advantage. Encouraging Japan to do more in areas that are both politically and economically feasible may result in real progress. Pushing Japan too hard in the wrong areas will only strain the relationship and encourage greater nationalism on both sides.

In a world of enormous capital flows and cross investments, the first dimension of a comprehensive strategy must be financial. Plainly, the U.S. budget deficit is one of the major causes of our trade deficit. Some economic estimates show that a reduction of the deficit by 20 percent would reduce the trade deficit by up to $15 billion.[22] Many Americans have failed to relate the ability to finance the U.S. deficit to the Japanese. According to *The Economist*, Japanese institutions hold approximately 30 to 40 percent of the bonds sold in recent years to fund the U.S. budget deficit.[23]

The next dimension of a comprehensive economic strategy is Japanese investment in the United States, which totals $135 billion.[24] Japanese companies in the United States employ over 240,000 Americans.[25] There is also a relationship between these jobs and the trade problem. To put it in perspective, every billion dollars' worth of exports generates an average 25,800 jobs. Thus, those jobs created by the Japanese companies in America make a contribution to our GNP that is the equivalent of $9.3 billion worth of exports. If Japanese foreign direct investment is omitted from our understanding of U.S.-Japanese relations, we ignore a major strategic dimension very much appreciated by governors but not so much by members of Congress.

The next dimension of a comprehensive strategy involves stimulating the Japanese economy. In January 1988, the new Japanese prime minister, Noboru Takeshita, brought with him to Washington statistics that showed Japanese progress in stimulating domestic demand, increasing manufactured imports, and reducing its structural dependence on exports. These improvements will only help to narrow the trade imbalance between the U.S. and Japan. Japan must, however, press forward in the areas of agriculture, housing, and tax reform. Although progress is being made, visible results may not be forthcoming for quite some time.

As the Japanese move to open their markets, it is important to remember that an increase in non-U.S. imports to Japan will take a significant burden off the United States. Currently the United States absorbs some 60 percent of the developing world's manufactured goods.[26] As we suffer from the effects of our trade deficit, the burden of importing from Third World countries takes a toll on the American economy. By buying more from Asian and Latin American countries, Japan is contributing to Third World development.

The fourth dimension relates to U.S.-Japanese cooperation in enhancing GATT. As a leading beneficiary of a free and open international economy, Japan has a clear obligation—and interest—in making its economy accessible to foreign competition. Japan has profited greatly from GATT and should work with the United States in modernizing GATT's mandate. Not only should Japan accept its rulings and judgments, even on difficult agricultural issues, but it should assume a greater leadership role.

Fifth, we must manage our technology more effectively. At a minimum, this means breaking down the barriers to the free exchange of information and technology while at the same time ensuring against another Toshiba affair. The Japanese have taken strong steps to address the illegal transfer of quiet-propeller technology to the Soviet Union by the Toshiba Corporation subsidiary. In February of 1988, when I met with the president of Toshiba, Joichi Aoi, I was briefed on the program Toshiba Corporation has developed to educate its employees and prevent a reoccurrence. It was my impression that Toshiba will soon be one of the most secure corporations in all of Japan. Nonetheless, the sale to the Soviet Union of state-of-the-art technology for manufacturing quiet submarines has damaged attempts to convince Congress of the advantages of technology cooperation with Japan.

Crisis also creates opportunity. Japan should take a lead to shore up what some of us have referred to as a "crippled" Coordinating Committee (COCOM). As I discussed in Chapter 17, COCOM is in dire need of revamping if it is to fulfill its mandate. Japan has the financial potential to do this, and such action would do much to offset the damage from the Toshiba affair as well as set COCOM back on track.

Once we restore confidence in our relations with Japan, we can encourage greater across-the-board cooperation in science and technology. This is the objective of the U.S.-Japan science and technology agreement recently concluded. The new agreement, signed in June 1988, promotes expanded exchanges, establishes the principal of "shared responsibilities and mutual and equitable contributions and benefits," and promises accelerated scientific progress. Another agreement between the U.S. and Japan in the technology area concerns the FSX fighter aircraft. The FSX will combine the General Dynamics F-16 air frame with Japanese avionics to produce what promises to be a superior plane. It is a great fear of the Soviet Union that the United States and Japan will coordinate their defense technology efforts, especially in the SDI area. In the future, cooperative agreements in a whole range of military and nonmilitary areas will only enhance our bilateral realtionship.

Many U.S. companies operating in Japan have benefited greatly from the intense competitive environment of the Japanese marketplace, which forces technological innovation. Companies like Procter & Gamble have taken the technology from the Japanese market and used it in their products around the world. Others, Dupont for example, have developed a technology center in Japan to take advantage of their advances and apply them globally. Joint ventures between Japanese and American companies have greatly contributed to the free flow of technology between both countries. The potential commercial as well as defense pay-offs from Japanese-U.S. efforts in such areas as superconductivity and fusion technology are phenomenal. In the future, the United States may have as much to gain from Japanese technology as the Japanese have gained from ours.

The sixth dimension of a U.S.-Japanese comprehensive strategy relates to security. Japan's security as well as that of Asia has been discussed at length in an earlier chapter. However, it is important to emphasize that our strategy should concentrate not so much on a greater Japanese defense budget but on exploiting collective defense capabilities in the smartest and most efficient manner. Japanese defense must focus on U.S.-Japanese vulnerabilities while avoiding any activity that might be perceived as a threat by other Asian countries.

That is, Japan needs to reduce the Asian perception of a Japanese threat, enhance Asian cooperation, and focus on Soviet vulnerabilities, thereby freeing up increasingly overstretched U.S. forces for other Asian commitments. By complementing U.S. forces in the Pacific, Japan makes a solid contribution to its own security and to the security of the free world.

In addition to the purely military contribution Japan makes to Western security, there are other contributions Japan can make. Taken together, they constitute what the Japanese call comprehensive security. Japan should increase aid to the arch of strategically pivotal nations that influence Japan's security, including the Philippines, Thailand, and Pakistan. Increased Japanese aid to Turkey would greatly benefit western security. U.S. security assistance and development aid has been drastically cut to the point of jeopardizing whatever concepts of the Nixon Doctrine remain. Assistance to other countries, many of which are engaged in low-intensity conflicts, has suffered greatly from the cuts. Congress has also cut back dramatically on non-earmarked funds, which has diminished our flexibility in timely allocations of security assistance to pivotal countries.

The most obvious and important area where Japan can use its economic power to take the strain off America and contribute to Asian security is in the Philippines. Japan should go beyond the current humanitarian aid to a program that recognizes the contribution U.S. bases in the Philippines make to Japan's security and to Asian security in general. U.S. facilities there protect Asian energy lifelines. Some 57 percent of Japanese oil comes through the Straits of Hormuz.[27] If democracy fails in the Philippines and we lose the bases, it would be a political and strategic blow to both Japan and the United States. American security assistance has undergone, and will continue to undergo, major cutbacks. If Japan does not pick up the slack, especially in Asia, our mutual security will come apart at the seams.

Japan should do much more to aid Third World countries. Presently, the terms on Japanese aid are among the tightest in the industrialized world. The grant element of Japanese overseas development assistance is inordinately small compared with other OECD countries. Also, Japanese aid is structured in a way that ties it to Japanese commercial interests, often placing American corporations at a disadvantage. As Japan increases its aid in the 1990s, considerable efforts must be made to address these shortcomings.

The seventh and final dimension of an economic program between the United States and Japan is joint management of the debt crisis. In the long run, our interest is, again, to preserve the international financial order. Latin American debt climbed from $280 billion in 1982 to almost $400 billion in 1987. The interest payments on Third World debts consume up to 50 percent of these countries' export revenue and 15 percent of their GNP. It is hard to believe that since 1983 there has been a net capital outflow from debtor nations. In 1986, rather than receiving new net funds, developing countries sent $26 billion to the industrialized world.[28]

Japan could be invaluable in acting to correct this threat to global security. With America, it could assume the financial leadership that would give the Third World a second chance at development. U.S. banks have their hands tied on Third World debt while Japanese financial institutions are prospering. Because a threat to the U.S. banking system is a threat to both economic superpowers, it is essential that the United States and Japan work together to avert a financial disaster.

20 Organizing for Strategy

DURING my 90 days at the White House, amidst a crisis that clearly reflected a need to rethink and reexamine the way we have organized our government, I asked for a copy of the Murphy Commission report. The report has a lot to offer on our conduct of foreign policy, and it was shocking that a copy couldn't be found in the White House. It addresses the crisis of strategy and organization that still confronts us today and lays out four foreign policy requirements I believe are almost entirely missing in the present-day process:

- To identify future trends and developments that, in the absence of action, will present major problems or missed opportunities
- To define comprehensively and precisely the long-term purposes and worldwide priorities of the United States
- To assure that day-to-day decisions take account of longer-term priorities
- To modify strategies and develop new courses in response to changing conditions and outcomes of past actions

The report points out that "those engaged in day-to-day operations, or those with limited jurisdictions, tend to neglect or resist these needs under the press of the demands of the moment. The reason for establishing planning or 'strategic thinking' as a separate function is precisely to overcome this deficiency and to compensate for such tendencies in the system as a whole." Planners must be insulated from operational tasks, but not isolated from operational realities. Planners must cut across traditional departmental borders and narrow interagency interests.

There were three parts to the commission's recommendations: First, it called for State of the World reports. With a strategic focus and containing an economic component, these would be developed under the secretary of state, drawing on his planning and NSC staffs. They would be issued at the start of each new presidential administration and updated annually thereafter.

Second, it called for a Global Systems Critical List. This would examine the world's physical resources and environment; possible catastrophic effects and major new opportunities arising from the use of these resources; and new developments in technology and science. Such an inventory would be an integral part of the "anticipation" role for policy planning. Responsibility for this list should be delegated to a "prestigious and independent organization of scientists."

Third, it addressed the organizational weaknesses within government. It recommended that planning for foreign policy be government-wide; that there be a strong Policy Planning Staff within the State Department; and that the president be given a greater role in planning policy. To achieve this, the president should create a Council of International Planning modeled on the Council of Economic Advisors and consisting of three to five respected "thinkers" with access to experts in and out of government.

When it comes to long-range research and planning, the executive branch generally remains focused on the latest tactical crisis, despite the State Department's Policy Planning Staff. Some committees, however, have begun to take a longer-range view in special hearings and research. The Congressional Research Service, the General Accounting Office, the Office of Technological Assessment, and the Congressional Budget Office all offer opportunities for longer-range analysis. What Congress cannot do, however, is to provide the overall focus and grand strategy.

President Eisenhower was intensely aware of the need for long-range planning and coordinating strategic policy. He restructured the National Security Council (NSC) and created two important groups: the National Security Planning Board, under Gordon Gray, to conduct interagency planning and policy development; and the Operations Coordinating Board, under Brigadier General Andrew Goodpaster, to oversee and coordinate policy implementation. Under this arrangement, the first oversaw the long-range planning of the NSC; the second, the day-to-day operations.

The National Security Act of 1947 established among other things the National Security Council, whose function would be "to advise the President with respect to the integration of domestic, foreign, and military policies relating to national security so as to enable the military services and other departments and agencies of the Government to cooperate more effectively in matters involving the national security."[1] The bright promise that this measure offered has never been fully realized, and it may be argued that recent administrations have become increasingly fragmented. Today's NSC is overcome, through no fault of its own, by day-to-day crisis management. As NSC staff are consumed by "fire fighting," there is no time for anticipatory analysis.

In the broader policy arena, cooperation on long-term policy development is hampered by mistrust—a fear in both parties that the other will use leaks for "partisan" reasons. A cult of secrecy has built up in recent administrations. There has been a general unwillingness to share either information or responsibility for policy failures. Congress has multiplied the number of oversight committees and used routine authorization and appropriation bills, the War Powers Act, media leaks, and legislative vetoes in an attempt to reassert its control and influence over foreign policy. Presidents, in turn, have built up the NSC as an isolated and autonomous operational agency; they appeal, over the heads of Congress, to the public and orchestrate their own leaks. This is the grim reality of chaotic strategy making in Washington.

This chapter is concerned with strategy objectives and the need for effective organization to carry them out. Later in this chapter, I recommend several specific steps we need to take in order to achieve this goal. But first we need to examine the relationship between leadership and organization. More than two decades ago, Senator Henry Jackson addressed this issue:

> A wise and courageous President, top executive branch officials effectively discharging their responsibilities, a Civil Service correctly interpreting and properly executing our policies, a Congress affirmatively and constructively playing its crucial role in the national security policy process, a citizenry alert to the great challenges of the time and willing

to make the sacrifices needed to meet them—*these are the prerequisites for a strategy equal to the challenge.* Lacking them, the organizational forms of policy-making will be ineffective—no matter how closely they may conform to the principles of sound management.[2]

Jackson was right. Effective strategy requires both good strategists and good machinery. With regard to the former, we must accept the president who is elected and the advisers he selects. Presidential personality is not subject to change. If a given president chooses to adopt a decision-making style that discourages the formation of integrated strategy, there is little to be done about it.[3] But structure and process can be changed. These are things we have control over, and we should seek to organize ourselves in the best way possible to establish and attain the objectives of our grand strategy.

No organizational arrangement can ensure that the president will always get the best possible advice or that he will make the best possible decision even with good advice. But that is not a prescription for despair. We need to organize our national security decision-making machinery so that it provides the president with the most accurate, considered advice possible; that permits the transmission of dissenting views; that provides decision makers with genuine options; that takes into account the problem of implementation; and that is conceived with conscious regard for clearly defined national goals.

My White House memorandum of February 1987, which I discussed in Chapter 1, pointed to the need to go beyond the Tower Board report in revamping the national security process. In the latter days of the Reagan administration, a remarkable team attitude developed among National Security Adviser Colin Powell; Frank Carlucci, by then Secretary of Defense; Chief of Staff Howard Baker; and Secretary of State George Shultz. It thereby became anything but a lame-duck administration. But this fortunate combination of personalities—while signifying the importance of people—must not obscure the systemic problems that have endured too long not to be decisively addressed.

The formulation of a grand strategy, what the National Security Act in effect called for, is the integration of domestic, foreign, and military policies, the cooperation of services, departments, agencies, *and*, I have added, the Congress. The achievement of this demands heroic measures. I recommend the following:

1. Personality and experience permitting, the vice president should be made more of an executive vice president. He should be given two special responsibilities: (1) to make sure the executive branch process works, and (2) to make sure that an executive-legislative partnership exists. The vice president presides in the Senate and should spend more time in his office just off the Senate floor. He should attend fewer overseas funerals and domestic political gatherings. By spending more time in Washington, he can invigorate an exchange between the administration and the Hill. He should have clear leadership responsibilities within the Cabinet, overarching the Chief of Staff and the National Security Adviser. If George Bush had been given these responsibilities, the Iran-Contra affair would never have gone as far as it did. Likewise, the economic and security policies of the administration might have been interrelated. The Congress and the Reagan administration have repeated the mistakes of Johnson's Vietnam—incurring huge national security costs without being able to pay for them.

In the midst of the personality crisis involving Secretary of State Al Haig and the White House, President Reagan assigned Vice President Bush to chair a crisis-management committee. This was a good step forward, but it had no continuing function. The vice president should chair a committee of the NSC that in effect conducts an audit of where the administration stands, what its strategy is, whether it is being executed effectively, and whether it is consistent with long-term goals. The Tower Board report noted the lack of "an effective audit" of policy relating to the opening toward Iran. But it is not just this administration but practically all administrations since that of Dwight Eisenhower that have needed this audit. Such an audit of policy was certainly lacking during the Johnson administration's piecemeal commitment of our forces to Vietnam, and during the Kennedy administration's planning for the Bay of Pigs operation.

2. On the National Security Council staff, there should be a division between policy and operations. When I speak of operations, I do not mean the kind of covert ones Oliver North ran. I mean, rather, the operations of the national security interagency process, which coordinates departmental positions and produces options for the president. This also involves crisis and major-event operations, including visits by heads of state, overseas treks by the president, or reactions to legislative fights.

Until one serves in the White House, or has been on the receiving end overseas, one does not realize how "next-event driven" the White House is. The eight o'clock morning staff meeting chaired by the chief of staff is devoted to the events of that day. And if events are crises, the administration too often reacts without having thought ahead. For this reason, President Eisenhower separated policy from strategy, with the executive secretary of the council—an unheard of position now—in charge of policy and strategy along with another individual in charge of operations. Under John Kennedy, with a well-known individual like McGeorge Bundy called the "National Security Adviser," the distinctions were lost.

Second, within the National Security Council staff, the president should assign the following people: (1) a national security adviser who takes charge of day-to-day operations and coordination; and, quite separate from this, (2) a presidential counsellor for policy integration and long range planning; he is, in effect, the grand strategist. His scope must include not only the national security cluster of departments and agencies, but also the economy as it relates to the total security of the nation. Both the national security adviser and the counselor should be present at all meetings regarding either agenda, so their efforts are always synchronized.

Vice President Nelson Rockefeller, while serving on the Murphy Commission with me, showed a deep interest in how the integration of defense and economics could be effected. He had several schemes for doing this. But before the report was concluded, he pulled back on the subject. I suspect the other parts of the White House complained he was rocking the boat.

As for a better audit of policy, the president's Foreign Intelligence Advisory Board of eight outside-of-government experts was first established by a wise President Eisenhower in 1957 to perform an overall audit of the workings and quality of our foreign intelligence community. This community now includes the Central Intelligence Agency, Defense Intelligence Agency, National Security Agency, and economic intelligence in general. A young, overconfident President Kennedy abolished the board not long before he fell into the Bay of Pigs disaster. He reestablished it soon thereafter, with the experienced Clark Clifford at its helm. Johnson maintained the board, headed by General Maxwell Taylor, but did not use it well. Under Nixon, Admiral George Anderson, and under Ford, Leo Cherne were talented chairmen. But Carter—not learning from Kennedy—abolished the board that conceivably could have saved him from the wrong assumptions he made regarding revolutionary Iran, which destroyed his presidency.

Reagan reestablished the board under a skilled chairman, Anne Armstrong, former ambassador to Great Britain. There was a scramble of people—over 100 candidates—to be appointed. The initial board was twenty-two, much too large. Chairman Armstrong was one of the most decisive I have known and later had the courage to have the board cut to a manageable size. This could have been the "auditing board"—the mechanism that would have saved the Reagan administration from the faulty intelligence assumptions of the Iran-Contra affair. Then CIA Director Bill Casey short-circuited it, never informing the chairman of his activities. President Reagan's successor should strengthen the board's mandate and ensure that such a bypassing never again happens.[4]

3. My proposed presidential counsellor should be given the authority to coordinate the efforts of the planning and analyses staffs in the areas of security and economics. Ideally the counselor could synchronize all of the best brains in strategic planning. Out of this cooperative effort could emerge not only the conceptual framework of our objectives in security matters, arms control, and economics, but also the opportunity for constant reexamination.

The groups coordinated for grand strategy making by the presidential counselor would include the president's science adviser, the Policy Planning Council of the State Department, the long-range planning section of the Joint Chiefs of Staff, the plans and analysis section of the Secretary of Defense, as well as appropriate people from the Arms Control and Disarmament Agency, the United States Information Agency, the Council of Economic Advisors, the Treasury Department assistant secretaries for international affairs and policy, and the intelligence community's long-range analysts. There is real brain power within these disparate groups, prepared to face the challenge of a comprehensive approach. In an era of constrained resources and dramatic budgetary cutbacks, this effort will help the president and Congress to think smarter rather than richer. This could also restore the type of conceptual Report of the President done under Henry Kissinger during the first Nixon years.

It may appear that this robs the secretary of state of his preeminent position as the president's chief representative in foreign affairs. This is not the intent nor would it be the result. He is the preeminent diplomat—the negotiator, the presidential adviser, the spokesperson. Diplomacy, as Foreign Service officers are taught, involves assessing, representing, and recommending to the president. Strategy, or at least grand strategy, is the art of harmonizing the nation's resources with the nation's commitments. A good secretary of state is so involved in specific negotiations that he has neither the time nor the perspective for such a comprehensive approach.

4. A special group should be constituted to maintain a list of global contingencies and possible responses to them. The gaming and simulation capabilities throughout the government should be marshaled in this continuing endeavor.

This would in no way relieve the Joint Chiefs of Staff of their role; rather, it lets them know that the president is going to take strategy making seriously. The Joint Chiefs will have to analyze mission components and deterrence and defense requirements as has not been effectively done in the past. The beginning must be short-term net assessments—how things stack up and the balance of risks—in areas where war might start. Here, the overseas commanders in chief—that is, in Europe, the Pacific, South America, and the Central Command for deployment to the Persian Gulf—must develop far more sophisticated net assessments than the present numbers-crunching approach. If this had been done effectively in the past, we would not have tolerated the shocking imbalance that exists in NATO's Northern Army Group, where much of our trillion-dollar defense investment could be invalidated by one short-warning blitzkrieg on that area.

An overall global net assessment, NSC 68, took place under the Truman administration. Today we must go far beyond its methodology. Strengths, vulnerabilities, incoherences, compartmentalizations all must become apparent. The dynamics of warning and timing become key to the process. Defense Secretary James Schlesinger first set up a net-assessment capability with its director, Dr. Andrew Marshall, in his immediate office. Successor secretaries downgraded the effort. Congressman Dave McCurdy introduced legislation in 1987 to require a net assessment by the Joint Chiefs of Staff. On the senate side, John McCain has been an adroit advocate. The president, however, should require of his secretary of defense an overall net assessment as the very foundation for developing better use of our defense resources. Key members of Congress should also be involved in this process so that it has Congressional acceptance.

This overall net assessment will encourage a new strategic approach. Congress has given the Joint Chiefs of Staff Chairman some new tools to strengthen his role in national security planning. The 1986 Goldwater-Nichols legislation made the chairman of the JCS the principal military adviser to the president, the NSC, and the secretary of defense,[5] and gave him greater authority over the JCS staff. Other bureaucratic changes—which the services will surely resist in spirit—include requiring JCS duty service for officers who seek promotion to general officer rank. Whether the changes being implemented as a result of legislation bring about a more collaborative officer corps remains uncertain for some time. In the past, the problem with allocating national resources to security is that the services have dominated the process. National strategy has been a collection of individual service doctrines. But the chairman of the JCS, backed by a corps of officers serving national security interests broadly conceived, needs to be in the forefront of developing military strategy. In this regard, there are two highly favorable developments: the law and the man. The new law clearly gives the chairman the responsibility for developing strategic plans and budgets. Second, the present chairman, Admiral William J. Crowe, Jr., combines political accumen, assertiveness, and an intellect honed by a Princeton doctorate. He is building momentum toward a unified strategic approach.

If one reads the initial strategy of the Reagan administration, its emphasis—indeed, its very strategy—is founded on the need to restore military strength, economic strength, international prestige, and personal motivation. It was a strategy of buildup across the board—*more* defense resources.[6] A resolute Caspar Weinberger deserves credit for restoring the fighting spirit and capabilities of the armed forces. But now the strategy of simply "more" is over. The need for a strategy of better use is upon us. The way of Ulysses S. Grant—the American way of war—is no longer affordable, and the way of Robert E. Lee is a necessity. But that strategy can only emerge from a close review of our commitments and a net assessment of our strengths and weaknesses, our maldeployments and misapplications.

The proposed Presidential counsellor must develop a conceptual framework to better involve the Congress in a partnership to support such elements in our national security that are essential for effectiveness. Personnel are important. One of the most self-destructive measures of our overall national security process since World War II has been the fiscal crisis imposed by Congress on the State Department. Congress must be encouraged to see that our professional Foreign Service and our State Department are integral to our national security effort. This goes hand in hand with the security assistance and related aid programs to pivotal areas of the world that give us the capability to be successful through indirect means, and save money in the long run. A third area of concern is the human side of intelligence work, where at all levels there is a paucity of capabilities and an increasing fear of exposure of our agents.

Perhaps the most difficult job for the new president is how to reconcile and relate the security strategy not just with international economic strategy but with the budget program and domestic costs in general. It is ironic that of the eight presidents since World War II, only one really understood and talked about the importance of economic health to national security; this was the one who had been a five-star general, Dwight Eisenhower. Early in his administration he warned of the dangers of fits and starts, peaks and valleys in defense spending, and of not paying for defense as we went along. In today's world, security *is* both economic and military, and the effect of our national debt on our security could be disastrous.

As for the options of organizing economic policy, a 1988 CSIS study led by former Labor Secretary Bill Brock and John Yochelson looked at three options: first, restoration of a Council for International Economic Policy, such as Nixon had with Peter Peterson and then Peter Flanigan at its head—an arrangement that was nevertheless dominated by Treasury Secretaries John Connolly and George Shultz; second, a treasury secretary who is an "economic czar" but with a White House mandate to integrate finance, trade, and competitiveness policies; third, more like the Rockefeller solution, an associate NSC adviser with economic credentials and staff.[7] My solution is to put such an associate with the proposed counselor for a grand strategy because at this end the economic issues dealt with should involve basic policy planning and not crisis management. I would also examine the reasons why the Council of Economic Advisors has not worked as a major policy player, and then reform it accordingly. Maybe too much of its effort goes into its public reports and too little into interfacing with the president in private. One requirement is absolutely certain in linking defense and economic policy: the secretary of the treasury should be made a statutory member of the NSC.

As discussed in Chapter 18, balancing the budget is essential, as is building a public strategy for consensus on domestic and security spending. There is hope if we have the right organization, strategy, and leadership. We have never had a more centrist Congress and public. Gone are the New Deal days of large spending advocates. Both Democrats and Republicans argue over the importance of balancing the budget, and there is a common foundation in both parties on which to build. The vice president in my proposed new capacity must bridge the economic and security gaps not only within the compartmentalized executive branch but within the compartmentalized Congress as well. Otherwise we may see a domestic financial recession that leads to a global depression and to financial crisis, with grave security implications. The defense budgets in all the allied nations would collapse. What is needed is a national security program and budget that are sustainable over the years with bipartisan support and paid for as we go. If the kind of coherent grand strategy that I've outlined is actually developed, the administration will be seen as a better steward of the taxpayer's money.

Lastly, we turn to the Congress—that coordinate branch of government that so perplexes allies and opponents. Justice Brandeis in 1926 said in a Supreme Court case: "The doctrine of the separation of powers was adopted by the Convention in 1787 not to promote efficiency but to preclude the exercise of arbitrary power. The purpose was not to avoid friction, but, by the means of the inevitable friction incident in the distribution of the governmental power among the three departments, to save the people from autocracy."[8] The Watergate episode and the Iran-Contra affair remain tragic reminders of the importance of those checks and balances that give rise to friction. But if this friction is allowed to give way to paralysis and uncertainty, we can indeed find ourselves in economic collapse, not to mention World War III. The Constitutional Fathers discarded the Articles of Confederation because just such a paralysis, in a different form, jeopardized the survival of the new Republic. They wanted the chief executive—whom they named the commander in chief—to be effective in both the diplomacy and the strategy arenas essential to the security and well-being of the new nation.

Without any question, Congress has become far too intrusive in the conduct of foreign affairs and national security policy—not by some grand design, but generally by ad hoc measures and by trying to make foreign policy by amendment. The house divided, and thus the house uncertain, is a dangerous thing. Some of that congressional intrusion came about because presidents did not consult, and even at times deceived, but above all because they did not make partners of Congress.

One consequence of the Vietnam experience was the adoption in 1973 of the War Power Resolution, which sought to prevent future administrations from using U.S. troops in war without explicit congressional—and implicit public—support. This act, which sought to foster congressional and executive branch cooperation, has, in fact, impeded it. It has, as Senator Nunn and others have suggested, encouraged confrontation at home and encouraged adversaries to trigger the 60-day withdrawal clock by firing on Americans deployed abroad.[9]

I agree with Sam Nunn's conclusion that procedural changes alone will not restore bipartisan consensus in foreign policy. But an intelligent Congress can find more realistic ways of making sure foreign policy is accountable to the will of the people. The president should work with congressional leaders to find an acceptable formula that encourages a genuine partnership in foreign policy.

The vice president, as the person responsible for process under our scheme, must have this partnership as his mission, so that the majority of Congress joins in a grand strategy for the 1990s. As has been pointed out, the president's power to command—often even when his own party controls Congress—has been diminished. Yet the power to persuade is tremendous, especially if the president is as effective a communicator as Roosevelt, Kennedy, and Reagan have been.

As the Murphy Commission recommended in 1975, the new president should embrace the idea of a newly constituted congressional leadership committee that meets with him regularly. The leadership of the Foreign Relations and Foreign Affairs committees, and the Intelligence Committees, should be involved in regular sessions with the president, vice president, and department secretaries. A house divided cannot be repaired in one or two sessions, and a consensus on a grand strategy requires continuous exchange.

At the same time, the new Congress must get its own house in order and must think anew on how to approach the challenges ahead. The two Intelligence Committees should work together. It may be that the security committees should come together—like the Joint Economic Committee—to commission basic evaluations of the long-range security environment to the year 2000. And just as the military services are asked to look beyond their own institutional self-interests, Congressmen who perpetuate an inefficient military structure for constituency reasons should recognize the harm being done to the Republic they serve.

This book has argued that economic war comes from barriers and compartments, and that shooting wars in this century have almost always evolved from uncertainty, division, and misperceptions. Unity and coherence must be the bedrock of our strategy. It must start with the presidency and Congress. As Justice Robert H. Jackson noted in 1952, the president achieves the strength of the sovereign when both branches act together. Unity must be exercised with and within Europe and Japan. But the reconstruction of unity and coherence must begin with America, for if the last, best hope of the world is in the balance, world peace is too. Ultimately, our task resides in leaders with both a vision and a determination to make the difference in a time of peril and promise.

Epilogue: To the Year 2000

As we approach the millenium, we confront a number of areas of extraordinary opportunity and danger. The 1990s portend a far more fluid environment than we have known since World War II. We may find that areas of opportunity can become areas of danger. If areas of danger converge, we can lose our freedom of action. On the other hand, if the opportunities of the 1990s can be exploited, the horizon is bright.

Clearly, the area of greatest challenge and opportunity, for both the U.S. president and Gorbachev, is the ferment and evolution of the Soviet state. Will Gorbachev survive politically until the year 2000? If he does, he may go a long way toward implementing the agenda for the Soviet state that he outlines in his book, *Perestroika*. If the Soviet state is successfully reinvigorated and transformed into an economic as well as a military superpower, it could pose a serious challenge in many areas of the globe unless there is a major reversal of historic Soviet intentions.

The alternative, in which Gorbachev's vision fails, could be equally alarming and even more chaotic. Gorbachev knows that the Soviet Union faces considerable problems as he tries to coax his economy into the twenty-first century while keeping nationalist tendencies in check and Eastern Europe in line. So far Gorbachev has shown an extraordinary ability to think and act like a grand strategist, often operating from positions of weakness. Nonetheless, despite his considerable abilities, uncontrollable forces may come to dominate him or his successor.

Some would argue that the ideal situation for the West is one of neither total success nor total failure, but instead a combination of the two that keeps the Soviets preoccupied with their domestic problems. But I am not so sure that there is a middle ground; rather, the inability to achieve overall success may in fact be tantamount to failure. This does not, however, necessarily mean a lose-lose situation for the West, because the dangers inherent in either outcome can be surmounted as long as we are prepared for the uncertainties

One certain factor, however, is that a new generation will be coming to power, one that did not experience Stalin's mass terror, the sacrifice of 20 million Russians in World War II, or the grand alliance with the West. It is a generation that will be shaped largely by the communications revolution in the East and between the East and the West. It is a generation nurtured on *glasnost* that, ironically, will know more about the dark corners of Soviet history than its predecessors. This generation and its successor will be ones of rising expectations. While Gorbachev is promoting this new generation, no one can forecast what it, in and out of power, will mean for Soviet policy.

Will this generation be less or more assertive externally? We do not know. We do know that the transition of Soviet leadership at the top has been rocky and unpredictable. The new generation, like the old, has the acute dilemma of competing priorities: guns, butter, and growth. The legitimacy of the Soviet system demands improved living standards. With approximately one-eighth of the Soviet GNP devoted to the military, this effort is hurt, and Gorbachev hopes to change that. There is a danger that he will fail, that growth could approach zero by the turn of the century and public expectations not be met. This could be an unprecedented crisis in the making.

A failure of reforms or a reaction against reforms could lead the Soviets to turn to external initiatives to maintain their image and legitimacy. A military superpower that is economically inferior or wounded might seek to compensate in the form of influence, by projecting the shadow of usable discriminate military force. Alternatively, a military superpower with dissatisfied nationalities and chaotic satellites faces the hard decision to let them go or bring them to heel. As we have seen, Poland has repeatedly been the hot hinge of the European power balance. The crisis in Poland could again become the crisis of Europe. A spillover could occur. The conventional power of the Soviet Union, whether blitzkrieg units or a northern "fleet in being," offers a far better means for pursuing compensatory external power than unusable SS-20s. Western Europe with its technology and industrial capacity was and is the Soviet prize. A NATO that loses its strength through U.S. troop withdrawals and that lacks cohesion in crisis becomes an easy target. Nations can be pinched off and coerced.

In Eastern Europe, the fault lines could become wider with the result that the Warsaw Pact allies could become less reliable. It would be unfortunate if, in crisis planning, NATO nations failed to loosen rather than push together this empire. While these fissures help to deter the Soviets, they also accentuate stress on quick rather than prolonged action.

What of the West? Will the United States find the leadership, the house united, the restored educational systems, the increased savings and productivity necessary to prevent loss of its freedom of action? Can the United States, in its own backyard, build economic complementarity with Mexico and ensure that Central American instabilities do not reach into the United States itself? Will the Pacific Rim and the European Community join hands with America in opening markets to mutual advantage? Or will intensified trading groups create protectionism? Will would-be security partners become economic combatants? The "crisis of capitalism" could indeed take place simultaneously with the final crisis of communism.

The danger is that such an unstable climate in the Soviet Union and in the West can lead to miscalculation or misperception, as in June 1914, the late 1930s, 1950 in Korea, or the Cuban missile crisis. There is even evidence that the Soviet Union also fears an uncontrollable chain of events, the "Sarajevo factor" of action and reaction that could lead to conflict.[1] An East in crisis and a West without a grand strategy while possibly suffering an economic breakdown is a prescription for either coercion or the World War III that nobody is planning. If we defy the lessons of World Wars I and II by dismantling the commitments and structure that have prevented World War III for forty years, we are creating a perilous unknown. This book argues that instead of dismantling, it is essential to overhaul the structure in order to eliminate the elements of crisis instability that could in the 1990s lead the superpowers and allies into a conflict that neither wants.

Just as miscalculation by our potential adversary can result from a weakened U.S. commitment, so the same is true if our allies do not take their own defense seriously. I am second to none in advocating the U.S. commitment of ground troops to Europe, both as a political symbol and as a military reality. Our forces are needed as we move to correct the dangerous instabilities on the central front. But although a cheerleader for NATO, I still disagree with those Europeans who say we will unconditionally keep forces in Europe simply because of our own national interest. I believe it is in the U.S. interest to keep them there only as long as European leaders want to defend Europe as much as we do. We must have an alliance, not of unilateral guarantee, but of genuine mutual security. A Western Europe so weak in defense that it invites miscalculation leading to nuclear war is in no one's interest and cannot be morally justified. The purpose of our troops in Europe is to prevent World War III, and this fundamental fact must not be forgotten. The same is true in Asia.

A hopeful sign for the 1990s is that Western negotiation strategy has begun to create a remarkably effective process. As a result of our past NATO alliance unity and strength as well as their own economic stress, the Soviets are making concessions previously inconceivable. There may be unique opportunities for fundamental East–West settlements. Our priorities must be to correct the threatening military imbalances in Europe and eliminate potential blitzkrieg capability as well as eliminate destabilizing strategic nuclear weapons. Broader opportunities include parallel actions in the Third World, such as in dealing with nuclear proliferation and nuclear terrorism. Settlements are possible: The Austrian State Treaty showed this in the 1950s, and the 1988 Soviet Afghanistan withdrawal is a more dramatic case in point. One can hope for the same, eventually, in Eastern Europe.

The world of the year 2000 will be more multipolar, with the United States, the Soviet Union, Japan, Europe, and the People's Republic of China each generating its own gravitational field. Power will be increasingly measured on multidimensional scales—military, economic, political, technological. Relatively speaking, both the United States and the Soviet Union will be less powerful. Many authorities think that this multipolar world will automatically subsume the Soviet problem, forgetting that 1914 was a time of a multipolar world and loose alliances.

To the contrary, the multipolar order conjures up visions of past centuries when war in Europe was indeed often limited, and dominance was checked by the balance-of-power system. The authoritative German historian Ludwig Dehio appropriately labeled his study of four centuries of European power struggle *The Precarious Balance*. In the 1990s, such a shifting balance, in place of our firm and clear alliances of democracies, could give a hard-pressed Kremlin an opening into a different kind of game of international maneuvering to build anew great power legitimacy. To exploit the Sino–Soviet split as Nixon and Kissinger did was a brilliant maneuver. But pursuing a strategy of continued maneuvering rather than the constant alliance of democracies is to defy every lesson of this century.

As we project toward the year 2000, there are often false assumptions made about the relationship between economic and military power. Plainly, economic power over the long term will determine the capability for military power. This is the message of the work relating economic and military power, *The Rise and Fall of the Great Powers* by Professor Paul Kennedy. The overcommitment of military power with its cost can cause or accelerate economic decline. Economic power—the productive and creative forces of a nation—must be at the heart of any sound grand strategy. Gorbachev recognizes this, and hence *perestroika* and military retrenchments. In a crisis, however, it is *usable* military power that counts, not economic potential. Simply the fact that the Soviets may face economic decline does not immediately translate into incapacity. In time, declining economic power will erode the capacity for military assertiveness, but in the process the declining power could lash out. During the decline, there could be an attempt to translate the military strength into political and economic benefit.

Our grand strategy must deal not with one but with many options. After World War II, in an act of unparalleled generosity, the United States devised a grand strategy not only to build democratic institutions in such nations as West Germany and Japan but to rebuild their strong economies as a part of Western security. As compared to the earlier frustrations over the divisions of Charlemagne's children, new movement is plainly taking place toward a single European market after 1992. In the Pacific, the economic superpower, Japan, has surpassed the Soviet Union. China, with a fifth of the world's population, is looking toward market solutions. Those Third World nations that tilted toward Marxism but now are in shambles are also driven to new approaches. The newly industrialized countries, especially Taiwan and Korea, which we helped restore, are strong economic competitors. In short, our postwar grand strategy worked brilliantly.

I feel that China offers a special hope because of a constellation of factors. In the Soviet Union, the nationalities and East European problems and the attempt to keep the world's last empire in place drive the Soviet government into a whirlpool. On the other hand, in China the outward pulls of the investment enclaves, the absorption of Hong Kong, the outreach to Taiwan, and the interlock with Western commerce become steadying factors.

From now to the year 2000 we must harmonize our economic strategy, with the principal pillars being the United States, Japan, and the European Community. Regional and global trends toward protectionism must be shoved aside as we seek a genuinely "level playing field" for trade and investment. This will unleash the powerful potential of the corporations from many nations, which can bridge national boundaries with ideas, goods, services, technology, and people. Using their international resources, they can help rescue the Third World, open the Second, and maximize the full potential of the First. The global economy is interlocked. International and local business can lead toward a greater creativity as we approach a stunning new revolution in the information age. But a corporate social conscience is essential.

The Third World challenge to the year 2000 is also one of opportunity and danger. Marxist and dictatorial governments in all forms have lost credibility. Democracy is being chosen as the pathway to deal with change, and the Marxist model, once embraced by many Third World countries, is recognized by them as irrelevant. The drama of the Philippine revolution and the transition in Korea, Taiwan, and many countries in Latin America are examples of democracy on the march.

In contrast to the good news in the Third World and NATO, with over forty years at peace, approximately twenty-five sizable wars are in progress worldwide. Use of chemical weapons and proliferation of nuclear ones are dark clouds on the horizon. Other problems abound: The Arab–Israeli conflict, the West Bank upheavals, religious fundamentalism, and the conflicts in southern Africa are triggers for ever larger conflict. Of a general order are the population explosions combined with poverty, pollution, AIDS, and the greenhouse effect. These add major new costs and burdens that can drive nations inward when outward cooperation and grand strategy are essential. It might just be that a more realistic, less political United Nations could successfully tackle more of these global problems.

As we march toward the millenium, our new grand strategy moves us from the postwar Pax Americana with its domination and its nuclear protection toward a Pax Amicorum; based on less Americanization and more partnership in decision making, we would seek to build genuine mutual security.

As I stated earlier, Pax cannot exist without Shalom. So far, I have concentrated on the peace of order and balance. But as we look toward the millenium, it is also essential to strive even for Shalom. There has been positive movement in that direction when it is possible for an Andrei Sakharov to hold a press conference in Moscow immediately following the Reagan–Gorbachev summit. But more than ever, we must heed his message: Human rights without institutional guarantees are an endangered species. This goes for rights and governments everywhere. But Shalom is more than human rights and justice. It must include economic and social well-being. Without Shalom, there will be no enduring Pax and no usable grand strategy.

The United States, the leader, however indirect, of the Western alliances and world economy in the 1990s, faces a time of crisis which, like the Chinese character for crisis, is a combination of danger and opportunity. The challenge for American leadership is this: Can we put our economic house in order? Can we renew and harmonize our security, economic, and moral capabilities in order to grasp the stunning new opportunities? Can we be grand strategists? Lincoln, struggling with a house divided, said to another generation, and to ours: "The dogmas of the quiet past are inadequate to the stormy present. The occasion is piled high with difficulty, and we must rise with the occasion. . . . As our case is new, so we must think anew and act anew. . . . Fellow citizens, we cannot escape history."[2]

Notes

Prologue: How War Comes

1. A combined figure of 57,968,000 deaths resulting from World Wars I and II
   is drawn from Ruth Leger Sivard, *World Military and Social Expenditures*
   (Washington, D.C.: World Priorities, Inc., 1986).
2. In response to the 1914 Austro-Hungarian ultimatum to Serbia, Russia mobilized to deter Austria from taking action. The Russian military told the
   reluctant czar that he, Cousin Nicky, must also mobilize against Cousin
   Wilhelm in Germany, who had pledged support for Vienna, so as not to leave
   Russia's flank exposed. Escalation of the conflict became automatic. The
   process was something no one thought through in advance.

   Through much of the fatal month of July, the Kaiser luxuriated in the
   Karlsbad spa, and the German Imperial Staff was on vacation. German
   intelligence did not indicate a high chance of war. Even if there were a
   war, almost everyone believed it would be limited and manageable, and
   Britain would not be involved. Despite a secret understanding with
   France, Sir Edward Grey had said openly that Great Britain had no firm
   commitment to the continent.
3. The battle of armies in World War I has long since ended, but the battle of
   books over the causes of the war continues unabated. In Article 231 of the
   Versailles Treaty, Germany accepted the sole responsibility for causing the
   war, and the first war histories published in Allied countries, of course,
   reflected this view. The German Foreign Office later financed a campaign to
   cite Russia and France for unleashing the war. The distinguished American
   historian S. B. Fay, in his *Origin of the First World War*, spread the blame.
   In the intervening years prior to World War II, it became generally accepted
   that Europe had, as Lloyd George said, "stumbled into the war nobody
   wanted." In 1959, Hamburg historian Fritz Fischer, with newly available

material and a broader socioeconomic analysis, challenged this view. In later writings, he charged that Germany actually desired and planned war. Other German historians, including Gerhard Ritter and Egmont Zechlin, counter-attacked Fischer's thesis and methodology. But even Fischer admits that Germany miscalculated the British decision to intervene.

It was, of course, true that the Second Reich was out to realize its *Weltpolitik*, or world power, perhaps at times even at the risk of war. Admiral Alfred von Tirpitz's daring naval program built up a direct challenge to Britain; and Field Marshal von Schlieffen's plan placed military ahead of diplomatic considerations. Germans increasingly believed they were being "encircled," and of course it was indeed the deviation from Bismarck's wise policies that had produced just that. But there were countervailing efforts and factors: for example, the eventual cooperation of Germany with Britain to limit the Balkans War of 1912; that same year the British attempt by Lord Haldane to develop with the Germans mutual restraints on naval building; expansion of commerce among all powers; and certainly the royal connections and relations with a great investment in the status quo. Of all the scholarly studies, the most exhaustive is that of the Italian Luigi Albertini. He finds Germany guilty of encouraging Austria-Hungary to attack Serbia but not of planning a world war. Albertini is certainly correct because no coordinated military plans between Austria-Hungary and Germany existed.

4. A similarly acrimonious debate has raged over the origins of the Second World War. While it is impossible here to provide a comprehensive survey of the literature, the following have been of particular interest and use to the author:

The best-known revisionist is, of course, A. J. P. Taylor (*The Origins of the Second World War*, first published by Hamish Hamilton, 1961 and in the U.S. by Atheneum), who argues that Hitler had no desire or coherent strategy for war; rather, he aimed at achieving his political and territorial objectives by intimidation short of war. Indeed, Taylor concludes that "in international affairs there was nothing wrong with Hitler except that he was a German"; he got as far as he did largely because of the way the Allies handled him in the late 1930s.

Arnold A. Offner (*The Origins of the Second World War: American Foreign Policy and World Politics, 1917–1941*. New York: Praeger, 1975) stresses the complexity of international interactions and the key role of mis-perception. See also Laurence Lafore (*The End of Glory*. New York: Lippin-cott/Harper and Row, 1970). Finally, Christopher Thorne (*The Approach of War 1938–1939*. London: Macmillan, 1967) engages in a balanced survey of the events leading up to the war, with very full references to the various contending approaches to its origins.

1: In Search of a Grand Strategy

1. There is, of course, a school of thought that maintains that Grant was a greater general than Lee. For example, see J. F. C. Fuller (*The Generalship of*

Ulysses S. Grant. London: John Murray, 1929) and the recent publication by
John Keegan (*The Mask of Command*. New York: Viking Publications, 1987,
pp. 164–229). Grant was far superior in competence than his predecessors
who Lincoln had replaced, but his forces far outnumbered those of Lee, as
did his casualties. His greatest strategic campaign was not his war of attrition
against Lee but his war of maneuver at Vicksburg.

2. George Shultz, in "Those to Whom 'Battle Royal' is Nothing New," *New York
   Times*, 28 July 1987, A7.

3. David Abshire, *Foreign Policy Makers: President vs. Congress* (London: Sage
   Publication, 1979), Washington Papers No. 66. Center for Strategic and
   International Studies, 5.

4. Arkady N. Shevchenko, *Breaking with Moscow* (New York: Ballantine Books,
   1985), p. 432.

5. In Abshire, *ibid.*, 70.

6. See Lloyd Cutler, "To Form a Government," *Foreign Affairs* 59, no. 1 (Fall
   1980).

7. White House memorandum, Washington, D.C., February 19, 1987, For:
   Mr. Donald Regan and Mr. Frank Carlucci; From: David M. Abshire; Subject: Beyond the Tower Board Report.

8. There is a telling story that, after the Vietnam War, a U.S. colonel visited
   Hanoi and commented to a Communist counterpart: "You know, you never
   defeated us on the battlefield." The response: "That may be so, but it is also
   irrelevant." Indeed the Americans won battles, had the so-called kill ratios in
   their favor, but lost the war. (The conversation took place on 25 April 1975,
   in Hanoi between Colonel Harry G. Summers, Jr., then Chief, Negotiations
   Division, U.S. Delegation, Four Party Joint Military Team; and Colonel Tu,
   Chief, North Vietnamese [DRV] Delegation. *On Strategy: The Vietnam War
   in Context*, 4th edition [Carlisle Barracks, Pa.: Strategic Studies Institute,
   U.S. Army War College, 1983], 1.)

9. Edward Luttwak, "Grand Strategy" (unpublished paper).

10. Mike Moodie, "NATO and the U.S. Grand Strategy" (paper at the CSIS
    Williamsburg Conference, Spring 1983).

11. Walter Lippmann, *Essays on the Public Philosophy* (Boston: Little, Brown
    and Co., 1955).

12. Article II of the NATO Treaty, *The North Atlantic Treaty Organization: Facts
    and Figures* (Brussels: NATO Information Service, 1984), 264.

13. This group consisted of Gaetano Martino of Italy, Halvard Lange of Norway,
    and Lester Pearson of Canada.

14. "Text of the Report of the Committee of Three on Non-Military Cooperation
    in NATO," 13 December 1956, *The North Atlantic Treaty Organization:
    Facts and Figures*. (Brussels: NATO Information Service, 1984), 270–88.

15. Ibid.

16. Ibid.

17. Ibid.

18. Ibid.

19. Article V of the NATO Treaty, op. cit., 264.

20. Ibid.
21. The series included four consecutive reports entitled "U.S. Foreign Policy for the 1970's: Building for Peace. A Report to the Congress by Richard Nixon, President of the United States." They were released respectively on: (I) 18 February 1970, (II) 25 February 1971, (III) 9 February 1972, (IV) 3 May 1973.
22. Fred Ikle and Albert Wohlstetter, "Discriminate Deterrence," report of the Commission on Integrated Long-Term Strategy, January 1988.
23. See "National Security Strategy Report," January 1988.

2: How NATO Works . . . Or Does It?

1. The North Atlantic Treaty Organization, founded in 1949, currently consists of 16 nations: Belgium, Canada, Denmark, France, Federal Republic of Germany, Greece, Iceland, Italy, Luxembourg, The Netherlands, Norway, Portugal, Spain, Turkey, United Kingdom, United States.
2. In keeping the mission working together, Ledogar had the strong support of my defense adviser, Dr. Larry Legere. Legere's ability to attract top-notch military officers was nothing short of phenomenal. The status of the U.S. mission to NATO in the State Department was such that it naturally attracted high-quality Foreign Service officers. But our military services have not traditionally rewarded officers sufficiently for accepting such postings, despite the tremendous contribution that they can make to national security in organizations like USNATO. Legere has a nose for talent and his ability to attract military officers with broad operational and educational experience (most of our Ph.D.s worked for Legere) continues to enrich U.S. participation at NATO.
3. The Rio Pact of September 2, 1947, predated the North Atlantic Treaty as the first regional collective security agreement in conformity with Article 51 of the United Nations Charter. However, unlike the North Atlantic Treaty, it has failed to protect its members against aggression.
4. The increased public and professional interest in NATO's nuclear policy, which arose out of the 1979 decision to deploy LRINF, was reinforced by the deployments themselves, and sustained by the debate over the INF Treaty, gave rise to an increasing number of publications that examined many aspects of the role of nuclear weapons in Europe, from order of battle to employment concepts to crisis management. See, for example, Ashton B. Carter, John D. Steinbruner, and Charles A. Zraket, eds., *Managing Nuclear Operations* (Washington: Brookings Institution, 1987), and especially Catherine McArdle Kelleher's article "NATO Nuclear Operations" in that book, which goes into some detail on nuclear authorization and release procedures. See also Stephen J. Cimbala, *Extended Deterrence* (Lexington, Mass.: Lexington Books, 1987), and Richard Ned Lebrow, *Nuclear Crisis Management: A Dangerous Illusion* (Ithaca: Cornell University Press, 1987). A more basic overview is presented in Lawrence Martin, *NATO and the Defense of the West* (New York: Holt, Rinehart and Winston, 1985), which includes a discussion of NATO nuclear consultation.

5. SACLANT in Norfolk has never had the alliance-wide visibility nor the prestige of SACEUR. This is largely because the command is distant from Europe and heavily involved with the unspectacular roles of logistics and reinforcement. It is also partly because the shortsighted U.S. Navy has filled this position with admirals still aspiring to the top U.S. job, who typically have had only two- or three-year tours of duty. Instead, they should be assigning a senior officer who might have already been chief of naval operations and who could build prestige and influence as SACLANT for four or five years or more, as SACEUR does.

   I took a special interest in the problems of SACLANT and CINCHAN and encouraged them to appear more often before the DPC. I also hosted, with SACLANT Admiral Lee Baggett and CINCHAN Admiral Sir Nicholas Hunt, a freewheeling seminar on maritime strategy at NATO with leading military experts and scholars.

6. Theoretically, the NATO Military Committee is superior in the chain of all NATO commands. Just as the NATO Council can meet at the highest level of presidents and prime ministers, so the Military Committee can meet at the levels of chiefs of defense staff. Those chiefs of staff meet twice a year. On a continuous basis, each nation assigns a permanent military representative and his supporting delegation to NATO Headquarters. When I arrived at NATO, our representative was my West Point classmate paratrooper General Roscoe Robinson, the highest ranking (four star) black general in the U.S. Army. Fine talent, only partially utilized, existed from other countries. When I arrived, the chairman of the Military Committee was the forthright Dutch General Cornelius de Jaeger, whose sincerity was a real asset when the peace movement was at its height.

3: The Moral Crossroads

1. An excellent discussion of this subject was offered in April 1983 at the Episcopal Church's National Conference on Peacemaking, where Professor Allan Parrent identified two traditional concepts.

2. For further reading see Gregory Flynn and Hans Rattinger, eds., *The Public and Atlantic Defense* (Totowa, N.J.: Roman and Allanheld, Atlantic Institute for International Affairs, 1985).

3. For further reading see Michael Howard, "Reassurance and Deterrence," *Foreign Affairs* 61, no. 2 (Winter 82–83), 309–24.

4. Jonathan Schell, *The Fate of the Earth* (New York: Alfred A. Knopf, Inc., 1982).

5. John O'Conner, quoted in David M. Abshire, "NATO at the Moral Crossroads," *Washington Quarterly* 7, no. 3 (Summer 1984), 7.

6. Ibid.

7. For further reading, see Roland H. Bainton, *Christian Attitudes Toward War and Peace* (New York: Abington Press, 1960); Howard Davis, ed., *Ethics and Defense* (New York: Basil Blackwell, Inc., 1987); Ernest W. Lefever and E. Stephen Hunt, eds., *The Apocalyptic Premise* (Washington, D.C.: Ethics and

Public Policy Center, 1982); William V. O'Brien and John Langan, S.J., eds., *The Nuclear Dilemma and the Just War Tradition* (Lexington, Mass.: Lexington Books, 1986); Michael Walzer, *Just and Unjust Wars* (New York: Basic Books, Inc., 1977).

8. Archbishop Robert Runcie, quoted in Abshire, op. cit., 12.
9. Walter Laqueur, *The Terrible Secret* (London: Weidenfeld and Nicholson, 1980).
10. *New York Times*, 5 June 1988.
11. It is interesting to note that in a subsequent book (reference note 4), Jonathan Schell recognizes the moral validity of the search for a defense against nuclear weapons. See Jonathan Schell, *The Abolition* (New York: Knopf, 1984).

4: Charlemagne's Children

1. Summary Report of the EuroGroup Seminar, chaired by the minister of defense of the Kingdom of the Netherlands and organized by the Center for Strategic and International Studies, 7 May 1987, Washington, D.C., 11.
2. William Pfaff, "Europe: A Slumbering, Politically Withdrawn Giant," *International Herald Tribune*, 23 June 1986.
3. It was estimated that holding European unemployment at the 1984 rate of 11.3% would require the creation of 6–7 million jobs through 1990. To reduce it to around 5.5% would require 14 million new jobs by 1990. The political and security ramifications of these trends are enormous. See Michael Moodie, "Economics and Security," *The Atlantic Papers*, No. 4 (Washington, D.C.: The Atlantic Council of the United States), 6.
4. Moodie, ibid., pp. 6–7.
5. *Science and Engineering Indicator–1987*, National Science Board (Washington, D.C.: U.S. Government Printing Office, 1987), 234.
6. Ibid., 103.
7. Christopher Tugendhat, *Making Sense of Europe* (New York: Viking Penguin, Inc., 1986), 42.
8. Ibid., 48.
9. Lord Peter Carrington, comments given to the EuroGroup Seminar, organized by the Center for Strategic and International Studies, Washington, D.C., 7 May 1987.
10. Further further reading, see Tugendhat, *Making Sense of Europe*, op. cit., 60.
11. "Bonn, Paris Widen Martial Cooperation," *Washington Post*, 25 September 1987, 27.
12. For text of de Gaulle's letter, see Don Cook, *Charles de Gaulle: A Biography* (London: Secker and Warburg, 1985), 382–83.
13. Robert Rudney, "French 1987–1991 Programming Law: An End to Independence," *Armed Forces Journal International*, January 1988, 30.
14. Assembly of Western European Union, "Platform on European Security Interests," Document 1122, The Hague, 27 October 1987.
15. Luigi Barzini, *The Europeans* (New York: Simon and Schuster, 1983), 193.

16. Paul Cole and William J. Taylor, Jr., "Northern Europe: The Politics and Economics of Coalition Defense" (draft paper, *NATO at Forty: Change, Continuity, and Implications for the Future,* ed. by the U.S. Military Academy, May 1987), 15.

5: To Withdraw or Recommit

1. Henry A. Kissinger. *The White House Years* (Boston: Little Brown and Company, 1979), 947.
2. Henry A. Kissinger. "A Plan To Reshape NATO," *Time,* 5 March 1984, 14–18.
3. For further reading see Senator Sam Nunn, "The Need to Reshape Military Strategy," The First David M. Abshire Endowed Lecutre given at The Center for Strategic and International Studies. Published under the same title in: Significant Issues Series, Volume X, Number 6 (Washington, D.C.: CSIS, 1983).
4. Under Secretary for Research and Engineering Dr. Richard DeLauer fought this trend and encouraged the Defense Science Board to commission what turned out to be a superb report on armaments cooperation, chaired by the very able Dr. Malcolm Currie. See the "Report of the Defense Science Board Task Force on Industry-to-Industry International Armaments Cooperation, Phase I, NATO Europe." Office of the Under Secretary of Defense for Research and Engineering, Washington, D.C., June 1983.
5. John Tower, *Congressional Record,* 20 June 1984, 7725.
6. Sam Nunn, *Congressional Record,* 20 June 1984, 7745.
7. William Cohen, *Congressional Record,* 20 June 1984, 7745.
8. David M. Abshire, "NATO on the Move," in *The Alliance Papers* (Brussels: Atlantic Council of the United States, in cooperation with United States Mission to NATO, 1985), 4–7.
9. For further reading on the Nunn amendment, see "DoD Allots $2.9-Billion for R&D with Allies over Next Five Years," *Armed Forces Journal International,* December 1986, 21. In the same issue, see interview with Ambassador David M. Abshire, 26; "Taft: 'Side-by-Side Testing a Key Solution' to Two-Way Street Issues," DoD news release, Office of Assistant Secretary of Defense (Public Affairs), 21 January 1987, no. 34–87.
10. The description is, of course, a simplistic presentation of the process of forming a congressional coalition behind NATO armaments cooperation. The approach of the landmark amendment to the 1986 DoD Authorization Act offered by Senators Nunn, Warner, and Roth was also strongly supported in the House by such powerful legislators as Bill Chappell (D–FL), chairman of the Defense Appropriations Subcommittee, and Charles Bennett (D–FL), of the Armed Services Committee.

    A related amendment to the 1986 Authorization Act, sponsored in the Senate by Dan Quayle (R–IN) and in the House by Sam Stratton (D–NY) and Marjorie Holt (R–MD), significantly reduced bureaucratic obstacles to expanded alliance armaments cooperation by allowing the secretary of defense to exempt cooperative projects from restrictions in the Arms Control Export Act.

Since 1986, $445 million has been appropriated for the Nunn Programs (including the side-by-side testing of off-the-shelf U.S. and European weapons and equipment). Indeed, the Department of Defense has planned to allocate $2.9 billion through 1992 to cooperative research and development programs with the NATO allies.

An important new congressional effort to energize NATO armaments cooperation is Senator Quayle's proposed NATO Defense Initiative. Quayle identifies a wide range of alliance procurement requirements for the 1990s, which provide significant new opportunities for harmonizing U.S. and allied advanced R & D.

6: Terrorism Strikes NATO

1. Statistics on incidents of terrorism and casualties were provided by the U.S. State Department's Office to Combat Terrorism.
2. "German and French Guerrilla Groups Announce Joint Anti-NATO 'Front,' " *International Herald Tribune,* 16 January 1985.
3. "Can Do," *Brussels Weekly,* JAS Personnel Office, American Embassy, 25 January 1985, no. 4.
4. "Belgium Arrests Bombing Suspects," *International Herald Tribune,* 17 December 1985.
5. "Combatting International Terrorism: U.S.-Allied Cooperation and Political Will." Policy Papers: Security Series (Washington, D.C.: Atlantic Council of the United States, November 1986), 45.
6. James Markham, op-ed, *New York Times,* June 1986.
7. Mary Kaldor and Paul Anderson, eds. *Mad Dogs: The U.S. Raid Against Libya* (London: Pluto Press, 1986), 7, 25.
8. Practically on the eve of the raid, Italian Prime Minister Craxi reportedly urged the United States to ask NATO to consider joint action against terrorism and also to consider defining terrorism as a threat to the alliance. When the Libyan raid occurred, the United States was charged with failure to respect the principle of "partnership" in the alliance. There had been no real consultations with NATO partners—only the request of the Walters mission to use U.K. facilities and to fly over France and Spain. Europeans were even more incensed that the raid went forward as European ministers were meeting in Brussels to discuss further action. But the other side of the coin is that the Europeans were not getting their act together, and the Craxi proposal would not have carried; France certainly would have blocked it. The charge of U.S. unilateralism was certainly correct, but only after Europe's failure to act. It was only the tremendous anti-French sentiment that had built up in the Congress that led the French at the forthcoming Tokyo summit to go along with placing terrorism on the agenda and in the communiqué. For further reading, see Frederick Zilian, Jr., "The U.S. Raid on Libya—and NATO," *Orbis,* Fall 1986, 518.

7: The Deterrence Debate

1. For a more detailed, but still brief, review of nuclear strategy, see Donald M. Snow, *National Security* (New York: St. Martin's Press, 1987), 189–98.
2. McGeorge Bundy, George F. Kennan, Robert S. McNamara, and Gerard Smith, "Nuclear Weapons and the Atlantic Alliance," *Foreign Affairs* 60, no. 4 (Spring 1982), 753–68.
3. At the nucler level, one way to restore flexible response was the enhanced radiation weapon, the so-called neutron bomb. Its deployment would have made first use a less hollow threat by substituting nuclear arms less suicidal and more militarily meaningful. As we know, the decision on deployment was fumbled in Washington and rejected in Europe, resulting in a lost opportunity to regain some flexibility at the theater nuclear level. The rejected weapon, wrongly labeled a monster weapon, would have been devastating to advancing Soviet tank columns, the very reason why France, independent in such matters, is developing a neutron bomb of its own. For further reading, see Fred Ikle, *Strategic Review* (Winter 1980).
4. Kenneth A. Myers, ed., *NATO: The Next Thirty Years* (Boulder, Colo.: Westview Press, 1980).
5. See Raymond Gartoff, *Reflections on the Cuban Missile Crisis* (Washington, D.C.: The Brookings Institution, 1987).
6. "National Security Strategy Report," January 1988.
7. Fred Ikle and Albert Wohlstetter, "Discriminate Deterrence," report of the Commission on Integrated Long-Term Strategy, January 1988, 2.
8. Michael Howard, Karl Kaiser, and Francois de Rose, "Deterrence Policy: A European Response," *International Herald Tribune*, 4 February 1988.
9. Zbigniew Brzezinski, Henry A. Kissinger, Fred C. Ikle, and Albert Wohlstetter, "Discriminate Deterrence Won't Leave Europe Dangling," *International Herald Tribune*, 24 February 1988.
10. Ibid.

8: What if War Comes?

1. The literature examining and measuring the conventional balance of forces in Europe or various aspects of it would fill several libraries. There is no single agreed assessment and, in fact, the issue is the subject of considerable debate. On the official level, the United States has done no unclassified "net assessment" of the European conventional balance, although Soviet forces are addressed in considerable detail in the various editions of *Soviet Military Power*. Under the terms of the 1987 DoD Reorganization Act, however, the Congress gave an explicit mandate to the chairman of the Joint Chiefs of Staff to do a dynamic net assessment. The first such net assessment has been completed on a classified basis.

   In the unclassified arena, Senator Carl Levin, chairman of the Senate Subcommittee on Conventional Forces, published under his own auspices "Beyond the Bean Count." Official unclassified non-American analyses include the German Ministry of Defense 1987 assessment of the balance, "Streitkraeftevergleich 1987: NATO-WARSCHAUER PAKT"; an assessment provided by the German Ministry of Defense, *Wehrtechnic* (December 1987) as a special issue; and a report of the Committee of the Western European Union titled "The Threat Assessment," report no. 1115, Parliamentary Assembly of the Western European Union, Committee on Defense Questions and Armaments, December 1987.

An earlier assessment was provided by NATO in *NATO and the Warsaw Pact: Force Comparisons* (Brussels: NATO Information Service, 1984), although political disputes between allies have prevented publication of an updated companion.

Critics of official, especially American, analyses of the balance in Europe have argued that such appraisals undervalue factors naturally favorable to NATO as the defender or that they do not adequately take into account nonquantifiable factors such as readiness and training. Many of these critics are regular contributors to *International Security*, the journal of Harvard's Center for Science and International Affairs. For the most important assessments in this regard, see John Mearsheimer, *Conventional Deterrence* (Ithaca, N.Y.: Cornell University Press, 1983); Mearsheimer's "Why the Soviets Can't Win Quickly in Central Europe," *International Security* 7, no. 1 (Summer 1982); Barry Posen, "Measuring the European Conventional Balance: Coping with Complexity in Threat Assessment," *International Security* 9, no. 3 (Winter 1984/85); and Joshua Epstein, *The 1988 Defense Budget* (Washington, D.C.: The Brookings Institution, 1987).

For other views of the conventional balance, see Phillip A. Karber, "In Defense of Forward Defense," *Armed Forces Journal International*, May 1984; William Mako, *U.S. General Forces and the Defense of Central Europe* (Washington D.C.: The Brookings Institution, 1983); and John Collins, *The U.S.-Soviet Military Balance, 1980–1985* (New York: Pergamon Brassey, 1985). For analyses of specific aspects of the balance, the Congressional Budget Office has conducted useful studies.

A significant literature has also developed on the methodology of measuring the conventional balance, including considerable operations research. See, for example, William W. Kaufman, "The Arithmetic of Force Planning," in John D. Steinbruner and Leon V. Sigal, eds., *Alliance Security: NATO and the No-First-Use Question* (Washington, D.C.: The Brookings Institution, 1983), 208–16; Joshua Epstein, *The Calculus of Conventional War* (Washington, D.C.: The Brookings Institution, 1985); and Stephen D. Biddle, "The European Conventional Balance: A Reinterpretation of the Debate," *Survival* 30, no. 2 (March/April 1988), 99–121.

2. This figure, like much of the analysis of the current balance of conventional forces that appears in these pages, is drawn from the ongoing work of the CSIS Project on a Resources Strategy for the United States and Its Allies, and specifically from its first report, "NATO: Meeting the Coming Challenge," published in December, 1987 (hereafter referred to as CSIS NATO Report). Begun when I returned to the Center in March 1987, this important study has

been generously supported by the John M. Olin Foundation of New York, the Sarah Scaife Foundation in Pittsburgh, and The Lynde & Harry Bradley Foundation of Milwaukee Wisconsin.

3. Ibid., 16. The overall balance of 2.2:1 is measured in Armoured Division Equivalents (ADEs).

4. David M. Abshire, Phil Karber, and Michael Moodie. *The Balance of Conventional Forces in Europe: A Comprehensive Appraisal.* Forthcoming book (Washington, D.C.: Center for Strategic and International Studies). All subsequent references to this source will be cited as CSIS Conventional Balance Appraisal.

5. CSIS NATO Report, 17.

6. For further reading, see Richard K. Betts, *Surprise Attack* (Washington, D.C.: The Brookings Institution, 1982).

7. CSIS Conventional Balance Appraisal.

8. Ibid.

9. *The Military Balance: 1987–1988* (London: International Institute for Strategic Studies, 1987), 63.

10. CSIS Conventional Balance Appraisal.

11. For an excellent analysis of the "fault line" in the Warsaw Pact, see E. B. Atkeson, *The Final Agreement of the Kings* (Fairfax: Hero Books, 1988), 223–244.

12. *Military Balance*, op. cit., 41.

13. CSIS NATO Report, 17.

14. The scenario of the Soviets generating a "fleet in being" is not uncontroversial. In the summer of 1985 the Soviets conducted their largest exercise ever in the Atlantic maritime theater. Labeled SUMMEREX 85 by NATO, over 50 Soviet surface combatants and 35 submarines deployed well south in the Norwegian Sea and into the North Atlantic in a relatively short time frame. Some of the forces then turned northward, presumably simulating Western naval forces in opposition to those arrayed farther north in a "defense of the homeland" role. Coordinated operations were then undertaken by "defensive" surface forces and submarines, in concert with land-based Soviet naval aviation units, against the northbound units. Some analysts estimated that SUMMEREX 85 was only a partial demonstration of Moscow's capability to deploy forces in such a manner. Indeed, some believe that as many as half their surface units could be sortied deep into the Norwegian Sea basin, with as many as 80 submarines at the Greenland-Iceland-United Kingdom (G-I-UK) gap within three days. SUMMEREX 85 raised the specter of possible similar Soviet naval force deployments in a NATO-Warsaw Pact crisis. The reasonableness of such an action is the issue under debate.

My view is that the exercise reflected possible Soviet intent of just such a deployment, *under the guise of an exercise,* in some future crisis to pressure Norway, Denmark, and, perhaps, Iceland. The problem for the 1990s is that NATO reaction to such Soviet deployments would be taken as provocative and, therefore, not initiated, at least until too late. Difficulties associated with arriving at a collective NATO decision in a time of rising tensions would reinforce reluctance to approve such a decision. If the crisis then escalated, Soviet naval forces would be positioned to disrupt, if not prevent, NATO reinforcement efforts, enabling the Warsaw Pact to buy time, possibly fragmenting NATO resolve and leading some members to capitulate to Pact pressure and declare neutrality. This view further holds that the Soviet "fleet in being" would be sufficiently dominant that any subsequent attempt to reinforce the northern allies would only be at very great cost in NATO lives and naval units. Moreover, if such an effort did succeed, it probably would not be early enough to prevent defeat in Central Europe.

The second school of thought argues that such a SUMMEREX-style deployment almost surely is not undertaken owing to the "target-rich environment" it would create for Western naval and air forces. Members of this school may believe the deep surge into the Atlantic and southern Norwegian Sea was only done to prepare for generating "Western" naval forces to oppose the "defense of the homeland" barriers farther north. This view holds that Soviet surface forces, although some possess impressive close-in air defense systems, would be no match for Western tactical air and submarine assets and would not survive against the range of capabilities NATO could bring to bear.

Without the range capability in their land-based tactical air assets to maintain air superiority in the Norwegian Sea basin, Soviet submarines would also be vulnerable to superior NATO maritime patrol aircraft, surface, and submarine ASW capabilities. They would stand to lose their surface fleet and a very high number of submarines, thus severely curtailing their ability to defend their SSBN force, a key requirement.

The results of past war games, engagement analyses, and exercises provide confidence that NATO naval forces, properly deployed in the Norwegian Sea and North Atlantic prior to the outbreak of hostilities, could prevail against Warsaw Pact naval forces and achieve most, if not all, of their wartime objectives. With 3–4 USN carrier battle groups and other NATO naval forces deployed to the eastern Norwegian Sea and North Atlantic, in concert with additional land-based tactical aircraft, MPA, and amphibious forces that could be brought to bear on short notice, NATO could contain and destroy the Northern and Baltic fleets, defend Norway against land and air attack, counter amphibious operations against Norway, prevent Soviet use of Norwegian bases, and deny the northern air corridor to the Soviets for air strikes against the UK. *The timely introduction of these forces (prior to hostilities) would very likely achieve the more desirable objective of deterring escalation to conflict.*

If, however, the Soviets deployed their Northern and Baltic Sea fleets into the Norwegian Sea and North Atlantic, *and the West did not respond,* a crisis escalating to conflict would present NATO with an extremely difficult dilemma. Although Soviet forces might suffer significant losses, it is unlikely that NATO forces would be able, without the NATO Strike Fleet and associated reinforcements, to defend northern Norway for more than 15–30 days. In addition to "giving up" Norway, Western naval operations to gain control of the Norwegian Sea probably could not be successful sufficiently early to provide critical reinforcement and resupply assets to Western Europe. A coordinated effort by NATO naval forces to fight their way into the Norwegian Sea could take as long as a month, before which NATO ground forces in Central Europe likely would have to resort to nuclear weapons.

In a NATO-Warsaw Pact crisis, the "time factor" and NATO decision making become all important. Events leading to the crisis are sure to influence NATO perceptions of threat development, and unilateral, bilateral, and multilateral decisions may suffice in developing initial maritime force counterdeployments. This method of force generation *will not be adequate,* however, to deal with the large-scale Soviet deployment envisioned in excess of the SUMMEREX 85 demonstration. Information supplied by Captain Richard E. Goolsby, U.S.N., Commanding Officer, U.S. Naval Air Station, Keflavik, Iceland.

15. Francois Heisbourg, quoted in Thomas A. Callaghan, Jr., "NATO's Collection of Forces: Falling Short of a Balanced, Conventional Defense," *Journal of Defense and Diplomacy* (July 1987), 19.

16. Thomas A. Callaghan, Jr., "The Structural Disarmament of NATO," *NATO Review,* no. 3 (June 1984), 3.

17. Ibid., 6.

18. Thomas A. Callaghan, Jr., statement before the Conventional Forces and Alliance Defense Subcommittee of the Senate Armed Services Committee, 7 October 1987, 2.

19. Thomas A. Callaghan, Jr., "Structural Disarmament: A Vengeful Phenomenon," *Journal of Defense and Diplomacy* 5, no. 9 (1987), 31.

9: U.S. Global Perspectives

1. For further reading, see Halford J. Mackinder, "The Geographical Pivot of History," *Geographical Journal* 23 (1904).

2. The "Pacific Basin" refers to countries in the Pacific Ocean. The "Pacific Rim" refers to countries with a border on the Pacific Ocean.

3. Ronald J. Hays, statement before the Defense Subcommittee of the House Appropriations Committee, 3 February 1988.

4. As President Nixon later explained, the idea of the Nixon Doctrine was that "in those lands to which we have obligations or in which we have interests, if they are ready to fight a fire, they should be able to count on us to furnish the hose and water." See C. L. Sulzberger, *The World and Richard Nixon* (New York: Prentice-Hall Press, 1987), 36, 241.

5. *The Military Balance: 1987–1988* (London: International Institute for Strategic Studies, 1987), 163–64.

6. Ibid., 162–63.

7. Ronald J. Hays, statement before the Defense Subcommittee of the House Appropriations Committee, 3 February 1988.

8. *The Military Balance: 1987/88* (London: The International Institute for Strategic Studies, 1987), 170.

9. Mikhail Gorbachev, Vladivostok speech, July 1986.

10. Ibid.
11. Pacific Area Update Briefing, U.S. Pacific Command, Honolulu, July 1987.
12. Ibid.
13. Ibid.
14. Ibid.
15. Ibid.
16. "Gulf Policy Said to Boost U.S. Credibility," *Washington Post*, 11 January 1988, A1.
17. Caspar W. Weinberger, "Annual Report to the Congress, Fiscal Year 1987," 5 February 1986, 184.
18. *Washington Post*, op. cit.
19. General George B. Crist, U.S. Marine Corps Commander and Chief U.S. Central Command, before the Defense Subcommittee of the House Appropriations Committee, 8 April 1987, 11–12.
20. Ibid., 12–13. For a more comprehensive review of Soviet military force structure in the Southern Strategic Theater, see *The Military Balance: 1987–1988*, International Institute for Strategic Studies, 43–44.
21. Crist statement, op. cit., 12. See also Joshua M. Epstein, *Strategy and Force Planning: The Case of the Persian Gulf* (Washington, D.C.: The Brookings Institution, 1987); Thomas L. McNaugher, *Arms and Oil: U.S. Military Strategy in the Gulf* (Washington, D.C.: The Brookings Institution, 1985).
22. Thomas H. Moorer and Georges A. Fauriol, *Caribbean Basin Security*. Washington Paper No. 104, by The Center for Strategic and International Studies. (Washington, D.C.: Praeger Special Studies, 1984), 11–23.
23. Douglas J. Murray, "The United States-Canadian Defense Relationship in Transition: An American Perspective," *Atlantic Community Quarterly* (Spring 1987), 70.
24. *Toronto Star* poll cited in David Buchan, "Fortress Canada Toughens Up," *Financial Times*, 5 August 1987, 13.
25. *Challenge and Commitment: A Defense Policy for Canada* (Ottawa: National Defense Publication, 1987), 67.

10: The Power Balancers: Japan and China

1. Ezra F. Vogel, *Japan as No. 1: Lessons for America* (Tokyo: Charles E. Tuttle Co., 1979).
2. Nathaniel Peffer, *The Far East* (Ann Arbor: University of Michigan Press, 1958).
3. Robert C. Christopher, *The Japanese Mind* (New York: Fawcett Columbine, 1983).
4. Chalmers Johnson, *MITI and the Japanese Miracle* (Tokyo: Charles E. Tuttle Co., 1982).
5. Peter F. Drucker, "Japan's Choices," *Foreign Affairs* (Summer 1987), 923–41.
6. "Novel Technique Shows Japanese Outpace Americans in Innovation," *New York Times*, 7 March 1988, 1.

7. Akio Morita, *Made in Japan* (New York: E. P. Dutton, 1986).
8. Nathaniel Peffer, *The Far East* (Ann Arbor: University of Michigan Press, 1958).
9. Allan Wallace, Under Secretary of State for Economic Affairs, address to the Federation of Economic Organizations (Keidenren), 18 April 1988.
10. See James Fallow, "The Rice Plot," *Atlantic* (January 1987), 22.
11. "Fiscal '88 Defense Budget to Hit Record 3.7 Trillion Yen," *Daily Yomiuri*, 29 December 1987, 1.
12. Pacific Area Update Briefing, United States Pacific Command, Honolulu, July 1987.
13. Worth H. Bagley, "U.S. Military Power in the Pacific: Problems and Prospects," *National Security in Northeast Asia* (New York: CAUSA Publications, 1987), 77–85.
14. Fred Ikle and Albert Wohlstetter, "Discriminate Deterrence," Report of the Commission on Integrated Long-Term Strategy, January 1988, 6–7.
15. Henry A. Kissinger, *The White House Years* (Boston: Little Brown and Company, 1979), 685.
16. Allen Whiting, *China Crosses the Yalu* (Stanford, Calif.: Stanford University Press, 1960), 85.
17. Kissinger, op. cit., 183.
18. Ibid., 164.
19. Zbigniew Brzezinski, *Power and Principle* (New York: Farrar, Straus, Giroux, 1983), Annex 1.
20. Eugene K. Lawson, ed., *U.S.-China Trade* (New York: Praeger Publishers, 1988), 298.
21. Fox Butterfield, "Mao and Deng: Competition for History's Judgement," *New York Times*, 15 November 1987, E2.
22. "Peking's Primary Goal," *Far Eastern Economic Review* (12 November 1987), 66.
23. Lawson, op. cit., pp. 298–299.
24. "The 13th Party Congress," Contingency Series paper (Washington, D.C.: Center for Strategic and International Studies, November 1987), 9.
25. Lawson, op. cit.
26. *Asian Security: 1987–88* (Tokyo: Research Institute for Peace and Security, 1987), p. 20.

11: Gorbachev's Superpower

1. One of Mikhail Gorbachev's earlier references to the "blank spaces" can be found in "Gorbachev Addresses Media Representatives" (translated from *Pravda*), Daily Report: Soviet Union, Foreign Broadcast Information Service (FBIS-SOV-87-031 3, no. 031) (17 February 1987), R1–R5.
2. Arkady N. Shevchenko, *Breaking with Moscow* (New York: Ballantine Books, 1985), 22.
3. Mikhail Gorbachev, speech to commemorate the seventieth anniversary of the October Revolution, 2 November 1987.

4. Hugh Seton Watson, *From Lenin to Malenkov* (New York: Praeger Publishers, 1956), vii.

5. Gorbachev, op. cit.

6. See Paul Johnson, *Modern Times* (New York: Harper Colophon Books, 1983), 303–34. Also Aleksandr I. Solzhenitsyn, *The Gulag Archipelago* (New York: Harper and Row, 1978), volumes 1–3.

7. Adam B. Ulam, *Stalin: The Man and His Era* (New York: Viking Press, 1973), 587.

8. Ibid., 608.

9. Harry S. Truman, *Memoirs* (Garden City, N.Y.: Doubleday, 1955–56), volume 1, 81–82.

10. Margaret Truman, *Harry S. Truman* (New York: William Morrow, 1973), 312.

11. Ulam, *Stalin*, op. cit., 658.

12. *The Military Balance: 1979–1980* (London: International Institute for Strategic Studies, 1987), 15–16.

13. Joseph L. Nogee and Robert H. Donaldson, *Soviet Foreign Policy since World War II*, second edition (New York: Pergamon Press, Inc., 1985), 125.

14. Stephen Sestanovich, "Net Assessment of the Soviet Future," working draft, August 1988, the Center for Strategic and International Studies.

15. For a more in-depth evaluation, see Thane Gustafson and Dawn Mann, "Gorbachev's First Year: Building Power and Authority," *Problems of Communism* (May-June 1986), 1; also, Thane Gustafson and Dawn Mann, "Gorbachev's Next Gamble," *Problems of Communism* (July-August 1987), 1.

16. Mikhail Gorbachev, *Perestroika* (New York: Harper & Row, Publishers, 1987), 17–24.

17. Sestanovich, op. cit., 1988.

The Grand Strategy

1. For further reading, see B. H. Liddell Hart, *Strategy* (New York: Frederick A. Praeger, 1954).

12: Political Strategy

1. "The Future Tasks of the Alliance" (Harmel Report), Report of the Council. annex to the final communiqué of the ministerial meeting, December 1967. In *The North Atlantic Treaty Organization: Facts and Figures* (Brussels: NATO Information Service, 1984), 289–91.

2. "Washington Statement on East-West Relations," text of the final communiqué from the North Atlantic Council that met in ministerial session in Washington, D.C., 29–31 May 1984. In *NATO Final Communiqués 1981–1985*, volume 3 (Brussels: NATO Information Service, 1986), 115–21.

3. See Patrick Cosgrove, *Carrington: A Life and A Policy* (London: J. M. Dent & Sons Ltd., 1985).

4. Christopher Bertram, "Europe's Security Dilemmas," *Foreign Affairs* 65, no. 5 (Summer 1987), 942–57.

5. Declaration of the Heads of State and Government Participating in the Meeting of the North Atlantic Council in Brussels, 3 March 1988, Paragraph 13.

6. Ronald Reagan, remarks by the president to the Center for Strategic and International Studies, the International Club, Washington, D.C., 14 December 1987.

7. "NATO in the 1990s: Towards a New Transatlantic Bargain," North Atlantic Assembly (report scheduled for publication May 1988).

8. *NATO in the 1990s*, Special Report by the North Atlantic Assembly Committee on NATO in the 1990s, May 1988.

9. Between 1975 and April 14, 1988, 173,332 Soviet Jews emigrated. Figures supplied by the Union of Councils for Soviet Jewry in Washington, D.C.

10. "Reagan Praises Helsinki Accords' Achievements," *Washington Post*, 28 May 1988, 1.

11. Ibid.

13: Public Strategy

1. Helsinki Final Act, cited in David M. Abshire, *International Broadcasting: A New Dimension of Western Diplomacy* (London: Sage Publications, 1976), The Washington Papers No. 35, by the Center for Strategic and International Studies, 11.

2. Abshire, op. cit.

3. Milton Eisenhower, "The Right to Know." Report of the Presidential Study Commission on International Radio Broadcasting (Washington, D.C.: U.S. Government Printing Office, 1973).

4. Abshire, op. cit., 35.

5. Ibid., 53.

6. Ibid., 79.

7. Ibid., 87.

8. Dante Fascell, remarks given at the Third Abshire Lecture, Center for Strategic and International Studies, Washington, D.C., 8 October 1985. For further reading, see Dante B. Fascell, ed., *International News: Freedom Under Attack* (London: Sage Publications, 1979), published in cooperation with the Center for Strategic and International Studies.

9. *The Alliance Papers*, Atlantic Council of the United States, in cooperation with the United States Mission to NATO, Brussels, nos. 1–12.

10. "A Sense of Strategy," *The New York Times*, July 24, 1987, 3.

11. USIA survey of July 16, 1987, titled "Europeans Skeptical about INF Agreement Being Signed in 1987; Soviets are credited with Proposing Zero Option," noted that most people in France, Britain, and the Federal Republic of Germany believed zero option was a Gorbachev initiative.

12. See Wilson P. Dizard and S. Blake Swensrud, "Gorbachev's Information Revolution: Controlling Glasnost in a New Electronic Era," Significant Is-

sue Series (Washington, D.C.: Westview Press, 1987). Published in cooperation with the Center for Strategic and International Studies.
13. See Stephen S. Rosenfeld, "The Winds of Exchange," *Washington Post,* 5
February 1988.
14. Even the total of 25 centers was down from a postwar high of 44. The 1951
budget was $51,814,815. Figures on personnel and centers supplied by
Hans Tuch, former counselor for public affairs in Bonn. Dollar figures are
from *The Organization of the Office of the U.S. High Commissioner for
Germany, 1949–52,* p. 6, Table I, published by Historical Division, Office
of U.S. High Commissioner for Germany, supplied by Martin Manning,
USIA archivist.
15. The total number of persons conducting public affairs work in Europe today
is 174. Figures supplied by USIA, Washington, D.C., April 1988.
16. The projected figures were supplied by Youth For Understanding, Washington, D.C., April 1988. In FY87, worldwide and including all forms of exchanges (youth exchange, Fulbright, International Visitors, etc.), the total
number of exchanges reaching the United States was 12,139. Figures supplied by USIA, April 1988.

14: Deterrence Strategy

1. Winston S. Churchill, *Their Finest Hour* (Boston: Houghton Mifflin, 1949),
47.
2. In the "first" year, there is a one-week HILEX exercise that tests procedures
against a precombat crisis scenario. In the following year, NATO holds a
two-week WINTEX/CIMEX exercise. In this exercise, the scenario spans
several days of "nuclear play." That is, SACEUR makes an initial request for
use of nuclear weapons as a result of the deterioration of the conventional
battlefield. A few weeks after the exercise, there is a "wash up" discussion
among the ambassadors for an hour or so.
3. U.S. Department of the Navy report to the Congress, Fiscal Year 1988, 5.

15: Negotiating Strategy

1. By way of a preface to the examination of our negotiating strategies, their
inadequacies, and reformulations for the future, a review of a 1986 Harvard
University study team headed by Albert Carnesale provides valuable in-
sights into the impact of arms control as a result of its study of twenty-five
years of arms-control negotiations. Most important, the study found that,
contrary to expectations of arms-control enthusiasts, the negotiations of the
1960s and 1970s had only a very limited impact on the arms race; however,
contrary to expectations of arms-control critics, there is little evidence that
those agreements have been detrimental to U.S. interests. None of them
required substantial changes in the nature or size of Soviet and U.S. forces.
The Harvard study also notes these three points: first, that arms-control
agreements have been concluded when neither side had an appreciable

advantage; second, unilateral constraint has not induced reciprocal Soviet behavior; and third, accords have helped stabilize military competition and lessened uncertainty in each side's threat estimate.

2. Henry A. Kissinger, *White House Years* (Boston: Little, Brown and Company), 1245.
3. Taken from *Congressional Record*, 11 August 1972, in *SALT Talks: Legislative History of the Jackson Amendment, 1972* (From the Office of Senator Henry M. Jackson), 53.
4. Zbigniew Brzezinski, *Power and Principle* (New York: Farrar, Straus, Giroux, 1983), 182.
5. Helmut Schmidt, lecture given at the International Institute for Strategic Studies, October 1977.
6. See Richard K. Betts, ed., *Cruise Missiles: Technology, Strategy, Politics* (Washington, D.C.: The Brookings Institution, 1981) for an analysis of the technological, military, and political dimension of the cruise missile debate as it appeared to observers at the beginning of the Reagan administration.
7. Ronald Reagan, speech given at the National Press Club, Washington, D.C., 18 November 1981.
8. Strobe Talbott, *Deadly Gambits* (New York: Alfred A. Knopf, 1984), 144.
9. Declaration from the Foreign Ministers Meeting (High Level Task Force), December 1986.
10. Ibid.
11. See, for example, James A. Thomson and Nanette C. Gantz, *Conventional Arms Control Revisited: Objectives in the New Phase*, Rand Note N-2697-AF (Santa Monica: The RAND Corporation), December 1987, p. 13.
12. Focusing on confidence-building measures (CBMs) could provide a credible negotiating option as long as they avoid the illusion of enhanced stability where none exists. CBMs are important politically because of the enhanced trust they can foster. Their military impact is limited, however, and NATO must be careful not to convey the impression that if additional CBMs can be agreed upon, long-term stability will have been achieved. CBMs would also offer difficulty, since they would involve "intrusive" measures that might be needed to verify reductions if they were agreed upon. Adequate verification of any reductions must be guaranteed or the confidence of the agreement could be eroded over time. I suspect that, even to its allies, the United States might look as if it is dragging its feet under the banner of verification. But if we have learned anything from our experiences in nuclear-weapons negotiations, it is that verification is often the key sticking point when it comes to debate over whether a treaty merits ratification.
13. See the *Statement by the Heads of State and Government Participating in the Meeting of the North Atlantic Council Meeting of the North Atlantic Council in Brussels*, 2–3 March 1988, and the *Declaration of the Heads of State and Government Participating in the Meeting of the North Atlantic Council Meeting of the North Atlantic Council* in Brussels, 2–3 March 1988.

16: Resources Strategy

1. These figures have been repeatedly cited throughout articles and papers by Thomas Callaghan, writer, lecturer, and consultant on allied and American armaments cooperation.
2. Years earlier, Marshall had been brought from the White House to the Pentagon by Secretary of Defense Schlesinger to serve in the new position of Director of Net Assessment. It was one of Schlesinger's many innovations as he sought to rebuild NATO after Vietnam-era neglect.
3. David M. Abshire, "NATO on the Move," in *The Alliance Papers*, no. 6 (Brussels: Atlantic Council of the United States, in cooperation with The United States Mission to NATO, September 1985), 5.
4. *Soviet Acquisition of Militarily Significant Western Technology: An Update* (Washington, D.C.: Department of Defense, 1985), 8.
5. Daniel Sneider, "Japan Disputes U.S. View of Damage done by Toshiba Sale," *Christian Science Monitor*, 20 July 1987, 11.
6. Jonathan Kapstein, "The West's Crackdown on High-Tech Smuggling Starts to Pay Off," *Business Week*, 29 July 1985, 47.
7. "Business Economists See U.S. Trade Gap Shrinking," *Wall Street Journal*, 10 June 1988, 1.
8. For a thorough listing of NATO cooperative research and development programs and Pentagon management of the effort, see "DoD Announces Formation of Defense Cooperation Working Group," Pentagon news release, 21 January 1987.
9. "Towards a Stronger Europe: Volume 1," report by an Independent Study Team established by Defense Ministers of Nations of the Independent European Programme Group, December 1986.
10. Ibid.
11. Ibid.
12. Figures supplied by the Department of Defense, April 1988. For information on recent U.S. efforts to advance cooperative development of the alliance's next generation fighter, see Dan Beyers, "U.S. Government and Industry Creating Stiff Competition for Europeans," *Defense News*, 4 January 1988; and John P. Morrocco, "U.S. Will Discuss Co-Development of Updated F/A-18 with Allies," *Aviation Week and Space Technology* (21 December 1987).

17: Technology Strategy

1. For an excellent discussion of the attitudes behind the Maginot Line concept, see Irving M. Gibson's chapter, "Maginot and Liddell Hart, The Doctrine of Defense," in Edward Mead Earle, *Makers of Modern Strategy* (Princeton: Princeton University Press, 1952), 365–75.
2. Fred Ikle and Albert Wohlstetter, "Discriminate Deterrence," report of the Commission on Integrated Long-Term Strategy, January 1988, 49–50.
3. See Martin van Creveld, "Mobilization Warfare," in Gordon H. McCormick

and Richard E. Bissell, eds., *The Strategic Dimensions of Economic Behavior* (New York: Praeger, 1984).

4. See General Andre Beaufre, *A Strategy of Action* (New York: Praeger, 1967). *Stratégie de l'action*, translated from the French by Major-General R. H. Barry.

5. *Red Star*, 9 May 1984, 3.

6. Andrew J. Pierre, ed., "Enhancing Conventional Defense: A Question of Priorities," in *Conventional Defense of Europe* (New York: Council on Foreign Relations, 1986).

7. Ibid.

8. William E. Snowden, "Technology, Conventional Defense, and the Balanced Technology Initiative" (unpublished paper).

9. David M. Abshire, interview in *Armed Forces Journal International*, December 1986, 26–34.

10. Admiral William J. Crowe, Jr., USN, statement before the Senate Armed Services Committee, 25 January 1988.

11. David M. Abshire, "Twenty Years in the Strategic Labyrinth," *Washington Quarterly* 5, no. 1 (Winter 1982).

12. Ikle and Wohlstetter, op. cit., 50–52.

18: Third World Strategy

1. Jerry F. Hough, *The Struggle for the Third World* (Washington, D.C.: The Brookings Institution, 1986), 272.

2. William P. Kintner, *Soviet Global Strategy* (Fairfax, Va.: Hero Books, 1987), 221–22.

3. *Congressional Record*, CX (August 7, 1964), 18471.

4. For further reading, see Dwight D. Eisenhower, *Mandate for Change 1953–1956* (Doubleday & Company, Inc.: New York, 1963), 332–75; and Robert F. Randle, *Geneva 1954: The Settlement of the Indo Chinese War* (Princeton, N.J.: University Press, Princeton, 1969) 72–135.

5. For a comprehensive review of both Caspar Weinberger's speech "The Uses of Military Power" (National Press Club, November 28, 1984) and George Shultz's speech "The Ethics of Power" (Yeshiva University, New York, December 9, 1984), see Ernest W. Lefever, *Ethics and American Power* (Washington, D.C.: Ethics and Public Policy Center, 1985).

6. Comments by Geoffrey Kemp to the CSIS Williamsburg Conference on April 17, 1988.

7. G. McMurtrie Godley, "Overtly Honest Covert Action," a letter to the editor, *Wall Street Journal*, 17 September 1987, 27.

8. Comments by Edward Luttwak to the CSIS Williamsburg Conference on April 16, 1988.

9. For further reading, see "Special Operations Command Reaches Turning Point in Bureaucratic Turf War," *Washington Times*, 10 May 1988, 4.; " 'Special Ops' Forces Harness Exotic Equipment," *Washington Times*, 10 May 1988, 6.; and "Special Forces Go to a Tough School," *Washington Times*,

11 May 1988, 5. For a recent and brief historical review of Special Operations forces, see Steven Emerson's adaptation from his book, *Secret Warriors: Inside the Covert Military Operations of the Reagan Era*, in *U.S. News and World Report* (21 March 1988), 24.

10. Robert H. Kupperman and William J. Taylor, Jr., eds., *Strategic Requirements for the Army to the Year 2000* (Lexington, Mass.: Lexington Books, 1984), 125–28, 512–14.

11. The Report to the President by the National Bipartisan Commission on Central America, 10 January 1984.

12. Paul M. Cole, "U.S.-European Relations and the 1988 Election," unpublished paper, 20 May 1988.

19: Economic Strategy

1. See "Wall Street's Wounds Have the World Bleeding," *Business Week* (2 November 1987), 54. Also "How the Crash has Hit Over Seas" (*Business Week*), 9 November 1987, 51.

2. "Congress Wrestles a Monster in Quest for Trade Reform," *Insight* (14 December 1987), 20.

3. If the United States were to stumble into such a trade war through a series of miscalculations and misperceptions, the history books would draw a direct comparison to the depression of the 1930s. Our young people would read about how the Congress of 1989 ignored the lessons learned from the protectionist Smoot-Hawley legislation of 1930. Students would point out that "beggarthy-neighbor" trade legislation brings about immediate retaliatory sanctions from trading partners, setting in motion a chain of events that inevitably leads to global depression. The Smoot-Hawley tariff was passed on June 17, 1930. By July, Spain passed the Wais tariff, which reacted to tariffs on grapes, oranges, corks, and onions. Switzerland—responding to U.S. tariffs on watches, embroideries, and shoes—boycotted all American imports. Italy retaliated against tariffs on olive oil and hats by imposing high tariffs on U.S. automobiles. Canada tripled its tariffs in response to U.S. tariffs on food, logs, and timber. Growth stopped and debtor nations could no longer service their debts.

4. The United States has experienced a rising oil imports bill up $14 billion since 1985, and this most likely will continue. If oil supplies were ever disrupted, it would send U.S. oil-import bills into the stratosphere. Each 1 mmbd of imports, even at $18 bbl, adds $6.5 billion to the nation's import bill.

5. Paolo Cecchini, *Cost of Non-Europe*, report by the European Communities, 1987.

6. *The Uruguay Round of Multilateral Trade Negotiations Under GATT: Policy Proposals on Trade and Services*, report of the Atlantic Council's Advisory Trade Panel (Washington, D.C.: Atlantic Council of the United States Policy Papers, 1987).

7. GATT Study, chaired by Maurice Greenberg, Center for Strategic and International Studies, 1982.

8. "Nations Owed $1.19 Trillion At End of '87," *The Wall Street Journal*, January 19, 1988, 3.

9. *Resolving the Global Economic Crisis: After Wall Street* (Washington, D.C.: Institute for International Economics, 1987), Special Report 6, 14.

10. In June 1987, I discussed with Prime Minister Nakasone my idea of establishing such a working group of the seven countries and suggested that the group meet at least every other month. I explained how important it was to have the representative of the European Communities represented as well. As former ambassador to NATO, it is easy for my suggestion to be misconstrued as involving Japan with NATO alliance matters. That is not the point and I think Nakasone understood that. Instead, the point is that global security and global strategy involve what the Japanese call "comprehensive security." It involves energy lifelines, sharing and protecting technology, global burden sharing as well as debt problems, and of course staving off protectionism. It must also include defense expenditures and cooperation at a time when the U.S. Congress, with our debt and deficits, increasingly sees allies—Atlantic and Pacific—as not carrying their fair share. By increasing the exchange of ideas and information among capitals, longer-term harmony and better use of overall resources will occur. Global strategy requires such a mechanism. One wonders whether the French would participate, but I suspect they would be at the table if the idea moves to an implementation phase.

11. David Rapp, "Deficit Limits Reagan's Options in 1989 Budget," *Congressional Quarterly*, 20 February 1988, 327–31.

12. *American Excellence in a World Economy*, report of the Business Round Table on International Competitiveness, Washington, D.C., 1987.

13. Ibid.

14. Gary F. Hufbauer and Howard Rosen, *Trade Policy for Troubled Industries* (Washington, D.C.: Institute for International Economics, 1984).

15. *United States Military Posture FY 1989*, prepared by the Joint Staff (no publication date), 13.

16. For further reading on Strategic Minerals, see "Key Metals Bind US to South Africa," *Chicago Tribune*, 27 August 1985, 9. For a critique, see "Whatever Happened to the Resources War?" by Jack Finlayson and David Hagland in *Survival*, International Institute for Strategic Studies 24, no 5. (September/October 1987), 403–13. The classic study is Uri Ra'anan and Charles M. Perry, eds., *Strategic Minerals and International Security* (Washington, D.C.: Pergamon-Brassey's, July 1985), by the Institute for Foreign Policy Analysis, Inc. Equally important is the fact that the United States has lost the processing capability of many minerals (e.g., ferro-manganese).

17. William Schneider, Jr., "Strategic Minerals: International Considerations," in Uri Ra'anan and Charles M. Perry, eds., *Strategic Minerals and International Security* (Washington, D.C.: Pergamon-Brassey's, 1985), by the Institute for Foreign Policy Analysis, 72.

18. Richard M. Morrow, chairman of the board, Amoco Corporation, estimates that "under the upper price scenario, imports are projected to increase to

about 10 million barrels per day, or 56 percent of U.S. consumption, by the year 2000. If the lower-price trend prevails, imports are projected to grow to 14 million barrels a day or 70 percent of consumption, at the end of the century," in "An Assessment of the American Energy Situation," address at the Centre for Geopolitics of Energy, University of Paris, 21 January 1988.

19. "America's Interests in the Persian Gulf Are Growing, Not Decreasing," *Armed Forces Journal International,* June 1987, 58.

20. For further reading, see "Not Enough Oil?" *Armed Forces Journal Intenational* (February 1988), 16.

21. George R. Packard, "The Coming U.S.-Japan Crisis," *Foreign Affairs* (Winter 1987/88), 348–67.

22. Dr. Saburo Okita, chairman of the Institute for Domestic and International Studies, has made such estimates.

23. "Hooked on T-bonds," *The Economist,* 7 February 1987, 75.

24. "Japanese Funds Still Pour In," *New York Times,* 7 April 1987, D5.

25. Figure supplied by the Japanese embassy in Washington, D.C., May 1988.

26. *American Excellence in a World Economy,* report of the Business Round Table on International Competitiveness, Washington, D.C., 15 June 1987, 23.

27. "How Japan Has Made Its Oil Suppliers Bow to Its Energy Needs," *Wall Street Journal,* 2 June 1987, 1.

28. See Henry A. Kissinger, "Brazil's Crisis: U.S. Must Lend a Hope, a Hand," *Los Angeles Times,* 24 May 1987.

20: Organizing for Strategy

1. National Security Act, Public Law 253, 80th Congress of the United States.

2. See Henry M. Jackson, ed., *The National Security Council; Jackson Subcommittee Papers on Policy-Making at the Presidential Level* (New York: Frederick A. Praeger, 1966).

3. It may be the case, for example, that President Johnson's personality and style were so potent that changing his national security advisory structure would have had little, if any, impact on the decisions he made. James David Barber (*The Presidential Character.* Englewood Cliffs, N.J.: Prentice-Hall, 1972, p. 82) relates two examples of the dilemma with which Johnson's advisers were often faced. Both involve Johnson's "polling technique," which he used as a device to build consensus. He relates one meeting during which McNamara, who had doubted the value of providing more troops to General Westmoreland, faced the following exchange:

"The troops that General Westmoreland needs and requests, as we feel it necessary, will be supplied," Johnson said, then asked, "Is that not true, General Westmoreland?"

"I agree, Mr. President."

"General Wheeler?"

"That is correct, Mr. President."

"Secretary McNamara?"
"Yes, sir," came the helpless reply.

Chester Cooper, a Johnson aide, also experienced similar situations:

> During the process I would frequently fall into a Walter Mitty-like fantasy:
> When my turn came I would rise to my feet slowly, look around the room
> and then directly at the President, and say very quietly and emphatically,
> "Mr. President, gentlemen, I most definitely do *not* agree." But I was
> removed from my trance when I heard the President's voice saying, "Mr.
> Cooper, do you agree?" And out would come a "Yes, Mr. President, I
> agree."

Presidential personality can render any advisory structure of limited utility.
In her biography of Johnson, Doris Kearns (*Lyndon Johnson and the American Dream*. New York: New American Library, 1976, pp. 334–37) contends
that as he became suspicious of the loyalties of those around him he narrowed
his circle of advisers to his trusted Tuesday lunch. Those who did not share
his beliefs soon stopped attending. Thus Johnson's policies evolved in an
increasingly isolated setting: loyalty, support, and secrecy became the by-
words of the day. Communication between decision makers and assistants
who were charged with implementing those decisions became strained. Policy formulation and policy implementation both suffered as a result.

4. It should be pointed out that a separate group, the three-person President's
   Intelligence Oversight Board—not the President's Foreign Intelligence Advisory Board—has the responsibility of conducting investigations and informing the President and the Attorney General of any intelligence activities that
   are in violation of the law.
5. See *Goldwater-Nichols Department of Defense Reorganization Act of 1986:
   Conference Report to Accompany H.R. 3622*, 99th Congress, Second session,
   House Report, 99-824, 1986.
6. See "National Security Strategy Report," January 1988.
7. CSIS Study chaired by William Brock and John Yochelson, 1988.
8. David Abshire, *Foreign Policy Makers: President vs. Congress* (London: Sage
   Publication, 1979), Washington Papers No. 66, Center for Strategic and
   International Studies, 8.
9. Sam Nunn, speech to Democratic Leadership Council in Williamsburg, Va.,
   29 February 1988.

Epilogue: To the Year 2000

1. Michael McGwire, *Military Objectives in Soviet Foreign Policy* (Washington,
   D.C.: Brookings Institute, 1988, pp. 272, 299, 362).
2. Philip Van Doren Stern, editor, *The Life and Writing of Abraham Lincoln*
   (New York: Modern Library, Random House, 1940), p. 745.

Index

About the Author

Davie Abshire has spent much of his life as an institution builder, working to bridge the worlds of ideas and action. He was a founder of the Center for Strategic and International Studies in Washington, D.C., in 1962 and has served as its president for many years.

After graduating from West Point in 1951, he served as a frontline platoon leader and company commander in Korea, and then on the division intelligence staff. He left active service to take a Ph.D. in history at Georgetown University, where he later served for twelve years as an adjunct professor at the School of Foreign Service. He entered government service as a professional staff member with the House of Representatives. Dr. Abshire has been especially involved in studying and overseeing the process of government, having served as a member of the Congressional Commission for the Conduct of Foreign Policy; the chairman of the U.S. Board for International Broadcasting; and a member of the President's Foreign Intelligence Advisory Board. His interest in cultural diplomacy has included service as vice-chairman of the trustees of Youth For Understanding.

His full-time government service has never been routine. As assistant secretary of state from 1970 to 1973, he was often in the eye of the storm of congressional debates related to U.S. troop withdrawals from Vietnam. He was also involved in the rescue of Radio Free Europe and Radio Liberty from a congressional funding cutoff. Dr. Abshire was the U.S. ambassador to NATO from 1983 to February 1987, a historically important period when the NATO allies began deployment of the intermediate-range missiles and the Soviets walked out of the Geneva negotiations. At the beginning of the Iran-Contra inquiry, President Reagan summoned Ambassador Abshire to the White House to serve as his special counsellor for the Iran-Contra inquiry, where he held full Cabinet rank and reported directly to the president.

Dr. Abshire has written extensively on foreign policy, the congress, and national security and is a founding editor of *The Washington Quarterly*. He is on several business, educational, and international boards and holds a number of awards for outstanding service in military and civilian life. He is also a John M. Olin Fellow.